Beauty Matters

Edited by **Peg Zeglin Brand**

INDIANA UNIVERSITY PRESS
BLOOMINGTON AND INDIANAPOLIS

This book is a publication of

Indiana University Press

601 North Morton Street

Bloomington, IN 47404-3797 USA

http://www.indiana.edu/~iupress

Telephone orders   800-842-6796

Fax orders   812-855-7931

Orders by e-mail   iuporder@indiana.edu

The paper used in this publication meets the minimum requirements of American National Standard for Information Sciences—Permanence of Paper for Printed Library Materials, ANSI Z39.48-1984.

Manufactured in the United States of America

Library of Congress Cataloging-in-Publication Data

Beauty matters / edited by Peg Zeglin Brand.

   p. cm.

  Includes bibliographical references and index.

  ISBN 0-253-33726-7 (cloth : alk. paper)—ISBN 0-253-21375-4 (paper : alk. paper)

1. Aesthetics. 2. Feminine beauty (Aesthetics)

I. Brand, Peggy Zeglin.

HQ1219 .B348 2000

305.42—dc21   99-056085

1   2   3   4   5   05   04   03   02   01   00

In memory of my late parents
Lillian M. and Joseph F. Zeglin
who were the first
to teach me
about beauty

What Is Beauty?

What exactly is beauty?
Who gets to decide whether or not we are beautiful?
We surely can't decide for ourselves for the world would scorn us as conceited.
Look in the mirror!
Trace the shape of your nose, run circles around your eyes, your lips.
Try to make your hair catch the light so it shines ever so perfectly.
You whisper under your breath, "I guess I am pretty," but is it you that gets the final say? . . .

Who decides whether or not we are beautiful?
Magazines that paste their air-brushed beauties for all to admire.
Movie stars who walk toward the camera, smiling, sucking in their stomachs and sticking out
        their boobs.
Who was the first person to claim that blondes had more fun?
Who was the first to say that white is better than black, skinny is better than fat,
        and tall is better than short?

The truth is, we all define beauty.
Every time you stand in front of a mirror
Every time you gain a few pounds and then step on the scale
Every time you dye your hair or pop in the colored contacts
Every time you look at yourself and smile and of course,
Every time you wish you were someone else.

—Laura L. Swain (at age 16)

CONTENTS

Contents

Acknowledgments

The editor of this volume gratefully acknowledges the following sources for permission to reprint previously published material:

An earlier version of "Introduction: How Beauty Matters," by Peg Zeglin Brand, originally appeared in a symposium entitled "Beauty Matters," in *The Journal of Aesthetics and Art Criticism* 57, no. 1 (Winter 1999): 1–10.

Chapter 1, "Kantian and Contextual Beauty," by Marcia M. Eaton, originally appeared in a symposium entitled "Beauty Matters," in *The Journal of Aesthetics and Art Criticism* 57, no. 1 (Winter 1999): 11–15.

Chapter 3, "Malcolm's Conk and Danto's Colors; or, Four Logical Petitions Concerning Race, Beauty, and Aesthetics," by Paul C. Taylor, originally appeared in a symposium entitled "Beauty Matters," in *The Journal of Aesthetics and Art Criticism* 57, no. 1 (Winter 1999): 16–20.

Chapter 6, "Beauty (Re)Discovers the Male Body," by Susan Bordo, originally appeared as "Gay Men's Revenge" in a symposium entitled "Beauty Matters," in *The Journal of Aesthetics and Art Criticism* 57, no. 1 (Winter 1999): 21–25. A longer version appears in Susan Bordo, *The Male Body: A New Look at Men in Public and in Private* (New York: Farrar, Straus and Giroux, 1999). A section entitled "Male Decorativeness in Cultural Perspective," on the varied history of Western attitudes toward male display and African American influences on fashion, has been omitted from this version of the essay.

Chapter 11, "A Man Pretending to Be a Woman: On Yasumasa Morimura's 'Actresses,'" by Kaori Chino, originally appeared in *Morimura Yasumasa: The Sickness unto Beauty — Self-Portrait as Actress* (Yokohama: Yokohama Museum of Art, 1996), pp. 157–162.

Foreword: Cutting Two Ways with Beauty

ELEANOR HEARTNEY

Recently, the *New York Times* ran an article reporting that supermodels are falling out of favor as magazine cover girls, and that their coveted slots are being filled instead by celebrities. This prompted one modeling agent to bemoan despairingly, "Where is the next generation of Linda Evangelistas going to come from?"

For the mere mortals who must view these unearthly creatures from the wrong side of the magazine racks, the news was unexpectedly cheering. Was it not a signal that our culture's relentless quest for physical perfection is faltering a bit? However, realism quickly set in. After all, celebrities, for the most part, are also impossibly beautiful. Still, the change did seem slightly positive—indicating a general desire to leaven beauty with a bit of "content."

Will we ever be at peace with beauty? Or must we always maintain an actively contradictory relationship to it, like my friend who proudly refuses to have the breast she lost in a mastectomy reconstructed, but who recently had a face lift?

Our present ambivalence about beauty has a variety of sources—social, psychological, political, even biological. From a philosophical point of view, it might be traced to contemporary society's discomfort with the utopian blandishments of the Platonic triad. The frightening consequences of the Aryan ideal, the obvious ethnocentrism of "universal" standards of beauty, and the absurdity of the notion of a beautocracy make it clear that the good, the true, and the beautiful are anything but kindred souls. In a pinch, we are more likely to agree with Adolf Loos's dictum, "Ornament is crime," than with Keats's ecstatic proclamation that the union of Beauty and Truth are "all ye know on earth and all ye need to know."

But in another sense, we have simply inverted the relationship between the beautiful and the good—substituting beauty's opposite to create a new triad consisting of the good, the true, and the ugly. Hence our fondness for the ideas that truth must be unvarnished and that the good must be without

Lisa Yuskavage, Blonde, Brunette, Redhead, 1995. *Oil on linen, 36 x 36 inches each. Courtesy of Marianne Boesky Gallery.*

illusions. In discussions of art, "too beautiful" has become a pejorative, while within the intellectual community at least, too much attention to personal appearance is considered a character flaw.

Thus, while the terms may have flipped, discussions of beauty remain deeply enmeshed in questions of morality. We are forever interrogating the guilty pleasures we derive from beauty with such questions as, Is beauty a form of tyranny? Is it exploitative? Is our response to beauty a moral choice, or is it externally determined—a matter of social conditioning, or a function of inalterable biological, physiological, or evolutionary factors? Is the embrace of beauty politically incorrect?

When the focus is turned specifically to physical beauty, the level of discomfort intensifies. Does our enjoyment of beauty reveal biases of class and race? What are implications of studies that find that attractive people are more trusted and successful than unattractive ones? In an era of widespread plastic surgery, what has become of Orwell's dictum: "After fifty, everyone has the face he deserves?" Does beauty undermine the egalitarian ideal?

But maybe it's time to cut beauty some slack. Perhaps it's not necessary to turn all questions of pleasure into questions of morality. Perhaps it's possible to be feminist and fashionable, for instance. Perhaps it's possible to loosen beauty's—or anti-beauty's—attachment to the good and the true. Perhaps the political danger inherent in the identification of beauty and morality is matched by the aesthetic danger of their opposition. (I'm thinking here of the flood of politically correct, aesthetically bereft artworks which washed through the art worlds of the 1980s and 1990s.)

Beauty seems in need of rehabilitation today as an impulse that can be as liberating as it has been deemed enslaving. Confident young women today pack their closets with miniskirts and sensible suits. Young female artists toy with feminine stereotypes in ways that make their feminist elders uncomfortable. They recognize that, like pornography, beauty can be a double-edged sword—as capable of destabilizing rigid conventions and restrictive behavioral models as it is of reinforcing them.

Why does beauty matter? Beauty flies in the face of a puritanical utilitarianism. It defies the reductiveness of both the political left and the political right in their efforts to bend it to a mission. Beauty subverts dogma by activating the realm of fantasy and imagination. It reminds us that the enjoyment of "mere" pleasure is an important element of our humanity. And it knits the mind and body together at a time when they seem all too easily divided.

Beauty is a contested category today because we both long for and fear its seductions. The essays in this volume interrogate beauty in all its complexity. But whether they construe it as friend or foe, they make it clear that beauty, and our preoccupation with it, cannot be wished away. Deeply embedded in that inchoate matter from which our judgments of value are formed, beauty is inseparable from all that is best and worst in human experience.

Peg Zeglin Brand

Introduction: How Beauty Matters

The image is simple, stark, yet stunning.

The photograph is untitled but well known to the art world as part of the Kitchen Table Series (1990) by Carrie Mae Weems. It is not only an instance *of* beauty but it is also *about* beauty—the adornment and display of the female body.

The space is balanced. The scene is quiet and unassuming. The luminescent skin tones of woman and child reflect the glow of a single light bulb. Time stands still for the brief and trivial act of applying lipstick. Absorbed in mirror-reflections, anticipation in the woman and girl grows as they imagine future judgments of their looks by others. Are they wearing the right color? Is it applied correctly? Their images are subdued in shades of gray. Applying lip color seems to enliven their faces, enhance their personalities, and, by extension, bring vitality to the starkness of their spartan surroundings.

Upon closer inspection, this is no trivial act. There is concentrated effort here: studied imitation, a deliberate process of replication bridging a generation gap between an adult notion of "beauty" and a child's notion, not yet formed. There is a ceremonial sharing of information, an induction into the secrets and codes of *beautification*, a transference of power. But, we begin to notice, this initiation rite is for women only.

The empty chair invites us in: to balance the triad, to partake in the ritual. But to assume the place of the third person at the table requires the revealing of one's self—male, female, white, black, old, young, observer,

1

Carrie Mae Weems, Untitled, *from the* Kitchen Table Series, *1990. Silver print, 28¹/₄ x 28¹/₄ inches. Courtesy of the artist and PPOW, New York.*

participant—each of whom has ideas about beauty. Given the ritual de-picted—of "applying one's face"—men cannot *really* participate, so they observe. As long-time observers of beauty, they have often regarded them-selves as highly qualified, cultured men of taste: men for whom beauty matters. Men have a long-established tradition of appreciating beauty in nature, art, and women that is chronicled in histories of art, philosophy, and literature. More recently, however, such men have been accused of enjoying much too heartily the privileged "male gaze": a look, some feminists claim, that objectifies, belittles, and silences the woman on display.

To sit at the table is even more complex for a woman since she cannot *simply* be an observer. Beginning at an early age, she must consciously *choose* to partake in the rites that involve beauty *matters* like lipstick, gloss, and liner. Some who refrain, to one degree or another, from wearing makeup and buying seasonal fashions, from exercise routines, or from cosmetic surgery have become vocal critics of such matters. Like Simone de Beauvoir, who in the 1940s accused women of complicity with men in their own oppression, they denounce women's participation in what Naomi Wolf has famously labeled "the beauty myth."[1] Beauty has become central to the topic of representation in general. Images of women in society, in advertising, in television, and in film, have placed the female body—long an icon of beauty and seduction—at the center of debates about pornography, girls' sports, and women's exercise routines. The pursuit of beauty and its attendant ideals lies at the center of controversy among women who disagree about the role of female agency in body-building, cosmetic surgery, and the act of wearing makeup. Women debate whether an elusive ideal of beauty is a menacing, male-fabricated myth that victimizes women or an avenue of self-realization by which women become empowered agents.[2] To think that issues of beauty within the worlds of fashion, popular culture, and the media fail to influence how beauty matters within the art world is to refuse to acknowledge the frequency and potency of cross-fertilization.

It is worth noting, however, that the topic of beauty—which has gradually come to the attention of feminist theorists—has been a staple of the content of artwork by women artists for decades. Feminist theorists have begun to view the female body as it has been depicted by male and female artists throughout recorded history as "contested territory"; their analysis of the portraiture of women artists highlights crucial links between issues of identity, sexuality, and empowerment.[3] Furthermore, beauty has come to operate in new and unusual ways; under the influence of the fashion world, artists are now making "girlie art" that represents "the perfected image of what beautiful is."[4] In "Cutting Two Ways with Beauty," Eleanor Heartney calls attention to the artistic production of younger women artists, who, "in miniskirts and makeup," invoke conflicting concepts of "beauty" in their work. She writes, "like pornography, beauty can be a double-edged sword—as capable of destabilizing rigid conventions and restrictive behavioral models as it is of reinforcing them." Clearly, the meaning of "beauty" has gained complexity amid the rhetoric of a "postfeminist" age in which women compete with men in an increasingly competitive, market-driven art world.

Weems, as an artist and woman, invites us to sit at the table and to share our thoughts about beauty. To do so, I believe, is to visually demonstrate *how beauty matters*. She invites a dialogue that precludes the standard philosophical response, that is, one based in a concept of *pleasure* that is *presumed* to be neutral, objective, and disinterested. Instead, she invites us to look at the representation of woman as she is situated *in context*: a context in which her beauty—and the value-laden concept of "beauty"—operates historically, culturally, and politically. As an artist, a woman, and an African American, she provides the setting that gives rise to many questions: What is beauty and how does it operate within the context of our particular culture? What are the ideals of feminine beauty and are they relevant to portraying beauty in art? How does skin color function as a "deviation" from the paradigm of white beauty, which has operated for so long in Western civilizations as the standard of all that is pure and good? How do inherited notions of physical beauty operate on girls who, at younger and younger ages, strive to control their bodies to the point of starvation? In an age of child pornography and sexual abuse of children, how can we ignore the effects of an industry that initiates infants as young as eight months into a cycle of beauty pageant competition. Recall JonBenet Ramsey was already a "winner" at age six, yet her murder is still unsolved. Given the extremes to which parents will go for the sake of improving their children's looks, how can an aesthetics of beauty—as it filters down to younger ages through advertising, peer, and parental pressure—ever be justified *apart from* ethics?

How beauty matters, therefore, is open to considerable debate. The essays in this volume seek to open the discussion about beauty—as based primarily in a philosophical tradition—to a larger audience. It is an attempt to invite various representatives to the table and begin a constructive dialogue about beauty *across* disciplinary boundaries. For example, feminist theorists who construct theories of the body and critique the beauty industry may come to better appreciate the work of women artists who offer viewers a subversive pleasure by using their bodies to visualize beauty for others. Art critics, literary theorists, and Cultural Studies scholars may come to recognize the important historical role of "beauty" in philosophical aesthetics, including the ways gender, race, and sexual orientation have informed the concept prior to the twentieth century. Women artists may come to re-examine the trend to borrow notions of "beauty" from the world of fashion and advertising, particularly as we come to better understand the harmful impact of such images on younger generations who excessively, and in imitation of their elders, strive for physical perfection.

This volume, moreover, is an attempt to expand the scope of traditional philosophical inquiry more substantively into the realms of contemporary women's art, art criticism, Cultural Studies, and feminist theory. Kant rubs shoulders with Calvin Klein. Beautification in Hegel's Third Realm operates alongside the practice of Chinese foot-binding. Plato confronts Picasso. New viewpoints extend "beauty" into the study of disabled bodies, women's intersubjectivity, and computer-generated hybridizations. There are analyses of kitsch, cross-dressing, and Karole Armitage.

The title, *Beauty Matters*, is intentionally ambiguous in the hope of yielding a multiplicity of meanings. First, "matters" can be interpreted as a verb, in which "beauty matters" reflects the historical importance of a concept that has provoked philosophical interest since the time of Plato and has motivated women worldwide to look better, more attractive, and more desirable. (Beautification rituals extend back to the time of Cleopatra, when varicose veins on legs and breasts were outlined in blue dye to enhance their appearance.) Alternately, "matters" can be read as a noun, in which "beauty matters" constitutes the tools of fashion, the materials of women's decoration, or, in another sense, the "talk" about (the business of) beautification. Given the central role women's bodies have played in the making of art (recall the many images of nudes, Venuses, and scenes of rape), the advent of photography and film (women in porn, film stars), and the fashion industry (runway and media models for predominantly male designers), it should come as no surprise that women have *not* dominated the academic "talk" about beauty, that is, the philosophical, art-historical, and art-critical discourses. Nor is there any strong indication that the trend will change in the near future. As outlined below, the history of the concept of beauty has been exclusively within the province of male philosophers; the current resurgence of theoretical interest in beauty is dominated by male critics; and the number of women who write in the fields of philosophy, art theory, and art criticism is still sorely disproportionate to the high numbers of men who write about beauty. We need more women to speak out about beauty and to engage in a productive dialogue (among themselves *and* with men) since it is *their* bodies that are routinely on display, under scrutiny, and the object of all who gaze. The call for more participation by women writers is in no way intended to deny the rich literature about women artists that has emerged in the last few decades; rather, it is to show that the burden of responsibility to engage dialectically with "beauty" has been shouldered—to a great degree—by women *artists* and it is their work that needs more attention, reflection, and critical review. For women, beauty has always mattered—in a personal way and as an inevitable and underlying sociopolitical framework for how they operate in the world. For women artists, beauty has mattered in the messages expressed through their art (common to much feminist art from the 1970s through the 1990s) or in the apolitical stance they strive to achieve today.

Beauty Is Back

Beauty, once deemed timeless, unchanging, and universal by the ancient Greek philosopher Plato, is currently back in fashion. Predicated on the success of art critic Dave Hickey's 1993 text, *The Invisible Dragon: Four Essays on Beauty*, and on the claims of 1995 Whitney Biennial curator Klauss Kertess who said, "The issue of the nineties is beauty," critic Peter Schjeldahl announced in a 1996 *New York Times Magazine* essay that "Beauty Is Back." He issued a call for the public to recognize "Beauty's malaise—the problem of worn-out philosophies that clutter its dictionary definition"—in order to overcome "the historically freighted, abstract piety of 'Beauty.'" ("Beauty" with a capital "B" is a reference to Plato's timeless and universal Form of Beauty, as opposed to instantiations of "beauty" of our own time or in our own sense of the term.) Not only did he confidently herald that "[a] trampled esthetic blooms again," but volunteered "to rescue for educated talk the vernacular sense of beauty."[5]

Equally dismissive of philosophy's contribution to the discussion of beauty, Dave Hickey bemoaned "our largely unarticulated concept of 'beauty'" and summarily discarded aesthetics as "old patriarchal do-dah about transcendent formal values and humane realism." More recently, Bill Beckley and David Shapiro, editors of a 1998 anthology of readings entitled *Uncontrollable Beauty*, located the origins of beauty in the nineteenth century. They also ignored a long and noteworthy history that included Aristotle, the eighteenth-century theorists of taste, and Kant.[6] Co-published with the School of Visual Arts in New York, the text, subtitled *Toward a New Aesthetics*, is unabashedly marketed toward "a new generation of artists."

Such narrowly conceived critical remarks are now being replicated in the press. One editor at a university press was quoted as saying, "We've had aesthetics for the last 200 years, but a lot has been missing from the definition." This was reported in an article entitled, "Wearying of Cultural Studies, Some Scholars Rediscover Beauty," in which aesthetics was described as emerging from its marginalized status in English and American Studies departments, where it had long been considered "the forbidden subject," that is, "the bad child no one wants to talk about."[7] What is common and noteworthy among these influential sources is that none of these authors consider the history of beauty in aesthetics seriously but have rather found it easier to haughtily dismiss its legacy and to urge others toward similar disdain. This irresponsibility is being transmitted to a new generation of artists who, in their naive assumptions, beliefs, and creative output, believe they are actually *discovering* beauty (for the first time) and uniquely determining the scope of its meaning. Perhaps they are; but if so, it is surely in the "vernacular sense" for which Schjeldahl had hoped, for the current connotation of "beauty" not only exceeds its prior definition(s), it is also by and large out of control. It is now the case that "beauty" can mean anything at all. Consider a few examples.

In response to charges of obscenity in his homoerotic photos of "The X Portfolio," Robert Mapplethorpe claimed to be "obsessed with beauty." Andres Serrano, famous for a large color photo of a crucifix submerged in urine, uses materials for shock value in his search for beauty. Damien Hirst's display of a fourteen-foot-long dead shark in a tank of formaldehyde was his way of expressing the feeling it evoked: "beauty combined with cruelty." (In a more recent show, his work was titled, "The Beautiful Afterlife.") As Kaori Chino points out in her essay in this volume, artist Yasumasa Morimura entitled a recent exhibition of photographs of himself in drag "The Sickness unto Beauty—Self-Portrait as Actress."

Art critics only add to, and simultaneously inspire, the confusion. According to Hickey, Mapplethorpe's disturbing images exemplify "formal beauty."[8] A Hirst sculpture consisting of shelving dotted with hundreds of cigarette butts impressed Roberta Smith as "strikingly beautiful."[9] In Lynn Gumpert's view, Morimura's impersonations raise "fundamental questions about the 'true' nature of beauty and selfhood."[10] Even novelist John Updike has joined the discussion. Writing about the erotic drawings of Egon Schiele, he invokes the disclaimer of Freud, who said, "the genitals themselves, the sight of which is always exciting, are nevertheless hardly ever judged to be beautiful," yet praises Schiele's drawings of women whose sex "is observed without being exploited." Beauty, he posits, "lies, perhaps, not in the eye of the beholder but in the hand of the creator."[11]

The most disturbing trend in contemporary art writing is the premeditated move to elide the beautiful with the sublime: a dangerous precedent that is noticeable among art critics, theorists, and artists alike. For instance, Hickey writes: "I rarely use the word beauty in reference to an image that isn't somehow dangerous or transgressive."[12] Schjeldahl finds beauty in "bizarre, often bleak, even grotesque extremes of visual sensation."[13] Recalling the title of his co-edited volume, Beckley casts beauty as "uncontrollable."[14] Even artist Cindy Sherman, in describing her photographs of bloody mannequin body parts amid scenes of vomit and dirt, describes the "grotesque, disastrous and disturbed" character of her work in similar terms:

> The world is so drawn toward beauty that I became interested in things that are normally considered grotesque or ugly, seeing them as more fascinating and beautiful. It seems boring to me to pursue the typical idea of beauty, because that is the easiest or the most obvious way to see the world. It's more challenging to look at the other side.[15]

This new model of beauty incorporates elements once confined to the distinct and contrasting philosophical notion of the sublime, which, again, most art critics fail to acknowledge or explore. Rather, they recast "beauty" as dangerous, transgressive, subversive, uncontrollable, grotesque. Beauty is no longer sought for the pure pleasure it gives; rather, in an era of un-licensed freedom to reproduce images of violence ad infinitum, beauty is cast in terms of the *dangerous* pleasure it gives, the way it pushes one to the edge, the way it allows us to safely taste the forbidden and evil under the guise of "beauty." Given the moral implications of a culture that finds the grotesque and dangerous beautiful, this dark side of beauty begs for critical analysis by scholars in art theory, ethics, social-political philosophy, and Cultural Studies. A look to the past is an essential component of informing ourselves toward that end.

Beauty's Past

In the process of addressing the deficiency of recent art writing about beauty, many essays in this volume use Immanuel Kant and other philo-sophical figures as either starting or reference points. A brief overview of the centrality of philosophy to the discussion of beauty will help place these essays in context. Questions about the types of qualities that inhere in objects of beauty (that is, in nature, in works of art, but also in bodies — male and female), the kinds of experiences they provoke, and the ways we come to value both, have occupied center stage in aesthetics. Plato linked beauty with love: first, the love of a beautiful body, and then, the beauty of one's soul, beautiful practices and customs, the beauty of knowledge, and ulti-mately the Form of Beauty. He also questioned the role of beauty in the physical world and within society at large since his goal was to urge all persons toward the attainment of knowledge of Beauty in the ideal (meta-physical) realm, where Virtue was the primary goal. Art, or *techne* (trans-lated more appropriately as "craft" than "art") was problematic; it could appeal to a person's passions rather than reason; it could deter one from the goal of being a virtuous citizen. Beautiful poems or statues in the "world of sense" (the world around us), therefore, invite suspicion. Poets and artists, although inspired by the gods, were not welcome in his utopian vision, the Republic. His legacy is a well-known distinction that contrasts a notion of timeless Beauty that *transcends* the physical world with a concept of beauty as the imitation and instantiation of Beauty in beautiful things *in* the world. Beautiful things, imitating and partaking in the Form of Beauty, share common characteristics like unity, measure, and proportion.

Common to both Beauty and beautiful things is the complex human act of *contemplation:* a component retained from Plato and elaborated in a cognitive-based notion of beauty by St. Thomas Aquinas. For Aquinas, beauty manifested itself in real-world objects through perfection, proportion, and clarity, and is tied to human perception and desire: "[T]he beautiful is that which calms the desire, by being seen or known." Thus beautiful things share objective features in the world of experience while persons experience the subjective property of pleasure, or the calming of desire. In the eighteenth century, a person's sense of taste came into play as the faculty that, singly or not, apprehends beauty, the sublime, or the picturesque. Nature, or the natural environment, played an important role by expanding the range of beautiful "objects" one might perceive. Landscapes, both actual and depicted, became the occasions of pleasurable experiences. But such pleasure was still devoid of desire; and thus disinterestedness—the exclusion of ethical, social, and political concerns—was introduced. Subjective theories came to occupy center stage as more emphasis was placed on the role of the perceiver ("Beauty is in the eye of the beholder") and less on the features of the object that triggered one's faculty of taste. The sublime came to replace beauty as the stronger of the two, and eventually (into the twentieth century) the notion of a sense of taste was replaced by that of the aesthetic attitude. Until the recent resurgence of interest in beauty, Ludwig Wittgenstein's mid-twentieth-century challenge to the use of basic philosophical terms had prompted an abandonment of the ongoing project of defining "art" and "beauty." Notable exceptions were Guy Sircello's 1975 analysis of the properties of beautiful objects and Mary Mothersill's revival of theories of taste in 1984.[16] As if to answer the question posed early in the 1990s, "Whatever Happened to Beauty?" numerous essays and several new texts on beauty have recently been published.[17]

It is important to note that as far back as Plato, gender and sexual orientation played a significant role in discussions of beauty. Plato's discussion of love in the *Symposium* operated within the context of a male-dominated, openly gay society. In the eighteenth century, by contrast, philosophers primarily used descriptions of women's bodies in their theories. Consider one example from Edmund Burke:

> Observe that part of a beautiful woman where she is perhaps the most beautiful, about the neck and breasts; the smoothness; the softness; the easy and insensible swell; the variety of the surface, which is never for the smallest space the same; the deceitful maze, through which the unsteady eye slides giddily, without knowing where to fix, or whither it is carried.[18]

Burke's remarks are startling: not so much in their frankness about how the male observer is seduced by "the deceitful maze," but how emphatically his "unsteady eye slides giddily" while the female is, as she is in most representations throughout the history of art, the passive object to be looked at. Burke signals another shift in thought from the classical era when he further observes:

> We shall have a strong desire for a woman of no remarkable beauty; whilst the greatest beauty in men, or in other animals, though it causes love, yet excites nothing at all of desire. Which shews that beauty, and the passion caused by beauty, which I call love, is different from desire, though desire may sometimes operate along with it.[19]

Reinforcing a norm that precludes the Greek ideal of desire, Burke demonstrates how the norms of desire, operating independently of beauty and love, become heterosexually coded. These codes were to remain dominant for centuries. Philosophical inquiry into heterosexual codes has been minimal; in this volume, Susan Bordo boldly re-opens the discussion of the desire for male bodies.

Race also plays a fascinating role in Burke's theory of beauty and in subsequent theories of the sublime. Burke tells the story of a white boy, blind since birth, who gains his sight and sees a black woman for the first time. The woman inspires both shock and terror in the boy; Burke interprets her deviance from a proper "white(s)-only" concept of feminine beauty as a transgression. The sublime comes to represent the dark, raced, terror that stands in contrast to the beautiful.[20] It is not surprising, given the religious and philosophical tenets of the day that held women to be vastly inferior to men, that the experience of the masculine sublime was ranked far above the (feminine) beautiful. Kant promoted the idea that blonde, blue-eyed women represented the ideal of female beauty, denigrating Africans and Indians to the status of "savages," but then postulated the notion of ideal beauty *within* individual races and cultures. Even Kant's inquiry into the beautiful and the sublime—considered by many to be the apex of aesthetic discourse—becomes inextricably tied to issues of gender, race, and cultural identity.

Beyond Kant

The authors in Section One start with Kant but move beyond standard notions of beauty that see the body as an external indicator of one's inner moral character. Marcia Eaton sympathizes with Tolstoy's rejection of Kant's pleasure-based theory and recommends a contextual approach. Suggesting that there are really two senses of beauty (only one of which is Kantian) she ties beauty to factual beliefs and moral attitudes. Noël Carroll is concerned with beauty and non-beauty (or, more specifically, beauty and ugliness) and the representation of ethnic and racial minorities. He notes how illustrations that evoke responses of horror or humor are routinely used to dehumanize, villainize, and show ugliness in the form of imperfect or defective human bodies. He suggests an analysis of depictions that play on the antinomy between the beautiful and the ugly in light of their Kantian connection to morality. Paul C. Taylor recalls a short story by Toni Morrison as an activist project that calls attention to a white-dominated culture that has *racialized* beauty. The internalization of such norms helps explain the desire of blacks to straighten their hair, as in the examples of Malcolm X or the many women who used Madame C. J. Walker's products early in the twentieth century.[21] Taylor suggests the recasting of philosophical aesthetics as a kind of cultural criticism, a suggestion supported by Arthur Danto, who turns away from Kant's influential dichotomy of artistic and natural beauty—as exemplified by fine art and the wonders of the natural world—toward Hegel's theorizing on decoration, adornment, and physical improvement. Danto argues for a concept of beauty that originates in Hegel's Third Realm, located *between* aesthetics and ethics: one that would include the clothing worn by Helen of Troy, the tattoos of New Zealand natives, *and* the straightening of African American hair.

Body Beautiful

In Part Two, Kathleen Higgins moves the discussion of how beauty matters in historical and philosophical terms to talk about matters of beauty in the world of fashion and advertising, where ideals of glamour and flawlessness function as paradigms that propel women into vicious cycles of emulation. She argues that women naively strive for characteristics more appropriately considered kitsch instead of beauty. This, in turn, has led philosophers to dismiss beauty—as it relates to women *today* and their concern over looks and dress—from the realm of serious philosophical concern.[22] Her probe into issues of power—long associated with beauty—and the desire it arouses, serves to enlighten the origin of the philosophical notion of disinterestedness. Susan Bordo's discussion of advertising and its preoccupation with beautiful bodies looks at gay consumer culture by turning our attention to male bodies that function as sex objects to elicit desire in both women *and* men. This dual marketing of "straight-looking, masculine men, with chiseled bodies" enables advertising to walk a fine line between homophobic rejection and successful sell. Such advertising complicates the cultural coding of gender, body stance, and other visual clues that inform the way bodies are portrayed, enabling Bordo to analyze both the pervasiveness of cultural norms of beauty and the ways in which they operate in gender-specific ways.[23] Dawn Perlmutter extends the discussion of how beautiful bodies are exploited as icons for consumerism and fame in our culture by revisiting the haunting murder of JonBenet Ramsey. Perlmutter traces the pursuit of bodily perfection through the history of beauty queen pageants and notes the trend of younger and younger girls becoming the contestants who parade and pose like adults. Denying the claims of promoters that beauty pageants offer a means of increased self-confidence and empowerment for girls, Perlmutter cites the pervasive "patriarchal notions of beauty, sex, youth, competition, and hierarchy" that routinely serve to demean and objectify the young women and girls who are involved.[24]

The essays by Eva Kit Wah Man and Anita Silvers serve as transitions between sections, linking the previous essays on beautiful bodies to those that explore the body in/as art. Man offers an insightful history of beauty that extends back to the Confucian era, follows its development through the courtesan culture of late Imperial China, and provides insights into contemporary notions of the beautiful woman in recent communist China. The Chinese emphasis on a paradigm of female beauty that requires women to be "young; small; slim," with "smooth white skin," "charming smiles" and "red lips" seems to have changed little over time. However, fashion—particularly Western fashion—has come to play a new role in China, enabling women to forge new identities and assimilate power previously unavailable to them. Anita Silvers also explores presumptions about beauty and the body that permeate artistic representations and real life. She asks why we enjoy the anomaly of a distorted face in a Picasso painting yet fail to admire such a face in real life. Kant has claimed that what is ugly can be portrayed as beautiful in art, but rejecting this binary distinction, Silvers invokes recent disability studies to question the current system of cultural representation in which disabled bodies operate. Noting that Eakins's depiction of a painted cadaver in 1875 was originally deemed repellent and only later considered "original" by art historians, she suggests the broadening of aesthetic strategies to enable us to view real people in morally and politically enriched ways. Our ability to view other humans more positively becomes, in effect, a case where beauty matters, apart from matters of art and aesthetics.

Body as Art

In light of the fact that we have looked at the return of "beauty" as it was defined by male artists, critics, and philosophers and have simultaneously called attention to women who are center stage in the fashion and beauty industry, one might ask, How have women artists dealt with issues of beauty and representation of the body? Is it a coincidence that the beautiful—first categorized as feminine—has now been recast as the (masculine) sublime? Has it been recast as dangerous and transgressive by (male) critics because of its past association with the feminine? Perhaps the work of women artists and feminist theorizing about the body can shed light on this complicated conceptual morass.

Much has been written about women's art of the 1970s and the role consciousness-raising played in addressing issues of identity and empowerment. Recent scholarship has unearthed fascinating histories of female surrealist artists, Unica Zürn and Francesca Woodman, who dealt with the many ways women's bodies were used in and as art in the history of art, early film, advertising, and eventually television.[25] The female body has come to occupy the intersection of feminist art, art criticism, and theoretical writing about beauty. Unlike male artists such as Mapplethorpe, Serrano, Hirst, and Morimura, who have only recently begun to appropriate the language of beauty in their art, women artists—in increasing numbers—have been exploring for decades the psychology and politics of beauty and the intimate connections between beauty, gender, race, and sexuality. Consider artists like Hannah Höch, a dadaist who in the 1920s arranged photos of white and black body parts in assemblages that interwove raced beauty ideals.[26] Or Carolee Schneeman, who posed nude in early performance pieces to critique the way women had been visually depicted by male artists.[27] The black and white "film stills" of Cindy Sherman (the same artist later responsible for the blood and vomit photos) imitated the filmic presence of the beautiful woman posed for male gazers. Her color photos of the 1980s, described as parodies of "soft-core pastiche," manipulated the erotics of the gaze within the "politics of representation of the body."[28] In the 1970s, Adrian Piper engaged the "conflicting standards of beauty and social acceptance on the most intimate level" by cross-dressing in her performance pieces and investigating the adage of the male-dominated Black Power movement, "black is beautiful."[29] Renee Cox photographed herself as a modern black Madonna with child. Orlan has undergone nine surgeries to reconstruct her face to imitate the ideals of female beauty represented by da Vinci, Botticelli, and Gerard in order to show that such male-defined ideals can never be attained (see the Orlan interview in this volume). Janine Antoni "paints" canvases with lipstick (see Robinson's essay) and sculpts self-portraits out of chocolate that she licks into human shape. The photographs of Nan Goldin catch heroin addicts in the act, elevating them to the status of "high art," while waif-like counterparts appear in dreary Calvin Klein ads as "heroin chic."[30]

These excursions into previously uncharted realms of physical and bodily beauty are uniquely female-based and feminine-oriented. Unlike the Body Art of Vito Acconci or Chris Burden, who sought to shock audiences with the graphic display and (ab)use of their bodies while pushing the limits of "art," women have placed an analysis of the many meanings and implications of "beauty" at the core of their work. Artworks created by women have manipulated and critiqued ideals of beauty to suit their own taste and expression and have wrested control of the representation of images *of* women from the hands of their male counterparts. These examples (which are only a few among many) clearly illustrate that beauty has been integral to women's art and discourse in innovative ways that still fail to gain a foothold in the thinking of most philosophers, art critics, and theorists. If these beauty matters—which inevitably carry over into the world of art and aesthetics—continue to be ignored, the projected new phase of "beauty" will remain as insular as before.

The essays in Part Three of this volume seek to remedy the deficiency and to move the dialogue in new directions. Continuing the theme of the human body in visual art, Hilary Robinson writes about woman's "sexualized subjective identity" in light of Luce Irigaray's notion of beauty which, for women, is "a potential state of being which can only come about as a result of rethinking political and cultural discourse." She analyzes the notions of corporeal, spiritual, and artistic beauty, all of which inevitably link the aesthetic with the ethical, political, and the ontological. Artworks, particularly representations *of* women and self-portraits, are seen not as objects of illusion but rather of mediation, offered by the artist to others who may then choose to accept or reject the connection.[31] Kaori Chino also focuses on the body as art in an investigation of the work of Yasumasa Morimura, an artist who has photographed himself in a series of impersonations of Hollywood actresses that includes Vivien Leigh, Elizabeth Taylor, and Marilyn Monroe. In spite of Japan's tradition of female impersonation in Kabuki and Noh theater, male viewers of Morimura's photographs were initially far less interested than were women, whose reactions ranged from awe and amusement to pure admiration. Chino describes the "Actresses" as beautiful, and offers a perspective that contrasts sharply with the well-known and accepted images of Marilyn Monroe by Andy Warhol: "Morimura receives the violent 'masculine gaze' often aimed at women with his exposed body, then the next moment laughs it away, and finally nullifies it."[32] Sally Banes sets the innovative work of Karole Armitage against a backdrop of nineteenth-century ballet and the work of Merce Cunningham and George Balanchine. The methods employed by Armitage spring from a brand of feminism shared by many artists of the 1960s and 1970s that empowered her to challenge and subvert the traditions of ballet that she had previously learned. But, as Banes argues, the beauty remains, albeit in new forms. The highly sexualized movements, bordering on the pornographic, are "mixed with icons of ravishing, transcendent beauty recognizable from the ballet canon."[33] Finally, the last essay is an interview conducted with a performance artist whose body also functions at the heart of her work. Orlan has reconfigured certain features of her face to resemble women depicted in famous artworks by artistic "masters." She draws attention to the futility of women's attempts to conform to male-defined standards of beauty and is critical of any (one) universal notion of beauty. She is an extreme example, surpassing Morimura, of measures undertaken by an artist, as she undercuts religious notions of the sanctity of the flesh and brazenly defies even the most liberal definitions of "art."

New-Age Beauty

Finally, given the goal of this volume—to bring together art, aesthetics, Cultural Studies, feminist theory, and fashion to the table of "talk" about beauty—it is fascinating (and fun) to find an entire line of cosmetics called "Philosophy" whose byline reads: "[T]he new age of beauty is the old age of beauty in disguise."[34] Described as a "fundamental physical science,"[35] the product line of "Philosophy" is divided into five areas: aesthetics (having to do with color), logic (skin care), metaphysics (fragrance for bed and bath), ethics (where profits are donated to nonprofit foundations or "individual people in need"), and epistemology (books and music). Recalling the untitled photograph by Weems with which we began this introduction, the advertising for one product in the extensive "Philosophy" line ties adult rituals of beautification to the unrealized aspirations of childhood: *"the coloring book* finally offers the artist in all of us a simple, convenient way to express our creativity and our beauty."* The product plays with the notion of a creative girl who grows up to be a busy woman with no time for creativity (crayons) or play, *except for* the application of color to her face every morning by means of her *coloring book:*

in the beginning . . .

There was a little girl, a poet, and an artist. the little girl loved playing with her doll. the poet loved expressing her deepest thoughts in her diary; and the artist, wild and imaginative, loved her coloring book and coloring crayons. there was true joy in being a girl and plenty of time to do so.

times changed . . .

the little girl sadly became less herself and more plastic, like her doll. the poet became an office memo queen; and the artist became increasingly more scattered as she dug through her makeup drawer every morning.

then there was an important discovery . . .

the discovery allowed the little girl to become "real" again. the poet would now have more time for poetry, and the artist had a brand new coloring book.

Invoking Plato's timeless and universal notion of "real" Beauty, *the coloring book* offers a diversified palette that contains "high-pigment, matte colors formulated to have a timeless, ageless, and universal appeal." The line includes "ten shades of eye shadow, four blushes, five lip colors, and two liner pencils plus seven professional makeup brushes for the tools of artful application"; color names range from "serenity" to "sensuality," from "passion" to "wisdom." Like Plato's focus on the beauty of one's soul, "Philosophy" offers "a way of life for the thinking mind and feeling heart in search of simplicity and balance."

Thus, the aesthetics component brings color to the monotony of gray in our lives (and faces); logic brings reason to dialectic; metaphysics posits Beauty that transcends the world around us; ethics reminds us of our responsibilities to others, including future generations who seek to imitate women they admire; and epistemology reminds us that, as Aquinas claimed, the beautiful is that which calms the desire by being seen or *known.* The new age of beauty recalls the old; it is only the disguise that misleads us into thinking it has never been seen or known before.

Has beauty become dangerous or has it always been so? I invite you to keep these basic philosophical notions in mind as you travel through the essays in this collection, in order to formulate your own thoughts on beauty, the passion of the soul it incites, the desire it calms, and the virtue it inspires in us all.

NOTES

1. Naomi Wolf, *The Beauty Myth: How Images of Beauty Are Used against Women* (New York: William Morrow, 1991). Sandra Lee Bartky criticizes the "fashion beauty complex" in *Femininity and Domination: Studies in the Phenomenology of Oppression* (New York: Routledge, 1990). See also Rose Weitz, ed., *The Politics of Women's Bodies: Sexuality, Appearance, and Behavior* (New York and Oxford: Oxford University Press, 1998). For a contrasting view that emphasizes empowerment, see Nancy Friday, *The Power of Beauty* (New York: HarperCollins, 1996), and Harriet Rubin, *The Princessa: Machiavelli for Women* (New York: Bantam Doubleday Dell, 1997). An additional bibliography follows these notes, organized according to category.

2. Kathy Davis, *Reshaping the Female Body: The Dilemma of Cosmetic Surgery* (New York and London: Routledge, 1995).

3. This phrase is captured in the title of a text by Judy Chicago and Edward Lucie-Smith, *Women and Art: Contested Territory* (New York: Watson Guptil, 1999). Several new texts have recently been published that highlight the representation of women in portraiture (see bibliography).

4. See Elizabeth Hayt, "The Artist Is a Glamour Puss," *New York Times*, April 18, 1999, Sunday Styles section, pp. 1, 4. A show of young women artists who dress like fashion models is reviewed; the author notes, "exuding glamour or sexuality is an extension of the themes in their work, the 90s being a decade in which many artists have made images of high fashion their point of departure."

5. See Dave Hickey's text, *The Invisible Dragon: Four Essays on Beauty* (Los Angeles: Art Issues, 1993); Kertess's quote is found in Paul Goldberger, "Klaus Kertess and the Making of the Whitney Biennial," *New York Times Magazine*, February 26, 1995, p. 61; Peter Schjeldahl, "Beauty Is Back: A Trampled Esthetic Blooms Again," *New York Times Magazine*, September 29, 1996, p. 161.

6. Bill Beckley and David Shapiro, eds., *Uncontrollable Beauty: Toward a New Aesthetics* (New York: School of Visual Arts and Allworth Press, 1998).

7. Scott Heller, "Wearying of Cultural Studies, Some Scholars Rediscover Beauty," *Chronicle of Higher Education*, December 4, 1998, pp. A15–A16.

8. Hickey, *Invisible Dragon*, p. 23.

9. Roberta Smith, "A Show of British Moderns Seeking to Shock," *New York Times*, November 23, 1995, sec. B., p. 6.

10. Lynn Gumpert, "Glamour Girls," *Art in America* 84 (July 1996): 62–65. The title of the show is a play on Kierkegaard's 1849 text, *The Sickness unto Death*.

11. John Updike, "Can Genitals Be Beautiful?" *New York Review of Books* 44, no. 19 (December 4, 1997): 10, 12.

12. Hickey, *Invisible Dragon*, p. 40.

13. Schjeldahl, "Beauty Is Back," p. 161; see also Schjeldahl, "Notes on Beauty," in *Uncontrollable Beauty*, p. 55.

14. Beckley and Shapiro, *Uncontrollable Beauty*, pp. x–xi.

15. Noriku Fuku, "A Woman of Parts," *Art in America* 85 (June 1997): 80. See also Zdenek Felix and Martin Schwander, eds., *Cindy Sherman: Photographic Work 1975–1995* (Munich: Schirmer Art Books, 1995).

16. Guy Sircello, *A New Theory of Beauty* (Princeton: Princeton University Press, 1975); see also his *Love and Beauty* (Princeton: Princeton University Press, 1989); Mary Mothersill, *Beauty Restored* (Oxford: Oxford University Press, 1984).

17. Danto addressed this question in an essay entitled "Beauty and Morality," in *Embodied Meanings: Critical Essays and Aesthetic Meditations* (New York: Farrar Straus Giroux, 1994), p. 375. He had attended a conference entitled "Whatever Happened to Beauty?" at the University of Texas–Austin in 1992. The essay is reprinted in Beckley and Shapiro, eds., *Uncontrollable Beauty*, pp. 25–37.

18. Edmund Burke, *A Philosophical Enquiry into the Origin of Our Ideas of the Sublime and Beautiful*, trans. J. T. Boulton (Notre Dame: University of Notre Dame Press, 1968), p. 115.

19. Ibid., p. 91.

20. See Meg Armstrong, "'The Effects of Blackness': Gender, Race, and the Sublime in Aesthetic Theories of Burke and Kant," *Journal of Aesthetics and Art Criticism* 54 (1996): 213–236. For the manifestation of this tendency in works of art, see, for example, Albert Boime, *The Art of Exclusion: Representing Blacks in the Nineteenth Century* (Washington, D.C., and London: Smithsonian Institution Press, 1990). Many more texts have appeared in the past decade.

21. In his notes, Taylor hints at the ongoing debate over Madam C. J. Walker's hair-straightening and skin-lightening products of the early 1900s. I would like to add a note about the socioeconomics of Walker's accomplishments. "Walker women," similar to women today who sell Avon products, were employed in large numbers at salaries that were higher than average for black women in the United States; by 1916, 20,000 were employed in the United States, Central America, and the Caribbean. Walker is heralded as "America's first black, self-made female millionaire" who actively engaged in and promoted philanthropy. See A'Lelia Perry Bundles, *Madam C. J. Walker, Entrepreneur* (New York and Philadelphia: Chelsea House, 1991).

22. See Karen Hanson, "Dressing Down Dressing Up: The Philosophic Fear of Fashion," in Hilde Hein and Carolyn Korsmeyer, eds., *Aesthetics in Feminist Perspective* (Bloomington and Indianapolis: Indiana University Press, 1993), pp. 229–241.

23. Recall Bordo's text on anorexia nervosa, *Unbearable Weight: Feminism, Western Culture, and the Body* (Berkeley: University of California Press, 1993).

24. See also Henry A. Giroux, "Innocence Lost: Child Beauty Pageants and the Politics of Abuse," *New Art Examiner* 25, no. 9 (June 1998): 26–31; and Joyce Carol Oates, "Who Killed JonBenet Ramsey?" *New York Review of Books* 46, no. 11 (June 24, 1999), pp. 31–37.

25. See for instance, Rosalind E. Krauss, *Bachelors* (Cambridge, Mass., and London: MIT Press, 1999).

26. Maud Lavin, *Cut with the Kitchen Knife: The Weimar Photomontages of Hannah Höch* (New Haven: Yale University Press, 1993).

27. A review of Schneeman's recent retrospective show is the subject of an essay by

Nancy Princenthal entitled "The Arrogance of Pleasure," *Art in America* 85 (October 1997): 106–109.

28. Laura Mulvey, "Cosmetics and Abjection: Cindy Sherman 1977–87," in *Fetishism and Curiosity* (Bloomington and Indianapolis: Indiana University Press, 1996), pp. 66, 69.

29. Lowery Stokes Sims, "The Mirror, The Other: The Politics of Aesthetics," *Artforum* 28 (March 1990): 111–115. See also Adrian Piper, *Out of Order, Out of Sight*, 2 vols. (Cambridge, Mass.: MIT Press, 1996).

30. See, for example, Goldin's "Getting High, New York City" (1979) or Mary Ellen Mark's "Heroin Addict on the Toilet" (1969) in Carmen Vendelin, "Junk Sells," *New Art Examiner* 25 (November 1997): 34–38.

31. For a fascinating anthropological view on why so-called Venus of Willendorf figures portray women with big breasts and stomachs, see Le Roy D. McDermott, "Self-Representation in Upper Paleolithic Female Figurines," *Current Anthropology* 37, no. 2 (April 1996): 227–275. McDermott suggests they were created by pregnant women to record their own bodies (as they looked down at them).

32. Morimura gained much attention when his exhibit, *Sickness unto Beauty—Self-Portrait as Actress*, traveled to the United States. According to one critic, the body of work was intended to "signal the artist's philosophical and almost perverse interest in the concept of beauty." See Gumpert, "Glamour Girls," p. 62.

33. The discussion of women's bodies in dance is infrequent in philosophy. For philosophical implications of Sally Banes's text, *Dancing Women: Female Bodies on Stage* (New York and London: Routledge, 1998), see my essay "Bodies, Agency, and Beauvoir," part of a symposium in *Dance Research Journal* 31, no. 2 (Fall 1999): 114–117.

34. The "Philosophy" line is available in department stores and at www.philosophy.com (1–888–2new-age). All quotes are taken from a catalog dated January 1998.

35. It is interesting that the ad uses the phrase, "fundamental physical science," since several books have just been published dealing with the evolutionary role of beauty and the attraction between sexes as an indicator of species survival. Examples include Nancy Etcoff, *The Survival of the Prettiest: The Science of Beauty* (New York: Doubleday, 1999); for a critique of beauty evolutionists, see Jacque Lynn Foltyn, *The Importance of Being Beautiful* (New York: HarperCollins, 1999). For a "new science of evolutionary psychology" see Natalie Angier, *Woman: An Intimate Geography* (Boston and New York: Houghton Mifflin, 1999).

ADDITIONAL BIBLIOGRAPHY

Philosophy

Brand, Peg Zeglin, and Carolyn Korsmeyer, eds. 1995. *Feminism and Tradition in Aesthetics.* University Park: Pennsylvania State University Press.

Budd, Malcolm. 1998. "Delight in the Natural World: Kant on the Aesthetic Appreciation of Nature." *British Journal of Aesthetics* 38. "Part I: Natural Beauty," pp. 1–18; "Part II: Natural Beauty and Morality," pp. 117–126; "Part III: The Sublime in Nature," pp. 233–250.

Carroll, Noël. 1991. "Beauty and the Genealogy of Art Theory." *Philosophical Forum* 22, no. 4 (Summer): 307–334.

Devereaux, Mary. 1998. "Beauty and Evil: The Case of Leni Riefenstahl's *Triumph of the Will.*" In Jerrold Levinson, ed., *Aesthetics and Ethics.* Cambridge: Cambridge University Press, pp. 227–256.

Eaton, Marcia Muelder, ed. 1997. *What about Beauty?* Minneapolis: University of Minnesota Department of Art.

Gaut, Berys, and Dominic McIver Lopes, eds. 2000. *Routledge Companion to Aesthetics.* London and New York: Routledge.

Hipple, Walter John, Jr. 1957. *The Beautiful, the Sublime, and the Picturesque in Eighteenth-Century British Aesthetic Theory.* Carbondale: Southern Illinois University Press.

Kelly, Michael, ed. 1998. *Encyclopedia of Aesthetics.* Oxford University Press.

Kirwan, James. 1999. *Beauty.* Manchester: Manchester University Press, St. Martin's Press.

Kivy, Peter, ed. 1992. *Essays on the History of Aesthetics.* New York: University of Rochester Press.

Korsmeyer, Carolyn, ed. 1998. *Aesthetics: The Big Questions.* Oxford: Blackwell Publishers.

Li, Zehou. 1994. *The Path of Beauty: A Study of Chinese Aesthetics.* Oxford: Oxford University Press.

Mattick, Paul, Jr., ed. 1993. *Eighteenth-Century Aesthetics and the Reconstruction of Art.* Cambridge: Cambridge University Press.

McMahon, Jennifer. 1999. "Towards a Unified Theory of Beauty." *The Journal of the Sydney Society of Literature and Aesthetics* 9 (October): 7–27.

Paulson, Ronald, ed. 1997. *William Hogarth: The Analysis of Beauty.* New Haven and London: Yale University Press.

Ross, Stephen David. 1996. *The Gift of Beauty: The Good as Art.* Albany: State University of New York Press.

Turner, Frederick. 1991. *Beauty: The Value of Values.* Charlottesville: University of Virginia Press.

Zemach, Eddy M. 1997. *Real Beauty.* University Park: Pennsylvania State University Press.

Cultural Studies

Gilman, Sander L. 1998. *Creating Beauty to Cure the Soul: Race and Psychology in the Shaping of Aesthetic Surgery.* Durham, N.C.: Duke University Press.

Levine, George, ed. 1994. *Aesthetics and Ideology.* New Brunswick, N.J.: Rutgers University Press.

Scarry, Elaine. 1994. *Resisting Representation.* New York: Oxford University Press.

———. 1999. *Dreaming by the Book.* New York: Farrar, Straus, Giroux.

———. 1999. *On Beauty and Being Just.* Princeton University Press.

Soderholm, James, ed. 1997. *Beauty and the Critic: Aesthetics in an Age of Cultural Studies.* Tuscaloosa: University of Alabama Press.

Taylor, Clyde R. 1998. *The Mask of Art: Breaking the Aesthetic Contract—Film and Literature.* Bloomington and Indianapolis: Indiana University Press.

Van Damme, Wilfried. 1996. *Beauty in Context: Towards an Anthropological Approach to Aesthetics.* Leiden and New York: E. J. Brill.

Gender Studies

Angier, Natalie. 1999. *Woman: An Intimate Geography.* Boston and New York: Houghton Mifflin.

Bordo, Susan. 1997. *Twilight Zones: The Hidden Life of Cultural Images from Plato to O.J.* Berkeley: University of California Press.

Brown, Lyn Mikel. 1998. *Raising Their Voices: The Politics of Girls' Anger.* Cambridge, Mass.: Harvard University Press.

Brumberg, Joan Jacobs. 1997. *The Body Project: An Intimate History of American Girls.* New York: Random House.

Chancer, Lynn S. 1998. *Reconcilable Differences: Confronting Beauty, Pornography, and the Future of Feminism.* Berkeley: University of California Press.

Etcoff, Nancy. 1999. *The Survival of the Prettiest: The Science of Beauty.* New York: Doubleday.

Folton, Jacque Lynn. 1999. *The Importance of Being Beautiful.* New York: HarperCollins.

Friday, Nancy. 1996. *The Power of Beauty.* New York: HarperCollins.

Frueh, Joanna. 2000. *Monster/Beauty: Building the Body of Love.* Berkeley: University of California Press.

Heywood, Leslie. 1996. *Dedication to Hunger: The Anorexic Aesthetic in Modern Culture.* Berkeley: University of California Press.

———. 1998. *Bodymakers: A Cultural Anatomy of Women's Body Building.* New Brunswick, N.J.: Rutgers University Press.

Lowe, Maria. 1998. *Women of Steel: Female Bodybuilders and the Struggle for Self-Definition.* New York: New York University Press.

Moore, Pamela, ed. 1997. *Building Bodies.* New Brunswick, N.J.: Rutgers University Press.

Nelson, Miriam E. 1997. *Strong Women Stay Young.* New York: Bantam Books.

Nussbaum, Emily. 1998. "Bodies That Matter." *Lingua Franca* 8, no. 7 (October): 53–60.

Pipher, Mary. 1994. *Reviving Ophelia: Saving the Selves of Adolescent Girls.* New York: Putnam.

Rubin, Harriet. 1997. *The Princessa: Machiavelli for Women.* New York: Bantam Doubleday Dell.

Weitz, Rose, ed. 1998. *The Politics of Women's Bodies: Sexuality, Appearance, and Behavior.* New York: Oxford University Press.

Wendell, Susan. 1996. *The Rejected Body: Feminist Philosophical Reflections on Disability.* New York: Routledge.

Woodward, Kathleen, ed. 1999. *Figuring Age: Women, Bodies, Generations.* Bloomington and Indianapolis: Indiana University Press.

Women in Art/Women Artists

Borzello, Frances. 1998. *Seeing Ourselves: Women's Self-Portraits.* New York: Harry N. Abrams.

Broude, Norma, and Mary D. Garrard. 1994. *The Power of Feminist Art: The American Movement of the 1970s, History and Impact*. New York: Harry N. Abrams.

Chadwick, Whitney, ed. 1998. *Mirror Images: Women, Surrealism, and Self-Representation*. Cambridge, Mass., and London: MIT Press.

Chicago, Judy, and Edward Lucie-Smith. 1999. *Women and Art: Contested Territory*. New York: Watson-Guptill.

Chino, Kaori. 1997. *Art and Gender*. Tokyo: Buryukke Publishers.

———. 1999. *Women? Japan? Beauty?* Tokyo: Keio University Press.

Deepwell, Katy, ed. 1995. *New Feminist Art Criticism: Critical Strategies*. Manchester: Manchester University Press.

Duby, Georges, and Michelle Perrot, eds. 1992. *Power and Beauty: Images of Women in Art*. London: I. B. Tauris.

Goldstein, Laurence, ed. 1991. *The Female Body: Figures, Styles, Speculations*. Ann Arbor: University of Michigan Press.

Jones, Amelia, ed. 1996. *Sexual Politics: Judy Chicago's "Dinner Party" in Feminist Art History*. Berkeley: University of California Press.

Kauffman, Linda S. 1998. *Bad Girls and Sick Boys: Fantasies in Contemporary Art and Culture*. Berkeley: University of California Press.

Kirsch, Andrea. 1993. *Carrie Mae Weems*. Washington, D.C.: National Museum of Women in the Arts.

Krauss, Rosalind. 1999. *Bachelors*. Cambridge, Mass.: MIT Press.

Larsen, Ernest. 1999. "Between Worlds" [on Carrie Mae Weems]. *Art in America* 87, no. 5 (May): 122–129.

Lavin, Maud. 1993. *Cut with the Kitchen Knife: The Weimar Photomontages of Hannah Höch*. New Haven and London: Yale University Press.

Lucie-Smith, Edward. 2000. *Judy Chicago: An American Vision*. New York: Watson Guptill.

Meskimmon, Marsha. 1996. *The Art of Reflection: Women Artists' Self-Portraiture in the Twentieth Century*. New York: Columbia University Press.

Pacteau, Francette. 1994. *The Symptom of Beauty: Essays in Art and Culture*. Cambridge, Mass.: Harvard University Press.

Piche, Thomas, Jr. 1998. *Carrie Mae Weems: Recent Work, 1992–1998*. New York: Everson Museum of Art, Syracuse University.

Pollock, Griselda. 1999. *Differencing the Canon: Feminist Desire and the Writing of Art's Histories*. New York: Routledge.

———. 1996. *Generations and Geographies in the Visual Arts: Feminist Readings*. London and New York: Routledge.

Slaven, Michael. 1998. "Jail Bait at the Millennium: Lolita's Grotesque Body." *New Art Examiner* 25, no. 9 (June): 14–19.

Fashion/Beauty Industry

Banet-Weiser, Sarah. 1999. *The Most Beautiful Girl in the World: Beauty Pageants and National Identity*. Berkeley: University of California Press.

Coleman, William P., III, William C. Hanke, III, William R. Cook, Jr., and Rhoda S. Body Narins. 1997. *Contouring: The New Art of Liposculpture*. Carmel, Ind.: Cooper Publishing Group.

Cooke, Kaz. 1996. *Real Gorgeous: The Truth About Body and Beauty.* New York: W.W. Norton.

Davis, Kathy. 1995. *Reshaping the Female Body: The Dilemma of Cosmetic Surgery.* New York and London: Routledge.

Gilman, Sander L. 1999. *Making the Body Beautiful: A Cultural History of Aesthetic Surgery.* Princeton, N.J.: Princeton University Press.

Haiden, Elizabeth. 1997. *Venus Envy: A History of Cosmetic Surgery.* Baltimore: Johns Hopkins University Press.

Mulvey, Kate, and Melissa Richards. 1998. *Decades of Beauty: The Changing Image of Women, 1890s–1990s.* New York: Facts on File.

Simon, Marie. 1995. *Fashion in Art.* London: Zwemmer.

Steele, Valerie. 1996. *Fetish: Fashion, Sex, and Power.* New York: Oxford University Press.

PART ONE

Beyond Kant

Marcia M. Eaton

1. Kantian and Contextual Beauty

Two conflicting but strongly entrenched intuitions about beauty hold sway in the hearts and minds of many. On the one hand, many people believe that attributions of beauty to objects or events are unmediated — that all that matters is one's direct, personal response. If something is beautiful, one just sees it; cognitive or ethical concerns matter little. On the other hand, many people are drawn to the view that the beautiful is not independent of other human values and attitudes — that our attributions of beauty are related to beliefs or moral judgments. At the end of the eighteenth century, Immanuel Kant represented the former view with such cleverness that his arguments continue to disturb even those who remain unconvinced by them. At the end of the nineteenth century, partly as a result of the influence of Kant's theory of beauty, Leo Tolstoy felt forced to downplay the importance of beauty's role in explaining the value of art — a trend that continued for several decades. At the end of the twentieth century, increasing numbers of aesthetic theorists and practitioners are persuaded that beauty *does* matter in art, and although many, including me, believe that beauty is a contextual property deeply connected to factual beliefs and moral attitudes, the tug of Kant's arguments remains strong.

I stand near the edge of one of Minneapolis's many urban lakes. A tall purple flower brightens the marshy shore. I recognize that it is purple loosestrife, an exotic plant species imported several years ago. I know that it tends to overtake areas where it takes root — that if left alone it will rapidly destroy the delicate ecosystem so important for water purification and for the support of a wide range of plant and wildlife. I know that this is a dangerous, even evil, plant. A friend of mine who is a landscape designer has a poster on her office door urging us to wipe it out. She tells me she finds it ugly—even repulsive. But as I stand near the lake, looking at the purple blossoms that stand out so vibrantly against the more or less uniformly colored background of the swamp, I cannot prevent myself from finding the plant quite beautiful.

This is anything but an isolated example of conflicting perceptions of beauty. From admiring wispy female actors who we are certain must be suffering from bulimia to glorying in ancient temples whose construction we have learned resulted in the deaths of hundreds of oppressed slaves, we often find that we cannot help ourselves—that Kant seems to be right to have insisted that where beauty is concerned, what we know and what we morally approve or disapprove seems irrelevant.

But then I think again of my ecologist friend. Does she not see what I see when she looks at the wetland? Is she truly un-seduced by the lush color? How, if Kant is right, does she see ugliness where I see beauty? And how, if Kant is right, do changes in my beliefs or moral assessments sometimes produce a change in my aesthetic views?

Kant argued that several features characterize a judgment that something is beautiful (*Critique of Judgment,* 1790). On occasion our imaginations take a holiday, as it were. When we apprehend the form of some objects or events, we feel pleasure in the purposive way the properties relate and realize that our pleasure is in no way dependent upon a particular interest, purpose, or concept. Because our pleasure is not in any way tied essentially to who we are as individuals, we expect that every other human being necessarily ought to feel pleasure as well upon apprehending this thing. We do not care what the object is (or even *that* it is—i.e., if we feel pleasure we do not really care whether the apparent cause of the pleasure actually exists), we do not have to know what it is, we do not care whether it is moral or immoral, we do not care who made it, or why. Judgments that something is ugly (not beautiful) will be like this, too—the only difference will be that we feel displeasure instead of pleasure.

Tolstoy believed that pleasure alone cannot account for the tremendous value that art has. Pleasure-based theories like Kant's led him to dismiss beauty as central to art. Just as one may forget, as one eats with pleasure, that the real value of food is bodily nutrition and not the enjoyment one derives, so one may be misled into thinking that the value of art is pleasure and not, as it were, the nutrition of the soul of an individual and of a community. For Tolstoy the source of the value of art is spiritual rather than hedonic, and thus any theory of art with a pleasure-based theory of beauty will be inadequate (*What Is Art?* 1896).[1]

To a great extent, Kant more than Tolstoy influenced twentieth-century aesthetics in Eurocentric cultures. Formalist theorists[2] insisted that disinterested apprehension of directly perceivable properties (color, rhythm, meter, balance, proportion, etc.) distinguished aesthetic experiences from all others. Kant never won the day in many non-Eurocentric cultures, however. Native Americans, for example, continued to connect aesthetic activity directly to "interested" and functional objects and events. Descriptions of objects or events as "beautiful" in most African cultures never required distinguishing "What is it for?" from "How does it look?" Even in Eurocentric cultures, outside the rather narrow "mainstream" art world (professional artists, critics, curators, etc.) formalism was never wholly accepted or practiced. Attributions of beauty made by ordinary persons-on-the-street have been unabashedly affected by moral values and factual beliefs. Recognition of this has resulted in what I have elsewhere described as a "contextual turn" in aesthetics. Feminists and ethnicists have contributed greatly to this turn. As the title of this symposium suggests, beauty matters (verb) and beauty matters (noun) have really never stopped being centrally important for a whole lot of reasons beyond the pleasure taken in morally and factually disinterested apprehension of form.[3]

Tolstoy thought that if Kant were correct, beauty could not matter — or at least could not matter enough. His tack was to look elsewhere to explain the importance of art. But suppose we go another way and say, *but beauty does matter.* Then Kant must not be correct. But just where did he go astray?

First, few people, in my experience, seem to agree that beauty is either universal or necessary. Being fully aware that my ecologist friend sees ugliness where I find beauty does not prevent me from making the judgment that the purple loosestrife is beautiful. The "beautiful people" that many of my generation see on some television advertisements seem positively repulsive, but we do not doubt for a moment that the younger audience to whom these marketing strategies are directed admire and strive to emulate them. Even in subcultures where one might expect agreement, one is disappointed. Attend a Women's Studies meeting at any university and one is struck with the differing degrees to which the women (and men) around the table buy into ideals of beauty extolled in commercial advertisements for everything from beer to running shoes. Many who wish that physical appearance mattered less in the United States find it hard not to hate our own bodies. The average size of a woman now is no smaller — in fact is

This Bwa "Plank Mask" is displayed in the African Gallery at the Minneapolis Institute of Arts, along with a photograph by art historian Christopher Roy that shows how such masks are used in Bwa ceremonies. Courtesy of the Minneapolis Institute of Arts and Dr. Christopher Roy.

probably larger—than it was during World War II. But the size-fourteen mannequins that looked beautiful in the 1940s have been replaced in store windows by size-six (or smaller) mannequins. It does no good, that is, neither assuages guilt nor prevents bulimia, to be reminded that Rubens' or even Renoir's "beautiful people" included "full-sized" women. As a society we seem unable to decide whether true self-esteem lies in accepting one's lumps and rolls or in managing to achieve the discipline it takes to get rid of them. However one answers this, one cannot help but be aware that the judgment is not shared by everyone; nor would most people insist that others ought to agree. I might prefer lunching with the folks on Renoir's boisterous boats to lunching with the people on Calvin Klein's dreary

A comparison of mannequin and dress sizes. Left: Halston dress, ca. 1970, New York, size 4. Right: Edward Molyneux dress, ca. 1925, Paris. Courtesy of Elizabeth Sage Historic Costume Collection. © Indiana University Art Museum. Photograph by Michael Cavanagh and Kevin Montague.

Papier-mâché mannequin, ca. 1940, created by Alice Bonabel, Paris. Post–World War II mannequins were inspired by the new Dior dress models, which were created with the measurements 36–22–37. Compare this size to standard-sized mannequins of the 1940s, which measured 35–24–36 ¹/₂. From Mannequins *(New York: Academy Editions; St. Martin's Press, 1982).*

urban streets—but I am certain that my preference is neither universal nor necessary. And just when we think we have found something that will please everyone—that beautiful wetland plant—we find someone who is distressed by it.

But Tolstoy, at least, did not reject beauty because it was not a universally or necessarily applied concept. He recognized that cultures and individuals will differ. The value of art is determined by the specific religious perceptions of a society, he claimed. He rejected beauty as central to art's value for conceptual and contextual reasons; he rejected it because he believed that art's importance in human lives depends upon seeing how it is tied to interests and beliefs that contribute to a community's sustainability.

So was Kant wrong to insist that when someone judges something to be beautiful it is independent of interests or purposes? My own experience — such as differing with my friend about purple loosestrife — leads to me think, with Tolstoy, that Kant was mistaken. Beliefs and moral value do, apparently, make a difference, at least sometimes to some people. "I used to think purple loosestrife was beautiful, but then I learned what it does to wetland ecosystems, and now I find it ugly." "Those melodies sung by Carmen sounded beautiful to me before I thought more deeply about what they imply about women's role; now they only make angry." "When I learned the 'painting' actually was blood and feces, not oil, on a canvas, the designs stopped being beautiful and became ugly for me."[4] That people make such statements cannot be denied. Of course, it is possible that when they say such things these speakers are all misusing the term "beautiful." But who gets to decide this? Surely just because Kant would say they have it wrong it does not follow that they do — not even if a majority of philosophers of art agree with him.

But, of course, just as many people — perhaps all of us on occasion — have experienced the disinterested, amoral, afactual pleasure Kant describes. What does one have to know about that sunset or that song to sense the beauty? Nothing, many respond. "I walked into the museum and there it was — that beautiful thing. I didn't know who made it or what it was, and I didn't care." "You don't have to know anything about geology to find the Grand Canyon beautiful." These statements also make perfectly good sense.[5]

So we are faced with a conflict:

1. One feels the pleasure required for the judgment that something is beautiful independently of what one knows or values.

2. The pleasure required for the judgment that something is beautiful diminishes, disappears, or is even replaced by displeasure as one's beliefs or values change.

The uses of "beauty" associated with these two phenomena are both entrenched in the language.[6] One is not puzzled to hear instances of statements that express either view. Nor do we feel inclined to correct people who use it either way (or both ways).

We can only conclude, I believe, that there are two related but different senses of the word. For want of better terms, I shall call these two senses the Kantian and the contextual. My own prejudices go in the direction of the contextual. That is, I am rather confused when someone claims that *no knowledge or moral stand at all is involved* in the judgment that something is beautiful. Surely one needs to know—at least usually does know—a great deal before one says that a poem or a horse or a dynamo or a mathematical proof is beautiful. Would one not be puzzled to hear a person insist that, although evil, the gas chambers used by Nazi Germans to commit genocide were nonetheless quite beautiful? Often a causal chain is involved; pleasure taken in apprehension of an object's form will occur only if attention is directed at that form, and this will often require knowledge of what in the form one is to look for or at. A concept (poem, horse, dynamo, proof) leads one to notice things (rhythm, muscle structure, organization of parts, organization of evidence), and the noticing is pleasurable. This explains why repeated exposure is frequently required before pleasure results— why, for example, one only hears that a particular musical composition is beautiful after one has listened to it several times. Understanding and even sympathizing with an author's moral point of view is sometimes required in order to notice relationships between characters. Changes in ecological and ethical beliefs and values have resulted in changing *perceptions* of wetlands in our own time.

Still, I am willing to admit that concepts and moral values may not always be necessary, indeed may sometimes be irrelevant. "Whatever that colorful shape is, it's beautiful." "Even if what I thought was a flower turns out to be a bird, it is still beautiful!"

I do think these "pure," conceptless, valueless uses of "beauty" are rare. It certainly has been a mistake for aestheticians to take this sense of beauty as the paradigmatic aesthetic concept—to act, that is, as if by giving an account of it one automatically has given an account for all aesthetic properties. Many, I would wager most, aesthetic terms are "impure"—they reflect, even require, beliefs and values: sincere, suspenseful, sentimental, shallow, sensitive, subtle, sexy, sensual, salacious, sordid, sobering, sustainable, skillful . . . and that, of course, only scratches the surface of the s-words! It would be better, that is, our conversations would be clearer and less misleading, if we were to admit that there are two strongly entrenched senses of the word "beauty" and were to move to replace one of them with another word. Most philosophers have given up (or should have given up by now) on urging language reform. Trying to find substitutes for terms as deeply entrenched in the language as is "beauty" presents particularly messy problems. Instead, we will have to live with the duality; but we must always be alert to it. In general, "beauty" will continue to refer to the pleasure one feels when attending to intrinsic properties of objects or events; but only on some occasions of its use will it also connote an absence of thought or moral judgment.

When one moves beyond Eurocentric cultures, it becomes an even greater mistake to take the Kantian sense of beauty as paradigmatic. Persons in other cultures *are* genuinely confused by (or downright contemptuous of) expressions of the Kantian "beauty-for-beauty's-sake" approach; that is, they think the word must be being misused. Why something is made, who is making it, what it is made from, and the satisfaction taken in the apprehension of and understanding of all these is as or more important than pleasure taken in the apprehension of formal qualities alone. Awareness of this gives support to those in Eurocentric cultures who have dissented from the Kantian line and insist that beauty—and art—cannot be sustained in anti-feminist, antisocial, anti-environmental contexts.

At the end of the eighteenth century, Kant thought he had solved one problem—the reconciliation of subjective and objective uses of "beauty," that is, the intuition that at one and the same time a person who says "That is beautiful" refers to his or her own particular inner pleasures, but also realizes that the judgment is, or at least should be, universal. He did it by insisting that the person who realizes that his or her response results from a shared humanity will believe that all people *ought* to agree. At the end of the nineteenth century Tolstoy wanted more, and I sense that growing numbers of us at the end of the twentieth century share his desire. How, if beauty is based on individual pleasure alone, can it contribute to the binding of communities that Tolstoy and many of us today long for? Believing that others will and must agree with me (even when I can believe that) is not sufficient. Believing that they ought to agree with me can even be dangerous. Action is required—action that leads to respect for and cooperation with others in personal and communal projects. Holmes Rolston III reports that his grandfather said that someone knows the meaning of life when he plants a tree whose shade he will not sit under.[7] The Kantian sense of "beauty" is unlikely to yield such a worldview, I think.

I have argued elsewhere[8] that there is a kind of beauty that requires health, namely the beauty attributed to sustainable environments. It is harder for me to root out purple loosestrife than it is for my ecologist friend. It is harder for all of us to fight bulimia as long as we prefer size-six models to size-fourteen models. The beauty that is required by healthy societies seems to have eluded us as well. Recently art critic Roberta Smith described an arrangement of cigarette butts as "strikingly beautiful."[9] I doubt that I would have been so struck. I am certain that most people in the

United States, let alone the world, would not see the beauty that Smith saw. And when the majority are struck by the beauty of something—by a Monet painting or a Yanni concert or a performance of *Riverdance*—they are often made to feel the brunt of contempt of professional critics. I doubt that Kant's definitions of "beauty" can do much to improve the health of marshes or nations. I do not see how that kind of beauty can matter—at least in the way I think beauty can and should. The formalists thought that beauty could matter only if it were given its own niche. But, made pure, given its own niche, beauty stops mattering.

Notes

1. Tolstoy claimed that art should express the religious perception of a culture. Today we would be more inclined, I think, to speak of spirituality—referring to that outside of oneself that one believes is important enough to serve and make sacrifices for.

2. For example, the theories of Clive Bell and Roger Fry in art criticism, Jerome Stolnitz in philosophy of art.

3. While working on this paper, I have also been writing a catalog for a series of lectures at the University of Minnesota entitled "What about Beauty?" The wording of the question plays on the persistence of a child's or an outsider's demand to be heard: "What about me?" But the consensus answer—"A lot about you"—suggests that beauty has never been the outsider in the lives of most people.

4. Kant distinguished between aesthetic and artistic value and recognized that cognitive and moral judgments can be relevant to *artistic* assessments. However, the Kantians or formalists that I contrast with contextualists in this paper do not make this distinction. Here, of course, I am discussing Kantians rather than Kant per se.

5. There are certainly many cultures in which beauty is tied to function, knowledge, morality, etc. But even there, I suspect, people might on occasion feel overpowering pleasure in the presence of natural formations or events about which they know little or nothing. Some landscape theorists explain this response in Darwinian terms; for example, we take pleasure in running water because it is pure, in a savannah landscape because it allows for both prospect and refuge. That is, certain natural environments provide a greater chance for human survival, so we naturally take pleasure in them. Whether this is true or not, of course, will require much more empirical research than has been done heretofore.

6. At least in the English language, and, I expect, in other Eurocentric languages.

7. Holmes Rolston III at a talk at a conference on Forest Aesthetics, Lusto, Finland, June 1996.

8. Marcia Muelder Eaton, "The Beauty That Requires Health," in *Placing Nature: Culture and Landscape Ecology*, ed. Joan Nassauer (Washington, D.C.: Island Press, 1997).

9. Roberta Smith, "A Show of British Moderns Seeking to Shock," *New York Times*, November 23, 1996, sec. B, p. 6.

2. Ethnicity, Race, and Monstrosity: The Rhetorics of Horror and Humor

There are many conceptions of beauty. Some associate beauty with proportion and harmony; some with pleasure taken in the appearance of things; and some, more narrowly, with *disinterested* pleasure. Kant, of course, uses disinterested pleasure as the central mark of what he calls free beauty. However, Kant also speaks of dependent or accessory beauty, which pertains to the aesthetic judgments we make about things in relation to the determinate concepts under which the objects in question fall.[1] Human beauty, for Kant, is of this sort.[2] We call a human beautiful, he suggests, insofar as a person approaches being a perfect example of the category or concept of human being.

This approach to human beauty has a corollary. It implies what shall count as *nonbeauty*. If human beauty is, at the limit, the perfect realization of the concept of human being, then nonbeauty is the imperfect or defective realization of the concept. That is, nonbeauty, the antithesis (or the family of antitheses) to beauty, is somehow an inadequate instantiation of the concept of human being. Moreover, these distinctions are relevant to our practices of representation: to represent a person or a group as beautiful, portray them as perfect or approximately perfect instances of the category human being (understanding that that category may be susceptible to cultural variation); to represent a person or a group as nonbeautiful, or as ugly (one of the most pertinent subcategories of nonbeauty), portray them as in some way or ways imperfect instances of the concept of the human.

In this essay, I am concerned with the representation of groups in popular culture. My interest has to do with the politics of representing people. The couplet beauty/nonbeauty (or, more specifically, beauty/ugliness) frequently figures importantly in the representation of groups, including most notably, for my purposes, ethnic and racial minorities. This couplet can be politically significant because beauty is often associated in our culture with moral goodness.[3] The beautiful exterior is taken as a sign of inward or moral goodness; the nonbeautiful or ugly exterior is often imagined to correlate with evil or depravity. Oscar Wilde's novel *The Picture of Dorian Gray* illustrates quite neatly this commonplace, which has had its philosophical defenders.

Thus, beauty and nonbeauty can serve as a basis for political rhetoric. The moral credentials of a group—an ethnicity or a race—can be endorsed by means of an association with beauty, or it can be demeaned by being represented as nonbeautiful or ugly. To show, in a caricature, a representative of an opposing faction as an ogre is to call into question the moral worth of that faction.

I suppose that this much is fairly obvious and unobjectionable. But it raises the question of how exactly this rhetoric works, at least some of the time. Part of the answer to that question, I conjecture, can be obtained by focusing on the notion of human beauty which identifies it with the perfect realization of the concept of human being. This line of speculation suggests that the way to represent a human group as depraved is to portray it as nonbeautiful or ugly, that is, as an imperfect or defective instantiation of the category of human being. If one concept of human beauty (which is connected to ideas of goodness) sees beauty as the instantiation or near approximation of the concept human being, then the related idea of human ugliness (which is connected with ideas of moral degradation) is rooted in problematic exemplifications of the concept of the human. These "problematic exemplifications" can take many forms. The two that will preoccupy me in this essay are the imperfect exemplifications of the human found in the popular genres of horror and humor.

Horror, Humor, and Concepts of the Human

One concept of beauty is applied to perfect or near-perfect examples of a kind. A perfect instance of an American Beauty Rose is called beautiful because it realizes the essential characteristics of its kind. This notion of beauty, which is fairly common in ordinary usage, is intimately connected with concepts. The beautiful object is one that at least accords maximally with the criteria for class membership for the category to which the item belongs. Often people refer to a picture as beautiful because it depicts a beautiful person, a person who is (or is thought to be) an exemplary specimen of the category of the human.

Finding a representation beautiful—or finding what is represented beautiful—is one kind of aesthetic response. There are others, such as finding a representation tragic or sublime. Of the variety of aesthetic responses we might undergo with respect to a representation, two that are especially interesting to consider in relation to finding an object beautiful are horror and comic amusement. These two responses are revealing when compared to the beauty response, because they too are intimately connected to concepts. However, while the beauty response is keyed to the perfect or exemplary realization of the relevant concept, horror and humor responses are connected to imperfect or defective instantiations of concepts. Horror and humor are, in this respect, antitheses of beauty, though antitheses that themselves diverge from each other as well in terms of their characteristic emotional timbres.

Perhaps the most straightforward way in which to substantiate this observation is to note that horror and humor both have as their natural terrain the ugly, even though they explore ugliness in different ways. The leading character in a horror movie, comic book, or the like is the monster, a creature most characteristically marked by ugliness so extreme that it is often capable of eliciting an aversive physical response.[4] Generally, the monster figure is explicitly aligned with the inhuman and its ugliness is a dramatic emblem for this.

Comedy, of course, has a more varied cast of characters. But one of particular interest is the clown type, who, like the monsters of the horror genre, is generally a subhuman being whose physical appearance deviates strikingly from the canons of human perfection: he or she is either too fat or too thin, or his or her parts (small heads, large torsos) combine disproportionately, and/or their features are vastly exaggerated—mouths, lips, and noses outsized; eyes miniscule. Clowns are designed to be ugly, though their ugliness is meant to be a source of mirth, whereas monsters are meant to horrify. Nevertheless, both monsters and clowns define themselves against the standards of humanity whose ideal approximation typically results in assessments of beauty (or, at least, dependent judgments of human beauty).[5]

Moreover, if we ask for an account of why horror and humor correlate regularly with ugliness, the answer would appear to be connected to the fact that horror and humor, like the kind of beauty we are considering, are also related to concepts. However, where beauty is connected with the perfect or near-perfect realization of concepts, horror and humor exploit intentionally pronounced deviations from concepts. Indeed, one might say that, albeit in different ways, horror and humor specialize in violating concepts.

Horror, at least in popular fictions, is a compound emotional response. It is made up of two components: fear and disgust. The horrific monster is fearsome. It kills people, maims them, possesses them, eats them. It is dangerous. But a horrific monster is not simply fearsome. It is also disgusting. Ideally, it makes our skin creep. It may make us gag. It is physically repulsive. Characteristically, we feel aversion for the monster in our body, where disgust, we might add, is a sensation that Kant himself singles out as a state that precludes the experience of beauty.[6]

But what is the basis of this feeling of revulsion? Speaking summarily, we can say that it is a reaction to the impurity of the monster. But why are monsters experienced as impure? Here it is useful to think in terms of categories and concepts. Horrific monsters violate our categories of things in various ways.

Many monsters are category errors; they contradict standing cultural concepts. They may be living and dead at the same time, like vampires and mummies, or they may be incongruous fusions of the animate and the inanimate, such as haunted houses possessed with wills of their own. Or, monsters may be interstitial figures, figures that blend, blur, or conjoin disparate categories: wolfmen, apemen, catwomen, and you-name-it-people that inhabit a conceptual space between recognized cultural categories. In addition, monsters may be incomplete realizations of standing cultural categories, like headless horsemen. That is why so many monsters are effectively amputees, like zombies without legs, missing vital parts that constitute our stereotypes for the kinds of beings in question. And, lastly, monsters may defy our standing categories and concepts by being altogether formless, shapeless, gelatinous masses of who-knows-what oozing their way to world conquest.

Where monsters are human-like, their impurity rests on their deviation from our norms of the human. They are violations of nature or, at least, of our conceptions of nature. Over the centuries, the creators of horror fictions have discovered an impressive variety of ways in which to violate our concept of the human, resulting in a bestiary of creatures that make our flesh crawl. In this respect, the popular genre of horror fiction stands outside what eighteenth-century French philosophers called the *beaux arts*.

Of course, this is no accident. Horror is a genre predicated on exploring our fascination with the ugly, the anomalous, and the category violation.

Humor, too, is deeply involved with category violation. Consider, for example, the simple children's riddle: "Why did the moron stay up all night? He was studying for his blood test." Here the humor revolves around incorrectly subsuming a blood test under the category of a scholastic examination. Likewise, the humorous saying "Comedy is when you fall down and break your neck; tragedy is when I prick my finger" provokes laughter, in part, because it exploits the conceptual incongruity of assimilating a pinprick under the category of the tragic. Whether or not conceptual incongruity explains every instance of humor is the source of much theoretical debate. However, it is clear that conceptual incongruity plays an important role in a great deal of comedy.

Where comedy is aimed at the appearance of its human objects, the notion of conceptual incongruity is particularly informative. "Funny-looking people," such as the clown figures who are designed to elicit laughter, diverge strikingly from our paradigms of the concept of the human. As noted above, they are too short or too tall, too fat or too thin, or their limbs or facial features violate the ideal proportions associated with our concept of the human. Whereas beauty converges on our ideal of the human, comedy, or at least the comedy of human appearances, is a travesty of that ideal, instantiating the concept of the human in a way that violates its canons of perfection.

The comic and horrific, with respect to human appearance, are antitheses of beauty. The monster is a violation of the concept of the human predicated on engendering fear and disgust. Comedy also indulges in transgressing the concept of the human. Comic butts and buffoons are frequently subhuman in their intellectual abilities, but, in addition, where the humor trades in appearances, comic figures are generally misshapen to the point of being studied transgressions of our stereotypical conceptions of the human form.

Horror and humor, of course, differ from each other. The conceptual anomaly of the monster is presented in a fearful context, and the result is horror. In comedy, the incongruity is presented in a context bereft of fear, and the result is comic amusement.[7] Nevertheless, both horror and humor explore the terrain of concepts anomalously exemplified. When the concept in question is our category of the human, horror and humor are antitheses of beauty, the latter epitomizing the human form, the former instantiating it freakishly in order to provoke anxiety, on the one hand, or laughter, on the other.

Ethnicity, Race, and Rhetoric

Inasmuch as there is an association between human beauty and good-ness, this opens the possibility of using nonbeauty and ugliness as a sign of a demoted moral status. Horror and humor are genres that specialize in nonbeauty and ugliness. Thus, it should come as no surprise that horror and humor are serviceable and frequently exploited strategies for demean-ing the ethical status of real or imagined political adversaries. This is readily borne out by the history of popular caricature, where it is common to rebuke pictorially the persons and factions the caricaturist suspects by rendering them either as monsters or as beings with comically exaggerated physiognomies, verging on and sometimes exceeding the clownish.

These strategies are often applied to individuals. But they can also be marshaled at the expense of entire groups—not only political parties and social classes, but ethnic and racial groups as well. In these cases, the rhetorics of horror and humor do double duty. For not only do they brand their objects as morally depraved, but they also figure their victims as subhuman and, therefore, as unworthy of the moral concern that befits a human person. That is, by portraying peoples of other ethnicities and races in terms of horrific and comic appearances, the notion that they are not quite human is literalized, while, at the same time, their distance from the canons of beauty, which symbolize our ideal concept of the human, mea-sure their remoteness from the good.

Undoubtedly it is because horror and the humor of appearances are, like beauty, so intimately connected to our concept of the human—at the level of what we might call folk biology—that these genres provide such an employable set of rhetorical strategies for ethnic and racial scorn. By por-traying their objects as antitheses of beauty, they not only associate them with evil, but render them not quite human—so far have they fallen short of our concept of humanity that they need not be treated morally. With the horror genre, the default is that we do not worry about the rights of mon-sters, while, with humor, the moral claims of comic butts can rarely be entertained without compromising the gag or the joke. Thus, in mobiliz-ing the visual vocabularies of horror and humor, the ideologue not only puts the relevant ethnicities and races beyond the human pale but also deprives them of the moral consideration appropriate to members of the class of human beings.

Recurrent examples of the use of horrific and/or humorous imagery against ethnic minorities can be found in British pictorial treatments of the Irish throughout the nineteenth century. In the June 18, 1881, issue of

Punch, John Tenniel produced an illustration entitled "The Irish Devil-Fish," which portrayed the Irish Land League as a composite figure, part octopus but with a grotesque human head where one might otherwise expect a tentacle.[8] The image is of the sort that one expects to find in a low-budget horror film. It is a literal fusion of the human with a mollusc, a violation of biological categories predicated on raising a sense of visceral disgust in the viewer—which disgust, of course, is designed to be transferred to the Irish in general.

This sort of composite figure is a staple of horror. Think how many horrific figures, like the Fly, are impossible hybridizations of discrete biological species. Fusions such as this raise a sense of impurity in us because they are category violations; they mix or blend biological features that we presume are, in the nature of things, separate. They are, for that reason, regarded as unnatural and monstrous, and when superimposed on an ethnic group that sense of impurity and monstrosity represents the relevant group as monstrous and impure in ways that are not only physically disturbing but that carry moral connotations as well.

In the case of "The Irish Devil-Fish," the pictorial logic works like a metaphor. The Irish are identified—through the rhetoric of the composite figure—with a non-human species, thereby taking on, by metaphorical transfer, salient features of octopi, like sliminess. At the same time, the Irish are represented literally as some sort of miscarriage of nature, absolutely alien to humanity and fit for suppression. Such images not only exploit culturally inculcated feelings of physical aversion toward the Irish and a sense of the impurity of the Other, but reinforce them as well.

The creation of visual category mistakes like this one is fundamental to the production of horror. A structurally comparable strategy for (mis)-characterizing and dehumanizing the Irish that appears again and again in British cartoons is simianization—the portrayal of the Irish as part human and part ape. Tenniel's "The Irish Frankenstein" appeared in *Punch* on May 20, 1882.[9] It portrays an Irish terrorist as the Frankenstein monster, already a horrific creature insofar as it is a contradictory being, both living and dead at the same time. What is additionally interesting about Tenniel's illustration here is that not only does he represent the Irish as Frankenstein's monster, but he depicts the monster in a decidedly ape-like way, hirsute and with a prognathous jaw.

The representation of the Irish as apes can also be seen in Tenniel's cartoon "Two Forces" in *Punch* (October 29, 1881), which L. Perry Curtis notes "reveals the almost complete simianization of Paddy. Tenniel has given his villain such proverbially ape-like features as the simous nose, long, projecting upper lip, shallow lower jaw, and fang-like teeth."[10] An even more pronounced example of this visual equation of the Irish with apes is Matt Morgan's "The Irish Frankenstein," which appeared in *The Tomahawk* on December 18, 1869, and which depicts the head of a gorilla superimposed on a human body, with "Fenian" written across its chest.[11] Nor is this treatment of the Irish unique to the British; in Thomas Nast's "The Day We Celebrate: St. Patrick's Day, 1867," which appeared in *Harper's Weekly* on April 6, 1867, several of the Irish rioters are depicted as horrifying apemen.[12]

In these examples, the fusion of the Irish with the ape are all horrific. They are designed to frighten and disgust readers—to associate a reflex of physical recoil at the thought of the Irish. Where the imagery of beauty attracts, the projection of ugliness repels. But this sort of composite image—this sort of visual category error—can also be given a comic spin. In Frederick B. Opper's "The King of A-Shantee," from *Puck* (February 15, 1882), an Irishman with the head of a monkey and a chamber pot for a hat sits outside his broken down shack smoking a clay pipe and lazing about.[13] In this picture, unlike the previous examples, the Irish-ape is not portrayed as dangerous or threatening. Any sense of fear has been excluded from the picture. Thus, though the figure is as monstrous as the one in Tenniel's "Two Forces," it is not horrific but humorous, its incongruous fusion of the human and the ape engendering ridicule rather than terror. Indeed, the fusion suggested by this cartoon goes beyond an association between the Irish and the ape, since the title notes that the Irishman is sitting before *a shanty*, the verbal wordplay invoking the name of an African tribe, and thereby suggesting an identity between the Irish and blacks as both interstitial category mongrelizations, at best missing links.

As this example indicates, transgressions of the concept of the human can be used not only as vehicles of ethnic prejudice but of racial prejudice as well. During the Second World War, for instance, simianization was a recurring strategy in Allied representations of the Japanese. In 1943, an illustration accompanying an article in the *New York Times Magazine* asks "How Tough Are the Japanese?" and answers it by saying "They are not tougher than other soldiers, says a veteran observer, but brutality is part of their fighting equipment."[14] Pictured above these captions is the image of a colossal Japanese soldier holding a handful of cringing humans in his paw after the fashion of King Kong. The arms of the Japanese soldier are elongated and touch the ground like a gorilla's. His shoulders are hunched like an ape's, and his mouth protrudes and is enlarged with giant teeth, bared as though ready to chomp on his victims. The picture leaves little doubt about what kind of brutality the Japanese specialize in; it is as "inhuman" morally as its ape-like exterior insinuates.

The Japanese, like other Asians, were equated not only with apes, but with monkeys and chimpanzees as well. In "The Monkey Folk," published in *Punch* in mid-January 1942, the Japanese advance down the Malay Peninsula was portrayed as a pack of chimpanzees swinging through the trees with helmets on their heads and submachine guns slung over their shoulders.[15] Here the iconography seems satiric rather than horrific; perhaps it is an instance of a pictorial wish fulfillment fantasy—by representing the Japanese as less-than-dangerous simians, their threat might be in some way be "magically" diminished.

Similarly, in David Low's cartoon "East or West," a monkey-like creature, labeled "Jap" and wearing spectacles, swings by its tail from a tree.[16] It has a wickedly shaped knife in its hand, and it hesitates as it decides whether to plunge the dagger into the back of a shirtless Anglo-Saxon sailor or a Russian soldier. In part, this cartoon is about the reputed duplicity of the Japanese, but equally important is the revulsion this species-crossed Japanese figure is intended to excite. There can be little doubt of the racial politics that underwrite this visual: in that the Japanese are at best incongruous instantiations of the category of the human, that they are impure, and, in this case, ridiculous, but also creepy; they are defective specimens of humanity. They are as morally deficient as they are grotesque; and, given that they are not quite human, they may be dealt with like animals. All this is etched in their ugliness, in their incongruous parody of the human form.

Not only Asians, but also blacks, have been recurrent targets of simianization. So frequent was this motif in the nineteenth century that upon seeing a lithograph that depicted a black public as dignified, Frederick Douglass was moved to write a congratulatory letter to the company that produced it—Prang's Chromo—because "we colored men so often see ourselves described and painted as monkeys."[17] The simianization of black people, as we have seen in our examples of the representation of the Irish and the Japanese, could take a comic form or a horrific one, but, in either case, the strategy relies upon superimposing the human with the animal in such a way that what results is a biological category error.

An example of the ostensibly humorous simianization of blacks can be found in a sketch by W. L. Sheppard for *Frank Leslie's Illustrated Newspaper* of April 27, 1872. Entitled "The Darwinian Theory Illustrated—A Case of Natural Selection," the street scene shows an organ grinder's monkey leaping onto the back of an onlooking black child, who flinches uncomfortably under the attack. What is intended to be the leading "joke" here, one surmises, is that the monkey has "naturally selected" to join some-one like himself in the crowd. However, there also seems to be a second "humorous aside" in the picture; on its right hand corner, there is an adult black male, dressed in military attire, watching the fracas. His heavy, hairy muttonchops and the articulation of the bottom part of his face suggest, for satiric purposes, a simian visage, as if he and his kind have more in com-mon with monkeys than with humans. The reference to Darwinism in this sketch also conjures up popular associations with the notion of a "missing link," where a missing link is by definition an imperfect realization of the category of the human.

Simianization can be orchestrated for horrific as well as comic effect. The drawings of George van Raemdonck for a Dutch comic book from 1927 bear the caption "a man-eater."[18] One of the pictures shows a naked black man walking on all fours, with his arms reaching the ground in the posture of an ape. Blood drips from his mouth, which is exaggerated and befanged, and he clutches a bone. An accompanying picture shows an enlarged black mouth—more of a maw—devouring two whites, clutched in each of the monster's hands, with their legs chewed off below the knees. Clearly this is an image meant to inspire horror in readers—meant to portray black Africans as thoroughly savage and inhuman, monstrous bio-logically and morally.

The association of the African with the simian, which recurs in popu-lar culture, appears in the supposedly scientific writings of the West as well. Linnaeus described his *Homo Africanus* as having an "ape-like nose"; Dar-win uncritically cited Robert Knox's description of the black face as akin to a baboon's; while Curvier alleged of blacks that "The projection of the lower parts of the face, and the thick lips, evidently approximate it to the monkey tribe."[19] If this "educated" correlation of blacks with simians did not cause the association of Africans and apes in popular culture, it surely reinforced it.

The association between blacks and simians, among other things, gave rise to the hypothesis that there was some transitional figure, some missing link, between humans and animals.[20] Edward Tyson proposed pygmies for that role; Bory St. Vincent suggested Hottentots.[21] Moreover, this transition between species was frequently "explained" by claiming that sexual inter-course between Africans and simians was not infrequent, the horror of racial mixing perhaps being projected onto a fantasy of sexual relations between apes and blacks.[22] Edward Long—planter, scholar, and adminis-trator of Jamaica—wrote: "I do not think that an orang-outang husband would be any dishonor to an Hottentot female [*sic*]."[23]

This delirium of species impurity is exemplified by a 1795 illustration from Britain entitled "The Orang-Outang Carrying Off a Negro Girl."[24] The "Orang-Outang," with his captive in hand, is prominently displayed climbing to the top of a tree, while, in the background, three strange-looking figures, neither human nor simian but a mixture of both, loll about, suggesting, perhaps with satiric intent, what will be the unnatural issue of rapes such as this one.[25]

Almost 150 years later, we see similar iconography repeated in a war-time Italian cartoon depicting a black GI as a gorilla, carrying off the *Venus de Milo* as part of his loot.[26] Here the black man, slouched and with elongated, hairy arms, is contrasted with one of the icons of Western beauty in order indicate the depths of American barbarity in contrast to an elevated Italian culture. But in its elision of barbarity with monstrosity—through the figure of the black apeman—the picture also reinforces the visual theme that African-Americans are at best defective people, interstitially blurring the categories of the ape and the human. Moreover, this picture is certainly intended to strike horror in the hearts of Italians at the prospect of an army of these black apemen, the very antithesis of Venus (the most beautiful of goddesses, according to Paris), invading and pillaging their cities.

The simianization of black people is also a feature of popular fiction. In Robert E. Howard's 1935 pulp fiction "Moon of Zambebwei," the first black character we encounter is described as apish in terms of his long arms and agility. This character is part of a black revolution, a revolution undertaken in the name of Zamba, who is described as "The *Black* God." It is hard not to interpret Zamba as a displacement for the allegedly apish blacks, such as the first one we meet, who follow Zamba. But what is Zamba? It is described thusly:

> a beast against nature—a beast that sought food strange to its natural species.
> The thing [Zamba] chained to the stake was an ape, but such an ape as the world at large never dreamed of, even in nightmares. Its shaggy grey hair was shot with silver that shone in the rising moon; it looked gigantic as it squatted ghoulishly on its haunches. Upright, on its bent gnarled legs, it would be as tall as a man, and much broader and thicker. But its prehensile fingers were armed with talons like those of a tiger—not the heavy blunt nails of the natural anthropoid, but the cruel scimitar-curved claws of the great carnivora. Its face was like that of a gorilla, low browed, flaring-nostriled, chinless; but when it snarled, its wide flat nose wrinkled like that of a great cat, and the cavernous mouth disclosed saber-like fangs, the fangs of a beast of prey. This was Zamba, the creature

sacred to the people of the land of Zambebwei—a monstrosity, a violation of an accepted law of nature—a carnivorous ape. . . .

The sight of the monstrosity filled McGrath [the hero] with revulsion; it was abysmal. . . . This thing was an affront to sanity.[27]

By calling Zamba the "black god," Howard plays on the ambiguity
between "the god of the blacks" and "the god who is black," albeit in a
symbolically exaggerated form. Given Howard's racist tendencies, evi-
denced in his other writings, I think that he intends us to think of Zamba
as a figure for black people, and, in this regard, he not only characterizes
the black race as an ape, but compounds that deliberate category error with
a further one, since Zamba is a also a violation of our concept of a gorilla,
being a man-eater, indeed a man-eater who incongruously resembles a
man in his upright position. Zamba also incarnates a black revolt, since he
is the cause of the black uprising, and the nearly physical aversion his
biologically anomalous status and horrific appearance is supposed to elicit
in the reader is intended, in turn, to attach to the sort of revolution whose
symbol he is.

I think that the simianization of black people may also explain one of
the more peculiar features of the iconography in *Blacula* and *Scream,
Blacula, Scream,* two Blaxploitation films of the 1970s. In both these films,
but more evidently in the original, something occurs that I believe is un-
precedented, though maybe only extremely rare, in vampire films. When
the vampire, Blacula, otherwise a handsome, courtly black aristocrat, goes
on the attack, he changes physically; what is particularly notable about this
transformation is that he grows an abundance of facial hair as his sideburns
spread across his cheeks.

I can think of no other example of this; it doesn't happen to white
vampires in the genre. Nor is it that Blacula is a werewolf; his makeup
doesn't resemble any of the standard strategies for portraying werewolves in
movies, nor is anything said about his being a werewolf. So why is Blacula
so hairy? I suggest that this involves, in part, tapping into the long-standing
association of the black person with the simian and monstrosity. Blacula is
not an apeman, but his makeup exploits a residue of that imagery for
horrific purposes.[28]

Of course, the point of this makeup, first and foremost, is to produce a
monster that is horrifying enough to engage horror fans. However, since
the monster character is black, and since the makeup toys with the traditional rhetoric of simianization, the film has the perhaps unintended consequence of sustaining a dehumanizing stereotype, a charge it would not
be liable to had Blacula remained as clean-shaven as Dracula.[29]

The horrific rhetoric of simianization works through appearances to provoke a gut response against blackness. It does this, in part, by representing blacks as category errors, as imperfect or incongruous realizations of the concept of the human. However, categorical incongruity can also be used for the purposes of a belittling variety of satirical humor. For example, Pat Turner has pointed out that in many nineteenth- and early-twentieth-century illustrations black children are depicted "like furry little animals," in order perhaps to mute the terrible things that happen to them, like being devoured by alligators, in the name of comic amusement.[30]

Nor is the simianization of the African-American for putatively comic purposes a thing of the past. It is thriving on the Internet on the Web site of Alpha, an organization that grew out of the United States of America Nationalist Party; their Web site is "dedicated to the countless Aryan men and women who have given their lives for our race."[31] The "humor" list on this Web site for September 6–13, 1998, contained three verbal jokes identifying blacks with simians of various sorts, including a parodic "definition" that states outright that blacks are apes. In addition, the Web site includes a cartoon that shows a black man with wild hair all over his face and arms, a simian facial structure (most notably around his mouth), and his left hand bent backward like a monkey's.[32] The text that accompanies this caricature begins "Coon, coon/Black Baboon," leaving no doubt as to how we are to interpret the distortions sketched on the black body next to the "poem." This is clearly humor of the Hobbesian variety, inviting the vicious laughter of superiority.

Simianization is not the only rhetoric of incongruous category instantiation used against blacks. The classical horror figure most closely associated with blacks is the zombie, a creature reputedly brought into being by voodoo. The zombie is an interstitial thing, neither living nor dead. Though white people can be zombies, zombies are most characteristically black. They are virtual automatons, moving mechanically with no will of their own, under control of those responsible for casting them into this state.

Though they need not be ugly, black zombies in movies are typically made up to appear grotesque. In I Walked with a Zombie, released in 1943 and considered a classic film in the genre, the zombified white wife of the plantation owner, though stiff, still retains vestiges of her beauty, whereas the black zombie, who guards the precincts of the voodoo worshipers, is intended to violate our stereotypes of the human—he is painfully gaunt, and his huge, exaggeratedly fixated white eyes pop out of the darkness preternaturally.[33]

The image of the zombie can be made to count doubly against blacks. There is the image of the zombie himself or herself, who can be made to function as an image of the black person as a mindless, subhuman slave. But there is also the priest or necromancer who has created the zombie by literally black arts, and where that priest is black, he serves as an icon of wickedness. In Wes Craven's film *The Serpent and the Rainbow*, the facially disfigured magician is also the chief of the secret police, projecting a fantasy of Caribbean politics as voodoo-like, unholy, unnatural, and altogether evil.

The zombie figure itself can be used to carry political rhetoric. In his 1936 short story "Black Canaan," Robert E. Howard returns to the theme of black revolt. A holy war is being raised in the name of Damballah. The troops are made up of black zombies. But these zombies are extra-anomalous conceptually. Not only are they neither living nor dead, but they live underwater, biologically on their way to becoming fish, and they rise up from beneath the swamp to take their victims unaware. When the hero grapples with one of these zombies and looks into its face, he notes "it was inhuman; as expressionless and soulless as that of a catfish; the face of a being no longer human, and no longer mindful of its human origin."[34]

Howard was a southerner who had inherited his culture's antebellum fear of black rebellion, reprisal, and revenge. The zombie serves as a symbol of his anxiety about the inhuman savagery that black vengeance would unleash. Blacks become the zombie menace, enabling him to portray the prospects of black vengeance with images predicated upon making the reader cringe viscerally. By dehumanizing blacks in this way, Howard rhetorically "justifies" not only keeping them down, but dealing with them brutally, a sentiment that the horrifically disgusted reader is invited to share.

That Howard chooses the zombie to exemplify black retribution is at least ironic, since one of the most salient features of zombies is that they are slaves. Thus, Howard's zombie revolutionaries bear the very mark of their history, their enslavement, which has brought them into opposition with whites. Moreover, insofar as Howard's story makes the master of these zombie slaves a black man, it is an exercise in pure projection.

In recent years, a new figure of black horror has emerged—The Candyman. Two films have been made in this series: *Candyman* and *Candyman: Farewell to the Flesh*. These films are based on Clive Barker's short story "The Forbidden." Oddly, the Candyman in Barker's original story is not black. He is not described as such, nor is anyone else so described. "The Forbidden" is set in London. But in the movie versions, both produced by

Barker, the story has been transposed to America. In the first film, the Candyman haunts Chicago—his lair is in the black housing project Cabrini-Green—and, in the second film he stalks New Orleans.

Along with these geographic relocations, the Candyman, whose intentionally vague origins contributed to the horrific effect of the story, has become in the film series a nineteenth-century black artist, born in the slave quarters of a plantation in Louisiana. Hired to paint the portrait of the southern belle of the big house, he fell in love with his model and she with him. When their affair was discovered, a white mob descended upon him. They severed his painting hand and then smeared his body with cloying honey. A swarm of bees congregated on his body and flayed him alive. After death, the Candyman metamorphosed into a revenant who, like so many fictional ghosts, is bent on revenge.

The Candyman is an interstitial figure, ambiguously straddling the conceptual distinction between living and dead. He is also an incomplete instantiation of the stereotype of a man since he is missing a hand, which he has replaced with a particularly nasty-looking hook. In most of his apparitions he is handsome, save for his hook; he is tall, he is strong, and his face has classical proportions. However, when he reveals his true nature, that is another story. When he opens his massive cloak, we see that his bloody torso has had the flesh torn from it and that bees nest in his rib cage. This reinforces his status as an incomplete being. It also explains why when he is cut, bees crawl from the wound, promoting a rather revolting image. Moreover, his "true face" looks as though it is melting off his skull, making his head a gooey, gelatinous, formless mass, less a head than a we-know-not-what.

The figure of the Candyman exploits stark contrasts between beauty and ugliness, as well as between sweetness and disgust, for horrific effect. Understood as a combinatory image, he conjoins opposites in a way that is initially attractive but then repelling. His physical appearance, it would seem, mirrors his moral status. On the one hand, his existential commitment to retribution may encourage some measure of sympathy—it is hard to think of many who have been treated so unjustly. But in his rage, he has become morally monstrous as well as physically so, since he kills indiscriminately; indeed, in the first film, he kills mostly black people.

His revenge is cosmic; he is not an avenger involved in paying back the wrongs of slavery. He seeks retribution from humanity at large, attacking innocents and even kidnapping a black infant. Thus, in terms of the moral calculus of the story, he is ultimately evil and must be destroyed. Though the film elicits an appreciable measure of empathy for the Candyman's heinous persecution, when all the moral accounts are in, it is finally the Candyman's vengeance that is represented as most horrifying and inhuman in the film.

In Howard's "Black Canaan," no thought is offered of motivating the black revolt in virtue of any claims of justice. Black retribution, personified by the zombies, is presented as unalloyed evil, which is associated graphically with and advanced by the iconography of ontological impurity. Through the zombies, the prospect of black reprisals is treated as horrifying—as both fearsome and disgusting. The *Candyman* films take black anger more seriously, but, in the last analysis, presuppose that humanity must oppose the Candyman and send him back to whence he came. His anger is exorbitant, monstrous in its proportions, and that moral monstrousness is symbolized by the horrific ugliness of his true appearance or essence, his transgression of the category of the human.

Conclusion

One leading concept of beauty associates beauty with the perfect realization of a concept; a beautiful Kentucky Walker is a perfect or approximately perfect example of its kind. When we say something is beautiful, in this light, we mean that it instantiates the conceptual category in this way. Human beauty has been characterized in this manner. At the same time, there is an enduring commonplace that beauty is connected to goodness: that the beautiful exterior reflects a righteous interior.

The link between beauty and goodness can yield a strategy of political rhetoric. In order to endorse a cause, portray it as beautiful. Thus, Liberty is pictured as a beautiful woman. But the couplet—the beautiful/the good —also suggests a further homology, viz., the beautiful/the good :: the ugly/the evil. And this homology affords an alternative political rhetoric. To portray something as evil, make it ugly.

Horror and humor are two genres that explore ugliness. Like beauty, horror and humor are essentially related to concepts including, notably, the concept of the human. Both create ugliness for their own unique purposes by violating, transgressing, blurring, contradicting, and/or otherwise jamming our concepts of the human. With horror, the results are monsters who are designed to frighten and disgust us. With humor, anomalous figures, like clowns, are designed to provoke laughter. Thus, where the iconography of beauty may be employed to advocate certain political persuasions, the imagery of horror and humor can be mobilized to stigmatize opposing political factions. Historically, the potentials of horror and humor to this end have been exploited frequently, often with reference to despised ethnic and racial groups, including the Irish, the Japanese, the African, and the African-American.[35]

As a rhetoric of hatred, horror and humor can be frighteningly effective. Like beauty, they do much of their work at the level of appearances, and they elicit a fast, visceral response from audiences. The almost immediate sense of aversion and disgust—along with fear—that arises in response to horrific monsters can be transferred smoothly from fictional apemen to what they stand for. Likewise, humor paints its assorted clowns and buffoons with bursts of ridicule that can attach to whole groups of people.

But, in addition to their immediate effects, horror and humor can stab even more deeply. Insofar as they traffic in the transgression of the concept of the human, often at the level of folk biology, they suggest that their targets are not human, and, therefore, not appropriate objects of human concern, particularly moral concern. Monsters and clown types are beneath or outside ethics. At the same time, their ugliness suggests their moral defectiveness and sometimes their evil in ways that indicate that they deserve whatever harsh treatment and punishment they receive. If beauty —the perfect realization of the concept of the human—rhetorically implies goodness, ugliness and category violation encourage the suspicion of evil and moral defectiveness. Where beauty can be used to valorize, horror and humor can be used to dehumanize and to vilify and, for that reason, they are diabolically effective levers of ethnic and racial hatred—ones that operate pretty close to our nerve endings.[36]

NOTES

I would especially like to thank Eric Foner, John Szwed, Sally Banes, S. T. Ross, and David Bordwell for all their help in the preparation of this essay, though, of course, only I am responsible for the errors herein.

1. Immanuel Kant, *Critique of Judgment*, trans. Werner S. Pluhar (Indianapolis: Hackett, 1987), p. 76.

2. Ibid., p. 77.

3. Ibid., pp. 83–84.

4. This characterization of horror is defended in Noël Carroll, *The Philosophy of Horror* (New York: Routledge, 1990).

5. The relation of horror to comedy and of the clown to the monster is explored at length in Noël Carroll, "Horror and Humor," *Journal of Aesthetics and Art Criticism* 57, no. 2 (Spring 1999): 145–160.

6. Kant, *Critique of Judgment*, p. 180.

7. See Carroll, "Horror and Humor," for a defense of this contrast.

8. See L. Perry Curtis, *Apes and Angels: The Irishman in Victorian Caricature* (Washington, D.C.: Smithsonian Institution Press, 1971), p. 44.

9. Ibid., p. 43.

10. Ibid., p. 42.

11. Ibid., p. 49.

12. Ibid., p. 59.

13. Ibid., p. 63.

14. John Dower, *War without Mercy: Race and Power in the Pacific War* (New York: Pantheon, 1986), p. 187.

15. Ibid., p. 183.

16. Ibid., p. 182.

17. A letter from Frederick Douglass, dated June 14, 1870, reproduced in Katharine Morrison McClinton, *Chromolithographs of Louis Prang* (New York: Clarkson N. Potter, 1973), p. 37.

18. Jan Nederveen Pieterse, *White on Black: Images of Africa and Blacks in Western Popular Culture* (New Haven: Yale University Press, 1992), p. 116.

19. Ibid., pp. 40–43.

20. Talk of "missing links" fired the popular imagination. For example, in the Circus Museum in Baraboo, Wisconsin, there is a replica of a freak show tent. The statues represent a collection of some of the most popular "freaks" displayed by the Ringling Brothers and Barnum and Bailey Circus. Among the figures is a "missing link," a smallish black man called Zip. That the basis of the comic address of this figure rests on categorical incongruity is supported by the accompanying promotional material which asks of Zip "What is it?" One also wonders whether Zip's name isn't also connected to the name of one of the staple characters of the minstrel stage, Zip Coon who, though not a biological missing link, was a satirical representation of the black man as an imperfect realization of the concept of a cultured gentleman, a sort of cultural missing link.

21. Pieterse, *White on Black*, pp. 40–43.

22. Here, as in many horror fictions, one supposes that cross-species hybridization stands in for the terror of miscegenation. This sort of conflation, it seems to me, occurs often in horror literature. It is especially evident in the writings of H. P. Lovecraft, whose racist tendencies are widely acknowledged. See, for example, his story "The Shadow over Innsmouth," in which the monstrous citizens of the town are a result of inbreeding between South Sea Islanders, New England stock, and something else. Their children look simian and "what kind of foreign blood—if any—these beings had, it was impossible to tell." H. P. Lovecraft, "The Shadow over Innsmouth," in *The Lurking Fear and Other Stories* (New York: Del Rey, 1971), p. 134.

23. Pieterse, *White on Black*, p. 41.

24. Ibid., p. 38.

25. For a history of cross-species unions in cinema, see Rhona J. Berenstein, "White Skin, White Masks: Race, Gender and Monstrosity in Jungle Horror Cinema," in her *Attack of the Leading Ladies: Gender, Sexuality, and Spectatorship* (New York: Columbia University Press, 1996), pp. 160–197.

26. Pieterse, *White on Black*, pp. 85 and 228.

27. Robert E. Howard, "Moon of Zambebwei," *Trails in Darkness* (Riverdale, N.Y.: Baen Publishing Enterprises, 1996), pp. 203–204.

28. Similarly, in another film in the same cycle, the 1973 *Blackenstein*, vestiges of the simianization motif surface. Eddie, the amputee whom Dr. Stein is reconstructing, is administered the wrong drug, one with a tendency to induce atavistic or "throwback" reactions. When the effects of this drug begin to manifest themselves, Eddie's two initial symptoms recall simian imagery. First his brow thickens, becoming Neanderthalish or apish. Next, hair sprouts on the back of his hands. Admittedly, as Eddie evolves (or devolves) into a black Frankenstein monster, his makeup progressively imitates (though poorly) the appearance of the Universal Studios horror films of the 1930s and 1940s. However, at least at first Eddie seems as though he is about to turn into an apeman.

29. Though I have been focusing on simianization, this is a subcategory of a wider strategy: the portrayal of the black man as beast. A discussion with examples of this figure can be found, among other places, in Marlon Riggs's TV documentary *Ethnic Notions* (KQED, 1987). See also Earl Ofari Hutchinson, "The Negro Beast or in the Image of God," in his *The Assassination of the Black Male* (Los Angeles: Middle Passage Press, 1994), pp. 7–17. Hutchinson argues that Rodney King was depicted in the vocabulary of the beast that was popularized in such texts as Charles Carroll's *The Negro a Beast, or, In the Image of God*, wherein it is alleged that "the black man was left out of human creation and was a sub-species of the animal world" (Hutchinson, "The Negro Beast," p. 8).

30. Pat Turner in *Ethnic Notions*, produced, written, and directed by Marlon Riggs.

31. See: www.alpha.org/jokes/jokes.html.

32. See: www.alpha.org/cartoons/cartoons1.htm/.

33. Zombies can also be turned into amusing figures when their lumbering gait and deadpan stoic expressionlessness are contrasted with the excited, cowardly terror of a comic actor like Mantan Moreland in films like the 1943 *Revenge of the Zombies*. In effect, Moreland uses the zombie as a straight man.

34. This association of the black person with the aquatic also appears in Howard's "Moon of Zambebwei," where a black man is described: "His bullet-head was set squarely between those gigantic shoulders, like that of a frog." Howard, "Moon over Zambebwei," p. 177. I have also noted that there are several composite figures of blacks and aquatic figures featured in *Ethnic Notions*. This leads me to wonder if there is recurring motif that equates blacks with marine species. This is a topic for future research. However, if there were such an association, it might reveal a further source of the horror of cross-species miscegenation found in Lovecraft stories such as "The Shadow over Innsmouth," where the monsters are described as frog-like and fish-like as well as simian.

35. This is not to suggest that this rhetoric is only used against ethnic and racial groups. It is also employed against gays. For examples, see Harry M. Benshoff, *Monsters in the Closet: Homosexuality and the Horror Film* (Manchester: Manchester University Press, 1997) and Noël Carroll, *The Philosophy of Mass Art* (Oxford: Clarendon Press, 1998), pp. 337–338.

36. Though I have stressed a recurring rhetorical association between horror and moral depravity in this essay, I should not be taken to be claiming that horrific ugliness always and necessarily connotes moral evil. There are standard deviations from this pattern. For example, there are many variations on the theme of beauty and the beast. Here the ugliness of the beast is to be taken initially as a sign of his moral depravity, but

then the unfolding particularities of the story eventually reverse this valuation. So a horrific depiction need not necessarily entail moral depravity. Its valuation can be redirected in the plot (though this is not always easy). All things being equal, horror will be a sign of moral defectiveness and beauty will be a sign of virtue. Those are our default assumptions. But sometimes all things are not equal, given the rest of the story. The comic book series *Spawn* is perhaps an example of this—an example where a black monster, as a result of the narrative, accrues a positive moral valuation.

That is, beauty, given the history of its association with moral goodness, is a *prima facie* cue for goodness; horrific imagery is a *prima facie* cue for moral depravity. These cues can either be reinforced or cancelled by the ensuing text (whether visual or verbal). Most frequently in popular culture, images of horror and ugliness will turn out to be evil, confirming our initial suspicion, based on the monster's ugliness. This initial suspicion can be reversed, but that takes extra work on the part of the artist. The homology—beauty/goodness :: ugliness/evil—provides the *initial* (or default) inference pattern that audiences generally use to decipher such imagery.

Paul C. Taylor

PAUL C. TAYLOR

3. Malcolm
Four Logic
B

It was
e·
littl
a·

as a condition to be despised, and
attitude to cover the physical fe·
black identity. So a central ass·
kinky hair, flat noses, thick·
are *ugly*. (I call to your a·
descriptive language:
lips, curly hair, an·
To make m·
took shape ·
teenth cen·
the "be·
phys·
is·

I have opened with this passage from Toni Morrison for a number of reasons. The passage reflects the long-standing preoccupation that African American activists have had with standards of physical beauty, a preoccupation that I will soon call *antiracist aestheticism*. The passage also captures in singularly effective language the existential, social, and psychological conditions that motivate this preoccupation and contributes the language of logical petitions that I will use to frame my discussion of aestheticism. Morrison's ugly little black girl, a character named Pecola, makes a request that would be ludicrous were it not for the nature of her circumstances. In this essay I want to consider how Pecola's circumstances motivate her petition and two others, after which I will offer my own petition concerning the practice of aesthetics.

First, a few words about the social and intellectual conditions that make Pecola's petition "logical." One of the cornerstones of the modern West has been the hierarchical valuation of human types along racial lines. (Unless I say otherwise, I will be concerned throughout with the modern West, particularly with England and its former possessions in the Americas.) The most prominent type of racialized ranking represents blackness

most tokens of this type extend this
...tures that are central to the ascription of
...mption has been that black folks—with our
...ips, dark skin, prognathism, and steatopygia—
...ttention the evaluative overtones of this standard
...magine the difference if I had said *broad* noses, *full*
...so on.)

...tters worse, the most prominent type of racialist thought
...nder the same intellectual circumstances that in the eigh-
...tury produced efforts to define an aesthetic morality centered on
...utiful soul" and in the nineteenth century led to the "science" of
...ognomy.[1] The circumstances that I have in mind consist, as much as
...pertinent for my purposes, of the widespread assumption that bodily
beauty and deformity covary with moral beauty and deformity as well as
with general cultural and intellectual capacity. This practice of conflating
different categories of value—of running together the good, the beautiful,
the intelligent, and the civilized—could only have made it easier for hierarchical racialism to become what I call *thick* racialism, which holds that
the physical differences between races are signs of deeper, typically intellectual and moral, differences. Thus it became part of the content of the
standard thick, hierarchical racialism—what I call *classical racialism*—
that the physical ugliness of black people was a sign of a deeper ugliness
and depravity.

The classical racialist order that presupposed the thoroughgoing odiousness of black people was composed of complex social formations that
brought about the inequitable distribution of social goods along racial
lines. (By "social goods" I mean material goods like property as well as other
goods like freedom, self-esteem, and the right to own property.) This distributive project was both facilitated and constituted by ideological projects
of justification that made the notion of black odiousness, inhumanity, and
inferiority a part of commonsense sociology. These justifying projects made
it possible for a humanist to be a slaveholder without contradiction, for the
dominance of capital and land to be concealed and maintained by the
social and moral authority of racial hegemony, and, most important here,
for imported Africans, stripped as much as could be of their own culture, to
be socialized (though not, of course, universally and seamlessly) into the
assumption of their own inferiority. Since the notion of black inferiority
typically involves inferiority with respect to beauty, the modern black experience has been intimately bound up with a struggle against the cultural
imperative to internalize the judgment of one's own thoroughgoing ugli-

Paul C. Taylor

3. Malcolm's Conk and Danto's Colors; or, Four Logical Petitions Concerning Race, Beauty, and Aesthetics

> *It was at once the most fantastic and the most logical petition he had ever received. Here was an ugly little girl asking for beauty. . . . A little black girl who wanted to rise up out of the pit of her blackness and see the world with blue eyes. . . . For the first time he honestly wished he could work miracles.*
>
> —TONI MORRISON, *The Bluest Eye*

I have opened with this passage from Toni Morrison for a number of reasons. The passage reflects the long-standing preoccupation that African American activists have had with standards of physical beauty, a preoccupation that I will soon call *antiracist aestheticism*. The passage also captures in singularly effective language the existential, social, and psychological conditions that motivate this preoccupation and contributes the language of logical petitions that I will use to frame my discussion of aestheticism. Morrison's ugly little black girl, a character named Pecola, makes a request that would be ludicrous were it not for the nature of her circumstances. In this essay I want to consider how Pecola's circumstances motivate her petition and two others, after which I will offer my own petition concerning the practice of aesthetics.

First, a few words about the social and intellectual conditions that make Pecola's petition "logical." One of the cornerstones of the modern West has been the hierarchical valuation of human types along racial lines. (Unless I say otherwise, I will be concerned throughout with the modern West, particularly with England and its former possessions in the Americas.) The most prominent type of racialized ranking represents blackness as a condition to be despised, and most tokens of this type extend this attitude to cover the physical features that are central to the ascription of black identity. So a central assumption has been that black folks—with our kinky hair, flat noses, thick lips, dark skin, prognathism, and steatopygia—are *ugly*. (I call to your attention the evaluative overtones of this standard descriptive language: imagine the difference if I had said *broad* noses, *full* lips, *curly* hair, and so on.)

To make matters worse, the most prominent type of racialist thought took shape under the same intellectual circumstances that in the eighteenth century produced efforts to define an aesthetic morality centered on the "beautiful soul" and in the nineteenth century led to the "science" of physiognomy.[1] The circumstances that I have in mind consist, as much as is pertinent for my purposes, of the widespread assumption that bodily beauty and deformity covary with moral beauty and deformity as well as with general cultural and intellectual capacity. This practice of conflating different categories of value—of running together the good, the beautiful, the intelligent, and the civilized—could only have made it easier for hierarchical racialism to become what I call *thick* racialism, which holds that the physical differences between races are signs of deeper, typically intellectual and moral, differences. Thus it became part of the content of the standard thick, hierarchical racialism—what I call *classical racialism*—that the physical ugliness of black people was a sign of a deeper ugliness and depravity.

The classical racialist order that presupposed the thoroughgoing odiousness of black people was composed of complex social formations that brought about the inequitable distribution of social goods along racial lines. (By "social goods" I mean material goods like property as well as other goods like freedom, self-esteem, and the right to own property.) This distributive project was both facilitated and constituted by ideological projects of justification that made the notion of black odiousness, inhumanity, and inferiority a part of commonsense sociology. These justifying projects made it possible for a humanist to be a slaveholder without contradiction, for the dominance of capital and land to be concealed and maintained by the social and moral authority of racial hegemony, and, most important here, for imported Africans, stripped as much as could be of their own culture, to be socialized (though not, of course, universally and seamlessly) into the assumption of their own inferiority. Since the notion of black inferiority typically involves inferiority with respect to beauty, the modern black experience has been intimately bound up with a struggle against the cultural imperative to internalize the judgment of one's own thoroughgoing ugliness—hence the widespread sentiment among black people, in the nineteenth century especially, that black features are a problematic link to a "dark past" and to uncivilized ways.[2]

Given these conditions, it is logical for Pecola to think of blackness as a pit and to petition for escape from it. It is logical for her dream of escape to be expressed as the desire to transcend the physical features that are usually the most obvious signs of blackness. And it is logical for her to conceive of the whole process of personal improvement as a movement from ugliness to beauty.

But it is also logical for people interested in bettering the black condition to do what Morrison has done: to ask that we critically examine the conditions that make Pecola's petition reasonable. *The Bluest Eye* is just one example, though a particularly salutary one, of a strong and varied strain in the black antiracist tradition, a strain that I promised at the outset to call *antiracist aestheticism.* The participants in this subtradition—a group that includes writers like Gwendolyn Brooks and Zora Neale Hurston, academics like bell hooks and Cornel West, and filmmakers like Julie Dash and Spike Lee—have a double motivation.[3] They are motivated first by the realization that a white-dominated culture has *racialized* beauty, that it has defined beauty per se in terms of white beauty, in terms of the physical features that the people we consider white are more likely to have. They are motivated also by the worry that racialized standards of beauty reproduce the workings of racism by weaving racist assumptions into the daily practices and inner lives of the victims of racism—most saliently here, by encouraging them to accept and act on the supposition of their own ugliness. The problem of *internalization* that these activists are concerned with manifests itself in a variety of ways, some of which we will come to. But we can most efficiently discuss this worry in the context of what I will call the *straight hair rule.*

The straight hair rule is the presumption, long embraced in African American communities (and, for not quite as long a time, in communities of African-descended peoples throughout the world), that straight hair is a necessary component of physical beauty. The necessity of this component is evident from the ordeals that people—including nonblack people unlucky enough to have curly hair[4]—will endure in its name. Consider Malcolm X's account of his first "conk," or chemically straightened hairstyle:

> The congolene just felt warm when Shorty started combing it in. But then my head caught fire. I gritted my teeth. . . . My eyes watered, my nose was running. I couldn't stand it any longer; I bolted to the washbasin. . . . My scalp still flamed, but not as badly. . . . My first view in the

mirror blotted out the hurting. . . . The transformation, after the lifetime of kinks, is staggering. . . . On top of my head was this thick, smooth sheen of shining red hair. . . . as straight as any white man's.[5]

The straight hair rule might be more precisely stated as the principle that *long* straight hair is a necessary component of *female* beauty. The aestheticist concern with beauty tends to be a concern with female beauty, as we might expect given the nature of the cultural forces at play; since current social conditions make physical appearance central to the construction of womanhood and femininity and fairly peripheral to the construction of manhood and masculinity, talk about physical beauty more or less reduces to talk about womanhood, femininity, and women. Participants in the aestheticist tradition tend either to conduct the race-based critique alongside the gender critique, or, too often, to discuss the racial issues without any regard for the gender dynamics. I mention all of this because I will express myself below as if the problems of female beauty can stand in for the problems of racialized aesthetic standards in general. This is an attempt on my part to capture the main concern of the aestheticist tradition, not a denial of the need for gender critique.

The straight hair rule dominates African American culture to such an extent that one commentator can meaningfully ask, "Have we reached the point where the only acceptable option for African American women is straight hair?"[6] This dominance should not be surprising, since the cultural imperative for black women to enact beauty engages most powerfully with the processes of racialization and internalization in connection with their hair. Until the fairly recent perfection of the technologies of colored contacts and cosmetic surgery, Pecola's dream of escape from the physical markers of blackness was most effectively focused on the hair, the part of the body that is most amenable to frequent, radical, and relatively inexpensive alteration in the direction of approximating "white" standards (since, at any rate, Madame C. J. Walker's work at the beginning of this century, about which more in a moment). Consequently, as Paulette Caldwell reports, "the writings of black women confirm the centrality of hair in the psychological abuse of black women. Virtually all novels and autobiographical works by black women writers contain some treatment of the issue of discrimination against black women because of . . . hair texture."[7]

In light of all this, the aestheticist tradition offers a logical petition of its own. The request is made in different forms by figures with different political affiliations, with different degrees of attachment to an essential black subject—the Form, as it were, of Blackness—and to one or another of the relevant psychological notions like pride or alienation. But the basic point remains the same. The aestheticist requests that we work to loosen the hold that hair-straightening has on the collective black consciousness, that we critically examine the conditions that make Pecola's request reasonable, and that we strive to cultivate the idea that we can be beautiful just as we are.

Stated broadly, the aestheticist account and critique should seem intuitively plausible. Given the present constitution of Western societies it seems right to say that the category of race tends to be central to the self-conception of the people we consider black, that physical features are central to the assignment and assumption of racial identities, and finally that, other things being equal, a person whose self-conception involves characteristics that she finds valuable is better off than someone whose identity is bound up with features she finds odious. But it is easy to narrow any broad statement of the aestheticist position in ways that make it more problematic. One might assume, for example, that the value of the aestheticist account is that it warrants inferences to the mental and moral states of individual agents; that it allows one to assume, in other words, that any person with straightened hair is, in the parlance of Spike Lee's *School Daze*, a "wannabee"—someone who wants to be white. On such a view, straightening involves the moral failing of groundlessly devaluing huge portions of the human family, and it involves the psychological problems of alienation and self-hatred—of devaluing one's *own* portion of the human family, and hence devaluing oneself.

Some people are moved by the dangers of this crude version of aestheticism to offer a third logical petition: They urge that we take seriously the complexity of the processes by which individuals participate in patterns of social meaning. They point out that people can participate in meaning-laden practices like hair-straightening while, or as a way of, *shifting* the meanings; or that hair-straightening itself has taken on such racialized significance that participation in the practice can be a way of expressing black pride rather than a way of precluding it. So, for example, when Malcolm X attacks his earlier self for the "self-degradation" of "burning my flesh to have it look like a white man's hair,"[8] historian Robin Kelley suggests that this interpretation is too beholden to Malcolm's later politics to do justice to his earlier behavior. Kelley explains:

> [T]o claim that black working-class males who conked their hair were merely parroting whites ignores the fact that specific stylizations created by black youth emphasized difference. . . . We cannot help but view the

conk as part of a larger process by which black youth . . . reinscribed coded oppositional meanings onto styles derived from the dominant culture.[9]

Noliwe Rooks makes a similar argument about Madame C. J. Walker, who amassed a fortune just after the turn of the twentieth century by popularizing the hot comb, the principal instrument for hair-straightening. Rooks explains that while "African Americans had long struggled with issues of inferiority, beauty, and the meaning of particular beauty practices . . . [Walker] attempted to shift the significance of hair away from concerns of disavowing African ancestry."[10] Walker, it turns out, even rejected the claim that hair-straightening was principally what she was up to; she argued instead that she provided a way for black women to keep their hair healthy and, not coincidentally, to expand their economic and social opportunities in the process by becoming hairdressers.

This request that we take seriously the complexity of the relations between individuals and their cultures is an important addition, both as a corrective to the potential oversights of the aestheticist account and as a clarification of the aestheticist project. Rooks and Kelley help to affirm that the aestheticist argument at its best involves political criticism of culture, not moral criticism of individuals. They show that the aim should be to consider the extent to which an individual's actions presuppose, reproduce, maintain, and re-fashion broader and perhaps troubling patterns of behavior and structures of meaning, both consciously and unconsciously. They show, in short, that antiracist aestheticism is an indigenous mode of cultural criticism, produced by efforts to come to grips with the uses and abuses of the concept of beauty in the experiences of black folks.

I want to insist for a moment on this last point, because it is the one that I have been aiming at all along. I have tried to discuss beauty here in a way that differs from what one usually finds in essays of philosophical aesthetics. Most often we consider beauty in its capacity as a property of artworks, either the property of general artistic merit or some more specific property that may not be necessary for the success of a work. But there is no reason for aestheticians to take up beauty only in the context of art—no reason, that is, apart from the widely held assumption that aesthetics just is the philosophy of art, an assumption that is deeply contingent as a matter of history and, though dominant, not universally accepted. I have discussed beauty in the context of cultural criticism because it seems to me that cultural criticism is one of the things that aesthetics can and should be. And that, of course, is the fourth of my eponymous petitions: that we explore the possibility that aestheticians can examine something broader than and, in a sense, prior to the arts—the reciprocally constitutive relationships between cultures and individuals.

This is not, of course, a radical proposal. No less a figure than Arthur Danto has argued that aesthetics is "virtually as wide in scope as experience itself, whether it be experience of art or of insects." Aesthetics, he says, has to do with the "encoloration" of human cognition and perception by historical meaning and cultural value: To attend to something aesthetically is "to suspend practicality, to stand back and assume a detached view of the object, see its shapes and colors, enjoy and admire it for what it is, subtracting all considerations of utility." He goes on to suggest that the future of the discipline of aesthetics lies not simply in continued examination of the philosophical issues arising from the practices of fine art, but also in showing cognitive scientists how they have undermined their own prospects for success by "treating us in abstraction from our historical and cultural locations." Aesthetics becomes for him, then, "a discipline which borders on philosophical psychology in one direction and the theory of knowledge in the other"—something like the under-laborer to cognitive science.[11]

I find Danto's proposal compelling except for the final step. Where he sees aesthetics bordering on the theory of knowledge and informing cognitive science, I see it bordering on political philosophy and informing social theory. I share his interest in the encoloration of cognition and perception by history and culture, but my concern has to do with how that process shapes our interactions with each other in the social realm. What more useful task could the discipline take up than that of excavating the hidden ways in which history and culture condition our choices, beliefs, desires, and preferences—such as the preference, say, for straight hair?

Recasting aesthetics as a kind of cultural criticism, as a discipline as ready to deal with the beauty of human bodies as with the beauty of art, would, I think, produce a number of benefits. First of all, cultural criticism relies heavily, and often obscurely, on the central aesthetic practice of interpretation. The much-ballyhooed (and sometimes overstated) clarity and rigor of philosophy could help to clear some of the ground here. Second, cultural criticism is, in the form of Cultural Studies, a thriving discipline in its own right. As such it represents a viable source of interdisciplinary cooperation, which makes it a useful intellectual and professional resource for a discipline that is often under attack both from the ax of downsizing administrations and from the arrogance of fellow philosophers. Finally, the move from aesthetics narrowly construed to an aesthetics "as broad in scope as experience itself" represents the opportunity to rebut once more the claim that philosophy is culturally detached and socially irrelevant.

I realize that I have said rather little about a number of crucial issues. I have simply gestured at what cultural criticism is; I have given no reason for the antiracist critic to stop at indexing judgments of beauty to racial body types instead of going on to question the whole framework of racialist (but, significantly, not necessarily *classical* racialist) thinking; and I have not been exactly clear about how the experience of being a black woman with hair that is not naturally straight, and can be made so only provisionally and with some expenditure of time and effort, differs from the experiences of similarly situated Jewish and Irish women. (As you might imagine, I mention these particular questions because I think I have answers to them, though I could not give them here.) My aim in this essay has not been to settle those issues but simply to point in a direction that seems to me to require, and likely to reward, further exploration. If I have done that adequately, then the rest can wait for another time.

NOTES

1. Robert E. Norton, *The Beautiful Soul: Aesthetic Morality in the Eighteenth Century* (Ithaca, N.Y.: Cornell University Press, 1995).

2. Noliwe Rooks, *Hair Raising* (New Brunswick, N.J.: Rutgers University Press, 1996), p. 35.

3. See especially Cornel West's essay "A Geneaology of Modern Racism," in *Prophesy Deliverance* (Philadelphia: Westminster, 1982), pp. 47–65.

4. See Susan Bordo, *Unbearable Weight: Feminism, Western Culture, and the Body* (Berkeley: University of California Press, 1993), p. 255.

5. Alex Haley and Malcolm X, *The Autobiography of Malcolm X* (1965; reprint, New York: Ballantine Books, 1973), pp. 53–54.

6. Rooks, *Hair Raising*, p. 132.

7. Paulette Caldwell, "A Hair Piece," *Duke Law Journal* 41, no. 2 (1991): p. 391.

8. Haley, *Autobiography of Malcolm X*, p. 54.

9. Robin D. G. Kelley, "The Riddle of the Zoot," in *Malcolm X*, ed. Joe Wood (New York: St. Martin's Press, 1992), pp. 161–162.

10. Rooks, *Hair Raising*, p. 52.

11. Arthur C. Danto, "A Future for Aesthetics," *Journal of Aesthetics and Art Criticism* 51 (1993): 274–275; and *The Transfiguration of the Commonplace* (Cambridge, Mass.: Harvard University Press, 1981), p. 22.

Arthur C. Danto

4. Beauty and Beautification

The history of aesthetic reflection moves from a discourse in which it is not perceived as especially relevant to efforts to distinguish natural from artistic beauty, through the recognition that there is a boundary between them, to the perception that they are separated by a more or less vast and largely unmapped territory, sharing boundaries with natural beauty on the one side and artistic beauty on the other. Beauty of what we may speak of as the Third Realm plays a far greater role in human conduct and attitude than either of the (philosophically) more familiar kinds, since most persons have little occasion to think about the fine arts, or to gaze upon natural wonders, though what Kant speaks of as the starry heavens above occasions awe and a sense of vastness in even the simplest of persons. By natural beauty it is perhaps best to think of beauty, the existence of which is independent of human will, like the night sky or the sunset, mighty seas or majestic peaks. So the beauty of a garden would not be natural beauty, leaving it a question of whether it belongs to art or to the Third Realm. No one can be unaware of Third Realm beauty in daily life, but the history of aesthetics, which has drawn examples from it, has often, perhaps typically, failed to note how different these are from either natural or artistic beauty.

Kant exemplifies the first moment of this history, as his choice of examples implies: he discusses green meadows just after discussing fine palaces, dissociating aesthetic judgment from whatever interest one may have in either. "A coat, a house, or a flower is beautiful," presumably in the same way; and Kant seems anxious that from the perspective of aesthetic analysis, no distinction is to be drawn between flowers and floral decorations ("free delineations, outlines intertwined with one another.") So "Nature is beautiful because it looks like art," while "Beautiful art must look like nature." Hence, from the perspective of beauty, the distinction between art and nature does not greatly signify.[1] In this Kant was very much a man of the Enlightenment, a period of cultivated taste, in which even the moderately affluent were liberated from the urgencies of immediate interest to the possibility of a disinterested contemplation of natural beauties and beautiful products of artistic genius. And the world was safe enough for people to travel about, to see the Alps or the artistic wonders of Italy.

Hegel defines the history's second moment, in that from the outset he finds it crucial to distinguish sharply between artistic beauty, on the one side, and "a beautiful color, a beautiful sky, a beautiful river; likewise beautiful flowers, beautiful animals, and even more of beautiful people."[2] Artistic beauty is "higher" than natural beauty, and is "born of the spirit." Like natural beauty, artistic beauty "presents itself to *sense*, feeling, intuition, imagination."[3] But it does more than gratify the senses: when "fine art is truly art" it "place[s] itself in the same sphere as religion and philosophy," bringing to our awareness "the deepest interests of mankind, and the most comprehensive truths of the spirit . . . displaying even the highest [reality] sensuously."[4] At a minimum, art has a content that must be grasped; it is, by contrast with skies and flowers, about something. Of course, the distinction would be obliterated if one thought of Nature as a Divine Visual Language, following Bishop Berkeley or the painters of the Hudson River School, who saw God addressing us through the medium of waterfalls or Catskill cliffs. Moreover, the idea of content arises late in our understanding of art, at that point—which Hegel identifies as the end of art—where art becomes a topic for intellectual judgment, rather than a sensuous presentation of what is taken to be a reality, which Hegel regards as art's "highest vocation."

There is in Hegel a kind of art which he mentions mainly to dismiss, as it does not qualify as a subject for "Science"—a term which has little to do with natural science, which is negligibly treated in his system. It designates, rather, "The Science of the *true* in its *true shape*," which is, after all, the way Hegel thinks of the processes through which Spirit arrives at an essential knowledge of its own nature. "Art can be used in fleeting play," he writes, "affording recreation and entertainment, decorating our surroundings, giving pleasantness to the externals of our life, and making other objects stand out by artistic adornment." Art so considered is not free but "ancillary"—it is *applied* to ends external to itself, whereas art *as* art is "free alike in its end and its means." It is only as such that it pertains, as with philosophy, to Absolute Spirit. Hegel is concerned to characterize art, which relies upon sensuous presentation, from thought. But there is a distinction to be made in regard to thought itself, which parallels entirely the distinction between fine and applied art: "Science may indeed be used as an intellectual servant for finite ends and accidental means"[5] he concedes, and not for the high purposes of Science (with a capital S). This would have been expected from the consideration that art and thought are one, with the difference that art uses sensuous vehicles for conveying its content. In any case, Hegel has identified what I have preemptively designated a third aesthetic realm, one greatly connected with human life and happiness. It is, in fact, coextensive with most forms of human life:

> Beauty and art does indeed pervade all the business of life like a friendly genius and brightly adorns all our surroundings whether inner or outer, mitigating the seriousness of our circumstances and the complexities of the actual world, extinguishing idleness in an entertaining way. . . . Art belongs rather to the indulgence and relaxation of the spirit, whereas substantial interests require its exertion. . . . Yet even though art intersperses with its pleasing forms everything from the war paint of the savages to the splendor of temples with all the richness of adornment, these forms themselves nevertheless seem to fall outside the true ends and aims of life.[6]

Someone who thought of art in these terms might consider it "inappropriate and pedantic to propose to treat with scientific seriousness what is not itself of a serious nature," as Hegel has set out to do in his *Lectures on Aesthetics*.[7] I am not certain Hegel disagrees with this proposition, despite his remarkably cosmopolitan personality. For he does not discuss art as applied art in the great work he devoted to the subject. Like philosophical thought, art is a modality of free spirit. So there can be no question of "the *worthiness* of art" to be treated as philosophically as philosophy itself. Art is *worthy* of philosophical address only under the perspective of its highest vocation, which it shares with philosophy. So Hegel spends little time in exploring the territory he has uncovered, in which art is applied to the enhancement of life, even if it may, in certain periods, like the Renaissance, have been difficult to distinguish it from Art (with a capital A). When Alberti was commissioned to give a new facade to Santa Maria Novella in Florence, was it upscale decoration or was it high art? We have such a problem today with the distinction between craft and art proper.

But the other border of what I shall designate the Third Realm is equally non-exclusionary, especially when we consider what Hegel singles out under the head of beautiful people—the kind of beauty possessed by Helen of Troy, say, which we must suppose a wonder of nature. But Helen's choice of hairstyles, makeup, or garments would have belonged to the Third Realm, since it would have been chosen for enhancement, like the setting of a jewel.

A great many of Kant's examples fall in this Third Realm—for example, coats and gardens. These could not have been examples of free art in Hegel's thought, and this somewhat helps distinguish our own situation from that of our great predecessors. In my own work, for example, I was from the first anxious to find a way of distinguishing real things from artworks when there was no obvious way of doing so by examination, as in the case (my favorite!) of Brillo boxes and Andy Warhol's *Brillo Box*—a problem that did not and perhaps could not have arisen in Hegel's time.[8] In 1828, for example, there was no way, as there is today, for a coat to be a work of art and subject to misuse if it was in fact used for the purpose of a coat. In seeking to distinguish artworks from what I termed "mere real things," I used *aboutness* as a principle of differentiation. It is a necessary condition for something to be an artwork that it be about something. Since something can possess aboutness without being art, more than content is accordingly needed to distinguish the artworks from mere real things. Aboutness, on the other hand, will not especially serve to distinguish art from applied art. Consider a wedding dress I recently saw exhibited at the Kunsthaus in Zurich by the French artist, Marie-Ange Guilleminot. It was not a work of art in the sense in which we praise wedding dresses generally as works of art—as marvelously designed, skillfully sewn and fitted, with appropriate rich fabrics and tasteful decorations. It was white, but rather plain and severe, and somewhat shroud-like. It could have been worn as a wedding dress, and was indeed so worn by the artist herself in a somewhat disturbatory performance work. We have reached a point in the history of art where there is no reason why a wedding dress—or a housedress, for that matter—cannot be a work of art, even if it is not a "work of art" in the commendatory vernacular sense in which we speak of the adorned bride as "looking like a work of art." What we are required to see is that Guilleminot's dress demands an interpretation, an ascription of meaning which explains its manifest properties. (It helps to know that she had sewn several kilos of lead under the skirt, perhaps to remind us of the weight, or burden, of marriage). The dress was, and this idea is hardly un-Hegelian, what I have termed an embodied meaning. As a garment, the meaning of a wedding dress is its use: it is worn to be married in and proclaims the purity of the wearer as well as the wealth of the bride's parents. That complex of symbolic uses is part of the meaning of the wedding dress as work of art,

Andy Warhol, Brillo Box, 1964. Synthetic polymer and silkscreen on wood, 17 x 17 x 14 inches. Courtesy of Andy Warhol Foundation for the Visual Arts.

Marie-Ange Guilleminot, Le Mariage de Saint Mauer à Saint Gallen, 1994. Courtesy of the artist.

which is not itself intended to be used for anything but art. If someone were to actually wear Guillminot's dress *to be married in,* that would be close to what Duchamp termed a "reverse ready-made," a little closer in this case to the artwork reversed than his own example of using a Rembrandt for the purpose of an ironing board.

Part of what makes Kant's aesthetics so inadequate to the art of our time is that a work like this falls under neither of the kinds of beauty he distinguishes. It is neither free nor dependent. A (real) wedding dress has dependent beauty, by virtue of its connection with ritual and use. But as art it falls outside the domain of application entirely. Beauty is free when it "presupposes no concept of what the object ought to be."[9] Kant uses as examples of free beauty that of flowers, birds, seashells, but also of "delineations *a la greque,* foliage for borders or wall papers."[10] Interestingly, Kant classes "all music without words" as exemplifying free beauty. The beauty of a wedding dress, on the other hand, is quite clearly connected with a concept. The concept governs who wears it when and for how long a time and what it means that it be white and its wearer veiled. But a wedding dress as art is not covered by that same concept. Rather, *it* covers the concept, in that it absorbs it as part of its meaning. It is plain from this that Kant has no independent concept of beautiful art, since art possesses neither kind of beauty. What Kant lacks is the concept of meaning. Hegel requires art to have content if the parallels between it and philosophical thought holds, but his emphasis upon adornment, ornamentation, the refreshment of the spirit through objects of applied art overlooks the role that meanings play in the Third Realm: think, once more, of *Brillo Box* and the Brillo boxes. They have entirely different kinds of meaning, as I have demonstrated elsewhere. The concept of art is part of the meaning of the former, but it is not part of the meaning of the Brillo carton as applied, or as commercial art. It is somewhat interesting to observe that Hegel thinks aesthetically of the objects of the Third Realm from Kant's perspective of free beauty. They *please,* like seashells and wallpaper borders, free from any concept and in themselves.

Nothing more sharply distinguishes the philosophy of art in Kant and in Hegel than the fact that *taste* is a central concept for Kant whereas it is not even discussed by Hegel. As I have suggested, taste was, as much as reason, the defining attribute of the Enlightenment. In *The Analysis of Beauty,* Hogarth draws attention to the serpentine line, whether it characterizes a dancing master's leg or the leg of a chair, a woman's figure or the shape of a teapot.[11] Hogarth argues that anybody, and not just "painters and connoisseurs," know what good taste is—much as his contemporary, Bishop Berkeley, argued that "The illiterate bulk of mankind complain not of any want of evidence in their senses, and are out of all danger of becoming skeptics."[12] He could argue this because English life embodied styles of dress, of decoration, and of craft to such a degree that an appropriately placed Englishman or Englishwoman would acquire taste as naturally as they would acquire their language. Or they could if they were situated in a fortunate social class, like their counterparts in Heian Japan, also a period of all-but-impeccable taste. All of this is absent from Hegel's analysis, and I consider this to be progress toward taking art seriously. The shift takes us from the sphere of the refinement of the senses to the sphere of meaning. The problem with Hegel's introduction of the Third Realm is that he tends to treat it from the eighteenth-century perspective rather than from that of the nineteenth century, where art is taken so seriously as to be coupled in solemnity with philosophy.

It is now time to address the Third Realm of beauty, which, though it embraces the domains of *Vanity Fair* and *Human, All Too Human*, has been the deer park of moralists and satirists down the ages and has only been taken *au serieux* by what in the past decade has been labeled Cultural Studies. It has certainly received relatively little in terms of direct philosophical attention. *Relatively* little, since pride (in Aristotle, Hume, and Davidson) and shame (in Sartre and perhaps in Kierkegaard) have generated a logical as well as a moralistic literature. It is as if philosophers, by shunning it, pay tacit homage to Hegel's thought that, since it is not entirely free, Third Realm beauty can have no claim to philosophical attention. It can certainly not be regarded as a displaced form of philosophy, as art in its "highest vocation" is claimed by Hegel to be. Third Realm beauty is the kind of beauty something possesses only because it was *caused* to possess it through actions whose purpose it is to *beautify*. It is the domain, in brief, of *beautification*. In this realm, things are beautiful only because they were beautified—and beautification has perhaps seemed, to a puritanical philosophical consciousness, to be—the term is Hegel's—*unworthy* of philosophical attention.[13] Morality has always been of central philosophical concern, but discussions of manners, which Hobbes sneers at as "small morals," have barely been noticed. And this somewhat parallels the distinction between considerations of beauty and beautification. The explanation of this perhaps goes back to the most ancient of philosophical distinctions—the distinction between reality and appearances—in that almost invariably Third Realm practitioners are bent on changing the appearances of things in order to beautify or prettify them without these changes penetrating what it really is: "Beauty is only skin-deep." Skills at inducing such changes are learned and applied by what in many languages are called *aestheticians* (or in English *beauticians*), and perhaps because beautification seems an exercise of frivolity, touching nothing fundamental or essential in those who pursue it, it is not difficult for philosophers to assimilate philosophical aesthetics as such to the study of beautification—to *aesthetics* as the practice of (for example) cosmetology—and hence to write the discipline off as having at best a marginal relationship to the True and the Good.

This would be, however, a piece of moral taxonomy, inasmuch as it expresses an unconscious disapproval of activities held to be unworthy of human beings. One gets a whiff of the grounds of such disapproval from Kant's remark on the use of a golden frame—"to merely recommend the painting by its *charm*." It is, Kant pronounces, "then called *finery* and injures genuine beauty." We can see exactly what Kant means when we consider the way certain curators hold picture frames in contempt and order their removal from around the paintings in their care. It is as if, instead of putting paintings in gold frames, we were to sew lace flounces around their edges, which would be—appealing to Webster on finery— "dressy or showy"—and hence an insult to the art. Finery is intended to produce a certain effect, hence it really is akin to rhetoric, the skills of which are bent on making the case look worse or better than it is. Finery, dressiness, show—these are expressions of moralistic disapproval, and in a way they imply an underlying imperative, that people should not appear other than the way God made them. The imperative is expressed in sumptuary codes, the purpose of which is not merely to regulate conduct, since all codes have that purpose, but to control any propensity toward extravagance or luxury. And of course to mislead viewers, who believe one's presented beauty to be one's own rather than due to artifice.

Beautification as a modality of moral self-consciousness presupposes a fairly complex epistemology and a metaphysics of the self, which may be made explicit by referring to the role the mirror image plays in its transactions. We look into the mirror not merely to see how we look, but how we expect others to see us, and, unless amazingly self-confident, we attempt to modulate our appearances in order that others shall see us as we hope to be seen. Happiness and unhappiness in this world is indexed to our appearances—which is perhaps why we have a concept of Heaven as a world in which happiness is not so indexed, since God sees us as we are without reference to how we appear.

If we assimilate our concept of art to the concept of beautification, then, Hegel writes, "it is not itself of a serious nature," though it can have serious consequences.

> On this view, art appears as a superfluity, even if the softening of the heart which preoccupation with beauty can produce does not altogether become deleterious as downright effeminacy. From this point of view, granted the fine arts are a luxury, it has frequently been necessary to defend them in their relationship to practical necessities in general and in particular to morality and piety, and since it is impossible to prove their harmlessness, at least to give grounds for believing this luxury of the spirit may afford a greater sum of advantages than disadvantages.[14]

I expect that the decision to establish a National Endowment for the Arts was justified by appeal to such considerations—that even if taxpayers ought not be asked to support luxury, an argument is available according to which art conduces to a certain softening of the human material. The ground disappeared from under this justification when the Endowment supported art which seemed to have the opposite moral effect, and the question, "why should we support art perceived as *harmful* to the fabric of political society?" could not be avoided.

What is evident through this entire discussion, then, is that the very existence of a third aesthetic realm is internally related to moral considerations in a way in which art in its highest vocation is not, nor is nature in its aspect as beautiful. Both of these, of course, can entail imperatives, especially when it becomes evident that preservation is in order when beauty is threatened. We cannot take it for granted that the beauties of nature or of art will be joys forever. But beautificatory practices themselves intersect every step of the way with various particular moral imperatives, which specify what we might call the bounds of taste (whose realm this is), viz., that something is too plain, or too ornate, or whatever. These aesthetic complaints can be, and typically are, overridden by moral considerations. "We could add much to a building," Kant wrote, "which would immediately please the eye if only it were not to be a church."[15] Its being a church in Königsburg sets boundaries to ornamentation, as if ornament were inconsistent with the momentousness of the house of God—as if the architects were bent on flattery. Consistently, it would similarly be prohibited to wear fine clothes to religious service, as if the church were, like a ball, the scene of flirtations or seduction. (There is a passage in *The Pillow Book* of Lady Sei Shonagun where she complains that a Buddhist monk is too good-looking for the exercise of piety, through his looks drawing her to the world from which his preaching is to liberate her. So beware handsome priests and beautiful nuns!)

God, it might be said, was not quite so austere in his tastes. There is a famous candelabrum in the Bible, one which a curiously finicky God orders Moses to construct. It is a very ornate candelabrum for what after all was a desert people, but it was to be placed in a sanctuary fit for God and was to represent an offering and a sacrifice on the part of the children of Israel "that I might dwell among them." The candelabrum was to be made of pure gold, and God specifies its structure in a brief sufficiently detailed that it might be in a contract with a goldsmith:

> Of beaten work shall the candlestick be made: his shaft and his branches, his bowls, his knops, his flowers, shall be of the same.
> And six branches shall come out of the sides of it: three branches of the candlestick out of the one side, and three branches of the candlestick out of the other side:
> Three bowls made like unto almonds, with a knop and a flower in one branch; and three bowls made like almonds in the other branch, with a knop and a flower: so in the six branches that come out of the candlestick. And in the candlestick shall be four bowls made like unto almonds, with their knops and flowers.
> And there shall be a knop under two branches of the same, and a knop under two branches of the same, according to the six branches that proceed out of the candlestick.
> Their knops and branches shall be of the same: all it shall be one beaten work of pure gold.
> And thou shalt make the seven lamps thereof: and they shall light the lamps thereof, that they may give light against it.[16]

The specification goes on, and it is clear that God means for the sanctuary, in which the candelabrum is to be placed, to be a simulacrum of God's own dwelling.

By the testimony of the book of Exodus, God was not an aesthetic minimalist. A candelabrum of the sort he demands placed a serious burden on his subjects, which meant that it was perceived as a sacrifice. And we see in religious custom practices entirely opposite to the puritanism of Prussia. It is not uncommon to create highly ornamental frames for certain holy pictures, not, as Kant says about golden frames, to recommend the painting, which needs no recommendation, but to pay homage, in the only way one knows how to, to the being of whom it is the picture—the *bambino sacro*, the merciful Madonna, or the *Nothilfige* saints to whom thanks are due for benign interventions. Appreciation is expressed through sometimes massive ornamentation that goes well beyond the boundaries of good taste and over into the realm of what we might consider bad taste, like lace on the wedding dress which crosses a border into froufrou. The artist Alexis

Smith, in her design for the dining room at the Getty Foundation in Santa Monica, asserts that bad taste is better than no taste at all. (A bit like the wry observation that if one did not have bad luck, one would have no luck at all.) The ornamental frame of the Pentecostal church has no business being tasteful because it has no business being bounded. If it is not too much then it is too little. The decorative programs of Flamboyant Gothic are quite clearly at odds with the anti-decorative program of Modernism, as in the writing of Adolf Loos—and in the architectural practice of Ludwig Wittgenstein—both of whom would have endorsed Kant's association of austerity with piety. The philosophical point, however, is that the exercise of taste is associated with how people believe they ought to live. ("If I have only one life to live," an advertisement read, "let me live it as a blonde!") Taste is not the mere application of discernment and fine discrimination. It belongs to ritual. If one thinks about it, church architecture belongs to applied religion, and differs from it as applied art differs from art "in its highest vocation," or as (continuing to follow Hegel) applied in contrast with pure thought. Each of the three moments of Absolute Spirit in fact has a practicum in the Third Realm where human life is actually lived. And every practice is connected with some vision of what a human life ought to be.

Kant offered a second example worth consideration here. "We could adorn a figure with all kinds of spirals and light but regular lines, as the New Zealanders do with their tattooing, if only it were not the figure of a human being."[17] The example is evidence that anthropological description had entered European consciousness; *Cook's Voyages* had recently been published. Hegel mentioned body painting, as we saw, but had, so far as I can tell, no special attitude toward it other than as a primitive form of beautification, a misguided form of gilding the lily. So I would infer that Hegel would have been relatively tolerant of face powder, lipstick, eyeshadow, and curled hair. For Kant, by contrast, the human form is like the form of a church. As the handiwork of God, it cannot be improved upon. It needs no finery, though his discussion of coats suggests that he was thinking of good tailoring and gold buttons. For both philosophers, anthropological knowledge exceeds anthropological understanding. Neither, for example, understands what it means painstakingly to cover the surface of the body with regular circular lines by tattooing—or to paint the body in ways Hegel must have seen in engravings of Micronesians or Africans. This cannot, I think, strictly be considered beautification because the paint or pattern serve important functions of a symbolic or magical kind. They involve

Head of a chief of New Zealand. A Journal of a Voyage to the South Seas, in His Majesty's Ship, The Endeavor. *Courtesy of the Lilly Library, Indiana University.*

ordeals for the sake of the power they confer. They connect the person who bears them to the greater forces of the universe: to spirits and deities. Taste has no application, though obviously ornamentation can be overdone. A heavily ornamental *mazuzzah* can in principle confer no higher power than the plainest of *mazuzzahs*. If it did, then all *mazuzzahs* should possess it. So it has to be gratuitous, which is what moralism holds in regard to beautification generally. It is mere luxury, toward which we can, with Kant, be negative or with Hegel be indifferent, or with Philip Johnson (when he fitted a pediment to the New York City AT&T Building) be positive. These are competing philosophies of taste which, in a cosmopolitan culture such as our own, exist side by side. Theories of taste, however, are not matters of taste: they bring with them entire philosophies of conduct and of life. The ornamentation of a Hindu statue or of a miraculous icon can be painful to a disapproving minimalist, just as the latter's austerity can be criticized as lack of gratitude for favors conferred. So the absence or presence of ornament always transcends questions of aesthetics alone. And this will be true of the enhancement of human beings, where the no-makeup look proclaims, or can proclaim, commitment to the view that 'tis a gift to be simple. Beautification may accordingly also carry symbolic weight, which can be perverted if something is used for looks alone. Were the long locks of the Chasidim to be accepted merely as coiffeur, as in "The Chasidic Look," they would for those who take them up as fashion not have any symbolic weight at all, and certainly would not express the commitment to an entire form of life which the Chasidim are presumed to have made. There would be a difference between circumcision "because it looks better" and circumcision as a condition for entering the covenant with God. Perhaps nothing cosmetic is without symbolic meaning.

The beautification of human beings is my main focus in what follows, primarily because of the somewhat complex relationship between the natural beauty possessed, say, by Helen of Troy, and the enhancing modifications induced by cosmetic intercession. I shall specifically be concerned with beautification which falsifies, by changing somebody's appearances — making them appear naturally beautiful, say, when in fact the look is the product of what moralists deprecate as paintpots, cunningly applied to make it look as if not applied at all.

When he discusses human beauty, Kant does not suppose that there is a single model for it, since he has become aware of racial differences, and recognizes that the different races will have non-congruent conceptions of human beauty. For any given race, the idea of a beautiful person, physiognomically considered, is the product of a kind of unconscious averaging, a statistical composite of the productive imagination which specifies a norm which "is at the basis of the normal idea of the beauty of the [human figure.]"[18] There are now computer programs which are capable of extracting the norm from as many images as one cares to scan into one's machine. The resultant morph is unlikely to match any individual we may encounter, and it is similarly unlikely that an individual human being will perfectly exemplify the prevailing idea of beauty. In fact, it has recently been demonstrated that a consolidated image of perhaps sixty people will be voted more attractive than the images of most of those who participated in the consolidation. But as a morph it will coincide with the idea of beauty at which everyone with a comparable degree of experience will have arrived. It is, within certain limits to be discussed shortly, universal, without corresponding to reality. To the degree that we appreciate symmetry and regularity as the coordinates of beauty, they really do define a norm which actual persons fall away from by various degrees, to the point where genuine ugliness attaches to asymmetry or irregularity. (One of the problems of living in a world where human beings are represented who are closely conforming to the norm, as in television, is that the rest of us feel inadequate or even villainous!) The limits on universality are set by the circumstance that the norm of beauty will vary from society to society, especially insofar as each society consists of members of a distinct racial type:

> Thus necessarily under these empirical conditions a Negro must have a different normal idea of the beauty of the [human figure] from a white man, a Chinaman a different normal idea from a European, etc. . . . It is the image for the whole race.[19]

There were probably very few "Chinamen" or "Negroes" in Königsburg or in most European centers in Kant's time, aside from seaports. But I would surmise that if the averaging crossed racial lines—if the morphing operation were extended to cover the Caucasian, the Negro, and the Oriental racial types—there would be a kind of hypermorph which members of various races might pick out as beautiful, regardless of the racial identity of the viewer. This is an entirely empirical matter; recently some computer-enhanced images of racially undifferentiated female heads were deemed most beautiful by Western and Japanese males. And by now, perhaps, through television and cinema, everyone has seen everything.

One supposes, if beautification is the aim, that everyone would want to approach the hypermorph in looks. Kant cites a work of Polycleitus, the *Doryphorus* or *Spear-carrier*, which came to be known as the *Canon*, inasmuch as it so perfectly embodied the correct proportions of the ideal male form as to serve as an atlas for sculptors. But normic beauty is curiously bland: an authority writes that "balance, rhythm and the minute perfection of bodily form . . . do not appeal to us as they did to the Greeks of the Fifth Century." Kant himself is anxious to press the point that we must "distinguish the *normal idea* of the beautiful from the *ideal*," which—uniquely in the case of human beings—lies in the expression of *moral* qualities. "This shows that a judgment in accordance with *such a standard can never be purely aesthetical and that a judgment in accordance with an ideal is not a mere judgment of taste.*"[20] So ideal beauty may involve a trade-off between normic beauty and the expression of what Kant enumerates as "goodness of heart, purity, strength, peace, etc.—visible as it were in bodily manifestations (as the effect of that which is internal.)"[21] Hegel characterizes Romantic Art as responsive to the demand for making inwardness visible, of showing what a person is so far as that person is coincident with his or her feelings. And that would explain why *The Spear Carrier* is bland: classical art, if Hegel is right, had no concept of inwardness. It explains as well why a contemporary artist, Orlan, who submits herself to plastic surgery in order to make herself conform to aesthetic prototypes, in fact looks, well, creepy. She shows no inwardness. And it explains why the life-likeness induced by mortuary intervention underscores the death of the body—even if the face is given a happy smile. It also explains, I think, why the case presented to Socrates by Adeimanthus in *The Republic* is less readily imagined than one might believe: a perfectly unjust man who appears to be perfectly just. We can, within limits, feign looks, but not consistently. The kind of person we are shows through the kind of person we appear to be; there is a limit to the possibilities of expressional cosmetics, of making ourselves look kind or thoughtful or sensitive. Someone may feel that the reason they are unloved is because they appear too fat, which may be true or false—true under the criterion of normic beauty, false under that of inner beauty, which may alert others to the fact that someone is cruel or vacuous, or their opposites. Kant is entirely right in his suggestion that inner beauty is not a matter of taste alone, as exhibited in adolescents, who fall in love with football heroes and prom queens, or by tycoons who marry models, whom they display as trophies. Inwardness sets a limit to how far hair transplants, nose jobs, liposuction, breast implants, and the like will carry one. But the literature of moralists and cynics, from ancient times, has been replete with applicable wisdom, whether or not it shows up in classical art.

There is a certain set of political considerations involved in beautification, which would not, I think, have shown up in this literature, inasmuch as they only began to enter consciousness in relatively recent times. They arise when members of a certain group begin to think that they have sought to conform to a norm of beauty which in fact was imposed upon them by a politically dominant class—by men in the case of women, or by whites in the case of blacks, or—a somewhat weaker case—by Caucasians in the case of Jews. As a corollary of contemporary feminism, it occurred to women that they aspired to an ideal of beauty which had been imposed upon them by men; or to blacks that they aspired to conform to a standard of beauty which in fact belonged to whites. When the possibility of imposition became a matter of a raised consciousness, beautificatory practices changed abruptly. In the case of blacks, as discussed in the article by Paul C. Taylor, even as militant a figure as Malcolm X went through a period in which he underwent a hair-straightening procedure, at considerable cost in pain, but one he felt to be worth it if in the end he would be perceived as not possessing the tight curls identified with negritude. So in terms of hair he would consider himself to be non-Negro (soft curls would be consistent with that). Hair is a very charged bodily part in black culture, mainly because kinked hair is part of the Negro stereotype—or because it would turn up in the averaging which defines the norm for the race, in Kant's view. But with the recognition that they had been applying a norm to themselves that was not their own, African Americans came to see kinked hair as something to be proud of (and a black born with straight hair might choose to rectify the situation). The Afro hairstyle became a weapon in the aesthetico-racial wars: it flaunted what under prevailing norms would have been held to be disfiguring, by others and by oneself, so long as one subscribed to the racial status quo. "Black is beautiful" is a political refusal not to be oppressed aesthetically. That is a return to Kant's distinctions; it entails accepting a norm of beauty specific to the race. Black culture radiated out from cosmetic changes: the choice of African names, the wearing of African costumes, changing one's religion from Christianity to Islam. The moral quandary of a black person who looks white is the perduring theme of Adrian Piper's art.

The case of feminism is different in certain ways, in that there was not a time in which women sought to define feminine beauty in terms of male beauty—though flattened breasts in the 1920s served to reduce to invisibility a traditionally feminine attribute. Women sought—and by the evidence of the literature they still seek—to define female beauty as men are perceived to define it, and hence become what men want them to be. Coeval with the Afro were the ritual "bra-burnings," in which a garment identified with femininity, and which served to construct a female figure along certain lines, was cast out and women's natural contours were flaunted. Breasts were allowed to swing freely, nipples to show through T-shirts. And, collaterally with the emergence of a politicized black culture, a politicized female culture appeared through which women sought to live in conformity with their own sexual reality as they perceived it, in which beauty as previously specified was now perceived as a trap.

None of this will be unfamiliar to anyone who lived through the 1970s and 1980s, nor is it unfamiliar in the forms it has assumed in the present decade. It is certainly subject to satire and caricature, but there can be little doubt that the struggle over whose canon of beauty we are to apply to ourselves goes well beyond what Kant described as taste, and well beyond the expression of moral states he felt must be adjoined to it. In a way, which I shall leave until a later occasion to examine, not allowing one's self-definition to be imposed from without is close enough to what Kant thought of as autonomy to suggest that there is a deep connection between the aesthetics of the Third Realm and the realm of ethics. It is to reject a categorical imperative with regard to how we shall appear and to endorse one restricted to who we are in terms of race and gender—and such other facticities as may in the course of time emerge politically. This has its dangers, and, especially in the case of women, it has some far from well-understood limits. The differences between races, while accounted for through evolution, are not required for human evolution. It is a difference more connected with variation than with speciation. With sexual difference, on the other hand, there has thus far been a bimorphic basis for generation. And this shows up in the role of sexual attraction. The human male is so constituted that he must be aroused, or there will be no erection, hence no pregnancies, hence no survival of the species. Feminine beauty is thus connected with the power to arouse and excite—and reproduce—and with the now legendary "male gaze" an agency of evolution.

This, of course, can change if the replenishment of the species can be detached from the psycho-chemistry of arousal. Viagra still requires sexual stimulation, but almost certainly there will be erectile prosthetics which dispense with this atavism, allowing the erection to be a matter of will, thus reproducing what Saint Augustine proposes was the condition of Adam before the Fall, his ability to plant his seed without the storms of passion.[22] When she is no longer under the imperatives of attractiveness, the human female will be free to appear as she cares to, indifferent to what turns men on. It is far from plain, moreover, that post-Adamic methods of impregnation are written into the genome. With cloning and the like, we can imagine and perhaps even foresee a time when men are sexually required only for sexual pleasure — or might even be cloned out because of social disorders blamed on testosterone. We are entering a brave new world, and Third Realm aesthetics becomes less and less frivolous every day.

NOTES

I am indebted to Peg Brand for encouraging me to comment on Paul Taylor's essay about some of the quandaries of black aesthetics, and of course I am indebted to Professor Taylor himself for entering into a territory of aesthetic analysis rarely explored by philosophers. There is an irony, I suppose, in the fact that Taylor uses a passage from one of my texts as license to deal with topics as remote from traditional aesthetic concern as hair-straightening, while I have used his study to generalize to a Third Realm of beauty, under which his inquiry can be subsumed. His essay, in any case, stimulated mine, even if I make use of his central example only by way of illustration. I have lately been interested in the ethics of appearance; see my "The Naked Truth" in Jerrold Levinson's anthology *Ethics and Aesthetics* (New York: Cambridge University Press, 1997). I would like to reclaim for philosophy some of the territory lost to Cultural Studies. Taylor is of course quite right to have turned to the latter for strategies, since philosophy has turned its back on personal appearance as, well, appearance.

1. Immanuel Kant, *Critique of Judgment,* trans. J. H. Bernard (New York: Hafner, 1951), sec. 4, p. 41.

2. G. W. F. Hegel, *Aesthetics: Lectures on Fine Art,* vol. I., trans. T. M. Knox (Oxford: Clarendon Press, 1975), p. 1.

3. Ibid., p. 2.

4. Ibid., p. 7.

5. Ibid.

6. Ibid., p. 3.

7. Ibid.

8. Arthur C. Danto, "Art Works and Real Things," in *The Transfiguration of the Commonplace* (Cambridge, Mass.: Harvard University Press, 1981).

9. Kant, *Critique of Judgment,* sec. 16, p. 65.

10. Ibid., sec. 16, p. 55.

11. William Hogarth, *The Analysis of Beauty,* ed. Ronald Paulson (New Haven: Yale University Press, 1997), chap. X.

12. George Berkeley, "Introduction," in A *Treatise concerning the Principles of Human Knowledge,* ed. Colin M. Turbayne (Indianapolis: Bobbs-Merrill Company, Inc., 1957), sec. 1, p. 5.

13. Hegel, *Aesthetics,* p. 5.

14. Ibid., p. 3.

15. Kant, *Critique of Judgment,* sec. 16, p. 66.

16. Exodus 25:31–37.

17. Kant, *Critique of Judgment,* sec. 16, p. 66.

18. Ibid., sec. 17, p. 72.

19. Ibid., sec. 17, p. 71.
20. Ibid., sec. 17, p. 72.
21. Ibid.
22. Saint Augustine, *The City of God*, trans. John Healey (London and New York: Everyman's Library, 1945), xiv, chap. 24.

PART TWO

Body Beautiful

Kathleen M. Higgins

5. Beauty and Its Kitsch Competitors

One of the reasons for the disappearance of beauty in the artistic ideology of the late twentieth century has been the seeming similarity of beauty to certain kinds of kitsch. Beauty has also been associated with flawlessness and with glamour. I will contend that the flawless and the glamorous are actually categories of kitsch, and that the dominance of these images in marketing has contributed to our societal tendency to confuse them with beauty. The quests for flawlessness and glamour are both self-sabotaging, a premise on which the marketing of beauty depends. These false paradigms of beauty have obscured the fact that human beauty manifests an ideal of balance and health that is neither self-conscious nor a consequence of deliberate effort. I will defend the relevance of this ideal to beauty to our personal and cultural well-being.

While my sister's daughter Allison was in pre-school, my sister told me that her teacher had given her an "A" when she graded the class's drawings. I congratulated Allison for her good work.

"Do you know why the teacher put a letter 'A' on my picture?" Allison asked me.

"Why?"

"Because I drew an angel, and angels are very beautiful."

Allison's explanation amused me, in part because of her naive belief that the referent of her drawing, independent of its execution, could compel her teacher's commendation. I was also entertained by the fact that her modesty regarding her artistry was effectively canceled by her evident pride that she had chosen so wisely.

On further reflection, however, it occurred to me that many adults hold similarly naive beliefs about the power of beauty, though with far less confidence that our choices aimed at beauty will actually achieve our goals. We share with Plato the belief that to recognize beauty is a matter of insight. Even when one's recognitions are rather self-directed and pedestrian—as when I am pleased to see my reflection when I've donned a well-fitting jacket—an aspect of the satisfaction is a sense of one's own good taste. The pleasing reflection in the mirror when one feels nicely dressed inspires double pride: pride in one's body *and* in one's mind.

Beyond pride, though, one feels a sense of invulnerability in being well-dressed. When I have to attend a meeting that I expect to be heated, I dress up somewhat. I put on war paint, literally. In general, we think of beauty as the best defense. We also consider beauty an assertion of power. Beauty is the irresistible weapon, the spiritual equivalent of the nuclear bomb. Beauty compels, and the beautiful being is, we imagine, all-powerful.

Consider the tale of Lucifer, literally the "light-bearer," the angel so beautiful that he imagined he could rival God. His attempt to dethrone God unsuccessful, he became Satan. Lucifer's story reminds us that beauty can be a temptation to hubris, but that the quest for divine omnipotence by means of beauty is ultimately deceptive and corrupting. Perhaps, then, our naive lust for power through beauty precedes a fall from grace. The continuing fascination with Oscar Wilde's *The Picture of Dorian Gray* suggests that our culture is suspicious of the beautiful person, even when that person holds us enthralled.

Traditionally, the notion of beauty as a means to power has been conjoined with the idea that beauty is also an occasion for insight. Plato considers beauty to be irresistible because it is the most salient manifestation of the absolute truth, the realm of forms. "But is not the right love a sober and harmonious love of the orderly and the beautiful?" asks Plato's Socrates.[1] Aristotle, although confining his analysis to the terrestrial plane, similarly sees beauty's effectiveness to be based upon its manifestation of principles with the status of universal truths, such as those of mathematics.

> The chief forms of beauty are order and symmetry and definiteness, which the mathematical sciences demonstrate in a special degree. And since these (e.g., order and definiteness) are obviously causes of many things, evidently these sciences must treat this sort of causative principle also (e.g., the beautiful) as in some sense a cause.[2]

Plotinus describes the power of beauty in terms of its manifestation of divine thought: "The material thing becomes beautiful—by communicating in the thought that flows from the Divine."[3]

In the medieval era, too, beauty was thought to facilitate insight into the divine. Thomas Aquinas included among his criteria for beauty such God-like attributes as perfection and "brightness, or clarity [*claritas*]."[4] James Joyce's character Stephen Dedalus elaborates on the Thomist notion of *claritas* in a manner that conjoins the ideas of insight into the divine and the power of beauty to transfix the human mind:

> The connotation of the word, Stephen said, is rather vague. Aquinas uses a term which seems to be inexact. . . . It would lead you to believe that he had in mind symbolism or idealism, the supreme quality of beauty being a light from some other world, the idea of which the matter is but the shadow, the reality of which it is but the symbol. . . . The instant wherein that supreme quality of beauty, the clear radiance of the esthetic image, is apprehended luminously by the mind which has been arrested by its wholeness and fascinated by its harmony is the luminous silent stasis of esthetic pleasure.[5]

In recent Western thought about beauty, however, the conjunction of insight and compulsion have been severed. For us, Lucifer has already lost the divine vision of heaven, but he retains his attractive power. One translation of the traditional baptismal vows in the Catholic Church includes renunciation of Satan's glamour. Lucifer's overwhelming beauty has become glamour, he himself the great Deceiver, whom we can resist only with an infusion of divine grace. This translation of the baptismal vows reflects what I think is a pervasive impression that is widespread in our culture: that beauty, or some near kin of it, is unsavory, a temptation that might get the soul off-track.

Our culture's suspicion of beauty might explain the relative absence of beauty from the agenda of contemporary American artists. I mentioned beauty to an artist friend recently, and he said, "I think it's a gimmick. It always makes me suspicious." Philosopher John Passmore, in his famous 1951 article "The Dreariness of Aesthetics," describes the artist's perspective similarly:

> I would suggest that there is something suspect ("phony") about "beauty". Artists seem to get along quite well without it; it is the cafe-haunters, the preachers, the metaphysicians, and the calendar-makers who talk of beauty. . . . "Beauty" is always nice, always soothing; it is what the bourgeois pays the artist for.[6]

Art critic Dave Hickey, enthusiast of beauty as "the issue for the nineties," contends that suspicion of beauty remains a common reaction among artists and others of influence in the contemporary art world. He analyzes the art world's rejection of beauty as inevitable, given the now-entrenched project of "honest" artistic expression.

> [T]he institution's curators hold a public trust . . . [and] must look carefully and genuinely care about what artists "really" mean—and therefore they must, almost of necessity, distrust appearances—distrust the very idea of appearances, and distrust most of all the appearance of images that, by virtue of the pleasure they give, are efficacious in their own right. The appeal of these images amounts to a kind of ingratitude, since the entire project of the new institution has been to lift the cruel burden of efficacy from the work of art and make it possible for artists to practice that "plain honesty" of which no great artist has yet been capable, nor ever wished to be. . . . [B]eauty is the *bête noire* of this agenda, the snake in the garden. It steals the institution's power, seduces its congregation, and, in every case, elicits the dismay of artists who have committed themselves to paint honestly and the efficacy of the institution.[7]

If Hickey is right, the current avoidance of beauty by artists is itself an indication of the presumption that beauty is coercive and manipulative. I find it hard to interpret this as a sign that artists have abandoned the will to overpower their audiences. Instead, it might indicate that they have upped the ante, now aiming to compel the audience outright without resorting to the camouflage that beauty has often achieved. Seen as a mode of camouflage, however, beauty is far from Plato's salient manifestation of absolute truth. Instead, it is an aesthetic form of lying.

Yet "a specifically aesthetic form of lying" is precisely Matei Calinescu's characterization of kitsch.[8] If beauty is now categorized by artists as among art's cheap tricks and deceptions, its project no longer seems distinct from that of kitsch. Kitsch, a category for a certain type of aesthetically deficient art, has often been categorized as deficient for eliciting emotional responses merely by treating subject matter that is associated with fundamental human concerns. Tomas Kulka, for example, offers such a characterization in his three criteria that make an object kitsch.

1. Kitsch depicts objects or themes that are highly charged with stock emotions.
2. The objects or themes depicted by kitsch are instantly and effortlessly identifiable.
3. Kitsch does not substantially enrich our associations relating to the depicted objects or themes.[9]

Kitsch typically treats stock themes such as the charming child, the adored housewife, or the adolescent dreaming of the future. Courtesy of Haussner Family Limited Partnership, Baltimore; In-Sink-Erator Corporation; and Lane Furniture.

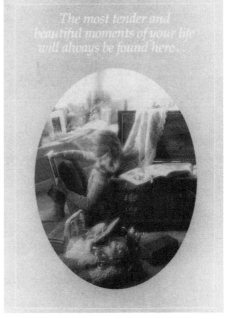

Kulka contends that "as long as its basic gestalt is preserved, alterations and transformations of a whole range of other features do not affect its aesthetic impact."[10] Consequently, "the effect of kitsch is totally parasitic on its referent."[11] Elsewhere, I, too, have suggested that the impact of kitsch depends on its presentation of an image which can be expected to arouse a strong emotional effect, regardless of how it is executed. My explanation is that kitsch presents an image, or icon, that makes reference to a culture's beliefs about the world and about what goals are desirable and attainable. These beliefs, which I call archetypes, are semiconscious and pervasively reinforced through cultural practices. The icon presents a part or an instance of the culture's network of archetypes. The icon heightens one's awareness of this background structure, and one's satisfaction in the object stems from its unchallenging reinforcement of culturally instilled beliefs one has about one's place in the world. One enjoys one's own feelings about the way the world should be, which seem to be affirmed by the kitsch object.[12]

I think that the impression that beauty is a cheap deception stems from our cultural failure to distinguish beauty from kitsch, a failure that is particularly evident in our ideology regarding female beauty.[13] This ideology tends to equate two fantasies with beauty: the flawless and the glamorous. Each of these fantasies, I will argue, is actually a species of kitsch; neither amounts to beauty. I will present my justifications for these claims and then go on to consider the possibility of a notion of beauty about which we need not be cynical.

"Beautiful," colloquially understood, is paradigmatically characteristic of a person. When I describe Plato's Form of Beauty for my introductory classes, students expect me to talk about people, not sunsets, and especially to talk about women.

What makes a woman beautiful? Plato, although probably concerned more directly with male beauty, sees beauty as a manifestation of spiritual reality through the physical in a way that inspires love.[14] Our popular culture has banalized Plato's account, but advertisements and women's magazines indicate the continued association between beauty and at least one aspect of love. Beauty arouses desire. Two of the recurrent themes in popular visions of beauty are the flawless and the glamorous. Flawless and glamorous women, sometimes women who are both at once, populate the pages of fashion magazines, particularly the advertisements.[15] Naomi Wolf contends that insinuations of this contrast are a staple of the beauty industry's marketing techniques. In her book *The Beauty Myth*, she recounts the pernicious psychological tactics that are used to sell products as means to achieve beauty, tactics that encourage women to feel insufficiently beautiful and to blame themselves for this "failure." Wolf describes the marketing of flawlessness in terms recalling the Platonic account:

> A woman enters a department store from the street, looking no doubt very mortal. . . . To reach the cosmetics counter, she must pass a deliberately disorienting prism of mirrors, lights, and scents. . . .

> On either side of her are ranks of angels—seraphim and cherubim—the "perfect" faces of the models on display. Behind them, across a liminal counter in which is arranged the magic that will permit her to cross over, lit from below, stands the guardian angel. The saleswoman is human, she knows, but "perfected" like the angels around her, from whose ranks the woman sees her own "flawed" face, reflected back and shut out. . . . [T]he mortal world disintegrates in her memory at the shame of feeling so out of place among all the ethereal objects. Put in the wrong, the shopper longs to cross over.[16]

Glamour, by contrast, does not seem angelic. The etymology of the term suggests its connection with darker forces. The word, according to *The New Shorter Oxford English Dictionary*, is an alternative form of "GRAMMAR with the sense of GRAMARYE."[17] The latter means "Grammar; learning," but also "occult learning; magic, necromancy.[18] The dictionary defines glamour, in its modern sense, as

> 1. Magic, enchantment. 2. (A) deceptive or bewitching beauty or charm; (a) mysteriously exciting or alluring physical attractiveness, esp. when artificially contrived. . . . B. 1. Enchant, bewitch. 2. Glamorize.[19]

These contemporary definitions retain the associations between glamour and black magic, mysterious learning that makes allure possible. While beauty's power arises from its idealization of realities, glamour's power derives from the arts of deception. Platonic beauty radiates "light from some other world," in Joyce's phrase; but glamour attaches directly to the body, which bewitches the beholder. The glamorous body's allure is not a spiritual radiance, but a sexual magnetism that pulls the enchanted viewer off-course.

Wolf's analysis of sexualized "beauty" ads suggests an appeal to glamour in this sense:

> In a crossover of imagery in the 1980s, the conventions of high-class pornographic photography, such as *Playboy*'s, began to be used generally to sell products to women. This made the beauty thinking that followed crucially different from all that had preceded it. Seeing a face anticipating orgasm, even if it is staged, is a powerful sell. In the absence of other

According to Naomi Wolf, such pre-orgasmic faces are effective marketing tools. Courtesy of Nine West and Elle. Photographs by Michel Comte and Christoph Cogner, respectively.

sexual images, many women came to believe that they must have that face, that body, to achieve ecstasy.[20]

The "staged" character of the apparent arousal in such advertisements does not defuse their persuasiveness. Instead, this deception makes one vulnerable to further falsehoods. The magic of advertising here is its ability to divert the viewer from a sense of ecstatic potential in one's own being to a lust for a body unencumbered by one's own inner life. One wants to don this body like a Greek tragic mask, the wearing of which transforms an actor into a god.

These images serve the aims of marketing by insinuating that an advertised product will give one a flawless or glamorous appearance that will provoke desire. Beauty's traditional role as guarantor of power has been usurped by each of these standards. Neither flawlessness nor glamour fulfills other traditional functions of beauty, however. Besides its overpowering character, as we have seen, the traditional vision of beauty holds that it is a manifestation of truth (divine or terrestrial), structured in an orderly fashion, perfected (i.e., complete, not lacking any element necessary for optimum impact), and radiant. With respect to the structure of beauty, philosophers from Aristotle through Kant have described the beautiful in terms of unity, something that is forged from a complex of elements.[21] Typically, too, beauty has been characterized as the worthy focus of love.[22]

Our cultural notion of beauty, then, is a cluster concept, involving a set of elements that together recur in most philosophical accounts. These elements include: (1) an orderly structure, (2) unity wrought from distinct elements, (3) perfection, (4) an occasion for epiphany, (5) radiance, (6) overpowering impact, and (7) the incitement of love, ideally, divorced from personal agendas. When beauty is characterized by this entire cluster, neither flawlessness nor glamour proves to be a form of beauty. I will consider these standards in turn.

Flawlessness implies that no element is defective and that no element interferes with a satisfactory impression of the whole. A scarred nose, for example, would be a flaw in a face, distracting attention from other features in a way that interferes with an impression of the whole. Accordingly, flawlessness is at least compatible with the achievement of two of the criteria in the beauty cluster. No element precludes the achievement of an orderly structure; and flawlessness is compatible with the recognition of unity among the elements.

However, flawlessness does not really *facilitate* the achievement of these criteria. Flawlessness frequently involves an evenness of features that is not conducive to the effect of a unified structure. Even features are indeterminate with respect to which are foreground and which are background. Fashion models who are relatively flawless can be "made over" into a wide variety of "looks" because their features do not tend clearly toward a definite unified structure.

There is no doubt that there is something fascinating about this potential for the same features to appear in a variety of ways. The beauty industry is not entirely deceptive when it recommends makeup as a means to reconfigure the apparent relation of facial elements. When we transform our appearances with cosmetics and clothing in a Halloween-like spirit, the "makeover" game need not be considered psychologically pernicious (although it may be unreasonably expensive).[23] However, it is rare for a woman in our society to approach clothes and cosmetics in a completely lighthearted manner.

The problem, as Wolf indicates, is the psychological message that unless you are physically flawless, you are deficient as a human being. Once one accepts this premise, no amount of effort to camouflage or reconfigure flaws will remove this deficiency. The more you work to conceal, in fact, the more you acknowledge your fundamental inadequacy. This cycle is reinforced by the fact that flawlessness is a negatively defined characteristic. One is flawless by virtue of lacking certain faults, not through any particular traits. As a goal, flawlessness is an empty achievement. This vicious circle is of great use to marketers. If a woman has purchased makeup from a feeling of inadequacy, the use of the makeup itself will likely be a further performative manifestation of her sense of inadequacy, and this reinforces the motive that may incite her to buy again.

Flawlessness falls short of beauty if we consider the entire cluster of associated ideas. In the first place, the presence of only flawless elements does not *necessarily* imply a unified, orderly structure. Well-formed elements do not necessarily result in a vital unity. The conjunction of elements may be inert; they may fail to be dynamically related.[24] Schopenhauer suggests a reason why the "flawless" beauty might fail to aesthetically captivate in his analysis of wax figures. Wax figures may depict human beings or fruits such as apples. Regardless of the beauty of the referent, the medium of wax fails aesthetically because the evenness of presentation leaves nothing to the imagination.

> [W]ax figures can never produce an aesthetic effect, and are therefore not real works of fine art, although it is precisely in them that the imitation of nature can reach the highest degree. For they leave nothing to the imagination. . . . The wax figure . . . gives everything, form and colour at the

same time; from this arises the appearance of reality, and the imagination is left out of account.[25]

Schopenhauer suggests here that beauty requires that imagination must be stimulated by structure, and that the presentation of well-formed parts can be an impediment to aesthetic satisfaction because it provides no room for the imagination to further elaborate.[26]

Kant offers an account that suggests a further explanation of why flawlessness will not suffice as a characteristic or species of beauty. He observes that the kind of standard we use in judging human beauty is an analytical construct on the order of a police composite, without instantiation in nature:

> Someone has seen a thousand adult men. If now he wishes to make a judgment about their standard size, to be estimated by way of a comparison, then (in my opinion) the imagination projects a large number of images (perhaps the entire thousand) onto one another. If I may be permitted to illustrate this by an analogy from optics: in the space where most of the images are united, and within the outline where the area is illuminated by the color applied most heavily, there the average size emerges, equally distant in both height and breadth from the outermost bounds of the tallest and shortest stature; and that is the stature for a beautiful man. . . . Now if in a similar way we try to find for this average man the average head, for it the average nose, etc., then it is this shape which underlies the standard idea of a beautiful man in the country where this comparison is made.

Kant goes on to distinguish the standard idea of a beautiful human being from the ideal instance of beauty.

> This *standard idea* is not derived from proportions that are taken from experience *as determinate rules*. Rather it is in accordance with this idea that rules for judging become possible in the first place. It is the image for the entire kind, hovering between all the singular and multiply varied intuitions of the individuals, the image that nature used as the archetype on which it based its productions within any one species, but which it does not seem to have attained completely in any individual. The standard idea is by no means the entire *archetype of beauty* within this kind, but is only the form that constitutes the indispensable condition of all beauty, and hence merely the correctness in the exhibition of the kind.[27]

In other words, this standard merely provides assurance that those presentations that approximate it will be well within the range of humankind. It does not, and cannot, specify the specific characteristics of an actually beautiful person (or thing).

It is precisely because of this, too, that the standard idea cannot contain any specific characteristics, since then it would not be the *standard idea* for that kind. Nor is it because of its beauty that we like its exhibition, but merely because it does not contradict any of the conditions under which alone a thing of this kind can be beautiful. The exhibition is merely academically correct.[28]

I think that flawlessness, treated as a criterion of beauty, is nothing more than the Kantian standard idea elevated to a principle of aesthetic correctness. The judgment that an object is flawless is a judgment that it approximates the standard idea, all of its elements corresponding roughly to the basic gestalt of the human form. Like politically correct language, flawlessness is "correct," but only to the extent that one cannot be shown to be at fault. Accordingly, flawlessness is not reliable as a guide to beauty. Insofar as our tradition's idea of beauty is a cluster concept, the flawless form is only a candidate for beauty, because no detracting feature precludes the possibility that its elements compose a well-integrated structure.

Flawlessness, like the Kantian standard idea, is a featureless concept because it provides no details about features.[29] It is an approximation that can be elaborated through features of many different sorts. When flawlessness is the most salient virtue of an object, there is a certain deficiency, particularly the absence of character.[30] This absence of character may explain why flawless features are considered desirable. Psychoanalysis suggests that a person's lack of apparent character can produce the effect of a blank screen, on which the beholder can project his or her own psychic contents with minimal constraint.[31] "Flawless" features, lacking definite indications of character, facilitate the beholder's projection of his or her own specific requirements because they do not assert incompatible traits.

The emptiness of the standard of flawlessness precludes its fulfillment of the traditional beauty cluster. Because it is empty and implies nothing positive about the features in question, it does not suggest any grounds for an occasion of epiphany. Even if we assume that radiance results from particular positively instantiated characteristics, we have no reason to suppose that mere fulfillment of the empty form of flawlessness will result in radiance. Properly viewed as a rough image of the average human type, the criterion of flawlessness does not assure an overpowering impact or the incitement of love. The beautiful, even when its object is not a human being, has sometimes been cited for its uniqueness,[32] and uniqueness would seem to be all the more important when one is speaking of a human being who is loved (Plato's Socrates notwithstanding to the contrary).[33] If beautiful objects are characteristically individual, flawlessness cannot be a sufficient criterion of beauty.

Seeing the criterion of flawlessness as an invocation of the Kantian standard idea, we are also able to see it as a criterion that promotes kitsch instead of beauty. Flawlessness appropriately serves as only a minimal standard for beauty, and then only when it is taken to be a rough approximation of the human gestalt. The standard established, therefore, is geared only to the preservation of a gestalt, not to any particular instantiation. The maintenance of a gestalt, Kulka observes, is the crucial achievement in kitsch.

Kulka's criteria of kitsch, although designed for artworks, apply well to the case of the flawless human being as well.[34] First, the appearance of flawlessness in a human being is highly emotionally charged. The suitability of the flawless person for projection virtually ensures the beholder's psychological investment, with the emotional charge that such investment entails.

Second, flawlessness is also effortlessly identifiable. If we are formulating aesthetic judgments of the human figure, presumably we already have a pattern in mind; and if so, we should not have much difficulty in recognizing those "flawless" faces and bodies that approximate the pattern. Finally, flawlessness, though compatible with many associations wrought by our own reveries, does not enrich our associations itself; it is an inherently negative characteristic.

Flawlessness may seem to be the property of an object, although we have suggested it is empty with respect to properties. Glamour, by contrast, is overtly a matter of atmosphere. While flawlessness can be static, like the sculptures in a wax museum, glamour is more dynamic, characteristically transferring its charge to the object it surrounds. The concept is ostensibly associated with power; and power is revealed only in its activity. The glamorous person is sexy, and sexiness is precisely the power that such a person exerts upon the beholder.

The fact that both flawlessness and glamour are paraded by advertisers as ideals of beauty is strange, for these standards are in some ways contrary to each other. Glamour exploits wild images (the staged "face anticipating orgasm," for example). Flawlessness is typically staid. Glamour often has overtones of sinfulness and forces contrary to nature. Flawlessness, by contrast, is associated with moral perfection and nature's achieved aim. Nevertheless, the same individual can sometimes be both. The reason may be that glamour, like flawlessness, is compatible with a wide variety of particular characteristics. Glamour does not determine specific traits, but only the nature of the atmosphere surrounding a person. Glamour, in this respect, is another featureless concept.

The quest for glamour, like the quest for flawlessness, typically engages a woman in a vicious circle. If one aspires to be glamorous, one seeks the mechanism for doing so. But if you are aware that you are trying to be glamorous by means of a deliberate technique, you cannot simultaneously observe yourself as simply ensconced by an atmosphere. Metaphorically, you must brush away the atmosphere to see the mechanism designed to produce it in its operation. But once you have dispelled the atmosphere, you cannot observe it surrounding you. To put the point less abstractly, the more you strive to be glamorous by means of clothes, for example, the less certain you can be that you have succeeded.

The cycle of perceived inadequacy that motivates purchases that reinforce one's perception of inadequacy, which we observed as incited by the goal of flawlessness, recurs in connection with glamour. Suppose I imagine that a certain dress will make me glamorous. I only entertain such fantasies to the extent that I feel unglamorous at present. I fantasize that a kind of chemical reaction will occur between me and the new dress, so that the glamour of the dress will become my own. This fantasy makes sense only because the dress possesses a power that I do not see as mine.

But what happens when I actually buy the dress? As soon as I consider it my possession, it no longer has the alien power that attracted me. Insofar as it is now connected to me, I can see my own unglamorous aura enveloping the dress, instead of the aura of the dress enveloping me. The dress becomes enfeebled almost as soon as it joins the ranks in my closet. Unless I consciously draw the obvious conclusion from this experience, that buying clothes will not give me glamour, I may well be motivated to shop again, fantasizing that I can gain the power of glamour through buying yet another glamorous item of clothing, which will fail me in the same way.

Glamour, when pursued through such artificial glamorizers, involves a performative contradiction for the person that aspires to it. If you feel you are the female equivalent of Walter Mitty in reality, you can envision yourself as powerful by means of fantasy. The props that render the fantasy convincing, marketers hope, are the clothing and cosmetics they sell. However, the acquisition of these props encourages self-doubt. Even if I succeed in getting others to respond to me as though I were glamorous, I can ask, "Is it me or is it my makeup?" And I am more likely to doubt that it is me the more I choose clothes and beauty products with glamour in mind.

Glamour operates through a metonymic borrowing of symbolic power. Borrowed symbolic power is what I seek when I buy a dress to make me glamorous. Certain roles also allow for power transference of a symbolic nature. High public office renders its holder glamorous, as does the fantasy that someone occupies a world unlike one's own, the basis for glamour in movie stars. Glamour is not about one's personal uniqueness, but about one's relationship to a larger complex of fantasy, one that is intriguing in part because of its unavailability. The president is glamorous because the White House is off-limits to most of us; movie stars are glamorous because they belong to an impenetrable social network that we see as symbolic of the high life.

The fact that most stars face the same freeway frustrations as the rest of us is irrelevant. Glamour is independent of the glamorous person's subjective experience. A person's glamour is evident only from a third-person perspective; a perspective that is unconcerned with that person's first-person subjectivity except insofar as that subjectivity gives us something to watch. Once glamour surrounds a person, even that person's frustration on the freeway can appear in a glamorous light. Glamour is a voyeuristic pleasure, sometimes heightened when a glamorous individual descends into our material world to drive, to shop, or to eat dinner. Far from dispelling the glamour of stars, talk shows that present stars as "just like us" contribute to their mystique. They seem so near, and yet so far. The conjunction is, for a large number of people, apparently riveting.

Glamour makes reference to the tail of a comet of unavailable power and experience, and this is its psychological hook. It is not dependent on a particularly attractive arrangement of features. Several of the traditional characteristics of beauty are unrelated to glamour. Glamour does not require an orderly structure or a unity wrought from distinct elements. Neither does it require perfection; even a sketchy impression is compatible with glamour. Because glamour depends on an object's implicit relationships rather than its individual character, it does not offer insight into the object, nor does it offer enough focus on the object itself to elicit love.

The two traditional features of beauty that glamour might seem to achieve are radiance and overpowering impact. These two characteristics of the beautiful object work in tandem. An object's radiance is the source of the impact that it has on us. Glamour seems to have impact and to make people radiant. Does glamour satisfy these two criteria of beauty?

Certainly, the atmosphere of glamour can be described as rendering a person "radiant." The term is not uncommon in fashion magazines, where models are posed as protagonists in a fictional world that is intended as attractive, but unavailable if only because it is fictional, offering no routes for us to enter it. When such models are called radiant, however, the "radiance" involved is not part of the traditional beauty-cluster. A beautiful object is radiant by virtue of something about its own nature; when an object is "radiant" through glamour, by contrast, it is by virtue of the surrounding atmosphere.

The "radiant" fashion model is sometimes so for a more literal reason as well. She is often synthetically lighted. Wolf points out that this manufactured radiance is offered as a substitute for genuine radiance, which she agrees is a characteristic of genuine beauty.

> People "light up" and objects don't. . . . [M]ost people are aware that a radiance can emerge from faces and bodies, making them truly beautiful. . . . If any general descriptions can be drawn, a sense of wholeness seems involved, and maybe trust. . . . The point is that you have seen it . . . and have probably been dazzled or excited or attracted; and that, according to the myth, it does not count. . . . The Rites of Beauty offer to sell women back an imitation of the light that is ours already. . . .
>
> Women "know" that fashion photographs are professionally lit to imitate this radiant quality. But since we as women are trained to see ourselves as cheap imitations of fashion photographs, rather than seeing fashion photographs as cheap imitations of women, we are urged to study ways to light up our features as if they were photographs marred by motion.[35]

Synthetic lighting encourages the impression that beauty is achieved by means of an atmosphere added from without. We might think of it as a form of "acting out" the ideology of glamour.

The mechanism that glamour uses is the characteristic maneuver of kitsch, the allusion to a gestalt without its specification in any particular object. Karsten Harries observes that kitsch typically creates an atmosphere that prevents engagement with a specific object. Remarking on the kitsch character of Canabal's *Birth of Venus*, he observes, "When we look at such a painting we don't really confront anything. In the end all that remains is an atmosphere, and it is precisely this atmosphere which Kitsch seeks to elicit." Harries goes on to contend that "aphrodisiac" is an appropriate characterization of kitsch, for it stimulates desire that is not centered in the object.[36]

The glamorous images of cosmetic and fashion ads have an aphrodisiac function. A sexualized atmosphere is suggested in the absence of any beloved person. The woman seeing the ad is supposed to provide the image of a particular beloved herself—or to envision herself surrounded by glamour and irresistible to any particular individual she desires. Glamour uses the atmosphere surrounding an object as occasion for its own fantasies, while beauty involves what Harries describes as an encounter between the beholder and a beautiful being.

Alexandre Cabanel, Birth of Venus, *1863. Courtesy of Musée d'Orsay, Paris.*

Glamour fits Kulka's three criteria for kitsch. First, glamour is highly charged emotionally, because it engages the observer in an activity of fantasizing that makes use of whatever psychic content the observer brings to it. Kitsch derives its emotional force from its allusion to a background structure of beliefs about the world. This metonymic character of glamour is another aspect of its kitsch character. Unlike soothing kitsch, in which the allusion to the background structure is reassuring, glamour alludes to a realm that is desirable but from which one is excluded. The metonymic reference is highly charged, for it taps into fantasies that concern one's desires, one's concern for status, and one's insecurities.

Second, glamour is effortlessly identifiable, given background awareness of the cultural vocabulary of presentation and/or well-known cultural symbols. One has to know that a person is the president or a movie star, but such knowledge is sufficient to create an atmosphere around such a person, be it an atmosphere of power, high living, or both. Finally, glamour does not enrich our associations with an object, for it serves merely as an occasion for our own reveries, not an encounter with the object.

What should we think about beauty? Should we consider beauty an inappropriate ideal or simply an ideal that is not promoted by an industry devoted to selling its surrogates? Like Wolf,[37] I think the latter, but I concur with her that we should rethink our personal ideals and those of our culture.

Wolf's comments on the "lighting up" of the truly beautiful person can help us in this project. Human beauty is not only skin deep; instead, it emerges from a condition of integration that encompasses body and soul, however the latter term is understood. It is epiphenomenal, as Wolf observes, to a sense of wholeness. Beauty is an ideal of balance and health that is neither self-conscious nor a direct consequence of deliberate effort. Kant remarks that beauty involves a "feeling of life's being furthered."[38] In connection with specifically human beauty, Nietzsche suggests that human fulfillment is gained by a relaxed gracefulness, characterized by energy but also by ease.[39]

Feminists and others concerned about human well-being have defended the ideal of a greater ease in the body than most women — and most men — experience in contemporary Western society.[40] But how does one do this? So far, these reflections may reduce to something like the following principles: don't worry, be happy, and calm down about clothes. The rub is that the project seems a bit like the project of not thinking of elephants. Worst of all, if the ideal remains that of being beautiful, the project seems to be that of trying not to try too hard, with interspersed self-examinations, "Am I doing it yet?"

The aim of trying not to try may sound self-contradictory. Yet this is precisely the status of one's aspirations in many human efforts, including some of the most spiritual. One ideally learns not to try in playing music; in doing archery; in any kind of focal activity that becomes "a part of you." When this happens, one has directed one's attention toward other things besides the difficulty of not trying. I think the ambition of personal beauty is also best pursued by redirecting attention.

Aristotle's suggestion that pleasure should not be one's aim, although everyone wants it, may be suggestive here. Aristotle sees pleasure as a by-product of the genuinely integrating goal for a human life, *eudaemonia*, but he argues that direct pursuit of pleasure undermines this integral goal. Human beauty, similarly, is a by-product of achieving wholeness of both body and soul, while focus on it as a primary goal undermines the wholeness that is the precondition. This is particularly the case when the direct pursuit focuses on the culturally encouraged surrogate ideas for beauty, those of glamour and of flawlessness.

I do not mean to suggest that beauty comes from inattention, or that giving any thought to one's appearance is harmful. Instead, I am claiming that one's health and beauty are best nurtured when they are not one's major conscious goals. Consider healthy living, for example. Hygiene, good nutrition, exercise, and avoidance of harmful drugs are among those practices that are conducive to health and beauty. My emphasis here is on "practice." The more routine healthy habits become, the less conscious effort is needed to maintain them. Considerable conscious effort may be necessary when initiating a new routine (such as taking vitamins) or when altering existing habits (the trauma of quitting smoking, for example). But for the majority of health-related matters, these efforts are most successful when they are habitual, integral elements of the "automatic pilot" of one's way of life.

Self-adornment and other attention to one's appearance of necessity involve some conscious effort, since they employ an artistic assessment of how one looks and what measures might be appropriately enhancing for the occasion. Neither is intrinsically counterproductive to health or bodily ease. Either can become so, however, if it becomes an end in itself, or a project of obsessive defense against one's flaws. Ideally, styled hair, jewelry, and cosmetics should function as a setting, like that for a gem, which directs attention to what it sets. These modes of artifice can help integrate the composition of one's appearance, and they can be gestures of thoughtfulness toward those with whom one deals, like a vase of flowers or pretty table setting when one is having guests. When it functions as a setting, self-adornment can enhance the interaction of individuals, for "dressing up" and its close cosmetic relatives serve as a gesture of honoring others ("I dressed up for you!"). It becomes a problem when it becomes a major purpose in one's interactions, as when "making an entrance" substitutes for inviting real encounter.

If the radiance that Wolf describes is the sign of true beauty, the wish to be beautiful should be subordinated into the larger aspiration for wholeness as a human being, a goal that involves a whole ethical agenda. This goal offers potential for fulfillment from a first-person point of view; it is not merely an image that appears desirable from the standpoint of others. I have suggested that flawlessness and glamour are mirages in part because they *are* merely images seen from a third-person point of view. Although beauty, too, is a judgment formulated at a distance, receptive appreciation of human beauty carries with it an impression that the person is more than an enjoyable image. One sees the beautiful person as radiant, and this radiance depends on a wholeness that we take to include the person's inner life.

Of course, given the self-inspection that we all, male and female, have learned to practice, beauty is a judgment that we hope we can make about ourselves as well. In order to keep the desire to be beautiful from being a perverse interest, we should simply take our beauty for granted. As it is healthy to assume that we are healthy unless we are sick, it is healthy to assume similarly that we are beautiful. That does not mean that we are perfect. This realization should be empowering, even while it is compatible with the recognition that there is room for improvement. But the fact that we might further enhance the satisfaction we take in being the person that we are does not mean that we are dissatisfied.

Further consideration of the notion of living well as a more fundamental goal than beauty and the place that beauty might play in life would, I think, be worthwhile. For example, we might profitably analyze what circumstances encourage beauty or radiance. Joy, presumably, would be a psychological state conducive to sensed well-being and to beauty. What conditions dispose people toward joy? What mental habits are involved? I would expect that among those that are centrally important are receptivity and flexibility. Appreciation enhances life and it also disposes us to beauty, at both the transmitting and the receiving ends. The conditions that enable non-defensive encounters are probably part of the story, too. Such encounters, in which one is open to an altered perspective, create the possibility for the transfigurations of the commonplace that Arthur C. Danto sees as the best achievements of modern art.[41] In this respect, artistic beauty might train our habits to be open to beauty throughout our experience. Indeed, I think that the "honesty" that is currently preferred to beauty in art is sometimes a glamorous posture, a gesture of power without the expectation of open encounter between the work and the observer. Dave Hickey describes the power play encouraged by contemporary artistic ideology:

> "Strength" is now ascribed to a work of art in terms of its bond with the artist; "weakness" is detected in terms of its bond with its beholder. . . . In this restructured dynamic, the function of the beholder is to be dominated and awestruck by the work of art, which . . . is recast as a simulacrum of the male artist's autonomous, impenetrable self.[42]

If the art world's current ideology promotes symbolic gestures of overpowering the observer, perhaps a return to the goal of beauty would encourage artistic encounters of a more fulfilling sort, for both artists and observers. For the observer, beautiful art encourages our reflection and rewards our willingness to see beyond ourselves and our own agendas. For the artists, too, the effort to create beautiful art might re-situate their conception of the place of artistic effort in the context of human experience and might reward them with a sense that their efforts have some impact toward furthering life.

Still, the program of ethical aspiration toward a more beautiful future is rather naive if we do not acknowledge the dynamics of power, played out in the realms of art, aesthetic marketing, and human interaction. In an era that has largely separated beauty's power from its potential to grant insight, it may seem impossible to focus on the latter without a sense that one is in a poorly defended position. Defensiveness contributes to our problem, in both beauty and in life more generally, yet defensiveness is certainly part of *our* problem. And as long as it is, glamour and cosmetic concealers will retain their allure.

The challenge is that of resisting our era's Satan, the illusion that the power of beauty is best sought without concern for well-being or integrity. When power remains the center of our concern for beauty, we are vulnerable to this temptation. As opposed to Lucifer's trajectory, we might consider the option he rejected, that of remaining angelic. In popular culture, angel images surround us, perhaps a sign that cultural reassessment of beauty and power is already underway.

Who are these angels, we might ask? Surely not the synthetically lit models who wore skimpy underwear in a recent ad campaign. Wim Wenders suggests in his film *Wings of Desire* that they are messengers of healing who make themselves present in order to transfigure the world in the eyes of those in spiritual trouble.[43] The film acknowledges that this mission, by itself, is not the entirety of human life; Wenders's angels want to celebrate the senses and have life stories, and in that, they are certainly like us.

Yet if these angels see their lives as imbalanced until they become as we are, perhaps we should see our embodied lives as incomplete without their mission as bearers of healing light. Rather than seek to manifest beauty as our ultimate means of control, the aim of Lucifer, we might better aim to embody the role of the angels as messengers of divine light. When we see ourselves as bearers of light, we live in an illumined world, aware of our own visible radiance and finding joy in the radiance of others.

NOTES

1. Plato, *Republic,* in *The Collected Dialogues of Plato, including the Letters,* ed. Edith Hamilton and Huntington Cairns, Bollingen Series LXXI (Princeton: Princeton University Press, 1961), III l. 403, p. 647.

2. Aristotle, *Metaphysics* (1078b 1–4), Book XIII, in *The Basic Works of Aristotle*, ed. Richard McKeon, trans. W. D. Ross (New York: Random House, 1941), pp. 893–894.

3. The *Enneads*, trans. Stephen MacKenna, rev. B. S. Page 1.6.2; cited by Lewis Rowell, *Thinking about Music: An Introduction to the Philosophy of Music* (Amherst: University of Massachusetts Press, 1983), p. 87.

4. See Thomas Aquinas, *Summa Theologica*, trans. by the Dominican Fathers (New York: Benziger Brothers, 1947–1948), 1. Q. 39, art. 8.

5. James Joyce, *A Portrait of the Artist as a Young Man* (New York: Viking, 1964), pp. 212–213.

6. John Passmore, "The Dreariness of Aesthetics," *Mind* 60, no. 239 (1951), p. 1.

7. Dave Hickey, "Enter the Dragon," in *The Invisible Dragon: Four Essays on Beauty* (Los Angeles: Art Issues Press, 1993), p. 16.

8. Matei Calinescu, *The Faces of Modernity: Avant-Garde, Decadence, Kitsch* (Bloomington: Indiana University Press, 1977), p. 229.

9. Tomas Kulka, *Kitsch and Art* (University Park: Pennsylvania State University Press, 1996), pp. 37–38. For my own, somewhat similar, analysis, see Kathleen Marie Higgins, "Sweet Kitsch," in *The Philosophy of the Visual Arts*, ed. Philip Alperson (New York: Oxford University Press, 1992), pp. 568–581. I disagree with Kulka, who seeks to identify particular objects as kitsch; I think that "kitsch" is a function to which objects can be put, and that objects commonly identified as "kitsch" are objects that are well-suited to such uses.

10. Kulka, *Kitsch and Art*, p. 73.

11. Ibid., pp. 78–79.

12. Higgins, "Sweet Kitsch," p. 572.

13. Ruth Lorand agrees that beauty should be distinguished from kitsch. She lists kitsch among beauty's opposites. See Ruth Lorand, "Beauty and Its Opposites," *Journal of Aesthetics and Art Criticism* 52, no. 4 (Fall 1994): 399–406. Nevertheless, she seems to consider the beautiful object to be suited to kitsch employment. "Kitsch may be characterized as a *misuse of beauty.* Kitsch exploits well-known and well-tested beautiful objects, natural or artificial, and uses their effects to flatter the spectator in order to get certain results" (p. 403).

14. See Mary Mothersill's summary: "Plato believed that beauty is (i) a kind of good (ii) which can be possessed by items of any kind and (iii) which is linked with pleasure and inspires love." (Mary Mothersill, *Beauty Restored* [Oxford: Clarendon, 1984], p. 262.) Plato does, as Mothersill indicates, consider beauty a property of other things besides individuals. In introducing the topic, however, he refers to the beauty of human beings, presumably expecting human beauty to be the paradigm in the minds of his others. Nietzsche is only somewhat exaggerating when he describes Plato's emphasis on the beautiful boy: "Plato . . . says with an innocence possible only for a Greek, not a 'Christian,' that there would be no Platonic philosophy at all if there were not such beautiful youths in Athens: it is only their sight that transposes the philosophers soul into an erotic trance, leaving it no peace until it lowers the seed of all exalted things into such beautiful soil. . . . queer saint! One does not trust one's ears, even if one should trust Plato. At least one guesses that they philosophized differently in Athens,

especially in public." (Friedrich Nietzsche, *The Twilight of the Idols*, in *The Portable Nietzsche*, trans. Walter Kaufmann [New York: Viking Press, 1968], p. 528).

15. Although I am discussing Western practices here, I do not mean to suggest that these visions are limited to Western society. I was startled while visiting India several years ago to see an advertisement for a product called "Ectobleach," a bleach for lightening one's skin. The advertising slogan was, "Twice a month—beautiful every-day." I found this ad particularly striking for its simultaneous similarity to and differ-ence from Western ads for tanning products.

16. Naomi Wolf, *The Beauty Myth: How Images of Beauty Are Used against Women* (New York: Doubleday, 1991), p. 107.

17. *The New Shorter Oxford English Dictionary on Historical Principles*, ed. Lesley Brown, 2 vols. (Oxford: Clarendon, 1993), vol. 1, p. 1096.

18. Ibid., p. 1128.

19. Ibid., p. 1096.

20. Wolf, *Beauty Myth*, p. 135.

21. Kant locates the beautiful in the representation within the mind, rather than in an external object; this is an important difference between Kant and earlier Western philosophers. Kant also attributes the unity of a beautiful representation to the impres-sion of a purposiveness in the arrangement of its elements. Nevertheless, although he offers a markedly different account of the "unity" of a beautiful object, Kant accepts the traditional characterization of beauty as the unity of elements.

22. Although Plato acknowledged that sexual desire is a natural response to beauty, he, like most subsequent philosophers who discussed the topic, considered lust an inferior reaction to transfixed appreciation. Optimally, the love inspired should be more spiritual than carnal. And later thinkers, like Kant and Schopenhauer, spoke of the optimum response as a disinterested satisfaction, a satisfaction that is independent of any personal agendas, lust being a personal agenda par excellence. For one of Schopenhauer's many characterizations of lust as the paradigm case of interest, or "will," in his metaphysical system, see Arthur Schopenhauer, *The World as Will and Representation*, ed. David Berman, trans. Jill Berman, abridged in one volume (Ver-mont: Charles E. Tuttle, 1995),vol. 1, §61, p. 209.

23. Cf. Wolf, *The Beauty Myth*, p. 290:

> A woman wins by giving herself and other women permission—to eat; to be sexual; to age; to wear overalls, a paste tiara, a Balenciaga gown, a second-hand opera cloak, or combat boots; to cover up or to go practically naked; to do whatever we choose in following—or ignoring—our own aesthetic. . . . But we can imagine, to save ourselves, a life in the body that is not value-laden; a masquerade, a voluntary theatricality that emerges from abundant self-love.

24. Nietzsche considers this one of two possibilities for a style that merely conjoins strong elements; the other is a war among the parts. See Friedrich Nietzsche, *The Case of Wagner* [together with *The Birth of Tragedy*], trans. and ed. Walter Kaufmann (New York: Random House, 1967), p. 170.

25. Arthur Schopenhauer, *The World as Will and Representation*, 2 vols. (New York: Dover Publications, 1958), vol. 2, p. 408.

26. This might seem to be contrary to the requirement of perfection in the beauty cluster that we have discussed. Traditionally, however, the notion of perfection involves the idea that every element contributes to the life of the whole, and that the elimination of any element would impoverish it. This does not require that the imagination has no work to do. Indeed, in the Kantian formula, the ideal configuration engages the imagination precisely *because* the elements all seem to further a common "purpose," but one which is not explicit. "Purposiveness" is evident in the arrangement, and evident precisely because the imagination can envision the arrangement as directed purposefully. The complete complement required by the criterion of perfection is an incitement to imagination, not a substitute for it.

27. Immanuel Kant, *The Critique of Judgment*, trans. Werner S. Pluhar (Indianapolis: Hackett, 1987), pp. 82–83.

28. Ibid.

29. Indeed, Kant also draws this conclusion with regard to human faces. See Kant, *Critique of Judgment*, p. 83n:

> It will be found that a perfectly regular face, such as a painter would like to have as a model, usually conveys nothing. This is because it contains nothing characteristic and hence expresses more the idea of the [human] kind than what is specific in one person. . . . Experience shows, moreover, that such wholly regular faces usually indicate that inwardly too the person is only mediocre. I suppose (if we may assume that nature expresses in [our] outward [appearance] the proportions of what is inward) this is because, if none of the mental predispositions stands out beyond the proportion that is required from someone to constitute merely a person free from defects, then we must not expect in him any degree of what we call *genius*; in the case of genius nature seems to depart from the proportions it usually imparts to our mental powers, instead favoring just one.

30. What the beauty industry assaults as wrinkles are also character lines.

31. See, for example, Sigmund Freud's description of projection as "to transpose outwards what becomes troublesome . . . from within" in "The Metapsychology of Dreams," in *The Standard Edition of the Complete Psychological Worlds of Sigmund Freud*, trans. James Strachey (London: Hogarth Press and the Institute of Psychoanalysis, 1957), vol. 14, p. 233. See also C. G. Jung on the topic of anima projection (the projection of contents from one's own psyche onto a member of the opposite sex) in *Aion: Researches into the Phenomenology of the Self*, in *The Collected Works of C. G. Jung*, ed. Herbert Read, Michael Fordham, and Gerhard Alder, trans. R. F. C. Hull, vol. 9, pt. II (London: Routledge and Kegan Paul, 1959), pp. 11–22.

32. Mary Mothersill, for example, asserts this view in connection with beautiful art: "[W]orks of art are beautiful or lay claim to beauty, and everything that is beautiful is unique" (Mothersill, *Beauty Restored*, p. 45).

33. In the *Symposium* Plato's Socrates contends that the beauty of individuals is only the individuals' participation in the Form of Beauty, and that love of individuals is ultimately the love of this universal Form. Martha Nussbaum has argued that Plato presents the speech of Alcibiades, which emphasizes the individuality of Socrates, as a rebuttal to Socrates' position. See Martha C. Nussbaum's article in *The Philosophy*

of (Erotic) Love, ed. Robert C. Solomon and Kathleen M. Higgins (Lawrence: University of Kansas Press, 1991).

34. Like Milan Kundera, I will construe the term "kitsch" to encompass other human productions besides art, narrowly construed. See Milan Kundera, *The Unbearable Lightness of Being* (New York: Harper and Row, 1984), pp. 248–254.

35. Wolf, *Beauty Myth*, pp. 104–105.

36. Karsten Harries, *The Meaning of Modern Art* (Evanston: Northwestern University Press, 1968), p. 79.

37. Wolf comments, "Are women beautiful or aren't we? Of course we are" (Wolf, *Beauty Myth*, p. 271).

38. Kant, *Critique of Judgment*, p. 98.

39. Nietzsche's character Zarathustra, similarly, ranks beauty as a greater achievement than the willingness to strain. Zarathustra admonishes the valiant hero, "To stand with relaxed muscles and unharnessed will: that is most difficult for all of you who are sublime. When power becomes gracious and descends into the visible—such descent I call beauty" (Friedrich Nietzsche, *Thus Spoke Zarathustra*, in *The Portable Nietzsche*, trans. and ed. Walter Kaufmann [New York: Viking, 1968], p. 230).

40. See, for example, Susan Sontag, "The Double Standard of Aging," in *Psychology of Women: Selected Readings*, ed. Juanita H. Williams (New York: W.W. Norton & Company, 1979), pp. 462–478; Adrienne Rich, *Of Woman Born* (New York: W.W. Norton & Company, 1976), pp. 20–22; Kartikeya C. Patel, "Women, Earth, and the Goddess: A Shakta-Hindu Interpretation of Embodied Religion," *Hypatia* 9, no. 4 (Fall 1994): 69–87; Sam Keen, *Hymns to an Unknown God: Awakening the Spirit in Everyday Life* (New York: Bantam Books, 1994), pp. 132–141; and Thomas Moore, *Care of the Soul: A Guide for Cultivating Depth and Sacredness in Everyday Life* (New York: HarperCollins, 1992), pp. 163–167.

41. See Arthur Danto, *The Transfiguration of the Commonplace: A Philosophy of Art* (Cambridge, Mass.: Harvard University Press, 1981).

42. Hickey, "Prom Night in Flatland," in *The Invisible Dragon*, p. 45.

43. Wim Wenders, director, *Wings of Desire*, Argos Films (Paris) and Road Movies (Berlin), together with Westdeustcher Runfunk, Köln, 1988.

Susan Bordo

6. Beauty (Re)Discovers the Male Body

Men on Display

Putting classical art to the side for the moment, the naked and near-naked female body became an object of mainstream consumption first in *Playboy* and its imitators, then in movies, and only then in fashion photographs. With the male body, the trajectory has been different. Fashion has taken the lead, the movies have followed. Hollywood may have been a chest-fest in the fifties, but it was male clothing designers who went south and violated the really powerful taboos—not just against the explicit depiction of penises and male bottoms but against the admission of all sorts of forbidden "feminine" qualities into mainstream conceptions of manliness.

It was the spring of 1995, and I was sipping my first cup of morning coffee, not yet fully awake, flipping through the *New York Times Sunday Magazine*, when I had my first real taste of what it's like to inhabit this visual culture as a man. It was both thrilling and disconcerting. It was the first time in my experience that I had encountered a commercial representation of a male body that seemed to deliberately invite me to linger over it. Let me make that stronger—that seemed to reach out to me, interrupting my mundane but peaceful Sunday morning, and provoke me into erotic consciousness, whether or not I wanted it. Women—both straight and gay—have always gazed covertly, of course, squeezing our illicit little titillations out of representations designed for—or pretending to—other purposes than to turn us on. *This* ad made no such pretense. It caused me to knock over my coffee cup, ruining the more cerebral pleasures of the *Book Review*. Later, when I had regained my equilibrium, I made a screen-saver out of him, so I could gaze at my leisure.

Ad for Calvin Klein underwear.

I'm sure that many gay men were as taken as I was, and perhaps some gay women, too. The erotic charge of various sexual styles is not neatly mapped onto sexual orientation (let alone biological sex). Brad Pitt's baby-butch looks are a turn-on to many lesbians, while I—regarded by most of my gay friends as a pretty hard-core heterosexual—have always found Anne Heche irresistible (even before Ellen did). A lesbian friend of mine, reading my reflections on how soft-core S&M in the biblical epics of the fifties had affected my adolescent sexuality, said the same movies influenced her later attraction to butch *women*. Despite such complications, until recently only heterosexual men have continually been inundated by popular cultural images *designed* with their sexual responses (or at least, what those sexual responses are imagined to be) in mind. It's not entirely a gift. On the minus side is having one's composure continually challenged by what Timothy Beneke has aptly described as a culture of "intrusive images," eliciting fantasies, emotions, and erections at times and in places where they might not be appropriate. On the plus side is the cultural permission to be a voyeur.

Some psychologists say that the circuit from eyes to brain to genitals is a quicker trip for men than for women. "There's some strong evidence," popular science writer Deborah Blum reports, citing studies of men's responses to pictures of naked women, "that testosterone is wired for visual response." Maybe. But who is the electrician here? God? Mother Nature? Or Hugh Hefner? Practice makes perfect. And women have had little practice. The Calvin Klein ad made me feel like an adolescent again, brought me back to that day when I saw Barry Resnick on the basketball court of Weequahic High and realized that men's legs could make me weak in the knees. Men's legs? I knew that *women's* legs were supposed to be sexy. I had learned that from all those hose-straightening scenes in the movies. But men's legs? Who had ever seen a woman gaga over some guy's legs in the movies? Or even read about it in a book? Yet the muscular grace of Barry's legs took my breath away. Maybe something was wrong with me. Maybe my sex drive was too strong, too much like a man's. By the time I came across that Calvin Klein ad, several decades of feminism and life experience had left me a little less worried about my sex drive. Still, the sight of that model's body made me feel that my sexual education was still far from complete.

I brought the ad to classes and lectures, asking women what they thought of him. Most began to sweat the moment I unfolded the picture, then got their bearings and tried to explore the bewitching stew of sexual elements the picture has to offer. The model—a young Jackson Browne look-alike—stands there in his form-fitting and rip-speckled Calvin Klein briefs, head lowered, dark hair loosely falling over his eyes. His body projects strength, solidity; he's no male waif. But his finely muscled chest is not so overdeveloped as to suggest a sexuality immobilized by the thick matter of the body. Gay theorist Ron Long, describing contemporary gay sexual aesthetics—lean, taut, sinuous muscles rather than Schwarzenegger bulk —points to a "dynamic tension" that the incredible hulks lack. Stiff, engorged Schwarzenegger bodies, he says, seem to *be* surrogate penises— with nowhere to go and nothing to do but stand there looking massive— whereas muscles like this young man's seem designed for movement, for sex. His body isn't a stand-in phallus; rather, he *has* a penis—the real thing, not a symbol, and a fairly breathtaking one, clearly outlined through the soft jersey fabric of the briefs. It seems slightly erect, or perhaps that's his non-erect size; either way, there's a substantial presence there that's palpable (it looks so touchable, you want to cup your hand over it) and very, very male.

At the same time, however, my gaze is invited by something "feminine" about the young man. His underwear may be ripped, but ever so slightly, subtly; unlike the original ripped-underwear poster boy Stanley Kowalksi, he's hardly a thug. He doesn't stare at the viewer challengingly, belligerently, as do so many models in other ads for male underwear, facing off like a street tough passing a member of the rival gang on the street. ("Yeah, this is an underwear ad and I'm half-naked. But I'm still the one in charge here. Who's gonna look away first?"). No, this model's languid body posture, his averted look are classic signals, both in the "natural" and the "cultural" world, of willing subordination. He offers himself non-aggressively to the gaze of another. Hip cocked in the snaky S-curve usually reserved for depictions of women's bodies, eyes downcast but not closed, he gives off a sultry, moody, subtle but undeniably seductive consciousness of his erotic allure. Feast on me, I'm here to be looked at, my body is for your eyes. Oh my.

Such an attitude of male sexual supplication, although it has (as we'll see) classical antecedents, is very new to contemporary mainstream representations. Homophobia is at work in this taboo, but so too are attitudes about gender that cut across sexual orientation. For many men, both gay and straight, to be so passively dependent on the gaze of another person for one's sense of self-worth is incompatible with being a real man. As we'll see, such notions about manliness are embedded in Greek culture, in contemporary visual representations, and even (in disguised form) in existentialist philosophy. "For the woman," as philosopher Simone de Beauvoir writes,

"... the absence of her lover is always torture; he is an eye, a judge. ... away from him, she is dispossessed, at once of herself and of the world." For Beauvoir's sometime lover and lifelong soulmate Jean-Paul Sartre, on the other hand, the gaze (or The Look, as he called it) of another person—including the gaze of one's lover—is the "hell" that other people represent. If we were alone in the world, he argues, we would be utterly free—within physical constraints—to be whomever we wanted to be, to be the creatures of our own self-fantasies, to define our behavior however we like. Other people intrude on this solipsism, and have the audacity to see us from their own perspective rather than ours. The result is what Sartre calls primordial Shame under the eyes of The Other, and a fierce desire to re-assert one's freedom. The other person has stolen "the secret" of who I am. I must fight back, resist their attempts to define me.

I understand, of course, what Sartre is talking about here. We've all, male and female alike, felt the shame that another pair of eyes can bring. Sartre's own classic example is of being caught peeking through a keyhole by another person. It isn't until those other eyes are upon you that you truly feel not just the "wrongness" of what you are doing, but—Sartre would argue—the very fact that you are doing it. Until the eyes of another are upon us, "catching us" in the act, we can deceive ourselves, pretend. Getting caught in moments of fantasy or vanity may be especially shameful. When I was an adolescent, I loved to pretend I was a radio personality, and talking into an empty coffee can created just the right sound. One day my mother caught me; speaking in the smooth and slightly sultry tones that radio personalities had even in those days. The way I felt is what Sartre means when he describes the Look of another person as the fulcrum of shame-making. My face got hot, and suddenly I saw how ridiculous I must have seemed, my head in the Chock Full O' Nuts, my narcissistic fantasies on full display. I was caught; I wanted to run.

The disjunction between self-conception and external judgement can be especially harsh when the external definitions carry racial and gender stereotypes with them. Sartre doesn't present such examples—he's interested in capturing the contours of an existential situation shared by all rather than in analyzing the cultural differences that affect that situation—but they are surely relevant to understanding the meaning of The Look of the Other. A black man jogs down the street in sweat clothes, thinking of the class he is going to teach later that day; a white woman passes him, clutches her handbag more tightly, quickens her step; in her eyes, the teacher is a potentially dangerous animal. A Latin American student arrives early the first day of college; an administrator, seeing him in the still-deserted hall, asks him if he is the new janitor. The aspiring student has had his emerging identity erased, a stereotype put in its place by another pair of eyes. When women are transformed from professionals to "pussies" by the comments of men on the street, it's humiliating, not so much because we're puritans but because we sense the hostility in the hoots, the desire to bring an uppity woman down to size by reminding her that she's just "the sex" (as Beauvoir put it).

We may all have felt shame, but—as the different attitudes of Beauvoir and Sartre suggest—men and women are socially sanctioned to deal with the gaze of the Other in different ways. Women learn to anticipate, even play to the gaze, trying to become what will please, captivate, turn shame into pride. (In the process, we also learn how sexy being gazed at can feel—perhaps precisely because it walks the fine edge of shame.) Many of us, truth be told, get somewhat addicted to the experience. I'm renting a video, feeling a bit low, a bit tired. The young man at the counter, unsolicited, tells me I'm "looking good." It alters everything, I feel fine, alive; it seems to go right down to my cells. I leave the store feeling younger, stronger, more awake. When women sense that they are not being assessed sexually—for example, as we age, or if we are disabled—it may feel like we no longer exist.

Women may dread being surveyed harshly—being seen as too old, too fat, too flat-chested—but men are not supposed to enjoy being surveyed *period*. It's feminine to be on display. Men are thus taught—as my uncle Leon used to say—to be a moving target. Get out of range of those eyes, don't let them catch you—even as the object of their fantasies (or, as Sartre would put it, don't let them "possess," "steal" your freedom). This phobia has even distorted scientific research. Evolutionary theorists have long acknowledged penile display as an important feature of courting behavior among primates—except when it comes to *our* closest ancestors. With descriptions of hominid behavior, male display behavior "suddenly drops out of the primate evolutionary picture" (Sheets-Johnstone, 95) and is replaced by the concept of year-round female sexual receptivity. It seems that it has been intolerable, unthinkable for male evolutionary theorists to imagine the bodies of their male ancestors being on display, sized up, dependent on selection (or rejection) by female hominids.

Scientists and "ordinary guys" are totally in synch here, as is humorously illustrated in Peter Cattaneo's popular 1997 British film *The Full Monty*. In the film, a group of unemployed metalworkers in Sheffield, England, watch a Chippendale's show and hatch the money-making scheme of presenting their own male strip show in which they will go right down to the "full Monty." At the start of the film, the heroes are hardly pillars of successful manliness (Gaz, their leader, refers to them as "scrap"). Yet even they have been sheltered by their guyhood, as they learn while putting the show together. One gets a penis pump. Another borrows his wife's face cream. They run, they wrap their bellies in plastic, they do jumping jacks, they get artificial tans. The most overweight one among them (temporarily) pulls out of the show. Before, these guys hadn't lived their lives under physical scrutiny but in male action mode, in which men are judged by their accomplishments. Now, anticipating being on display to a roomful of spectators, they suddenly realize how it feels to be judged as women routinely are, sized up by another pair of eyes. "I pray that they'll be a bit more understanding about us" than they've been with women, David (the fat one) murmurs.

They get past their discomfort, in the end, and their show is greeted with wild enthusiasm by the audience. The movie leaves us with this feel-good ending, not raising the question obvious to every woman watching the film: would a troupe of out-of-shape women be received as warmly, as affectionately? The climactic moment when the men throw off their little pouches is demurely shot from the rear, moreover, so we—the audience—don't get "the full Monty." Nonetheless, the film gently and humorously makes an important point: for a heterosexual man to offer himself up to a sexually evaluating gaze is for him to make a large, scary leap—and not just because of the anxieties about penis size (the guy who drops out of the show, remember, is embarrassed by his fat, not his penis). The "full Monty" —the naked penis—is not merely a body part in the movie (hence it doesn't really matter that the film doesn't show it). It's a symbol for male exposure, vulnerability to an evaluation and judgement that women—clothed or naked—experience all the time.

I had to laugh out loud at a 1997 *New York Times Magazine* "Style" column, entitled "Overexposure," which complained of the "contagion" of nudity spreading through celebrity culture. "Stars no longer have private parts," the author observed, and fretted that civilians would soon also be measured by the beauty of their buns. I share this author's concern about our body-obsessed culture. But, pardon me, he's just noticing this now??? Actresses have been baring their breasts, their butts, even their bushes, for some time, and ordinary women have been tromping off to the gym in pursuit of comparably perfect bodies. What's got the author suddenly crying "overkill," it turns out, is Sly Stallone's "surreally fat-free" appearance on the cover of *Vanity Fair*, and Rupert Everett's "dimpled behind" in a Karl Lagerfield fashion spread. Now that *men* are taking off their clothes, the culture is suddenly going too far. Could it be that the author doesn't even "read" all those naked female bodies as "over-exposed"? Does he protest a bit too much when he declares in the first sentence of the piece that he found it "a yawn" when Dirk Diggler unsheathed his "prosthetic shillelagh" ("penis" is still a word to be avoided whenever possible) at the end of *Boogie Nights*? A yawn? My male companion's palms were sweating profusely, and I was not about to drop off to sleep, either.

As for dimpled behinds, my second choice for male pinup of the decade is the Gucci series of two ads in which a beautiful young man, shot from the rear, puts on a pair of briefs. In the first ad, he's holding them in his hands, contemplating them. Is he checking out the correct washing machine temp? It's odd, surely, to stand there looking at your underwear, but never mind. The point is: his underwear is in his hands, not on his butt. *It*—his bottom, that is—is gorgeously, completely naked—a motif so new to mainstream advertising (but since then catching on rapidly) that several of my friends, knowing I was writing about the male body, E-mailed me immediately when they saw the ad. In the second ad, he's put the underwear on, and is adjusting it to fit. Luckily for us, he hasn't succeeded yet, so his buns are peeking out the bottom of the underwear, looking biteable. For the *Times* writer, those buns may be an indecent exposure of parts that should be kept private (or they're a boring yawn—I'm afraid he can't have it both ways), but for me—and for thousands of gay men across the country—this was a moment of political magnitude, and a delicious one. The body parts that *we* love to squeeze (those plastic breasts, they're the real yawn for me) had come out of the closet and into mainstream culture, where *we* can enjoy them without a trip to a specialty store.

But all this is very new. Women aren't used to seeing naked men frankly portrayed as "objects" of a sexual gaze (and neither are heterosexual men, as that *Times* writer makes clear). So pardon me if I'm skeptical when I read arguments about men's greater "biological" responsiveness to visual stimuli. These "findings," besides being ethnocentric (no one thinks to poll Trobriand islanders), display little awareness of the impact of changes in cultural representations on our capacities for sexual response. Popular science writer Deborah Blum, for example, cites a study from the Kinsey Institute which showed a group of men and women a series of photos and drawings of nudes, both male and female:

> Fifty-four percent of the men were erotically aroused versus twelve percent of the women—in other words, more than four times as many men. The same gap exists, on a much larger scale, in the business of pornography, a $500-million-plus industry in the U.S. which caters almost exclu-

Ad for Gucci underwear.

sively to men. In the first flush of 1970s feminism, two magazines—*Playgirl* and *Viva*—began publishing male centerfolds. *Viva* dropped the nude photos after surveys showed their readers didn't care for them; the editor herself admitted to finding them slightly disgusting.

Blum presents these findings as suggestive of a hard-wired difference between men and women. I'd be cautious about accepting that conclusion. First of all, there's the question of which physiological responses count as "erotic arousal" and whether they couldn't be evidence of other states. Clearly, too, we can *learn* to have certain physiological responses—and to suppress them—so nothing biologically definitive is proved by the presence or absence of physical arousal.

Studies that rely on viewers' *own* reports need to be carefully interpreted, too. I know, from talking to women students, that they sometimes aren't all that clear about *what* they feel in the presence of erotic stimuli, and even when they are, they may not be all that comfortable admitting what they feel. Hell, not just my students! Once, a lover asked me, as we were about to part for the evening, if there was anything that we hadn't done that I'd really like to do. I knew immediately what that was: I wanted him to undress, very slowly, while I sat on the floor and just watched. But I couldn't tell him. I was too embarrassed. Later, alone in my compartment on the train, I sorely regretted my cowardice. The fact is that I love to watch a man getting undressed, and I especially like it if he is conscious of being looked at. But there is a long legacy of shame to be overcome here, for both sexes, and the cultural models are only now just emerging which might help us move beyond it.

Perhaps, then, we should wait a bit longer, do a few more studies, before we come to any biological conclusions about women's failure to get aroused by naked pictures? A newer (1994) University of Chicago study found that 30 percent of women ages eighteen to forty-four and 19 percent of women ages forty-five to fifty-nine said they found "watching a partner undress" to be "very appealing" ("Not a bad percentage," Nancy Friday comments, "given that Nice Girls didn't look.") There's still a gender gap—the respective figures for men of the same age groups were 50 percent and 40 percent. We're just learning, after all, to be voyeuses. Perhaps, too, heterosexual men could learn to be less uncomfortable offering themselves as "sexual objects" if they realized the pleasure women get from it. Getting what you have been most deprived of is the best gift, the most healing gift, the most potentially transforming gift—because it has the capacity to make one more whole. Women have been deprived not so much of the *sight* of beautiful male bodies as the experience of having the male body *offered* to us, handed to us on a silver platter, the way female bodies—in the ads, in the movies—are handed to men. Getting this from her partner is the erotic equivalent of a woman's coming home from work to find a meal prepared and ready for her. Delicious—even if it's just franks and beans.

Thanks, Calvin!

Despite their bisexual appeal, the cultural genealogy of the ads I've been discussing and others like them is to be traced largely through gay male aesthetics, rather than a sudden blossoming of appreciation for the fact that women might enjoy looking at sexy, well-hung young men who don't appear to be about to rape them. Feminists might like to imagine that Madison Avenue heard our pleas for sexual equality, and finally gave us "men as sex objects." But what's really happened is that women have been the beneficiaries of what might be described as a triumph of pure consumerism—and with it, a burgeoning male fitness and beauty culture—over homophobia and the taboos against male vanity, male "femininity," and erotic display of the male body that have gone along with it.

Throughout this century, gay photographers have created a rich, sensuous, and dramatic tradition which is unabashed in eroticizing the male body, male sensuousness, and male potency, including penises. But until recently, such representations have been kept largely in the closet. Mainstream responses to several important exhibits which opened in the seventies—featuring the groundbreaking early work of Wilhelm von Gloeden, George Dureau, and George Platt Lynes, as well as then-contemporary artists such as Robert Mapplethorpe, Peter Hujar, and Arthur Tress—would today probably embarrass the critics who wrote about them when they opened. John Ashbery, in *New York Magazine*, dismissed the entire genre of male nude photography with the same sexist tautology that covertly underlies that *Times* piece on cultural "overexposure": "Nude women seem to be in their natural state; men, for some reason, merely look undressed. . . . When is a nude not a nude? When it is male." (Substitute "blacks" and "whites" for "women" and "men" and you'll see how offensive the statement is.).

For other reviewers, the naked male, far from seeming "merely undressed," was unnervingly sexual. *New York Times* critic Gene Thompson wrote that "there is something disconcerting about the sight of a man's naked body being presented as a sexual object"; he went on to describe the world of homoerotic photography as one "closed to most of us, fortunately."

Vicki Goldberg, writing for the *Saturday Review*, was more appreciative of the "beauty and dignity" of the nude male body, but concluded that so long as its depiction was erotic in emphasis, it will "remain half-private, slightly awkward, an art form cast from its traditions and in search of some niche to call its home."

Goldberg needed a course in art history. It's true that in classical art, the naked human body was often presented as a messenger of spiritual themes, and received as such. But the male bodies sculpted by the Greeks and Michelangelo were not exactly non-erotic. It might be more accurate to say that in modernity, with the spiritual interpretation of the nude body no longer a convention, the contemporary homophobic psyche is not screened in the same way from the sexual charge of the nude male body. Goldberg was dead wrong about something else too. Whatever its historical lineage, the frankly sexual representation of the male body was to find, in the next twenty years, a far-from-private "niche to call its home": consumer culture discovered its commercial potency.

Calvin Klein had his epiphany, according to one biography, one night in 1974 in New York's gay Flamingo bar:

> As Calvin wandered through the crowd at the Flamingo, the body heat rushed though him like a revelation; this was the cutting edge. . . . [The] men! The men at the Flamingo had less to do about sex for him than the notion of portraying men as gods. He realized that what he was watching was the freedom of a new generation, unashamed, in-the-flesh embodiments of Calvin's ideals: straight-looking, masculine men, with chiseled bodies, young Greek gods come to life. The vision of shirtless young men with hardened torsos, all in blue jeans, top button opened, a whisper of hair from the belly button disappearing into the denim pants, would inspire and inform the next ten years of Calvin Klein's print and television advertisements.

Klein's genius was that of a cultural Geiger counter; his own bisexuality enabled him to see that the phallic body, as much as any female figure, is an enduring sex object within Western culture. In America in 1974, however, that ideal was still largely closeted. Only gay culture unashamedly sexualized the lean, fit body that virtually everyone, gay and straight, now aspires to. Sex, as Calvin Klein knew, sells. He also knew that gay sex wouldn't sell to straight men. But the rock-hard, athletic gay male bodies that Klein admired at the Flamingo did not advertise their sexual preference through the feminine codes—limp wrists, raised pinkie finger, swishy walk—which the straight world then identified with homosexuality. Rather, they embodied a highly masculine aesthetic that—although definitely exciting for gay men—would scream "heterosexual" to (clueless) straights. Klein knew just the kind of clothing to show that body off in, too. As Steven Gaines and Sharon Churcher tell it:

> He had watched enough attractive young people with good bodies in tight jeans dancing at the Flamingo and Studio 54 to know that the "basket" and the behind was what gave jeans sex appeal. Calvin sent his assistants out for several pairs of jeans, including the classic five-button Levi's, and cut them apart to see how they were made. Then he cut the "rise," or area from the waistband to under the groin, much shorter to accentuate the crotch and pull the seam up between the buttocks, giving the behind more shape and prominence. The result was instant sex appeal—and a look that somehow Calvin just *knew* was going to sell. (*Obsession*, 235)

So we come to the mainstream commercialization of the aesthetic legacy of Stanley Kowalski and those inspired innovations of Brando's costumer in *A Streetcar Named Desire* (Brando as Kowalski had been the first to wear jeans fitted rather than baggy, with a tight T-shirt, shrunk to cling). When I was growing up, jeans were "dungarees"—suitable for little kids, hayseeds, and juvenile delinquents, but not for anyone to wear on a date. Klein transformed jeans from utilitarian garments to erotic second skins. Next, Klein went for underwear. He wasn't the first, but he was the most daring. In 1981, Jockey International had broken ground by photographing Baltimore Oriole pitcher Jim Palmer in a pair of briefs (airbrushed) in one of its ads—selling $100 million worth of underwear by year's end. Inspired by Jockey's success, in 1983 Calvin Klein put a forty-by-fifty-foot-high Bruce Weber photograph of Olympic pole vaulter Tom Hintinauss in Times Square, Hintinauss's large penis clearly discernible through his briefs. The Hintinauss ad, unlike the Palmer ad, did not employ any of the usual fictional rationales for a man's being in his underwear—for example, the pretense that the man is in the process of getting dressed—but blatantly put Hintinauss's body on display, sunbathing on a rooftop, his skin glistening. The line of shorts "flew off the shelves" at Bloomingdale's and when Klein papered bus shelters in Manhattan with poster versions of the ad they were all stolen overnight.

Images of masculinity that will do double (or triple or quadruple) duty with a variety of consumers, straight and gay, male and female, are not difficult to create in a culture like ours, in which the muscular, male body has a long and glorious aesthetic history. That's precisely what Calvin Klein was the first to recognize and exploit—the possibility and profitability of what is known in the trade as a "dual marketing" approach. Since then,

Calvin Klein Underwear

Bronzed and beautiful Tom Hintinauss. A breakthrough ad for Calvin Klein — and the beginning of a new era for the unabashed erotic display of the male body.

many advertisers have taken advantage of Klein's insight. A recent Aber-crombie & Fitch ad, for example, depicts a locker room full of young, half-clothed football players getting a postmortem from their coach after a game. Beautiful, undressed male bodies doing what real men are "sup-posed to do." Dirty uniforms and smudged faces, wounded players, hel-mets. What could be more straight? But as iconography depicting a culture of exclusively male bodies, young, gorgeous, and well-hung, what could be more "gay"?

It required a Calvin Klein to give the new vision cultural form. But the fact is that if we've entered a brave new world of male bodies it is largely because of a more "material" kind of epiphany—a dawning recognition among advertisers of the buying power of gay men. For a long time preju-dice had triumphed over the profit motive, blinding marketers to just how sizable—and well-heeled—a consumer group gay men represent. (This has been the case with other "minorities" too. Hollywood producers, never bothering to do any demographics on middle-class and professional Afri-can American women—or the issues that they share with women of other races and classes in this culture—were shocked at the tremendous box office success of *Waiting to Exhale*. They won't make that particular mis-take again.) It took a survey conducted by *The Advocate* to jolt corporate America awake about gay consumers. The survey, done between 1977 and 1980, showed that 70 percent of its readers aged twenty to forty earned incomes well above the national median. Soon, articles were appearing on the business pages of newspapers, like one in 1982 in the *New York Times Magazine*, which described advertisers as newly interested in "wooing . . . the white, single, well-educated, well-paid man who happens to be homo-sexual."

"Happens to be homosexual": the phrasing—suggesting that sexual identity is peripheral, even accidental—is telling. Because of homopho-bia, dual marketing used to require a delicate balancing act, as advertisers tried to speak to gays "in a way that the straight consumer will not notice." Often, that's been accomplished through the use of play and parody, as in Versace's droll portraits of men being groomed and tended by male servants and Diesel's overtly narcissistic gay posers. "Thanks Diesel, for making us so very beautiful," they gush. Or take this ad, with its gorgeous, mechani-cally inept model admitting that he's "known more for my superb bone construction and soft, supple hair than my keen intellect." The playful tone reassures heterosexual consumers that the vanity (and mechanical incom-petence) of the man selling the product is "just a joke." For gay consumers, on the other hand, this reassurance is *itself* the "joke"; they read the humor

"I'm known more for my superb bone construction and soft, supple hair than my keen intellect.

But even I can hook up Kenwood's Centerstage Home Theater System in a few minutes."

You don't need a Ph.D in quantum mechanics to enjoy true home theatre sound. Heck, you don't even have to know how to spell Ph.D. Introducing Kenwood's revolutionary Centerstage Home Theater System. It's a complete system with all the Dolby* electronics and amplifiers built into four easy-to-connect speakers. All you do is plug it in to your VCR or TV and you're done. There's no need for anything else. And the whole system is only about $400. Which means that even if you're not a model, but just look like one, you can probably afford it. For the nearest dealer call 1-800-KENWOOD. Or visit our new web site www.kenwoodusa.com

KENWOOD
HOME AUDIO CAR AUDIO COMMUNICATIONS

"I'm known more for my superb bone construction and soft, supple hair than my keen intellect."

in the ad as an insider wink, which says "This is for *you*, guys." The joke is further layered by the fact that they know the model in the ad is very likely to be gay.

Contrast this ad to the ostentatious heterosexual protest of a Perry Ellis ad which appeared in the early 1990s (and no, it's not a parody):

> *I hate this job. I'm not just an empty suit who stands in front of a camera, collects the money and flies off to St. Maarten for the weekend.*
>
> *I may model for a living, but I hate being treated like a piece of meat. I once had a loud-mouthed art director say "Stand there and pretend you're a human." I wanted to punch him, but I needed the job.*
>
> *What am I all about? Well, I know I'm very good-looking, and there are days when that is enough. Some nights, when I'm alone, it's not.*
>
> *I like women—all kinds.*
>
> *I like music—all kinds.*
>
> *I like myself so I don't do drugs.*
>
> *Oh yeah, about this fragrance. It's good. Very good.*
>
> *When I posed for this picture, the art director insisted that I wear it while the pictures were being taken. I thought it was silly, but I said "What the hell? It's their money."*
>
> *After a while, I realized I like this fragrance a lot. When the photo shoot was over, I walked right over, picked up the bottle, put it in my pocket and said "If you don't mind, I'd like to take this as a souvenir." Then I smiled my best f— you smile and walked out.*
>
> *Next time, I'll pay for it.*
>
> *It's that good.*

Today, good-looking straight guys are flocking to the modeling agencies, much less concerned about any homosexual taint that will cleave to them. It's no longer necessary for an ad to plant its tongue firmly in cheek when lavishing erotic attention on the male body—or to pepper the ad with proofs of heterosexuality. It used to be, if an advertisement aimed at straight men dared to show a man fussing over his looks with seemingly romantic plans in mind, there had better be a woman in the picture, making it clear just *whom* the boy was getting pretty for. To sell a muscle-building product to heterosexuals, of course you had to link it to virility and the ability to attract women on the beach. Today, muscles are openly sold for their looks; Chroma Lean nutritional supplement unabashedly compares the well-sculpted male body to a work of art (and a gay male icon, to boot)— Michelangelo's *David*. Many ads display the naked male body without shame or plot excuse, and often exploit rather than resolve the sexual ambiguity that is generated.

Today, too, the athletic, muscular male body that Calvin plastered all over buildings, magazines, and subway stops has become an aesthetic norm, for straights as well as gays. "No pecs, no sex," is how the trendy David Barton gym sells itself: "My motto is not 'Be healthy'; it's 'Look better naked,'" Barton says. The notion has even made its way into that most determinedly heterosexual of contexts, a Rob Reiner film. In *Sleepless in Seattle*, Tom Hanks's character, who hasn't been on a date in fifteen years, asks his friend (played by Rob), what women are looking for nowadays. "Pecs and a cute butt," his friend replied without hesitation. "You can't even turn on the news nowadays without hearing about how some babe thought some guy's butt was cute. Who the first woman was to say this was I don't know, but somehow it caught on." Should we tell Rob that it wasn't a woman who started the craze for men's butts?

Rocks and Leaners

We "nouvelles voyeuses" thus owe a big measure of thanks to gay male designers and consumers, and to the aesthetic and erotic overlap—not uniform or total, but significant—in what makes our hearts go thump. But although I've been using the term for convenience, I don't think it's correct to say that these ads depict men as "sex objects." Actually, I find that whole notion misleading, whether applied to men or women, because it seems to suggest that what these representations offer is a body that is inert, deper-sonalized, flat, a mere thing. In fact, advertisers put a huge amount of time, money, and creativity into figuring out how to create images of beautiful bodies that are heavy on attitude, style, associations with pleasure, success, happiness. The most compelling images are suffused with "subjectivity"— they *speak* to us, they seduce us. Unlike other kind of "objects" (chairs and tables, for example) they don't let us use them in any way we like. In fact, they exert considerable power over us—over our psyches, our desires, our self-image.

How do male bodies in the ads speak to us nowadays? In a variety of ways. Sometimes the message is challenging, aggressive. Many models stare coldly at the viewer, defying the observer to view them in any way other than they have chosen to present themselves: as powerful, armored, emotionally impenetrable. "I am a rock," their bodies (and sometimes their genitals) seem to proclaim. Often, as in the Jackson Browne look-alike ad, the penis is prominent, but *unlike* the penis in that ad, its presence is martial rather than sensual. Overall, these ads depict what I would describe as "face-off masculinity," in which victory goes to the dominant contestant in a game of will against will. Who can stare the other man down? Who will avert his eyes first? Whose gaze will be triumphant? Such moments—

129

Face-off masculinity.

"facing up," "facing off," "staring down"—as anthropologist David Gilmore has documented, are a test of macho in many cultures, including our own. "Don't eyeball me!" barks the sergeant to his cadets-in-training in *An Officer and a Gentleman*; the authority of the stare is a prize to be won only with full manhood. Before then, it is a mark of insolence—or stupidity, failure to understand the codes of masculine rank. In *Get Shorty*, an unsuspecting film director challenges a mob boss to look him in the eye; in return, he is hurled across the room and has his fingers broken.

"Face-off" ads, except for their innovations in the amount of skin exposed, are pretty traditional—one might even say primal—in their conception of masculinity. Many other species use staring to establish dominance, and not only our close primate relatives. It's how my Jack Russell terrier intimidates my male collie, who weighs over four times as much as the little guy but cowers under the authority of the terrier's macho stare. In the doggie world, size doesn't matter; it's the power of the gaze—which indicates the power to stand one's ground—that counts. My little terrier's dominance, in other words, is based on a convincing acting job—and it's one that is very similar, according to William Pollack, to the kind of performance that young boys in our culture must learn to master. Pollack's studies of boys suggest that a set of rules—which he calls "The Boy Code"— govern their behavior with each other. The first imperative of the code —"Be a sturdy oak"—represents the emotional equivalent of "face-off masculinity": Never reveal weakness. Pretend to be confident even though you may be scared. Act like a rock even when you feel shaky. Dare others to challenge your position.

The face-off is not the only available posture for male bodies in ads today. Another possibility is what I call "the lean"—because these bodies are almost always reclining, leaning against, or propped up against something in the fashion typical of women's bodies. James Dean was probably our first pop culture "leaner"; he made it stylish for teenagers to slouch. Dean, however, never posed as languidly or was as openly seductive as some of the high-fashion leaners are today. A recent Calvin Klein "Escape" ad depicts a young, sensuous-looking man leaning against a wall, arm raised, dark underarm hair exposed. His eyes seek out the imagined viewer, soberly but flirtatiously. *"Take Me,"* the copy reads.

Languid leaners have actually been around for a long time. Statues of sleeping fauns, their bodies draped languorously, exist in classical art alongside more heroic models of male beauty. I find it interesting, though, that Klein has chosen Mr. Take Me to advertise a perfume called "Escape." Klein's "Eternity" ads usually depict happy, heterosexual couples, often

"Take me" ad.

with a child. "Obsession" has always been cutting-edge, sexually ambiguous erotica. This ad, featuring a man offering himself up seductively, invitingly to the observer, promises "escape." From what? *To* what? Men have complained, justly, about the burden of always having to be the sexual initiator, the pursuer, the one of whom sexual "performance" is expected. Perhaps the escape is from these burdens, and toward the freedom to indulge in some of the more receptive pleasures traditionally reserved for women. The pleasures, not of staring someone down but of feeling one's body caressed by another's eyes, of being the one who receives the awaited call rather than the one who must build up the nerve to make the call, the one who doesn't have to hump and pump, but is permitted to lie quietly, engrossed in reverie and sensation.

Some people describe these receptive pleasures as "passive"—which gives them bad press with men, and is just plain inaccurate, too. "Passive" hardly describes what's going on when one person offers himself or herself to another. Inviting, receiving, responding—these are active behaviors, too, and rather thrilling ones. It's a macho bias to view the only *real* activity as that which takes, invades, aggresses. It's a bias, however, that's been with us for a long time, in both straight and gay cultures. In many Latin cultures, it's not a disgrace to sleep with other men, so long as one is *activo* (or *machista*)—the penetrator rather than the penetratee. To be a *pasivo*, on the other hand, is to be socially stigmatized. It's that way in prison cultures, too—a good indication of the power hierarchies involved. These hierarchies date back to the ancient Greeks, who believed that passivity, receptivity, penetrability were marks of inferior feminine being. The qualities were inherent in women; it was our nature to be passively controlled by our sexual needs. (Unlike us, the Greeks viewed women—not men—as the animalistic ones.) Real Men who, unlike women, had the necessary rationality and will were expected to be judicious in the exercise of their desires. But being judicious and being "active"—deciding when to pursue, whom to pursue, making advances, pleading one's case—went hand in hand.

Allowing oneself to be pursued, flirting, accepting the advances of another, offering one's body—these behaviors were permitted also (but only on a temporary basis) to still-developing, younger men. These young men—not little boys, as is sometimes incorrectly believed—were the true "sex objects" of elite Greek culture. Full-fledged male citizens, on the other hand, were expected to be "active," initiators, the penetrators not the penetratees, masters of their own desires rather than the objects of another's. Plato's *Symposium* is full of speeches on the different sexual behaviors appropriate to adult men with full beards and established professions and glamorous young men still revered more for their beauty than their minds. But even youth could not make it okay for a man to behave *too* much like a woman. The admirable youth was the one who—unlike a woman—was able to remain sexually "cool" and remote, to keep his wits about him. "Letting go" was not seemly.

Where does our culture stand today with respect to these ideas about men's sexuality? Well, to begin with consider how rarely male actors are shown—on their faces, in their utterances, and not merely in the movements of their bodies—having orgasms. In sex scenes, the moanings and writhings of the female partner have become the conventional cinematic code for heterosexual ecstasy and climax. The male's participation is largely represented by caressing hands, humping buttocks, and—on rare occasions—a facial expression of intense concentration. She's transported to another world; he's the pilot of the ship that takes her there. When men are shown being transported themselves, it's usually been played for comedy (as in Al Pacino's shrieks in *Frankie and Johnny*, Eddie Murphy's moanings in *Boomerang*, Kevin Kline's contortions in *A Fish Called Wanda*), or it's coded to suggest that something is not quite normal about the man—he's sexually enslaved, for example (as with Jeremy Irons in *Damage*). Mostly, men's bodies are presented like action hero toys—wind them up and watch them perform.

Hollywood—still an overwhelmingly straight male–dominated industry—is clearly not yet ready to show us a man "passively" giving himself over to another, at least not when the actors in question are our cultural icons. Too feminine. Too suggestive, metaphorically speaking, of penetration by another. But perhaps fashion ads are less uptight? I decided to perform an experiment. I grouped ads that I had collected over recent years into a pile of "rocks" and a pile of "leaners" and found, not surprisingly, that both race and age played a role. African American models, whether in *Esquire* or *Vibe*, are almost always posed facing off. And leaners tend to be younger than the rocks. Both in gay publications and straight ones, the more languid, come-hither poses in advertisements are of boys and very young men. Once a certain maturity line is crossed, the challenging stares, the "face-off" postures are the norm. What does one learn from these ads? Well, I wouldn't want to claim *too* much. It used to be that one could tell a lot about gender and race from looking at ads. Racial stereotypes were transparent, the established formulas for representing men and women were pretty clear (sociologist Erving Goffman even called ads "gender advertisements"), and when the conventions were defied it was usually

A youthful, androgynous "leaner"—appropriately enough advertising a fragrance "for a man or a woman."

because advertisers sensed (or discovered in their polls) that social shifts had made consumers ready to receive new images. In this "postmodern" age, it's more of a free-for-all, and images are often more reactive to each other than to social change. It's the viewers' jaded eye, not their social prejudices, that is the prime consideration of every ad campaign, and advertisers are quick to tap into taboos, to defy expectations, simply in order to produce new and arresting images. So it wouldn't surprise me if we soon find languid black men and hairy-chested leaners on the pages of *Gentleman's Quarterly*.

But I haven't seen one yet. At the very least, the current scene suggests that even in this era of postmodern pastiche racial clichés and gender taboos persist; among them, we don't want grown men to appear too much the "passive" objects of another's sexual gaze, another's desires. We appear, still, to have somewhat different rules for boys and men. As in ancient Greece, boys are permitted to be seductive, playful, to flirt with being "taken." *Men* must still be in command. Leonardo DiCaprio, watch out. Your days may be numbered.

"Honey, What Do I Want to Wear?"

The male fashion scene of the nineties involves a kind of contest for the souls of men. Calvin Klein, Versace, Gucci, Abercrombie & Fitch have not only brought naked bottoms and bulging briefs onto the commercial scene, they present underwear, jeans, shirts, and suits as items for enhancing a man's appearance and sexual appeal. They suggest it's fine for a man to care about how he looks, and to cultivate an openly erotic style. In response, aggressively heterosexual Dockers and Haggar ads compete—for the buying dollar of men, but in the process for their gender-consciousness, too—by stressing the no-nonsense utility of khakis. Consider this Haggar casuals advertisement, and what it says about how "real men" are supposed to feel about their clothes:

"I'm damn well gonna wear what I want. . . . Honey, what do I want?"

Looked at in one light, the man in the advertisement is being made fun of, as a self-deceived blusterer who asserts his independence "like a man" and in the next breath reveals that he is actually a helpless little boy who needs his mommy to pick out his clothes for him. But fashion incompetence is a species of helplessness that many men feel quite comfortable with, even proud of. Recognizing this, Haggar and Dockers are among those manufacturers who have put a great deal of effort into marketing "non-fashion guy fashion" to a niche of straight men—working-class and

"I'm damn well gonna wear what I want. . . . Honey, what do I want?"

yuppie—who, they presume, would be scared off by even a whiff of "feminine" clothes-consciousness. Here's another one from Haggar:

"In the female the ability to match colors comes at an early age. In the male it comes when he marries a female."

The juxtaposition of inept male/fashion-conscious female, which with one stroke establishes the masculinity *and* the heterosexuality of the depicted man, is a staple of virtually every Haggar ad. In a Haggar television spot with voice-over by John Goodman (Roseanne's beefy ex–television husband), a man wakes up, sleepily pulls on a pair of khakis, and goes outside to get the paper:

137

"I am not what I wear. I'm not a pair of pants, or a shirt." (He then walks by his wife, handing her the front section of the paper.) *"I'm not in touch with my inner child. I don't read poetry, and I'm not politically correct."* (He goes down a hall, and his kid snatches the comics from him.) *"I'm just a guy, and I don't have time to think about what I wear, because I've got a lot of important guy things to do."* (Left with only the sports section of the paper, he heads for the bathroom.) *"One-hundred-per-cent cotton wrinkle-free khaki pants that don't require a lot of thought. Haggar. Stuff you can wear."*

Yes, it's a bit of a parody, but that only allows Haggar to double its point that real guys have better things to do than think about what they are going to wear or how they appear to others. The guy who would be so worried about his image that he couldn't poke fun at himself wouldn't be a real guy at all. Real guys don't take themselves so seriously! That's for wimps who favor poetry, self-help psychology, and bleeding-heart politics. That's for girls, and for the men who are pussy-whipped by them.

In Haggar's world, real guys don't choose clothing that will enhance the appearance of their bodies or display a sense of style; real guys just put on some "stuff" to wear because they have to, it's socially required. The less decorative, the better. "We would never do anything with our pants that would frighten anyone away," says Dockers designer Gareth Morris, as reported in a 1997 piece in *The New Yorker*, "We'd never do too many belt loops, or an unusual base cloth . . . [or] zips or a lot of pocket flaps and details on the back." Pocket flaps, the ultimate signifier of suspect sexuality! In such ads, male naiveté about the sexual potency of clothes, as agency maven David Altschiller claims, is critical. "In women's advertising," he points out, "self-confidence is sexy. But if a man is self-confident—if he knows he is attractive and is beautifully dressed—then he's not a man anymore. He's a fop. He's effeminate." In Dockers' "Nice Pants" television ads, for example, it's crucial that the guy not *know* his pants are "nice" until a gorgeous woman points it out to him.

It's no accident that the pants are described via the low-key understatement "nice" (rather than "great," for example, which would suggest that the guy was actually *trying* to look good.) For the real man (according to Dockers), the mirror is a tool, not a captivating pool; if he could, he'd look the other way while he shaves. Many other advertisers capitalize on such notions, encouraging men to take care of their looks, but reassuring them that it's for utilitarian or instrumental purposes. Cosmetic surgeons emphasize the corporate advantage that a face-lift or tummy-tuck will give the aging executive: "A youthful look," as one says, "gives the appearance of a more dynamic, charging individual who will go out and get the business." Male grooming products too are often marketed by way of "action hero" euphemisms which obscure their relation to feminine versions of the same product (a male girdle marketed by BodySlimmers is called the "Double Agent Boxer") and the fact that their function is to enhance a man's appearance: hair spray as "hair control," exfoliating liquid as "scruffing lotion," astringents as "scrubs," moisturizers and fragrances as "after" or "pre"-accompaniments to that most manly of rituals, the shave. They often have names like Safari and Chaps and Lab Series, and come in containers shaped like spaceships and other forms a girl could have some fun with.

The notions about gender that are maintained in this marketing run deeper than a refusal to use the word "perfume" for products designed to make men smell good. In the late seventies, coincident with the development of feminist consciousness about these matters, art historian John Berger discovered what he argued were a set of implicit cultural paradigms of masculinity and femininity, crystallized in a visual "rule" of both classical painting and commercial advertisements: *men act and women appear.* Here's a contemporary illustration:

The man in the Nautica ad, rigging his sail, seems oblivious to his appearance; he's too busy checking the prevailing winds. The woman, in contrast, seems well aware and well pleased that her legs have caught the attention of the men gaping at her. A woman's *appearance*, Berger argued, has been socially determined to be "of crucial importance for what is normally thought of as the success of her life." Even walking on a city street, headed for their high-power executive jobs, women exist to be seen, and they *know* it—a notion communicated by the constant tropes of female narcissism: women shown preening, looking in mirrors, stroking their own bodies, exhibiting themselves for an assumed spectator, asking to be admired for their beauty.

With depictions of men, it's just the opposite. "A man's presence," Berger wrote, "is dependent upon the promise of power which he embodies . . . what he is capable of doing to you or for you." Thus, the classic formula for representing men is always to show them in action, immersed in whatever they are doing, seemingly unaware of anyone who might be looking at them. They never fondle their own bodies narcissistically, display themselves purely as "sights," or gaze at themselves in the mirror. In everything from war paintings to jeans and cologne ads, men are portrayed as utterly oblivious to their beauty (or lack of it), intent only on getting the job done—raising the flag, lassoing a steer, busting up concrete. The ability to move heavy things around, tame wild creatures—that's manly business.

Men act and women appear.

Fretting about your love handles, your dry skin, your sagging eyelids? That's for girls.

Women in ads and movies thus require no plot-excuse to show off their various body-parts in ads, proudly, shyly, or seductively; it's the "business" of *all* of us to be beautiful—whether we are actresses, politicians, home-makers, teachers, or rock stars. This has changed very little since Berger came up with his formula. When *Time* magazine did a story on the new dominance of female stars in the rock world, its cover featured singing star Jewel, not performing, but in a dewy close-up, lips moist and soft eyes smiling from behind curled lashes. This formidable new "force" in the rock world might as well have been modeling Maybelline. True, a beautiful woman today may be depicted puffing away on a cigar, getting "in touch with her masculine side." But in expression she's still a seductress, gazing through long lashed lids into the eyes of an imagined viewer. "Do you like what you see?" the expressions of the models seem ask.

Men, according to Berger's formula, must never seem as though they are asking this question, and may display their beauty only if it is an un-avoidable side effect of other "business." Thus, a lot of the glistening, naked male chests in the movies of the fifties and sixties were on the bodies of warriors, prisoners, slaves, and prizefighters. No one could claim there was vanity in such nakedness. (No time for preening while nailing spikes on a chain gang or rowing in a slave galley.) So a strong dose of male skin could be sneaked into a movie without disturbing the gender rules. The physical presence of an actor like Richard Gere, who emanates consciousness of his body as the erotic focus of the gaze and invites it, has always annoyed and disconcerted critics. The pomposity of Charlton Heston, on the other hand, his naked (and actually rather gorgeous) chest puffed up in numer-ous biblical epochs, goes unnoticed, because he's doing it all in a builder-of-the-universe rather than narcissus-in-the-mirror mode.

Saturday Night Fever (1977) deserves mention here for openly break-ing with this convention. Tony Manero (John Travolta), a disco-dancing dandy who knows how to use his walk, was a man who *really* needed a course in masculinity-according-to-Haggar. He blows all his wages on fan-cy shirts and shoes. On Saturday night, he prepares his body meticulously, shaving, deodorizing, blow-drying, choosing just the right combination of gold chains and amulets, torso-clinging pants, shiny platforms. Eating din-ner with his family, he swaths himself in a sheet like a baby to protect his new floral shirt; when his father boxes his ear roughly, his only thought is for his pompadour: "Just watch the hair! I work on my hair a long time and you hit it. He hits the hair!" Manero spends much of his time in front of the mirror, getting himself pretty, posing, anticipating the impression he's going to make when he enters the disco or struts down the street.

Never before *Saturday Night Fever* had a heterosexual male movie hero spent so much time on his toilette. (Even Cary Grant's glamorous looks were never shown as requiring any conscious effort or attention; in *The Awful Truth* he sits under a tanning lamp—but that's to fake a trip to Florida.) Although this was the polyester seventies, and men like Sonny Bono dressed like Tony on television, Bono was very careful (as the Beatles were, too) to treat his flamboyant ruffles as show-biz costumes, while Cher proudly strutted her feathers and finery as a second skin for her body and sexuality. Tony, like Cher, chooses his clothes to highlight his sinuous form.

Manero was, in many ways, the cinema equivalent (reassuringly straight and working-class) of the revolution that Calvin Klein was making in more sexually ambiguous form in the fashion world. As a dancer, Tony is unembarrassed—and the camera isn't embarrassed either—to make his hips, groin, and buttocks the mesmerizing center of attention. Travolta was also the first actor to appear on-screen in form-fitting (if discreetly black) briefs. One scene finds him asleep in his underwear, blanket between his legs, hip jutting upward; the camera moves slowly down the length of his body, watches as Tony rouses, sits up, pulls the blanket from between his legs and puts his hand in his briefs to adjust his penis. (The script originally had called for Travolta to appear naked in a later scene; he balked, suggesting the early morning scene as a compromise.) We then follow him to the mirror (where he compares himself admiringly to a poster of Al Pacino) and into the hall, where he flexes teasingly for his shocked grandmother. This was new stuff, and some people were a bit taken aback by such open male vanity and exhibitionism. (Pauline Kael, for one, seemed to need to convince herself of Tony's sexual orientation. "It's a straight heterosexual film," she wrote, "but with a feeling for the sexiness of young boys who are bursting their britches with energy and desire.")

True, there is the suggestion, in the film, that Tony may grow out of his narcissism once he leaves Brooklyn and the gold-chain crowd. Hollywood, of course, had shown men preening, decorating and oiling themselves before—pimps and homosexuals, usually, but also various unassimilated natives (Blacks, Puerto Ricans, Italians) depicted as living more fully in their bodies, with a taste for flashy clothes that marks them as déclassé. Manero fits those stereotypes—but only up to a point. He may have awful taste in jewelry, but he also has boyish charm and "native" intelligence. Unlike his friends—a pathetic trio of racist, homophobic, sexist homeboys—Tony has integrity. He is enraged when, at the "2001" dance contest, racism and favoritism land him first prize over a Puerto Rican couple. He's also the only one of his friends who doesn't taunt a gay couple as they pass on the street. The movie may poke affectionate fun at him, but it also admires him. A hero-narcissus—a very new image for postwar Hollywood.

Of course, most men, gold chains or not, straight or gay, *do* care how they "appear." The gender differences described in Berger's formula and embedded in the Dockers and Haggar advertisements are "fictional," a distillation of certain *ideas* about men and women, not an empirical generalization about their actual behavior. This doesn't mean, however, that they have no impact on "real life." Far from it. As embodied in attractive and sometimes highly manipulative images, "men act and women appear" functions as a visual instruction. Women are supposed to care very much about fashion, "vanity," looking good, and may be seen as unfeminine, man-hating, or lesbian if they don't. The reverse goes for men. The man who cares about his looks the way a woman does, self-esteem on the line, ready to be shattered at the slightest insult or increase in weight gain, is unmanly, sexually suspect.

So the next time you see a Dockers or Haggar ad, think of it not only as an advertisement for khakis, but also as an advertisement for a certain notion of what it means to be a man. The ad execs know that's what's going on; they're open about not wanting to frighten men off with touches of feminine decorativeness. What they are less open about is the fact that such ads don't just cater to male phobias about fashion but also perpetuate them. They have to. Nowadays, the Dockers man is competing against other models of masculinity, laughing at him from both the pages of history and from what was previously the "margin" of contemporary culture. Can you imagine Cary Grant, Rupert Everett, or Michael Jordan as the fashion-incompetent man in a Dockers ad? The stylish man, who began to make a new claim on popular cultural representations with the greater visibility of black and gay men—the men consumer culture once ignored—was chiseling cracks in the rule that "men act and women appear" even as Berger was formulating it.

My World . . . and Welcome to It?

Despite everything I've said thus far, I feel decidedly ambivalent about consumer culture's inroads into the male body. I *do* find it wonderful that the male form, both clothed and unclothed, is being made so widely available for sexual fantasy and aesthetic admiration. I like the fact that more and more heterosexual white guys are feeling permission to play with fashion, self-decoration, sensual presentation of the self. Even Dockers has become a little less "me a guy . . . duh!" in its ads and spreads for khakis, which now include spaced-out women as well as men.

But I also know what it's like to be on the other side of the gaze. I know its pleasures, and I know its agonies—intimately. Even in the second half of the twentieth century, beauty remains a prerequisite for female success. In fact, in an era characterized by some as "postfeminist," beauty seems to count more than it ever did before, and the standards for achieving it have become more stringent, more rigorous, than ever. We live in an empire ruled not by kings or even presidents, but by images. The tight buns; the perfect skin; the firm breasts; the long, muscled legs; the bulgeless, sagless bodies are everywhere. Beautiful women, everywhere, telling the rest of us how to stand, how to swing our hair, how slim we must be.

Actually, all this flawless beauty is the product of illusion, generated with body doubles, computers, artful retouching. "Steal this look!" the lifestyles magazines urge women; it's clear from the photo that great new haircut of Sharon Stone's could change a woman's life. But in this era of digital retouching not even Sharon Stone looks like Sharon Stone. (Isabella Rossellini, who used to be the Lancôme girl before she got too old to be beautiful, has said that her photos are so enhanced that when people meet her they tell her "Your sister is so beautiful.") Still, we try to accomplish the impossible, and often get into trouble. Illusions set the standard for real women, and they spawn special disorders and addictions: in trying to become as fat-free and poreless as the ads, one's fleshly body is pushed to achieve the impossible.

I had a student who admitted to me in her journal that she had a makeup addiction. This young woman was unable to leave the house—not even to walk down to the corner mailbox—without a full face and body cover-up that took her over an hour and a half to apply. In her journal, she described having escalated over a year or so from minimal "touching-up" to a virtual mask of foundation, powder, eyebrow pencil, eyeshadow, eyeliner, mascara, lipliner, lipstick—a mask so thorough, so successful in its illusionary reality that her own, naked face now looked grotesque to her, mottled, pasty, featureless. She dreaded having sex with her boyfriend, for fear some of the mask might come off and he would see what she looked like underneath. As soon as they were done, she would race to the bathroom to reapply; when he stayed over, she would make sure to sleep lightly in order to wake up earlier than him. It's funny—and not really funny. My student's disorder may be one generated by a superficial, even insane culture, a disorder befitting the Oprah Show rather than a PBS documentary. But a disorder nonetheless. Real. Painful. Deforming of her life.

So, too, for the eating disorders that run rampant among girls and women. In much of my writing on the female body, I've chronicled how these disorders have spread across race, class, and ethnic differences in this culture. Today, serious problems with food, weight, and body image are no longer (if they ever were) the province of pampered, narcissistic, hetero-sexual white girls. To imagine that they are is to view black, Asian, Latin, lesbian, and working-class women as outside the loop of the dominant culture and untouched by its messages about what is beautiful — a mistake that has left many women feeling abandoned and alone with a disorder they weren't "supposed" to have. Today, eating problems are virtually the norm among high school and college women — and even younger girls. Yes, of course there are far greater tragedies in life than gaining five pounds. But try to reassure a fifteen-year-old girl that her success in life doesn't require a slender body, and she will think you dropped from another planet. *She* knows what's demanded; she's learned it from the movies, the maga-zines, the soap operas.

There, the "progressive" message conveyed by giving the girls and women depicted great careers or exciting adventures is overpowered, I think, by the more potent example of their perfect bodies. The plots may say: "The world is yours." The bodies caution: "But only if you aren't fat." What counts as "fat" today? Well, Alicia Silverstone was taunted by the press when she appeared at the Academy Awards barely ten pounds heavier than her (extremely) svelte self in *Clueless.* Janeane Garofalo was the "fat one" in *The Truth About Cats and Dogs.* Reviews of *Titanic* described Kate Winslet as plump, overripe, much too hefty for ethereal Leonardo Di-Caprio. Any anger you detect here is personal, too. I ironed my hair in the sixties, have dieted all my life, continue to be deeply ashamed of those parts of my body — like my peasant legs and zaftig behind — that our culture has coded as ethnic excess. I suspect it's only an accident of generational timing or a slight warp in the fabric of my cultural environment that prevented me from developing an eating disorder. I'm not a makeup junkie like my student, but I am becoming somewhat addicted nowadays to alpha-hy-droxies, skin drenchers, quenchers, and other "age-defying" potions.

No, I don't think the business of beauty is without its pleasures. It offers a daily ritual of transformation, renewal. Of "putting oneself together" and walking out into the world, more confident than you were, anticipating attraction, flirtation, sexual play. I love shopping for makeup with my friends. (Despite what Rush Limbaugh tells you, feminism — certainly not feminism in the nineties — is not synonymous with unshaved legs.) Women bond over shared makeup, shared beauty tips. It's fun. Too often, though, our bond is over shared pain — over "bad" skin, "bad" hair, "bad" legs. There's always that constant judgement and evaluation — not only by actual, living men, but by an ever-present, watchful cultural gaze which always has its eye on our thighs — no matter how much else we accomplish. We judge each other that way, too, sometimes much more nastily than men. Some of the bitchiest comments about Marcia Clark's hair and Hillary Clinton's calves have come from women. But if we are sometimes our "own worst enemies," it's usually because we see in each other not so much competition as a reflection of our fears and anxieties about ourselves. In this culture, all women suffer over our bodies. A demon is loose in our consciousness and can't easily be controlled. We see the devil, fat calves, living on Hillary's body. We point our fingers, like the accusers at Salem. Root him out, kill *her*!

And now men are suddenly finding that devil living in their flesh. If someone had told me in 1977 that in 1997 *men* would comprise over a quarter of cosmetic surgery patients, I would have been astounded. I never dreamed that "equality" would move in the direction of men worrying *more* about their looks rather than women worrying less. I first suspected that something major was going on when the guys in my gender classes stopped yawning and passing snide notes when we discussed body issues, and instead began to protest when the women talked as though they were the only ones "oppressed" by standards of beauty. After my book *Unbearable Weight* appeared, I received several letters from male anorexics, reminding me that the incidence of such disorders among men was on the rise. Today, as many as a million men — and eight million women — have an eating disorder.

Then I began noticing all the new men's "health" magazines on the newsstands, dispensing diet and exercise advice ("A Better Body in Half the Time," "50 Snacks that Won't Make You Fat") in the same cheerleaderish mode that Betty Friedan had once chastised the women's magazines for: "It's Chinese New Year, so make a resolution to custom-order your next takeout. Ask that they substitute wonton soup for oil. Try the soba noodles instead of plain noodles. They're richer in nutrients and contain much less fat." The "real man" is no longer required to shun broccoli in favor of beef (although quiche is much too fattening).

It used to be a truism among those of us familiar with the research on body image problems that most men (that is, most straight men, on whom the studies were based) were largely immune. Women, research showed,

Men's Fitness *magazine cover. Reprinted with
permission of the USA edition of* Men's Fitness,
copyright 1999. All rights reserved.

were chronically dissatisfied with themselves. But men tended, if anything, to see themselves as better-looking than they (perhaps) actually were. Peter Richmond, in a 1987 piece in *Glamour,* describes his "wonderful male trick" for seeing what he wants to see when he looks in the mirror:

> I edit out the flaws. Recently, under the influence of too many Heinekens in a strange hotel room, I stood in front of a wraparound full-length mirror and saw, in a moment of nauseous clarity, how unshapely my stomach and butt have become. The next morning, looking again in the same mirror, ready to begin another business day, I simply didn't see these offending areas.

Notice all the codes for male "action" that Richmond has decorated his self-revelation with. "Too many Heinekens," "another business day" — all reassurances that other things matter more to him than his appearance.

But a decade later, it's no longer so easy for men to perform these little tricks. Getting ready for the business day is apt to exacerbate rather than divert male anxieties about the body, as men compete with fitter, younger men and fitter, more self-sufficient women. In a 1994 survey, 6,000 men ages eighteen to fifty-five were asked how they would like to see themselves. Three of men's top six answers were about looks: attractive to women, sexy, good-looking. Male "action" qualities—assertiveness, decisiveness—trailed at numbers eight and nine.

"Back when bad bodies were the norm," claims *Fortune* writer Alan Farnham (again, operating with the presumption of heterosexuality), "money distinguished male from male. Now muscles have devalued money," and the market for products and procedures "catering to male vanity" (as *Fortune* puts it) is $9.5 billion or so a year. "It's a Face-Lifted, Tummy-Tucked Jungle Out There," reports the *New York Times.* To compete, a man

> could buy Rogaine to thicken his hair. He could invest in BodySlimmers underwear for men, by the designer Nancy Ganz, with built-in support to suck in the waist. Or he could skip the aloe skin cream and go on to a more drastic measure, new to the male market: alpha-hydroxy product that sloughs off dead skin. Or he could rub on some belly- and thigh-shrinking creams. . . . If rubbing cream seems too strenuous, [he] can just don an undershirt from Mountainville House, to "shape up and pull in loose stomachs and sagging chests," with a diamond-shaped insert at the gut for "extra control." . . . Plastic surgery offers pectoral implants to make the chest appear more muscular, and calf muscle implants to give the leg a bodybuilder shape. There is liposuction to counter thickening middles and accumulating breast and fatty tissue in the chest . . . and a half-dozen surgical methods for tightening skin.

Some writers blame all this on sexual equality in the workplace. Anthropologist Lionel Tiger offers this explanation. "Once," he says, "men could fairly well control their destiny through providing resources to women, but now that the female is obliged to earn a living, he himself becomes a resource. He becomes his own product: Is he good-looking? Does he smell good? Before, when he had to provide for the female, he could have a potbelly. Now he has to appear attractive in the way the female had to be." Some evidence does support this. A *Psychology Today* survey found that the more financially secure the woman, the more important a man's looks were to her.

I, however, tend to see consumer capitalism rather than women's expectations or proclivities as the true motor driving male concern with appearance. Calvin gave us those muscled men in underwear. Then, the cosmetics, diet, exercise, and surgery industries elbowed in, providing the means for everyone to develop that great Soloflex body. After all, why should they restrict themselves to female markets if they can convince men that their looks need constant improvement too? The management and enhancement of the body is a gold mine for consumerism; one whose treasures are inexhaustible, as women know. Dieting and staving off aging are never-ending processes. Ideals of beauty can be endlessly tinkered with by fashion designers and cosmetic manufacturers, remaining continually elusive, requiring constant new purchases, new kinds of work on the body.

Thomas Berger's opposition of "acting" and "appearing," this body-work reveals, is something of a false duality—and always has been. "Feminine" attention to appearance is hardly the absence of activity, as men are learning. It takes time, energy, creativity, dedication. It can *hurt*. Nowadays, the "act/appear" duality is even less meaningful, as the cultivation of the suitably fit appearance has become not just a matter of sexual allure but also a demonstration that one has the "right stuff": will, discipline, the ability to stop whining and "just do it." When I was growing up in the sixties, a muscular male body meant beefy but dumb jock; a middle-class girl could drool over him but probably wouldn't want to marry him. Today, with a booming "gymnasium culture" existing (as in ancient Greece) for professional men, and with it a revival of the Greek idea that a good mind and a good body are not mutually exclusive, even Jeff Goldblum has muscles, and the only type of jock he plays is a computer jock.

All of this, as physicians have begun to note, is landing more and more men straight into the formerly female territory of body image dysfunction, eating disorders, and exercise compulsions. Last year, I read a survey that reported that 90 percent of male undergraduates believe that they are not muscular enough. That sent warning bells clanging in my mind, and sure enough, there's now a medical category for "muscle dysmorphia" (or "bigorexia," as it's actually sometimes called!) a kind of reverse anorexia in which the sufferer sees his muscles as never massive enough. Researchers are "explaining" bigorexia in the same dumb way they've tended to approach women's disorders—as a combination of bad biochemistry and "triggering events," such as being picked on. They just don't seem to fully appreciate the fact that "bigorexia"—like anorexia—only blooms in a very particular cultural soil. Not even the ancient Greeks—who revered athletic bodies and scorned weaklings, but also advised moderation in all things—produced "muscle dysmorphics." (Or at least, none of the available medical texts mention anything like it.) Anorexia and bigorexia, like so many contemporary disorders, are diseases of a culture that doesn't know when to stop.

Those beautiful bodies of Greek statues may be the historical inspiration for the muscled men in underwear of the Calvin Klein ads. But the fact is that studying the ancient Greeks reveals a different set of attitudes toward beauty and the body than our contemporary ideals. As is well known by now (although undiscussed when I studied philosophy as an undergraduate), Plato was not above appreciating a beautiful young body. In the *Symposium*, he describes the beauty of the body as evidence of the presence of the divine on earth and the original spur to all "higher" human endeavors (as well as earthly, sexual love). We see someone dazzling, and he or she awakens the soul to its natural hunger to be lifted above the mundane, transitory, mortal world. Some people seek that transcendence through ordinary human intercourse and achieve the only immortality they will know through the begetting of human offspring and the continuation of the human race. For others, the beautiful body of another becomes the inspiration for a lifelong search for beauty in all its forms, the creation of beautiful art, beautiful words, beautiful ideals, beautiful cities. They will achieve their immortality through communion with something beyond the body—the idea of Beauty itself.

So human beauty is a pretty far-ranging and powerful thing for Plato, capable of evoking worlds beyond itself, even recalling a previous life when we dwelt among timeless, perfect forms. But human beauty, significantly (in fact, all earthly beauty), can only offer a glimpse of heavenly perfection. It's our nature to be imperfect, after all, and anyone who tries to overcome that limitation on earth is guilty of hubris—according to the Greeks. Our own culture, in contrast, is one without "limits" (a frequent theme of advertisements and commercials) and seemingly without any fear of hubris. Not only do we expect perfection in the bodies of others (just take a gander at some personal ads), we are constantly encouraged to achieve it ourselves, with the help of science and technology and the products and services they make available to us. "This body could be yours," the chiseled Greek statue in the Soloflex commercial tells us (and for only twenty minutes three times a week—give me a break!) "Timeless Beauty Is Within Your Reach," reads an ad for cosmetic surgery. Plato is rolling over in his grave.

For Plato (unlike Descartes) there are no "mere" physical bodies; bodies are lit with meaning, with memory. Our culture is more Cartesian; we like to think of our bodies as so much stuff, which can be tinkered with without any consequences for our soul. We bob our "family noses," lift our aging faces, suction extra fat, remove minor "flaws" with seemingly little concern for any "deep" meaning that our bodies might have, as repositories of our histories, our ethnic and racial and family lineage, our personalities. Actually, much of the time our intentions are to deliberately shed those meanings: to get rid of that Jewish nose, to erase the years from our faces. Unlike the Platonic philosopher, we aren't content to experience timelessness in philosophy, art, or even the beautiful bodies of others; we want to stop time on our own bodies, too. In the process, we substitute individualized beauty—the distinctive faces of the generation of beautiful actresses of my own age, for example—for generic, very often racialized, conventionalized, reproducible codes of youth.

The fact is that we're not only Cartesian but Puritan in our attitudes toward the body. The Greeks went for muscles, sure, but they would have regarded our exercise compulsions as evidence of a system out of control. They thought it unseemly—and a failure of will—to get too self-obsessed with *anything*. They were into the judicious "management" of the body (as French philosopher Michel Foucault has put it), not its utter subjugation. We, on the other hand, can become what our culture regards as sexually alluring only if we're willing to regard our flesh as recalcitrant metal, to be pummeled, burned, and tempered into steel, day in and day out. No pain, no gain. Obsessively pursuing these ideals has deprived both men *and* women of the playful eros of beauty, turned it all into constant, hard work. I love gay and black body-cultures for their flirtatiousness, their tongue-in-cheekness, their irony, their let's-dress-up-and-have-some-fun attitudes. Consumer culture, unfortunately, can even grind playfulness into a commodity, a required item for this year's wardrobe.

For all its idealization of the beauty of the body, Greek culture also understood that beauty could be "inner." In the *Symposium*, a group of elite Greeks discourse on the nature of love. Everyone except for Socrates and Aristophanes is in love with someone else at the party, and they're madly flirting, advancing their own romantic agendas through their speeches. Among the participants are the most beautiful young men of their crowd. Socrates himself is over fifty at the time, and not a pretty man to look at (to put it generously). Yet as we're told at the beginning (and this seems to have been historically true), nearly everyone has at one time or another been "obsessed" with him, "transported, completely possessed"—by his cleverness, his irony, his ability to weave a spell with words and ideas. Even the most dazzling Athenian of them all—soldier superhero Alcibiades, generally regarded as one of the sexiest, handsomest men in town, who joins the party late (and drunk) with a beautiful wreath of violets and ivy and ribbons in his hair—is totally, madly smitten with Socrates.

Alcibiades's love for Socrates is *not* "Platonic" in the sense in which we have come to understand that term. In fact, Alcibiades is insulted because Socrates has refused to have sex with him. "The moment he starts to speak," he tells the crowd of his feelings for Socrates, "I am beside myself: my heart starts leaping in my chest, the tears come streaming down my face." This is not the way it usually goes. In the more normal Greek scheme of things, it's the beautiful young man—like Alcibiades—who is supposed to start the heart of the older man thumping, and who flirtatiously withholds his favors while the older lover does his best to win him. Alcibiades is in a state about this role reversal, but he understands why it has happened. He compares Socrates to a popular kind of satyr statue, which (like the little lacquered Russian dolls we're more familiar with) could be opened to reveal another figure within. Socrates may be ugly as a satyr on the outside, but "once I had a glimpse of the figures within—they were so godlike, so bright and beautiful, so utterly amazing—that I no longer had a choice—I just had to do whatever he told me."

We pay constant lip service to beauty that is more than skin-deep. The talk shows frequently parade extreme May-December matings for our ogling, too. But the fact is that the idea of a glamorous young man being romantically, *sexually* obsessed with someone old and "ugly"—same-sex or other-sex, and no matter what other sterling qualities he or she may have— is pretty much beyond us. Historically, men have benefited from a double standard which culturally codes their gray hair, middle-aged paunches, and facial lines as signs of wisdom and experience rather than advancing decrepitude. My older gay male friends lament that those days are over for them. And if those new polls about women's attitudes are to be believed, the clock is ticking on that double standard for heterosexual men too—no matter how hard Hollywood tries to preserve it. With more and more expectation that men be as physically well-tended as women, those celluloid pairings of Woody Allen and women half as old and forty-six times as good-looking are becoming more of a hoot every day.

There is something anti-sensual to me about current aesthetics. There's so much that my younger friends go "uggh" over. Fat—yecch! Wrinkles— yuck! They live in a constant state of squeamishness about the flesh. I find that finely muscled, young Calvin Klein model beautiful and sexy, sure. But I also was moved by Clint Eastwood's aging chest in *Bridges of Madison County*. Deflated, skin loose around the waistband of his pants, not a washboard ridge in sight—for me, they signaled that Eastwood (at least for this role) had put Dirty Harry away for good, become a real, warm, penetrable, vulnerable human being instead of a make-my-day machine. Call me old-fashioned, but I find that very sexy. For a culture obsessed with youth and fitness, in contrast, sagging flesh is almost the ultimate signifier of decay and disorder. We prefer the clean machine—and are given it, in spades. Purified of "flaws," all loose skin tightened, armored with implants, digitally enhanced, the bodies of most movie stars and models are fully dressed even when naked.

In *Saturday Night Fever*, John Travolta was trim, but (by contemporary standards) a bit "soft." Six years later, Travolta recreated Tony Manero in the sequel, *Staying Alive*. This time, however, the film was directed by Sylvester Stallone, who showed Travolta a statue of a discus thrower and asked: "How would you like to look like that?" "Terrific," replied Travolta, and embarked on a seven-month program of fitness training that literally redesigned his body into a carbon copy of Sly's. In the film, his body was "perfect": gleaming and muscular, without an ounce of fat. He was nice to look at. But if I had to choose between the Tony Manero of *Fever* and the Tony Manero of *Staying Alive*, it'd be no contest. I'd rather spend time (and have sex) with a dancing man with love handles than with a Greek statue who gets in a nasty mood if he misses a workout.

BIBLIOGRAPHY

Beauvoir, Simone de. 1952. *The Second Sex*. New York: Vintage Books.

Berger, John. 1972. *Ways of Seeing*. Great Britain: Penguin.

Blum, Deborah. 1997. *Sex on the Brain: The Biological Differences between Men and Women*. New York: Viking.

Boyd, Herbert and Robert Allen, eds. 1995. *Brotherman*. New York: Ballantine.

Clark, Danae. 1995. "Commodity Lesbianism." In *Free Spirits*, ed. Kate Meuhuron and Gary Persecute. Englewood Cliffs, N.J.: Prentice Hall, pp. 82–94.

Clarkson, Wensley. 1997. *John Travolta: Back in Character*. Woodstock: The Overlook Press.

Ellenzweig, Allen. 1992. *The Homoerotic Photograph*. New York: Columbia University Press.

Farnham, Alan. 1996. "You're So Vain." *Fortune*, September 9, pp. 66–82.

Foucault, Michel. 1985. *The Use of Pleasure*. New York: Vintage Books.

Friday, Nancy. 1996. *The Power of Beauty*. New York: HarperCollins.

Gaines, Steven, and Sharon Churcher. 1994. *Obsession: The Lives and Times of Calvin Klein*. New York: Avon.

Gilmore, David. 1990. *Manhood in the Making*. New Haven: Yale University Press.

Gladwell, Malcolm. 1997. "Listening to Khakis." *The New Yorker*, July 28, pp. 54–58.

Hollander, Anne. 1994. *Sex and Suits: The Evolution of Modern Dress*. New York: Kodansha International.

Long, Ron. 1997. "The Fitness of the Gym." *Harvard Gay and Lesbian Review* 4, no. 3 (Summer): 20–22.

Majors, Richard, and Janet Mancini Billson. 1992. *Cool Pose: The Dilemmas of Black Manhood in America.* New York: Lexington Books.

Peiss, Kathy. 1998. *Hope in a Jar: The Making of America's Beauty Culture.* New York: Metropolitan Books.

Pieterse, Jan Nederveen. 1990. *White on Black: Images of Africa and Blacks in Western Popular Culture.* New Haven: Yale University Press.

Plato. 1989. *Symposium.* Trans. by Alexander Nehamas. Indianapolis: Hackett Publishing.

Richmond, Peter. 1987. "How Do Men Feel about Their Bodies?" *Glamour,* April, pp. 312–313, 369–372.

Rotundo, E. Anthony. 1993. *American Manhood: Transformations in Masculinity from the Revolution to the Modern Era.* New York: Basic Books.

Sartre, Jean-Paul. 1966. *Being and Nothingness.* New York: Washington Square Press.

Shaw, Dan. 1994. "Mirror, Mirror." *New York Times,* May 29, sec. 9, pp. 1, 6.

Sheets-Johnstone, Maxine. 1994. *The Roots of Power: Animate Form and Gendered Bodies.* Chicago: Open Court.

Spindler, Amy. 1996. "It's a Face-Lifted Tummy-Tucked Jungle Out There." *New York Times,* June 9, sec. 3, pp. 1, 8.

Taylor, John. 1995. "The Long Hard Days of Dr. Dick." *Esquire,* September, pp. 120–130.

White, Shane, and Graham White. 1998. *Stylin'.* Ithaca, N.Y.: Cornell University Press.

7. Miss America: Whose Ideal?

There she is: Miss America.
There she is: your ideal.
The dreams of a million girls who are more than pretty
    may come true in Atlantic City
For they may turn out to be the queen of femininity.
There she is: Miss America.
There she is: your ideal.
With so many beauties she'll take the town by storm
    with her all-American face and form.
There she is, walking on air she is, fairest of the fair she is:
    Miss America.[1]

The familiar lyrics heard each year during the crowning of Miss America are usually stifled by the adoration of the crowd and the tears of the latest winner as she strolls down the runway. But this song composed by Bernie Wayne is not as innocent as it sounds — it encompasses attitudes that are racist, sexist, and classist. Unfortunately it is an accurate depiction of the pageant it represents. This constitutes a significant problem since the pageant is viewed each year by over fifty million people and is hailed as an American tradition. The word "ideal" in the context of this trademark song is a question of not just aesthetic value but also of the value of women. So when the emcee is singing "There she is: *your* ideal," the question that needs to be explored is, *Whose* ideal, whose values?

Class discrimination has been an intrinsic part of the Miss America Pageant from its very inception. But it also had a significant effect in shaping the content of this event. The expression "beauty queen," alluded to in the song as the queen of femininity, historically originates from May Day celebrations when the favorite girl was crowned Queen of the May. In 1921, when the pageant began, it was socially acceptable for a woman to participate as a queen for May Day celebrations, tournaments, and festivals. Beauty contests, however, were morally unacceptable for so-called refined women.[2] The prevalent attitude was that upper-class refined women simply did not display themselves before judges or the public. The shaping of the pageant evolved from attempts to legitimize the contest in the eyes of the upper classes. This was achieved by the emphasis promoters placed on specific characteristics such as wholesomeness, physical fitness, and clean-cut natural qualities that personified innocence. So the "type" of Miss America contestant was a direct response to upper-class ideals of what constituted an acceptable woman. That these ideals could not easily be achieved was demonstrated by the fact that the contest was canceled from 1928 until 1935 because it still retained the feel of what was referred to as a "lower class carnival."[3] The promoters' campaign of deliberately using rhetoric that stressed the wholesome, natural qualities and athletic abilities of the contestants eventually won out and the pageant resumed.[4] Over the years the promoters had to keep up with the changing values of what was expected of an upper-class woman; hence, talent competitions, question-and-answer sections, and college scholarships were eventually added to the pageant so it would retain the reputation of a "classy" event. In her book *American Beauty*, Lois W. Banner states:

> [A]lthough the contest rhetoric, the composition of the parade, and the festival setting were all attempts to make a display of women's bodies respectable, they did not overshadow the fact that contestants were being judged on how they looked in bathing suits. Even when later pageants added talent divisions and gave college scholarships as prizes, the review of the contestants in bathing suits was still the most important part of the competition. Despite pretensions to intellect and talent, physical beauty remained the overriding feature of the ideal American woman.[5]

Although it may appear that the Miss America Pageant is responsible for breaking down class barriers, the fact is that the pageant was always governed by upper-class patriarchal values of what constitutes the proper woman. Ironically, the pageant only managed to serve the purpose of reflecting the change in the class of women who are allowed to be paraded in public. Instead of the contest being socially designated to so-called lower-class unrefined women, now the contestants are mostly college educated and hail from upper-class homes. Either way, the Miss America Pageant fosters sexist practices. In 1921 it was unacceptable for men to marry women who were ogled by other men; in 1996 if a man marries a beauty queen, he literally takes home the trophy, tiara and all.

While May Day queens have their origins in pagan fertility rituals, the concept of a "Queen" in the context of the Miss America Pageant is more representative of royalty, exemplified by the symbolism of the ceremony of the robing and crowning of new winners. Terminology such as "queen," "throne," "scepter," and expressions such as "Miss America's reign" and references to the runners-up as her "court" evoke notions of a ruling class and the values of monarchies and hierarchies. This is only one of the many troubling aspects to consider when questioning whose ideals are represented in this event.

When the judges are deciding who is the fairest in the land, this can be taken literally. In her book *Beauty Bound*, Rita Freedman states that "Approximately one out of three Miss America contestants has been blonde. . . . Since blondness occurs mainly among Caucasians, it also carries with it the high status of the dominant group in a racist culture like ours."[6]

Let's look at the history of African Americans in the Miss America Pageant. In 1970, Cheryl Browne, Miss Iowa, was the first African American woman to win a state title. In 1976, Deborah Lipford, Miss Delaware, was the first to make the top ten, and in 1980, Lencola Sullivan, Miss Arkansas, was the first to make the top five. In 1983, Vanessa Williams was the first African American woman to become Miss America; the first runner-up, Suzette Charles, was the second to wear the crown when she reigned during the last eight weeks of the same year. In 1990, the third African American woman to be crowned Miss America was Debbye Turner, and the 1991 winner, Marjorie Vincent, was not only black but the daughter of Haitian immigrants. In 1994 Kimberly Aiken was the first black contestant from a former Confederate state to become Miss America.[7] Why did it take until 1970 for an African American woman to participate in the Miss America Pageant? The answer is quite simple; it was right there in the rule book. Rule number seven states: "Contestants must be of good health and of the white race."[8] Of course this does not mean that African Americans never participated in the pageant; a 1921 photograph depicts black men serving as slaves in the Court of King Neptune and Miss America; they also participated in the pageant by "pushing the chairs on the boardwalk, and playing the banjo or horn on early floats in the parade."[9] The Miss America Organization, aware of the contest's history, has recently been forthright about its tainted past. In fact, the previous information was cited from a book entitled *Miss America: The Dream Lives On—A 75 Year Celebration*, which is published by and can be purchased through their organization. It was a politically advantageous move to admit to controversy by publishing inflammatory information before critics could take them to task. Because they controlled the presentation of the data, the public is invited to take the attitude of "See, they admit what they did. They let black girls in now, and fifty years of discrimination can be forgiven."

As I perused the organization's anniversary book and looked at the photographs of the African American women who managed to get accepted into the pageant, a significant detail stood out: all the black women are light skinned with Caucasian features and the style of their hair is characteristically that of white women. The African American women who were allowed into the pageant could pass for white. "Passing for white" is a loaded term with its own history but basically it means that white dominant society thinks you look enough like them to bend the rules and "pass." So when Bert Parks was crooning, "There she is, walking on air she is, there so fair she is," the lyrics applied literally to the African American women who became Miss America. Even with the organization's forthrightness in the face of charges of racism, you still have to question whose ideal, whose values are being perpetuated in this pageant.

In 1994, there was another first in the Miss America Pageant: the crowning of Heather Whitestone, who is hearing impaired. The Miss America Organization can now advertise not only that it is culturally diverse but also that it does not discriminate on the grounds of physical impairment; it is an equal opportunity beauty pageant. But just as the African American women who participated could pass for white, so also can a woman with a hearing impairment pass for one who is physically intact. In terms of visual imagery, being deaf is just not the same as being a quadriplegic. In our society hearing impairment is the most socially acceptable physical disability because it is invisible and hence does not cause visual discomfort to the viewer. So even with her physical impairment, Heather Whitestone still serves to perpetuate the values of the patriarchy. Indeed, if her disability were of such a nature that she couldn't speak she would be the ultimate example of the desirable woman—a beautiful object that can't express any opinions.

To exemplify my point let's imagine a scenario in which Miss America is somehow disfigured. This doesn't have to be anything as serious as a car accident or a fire; perhaps she developed some kind of lingering skin rash to the cloak in which she was wrapped, or the crown fell off her head when she was walking down the runway in such a manner as to scratch and scar her face. The point is to imagine that she is no longer the perfect unblemished image of female beauty. Is her title revoked and all her engagements canceled? Most likely. After all, it would make everyone feel so uncomfortable to have to witness a tarnished beauty. The grounds used to dismiss her could be rationalized by saying that young girls might intentionally scar their faces so they too could be as beautiful as the fairest in the land. A disfigured beauty queen is unacceptable in a culture whose ideal beauty is supposed to remain intact, if only for one year.

In 1996 beauty pageant ethics were put to the test when an international scandal erupted concerning Alicia Machado, the reigning Miss Universe. The nineteen-year-old former Miss Venezuela had the audacity to gain weight during her reign as Miss Universe. When she won the title on May 17, 1996, she weighed 112 pounds at 5'7". By August, the media reported she had "gained weight during the summer" and, while refusing to reveal her current weight, was "given an ultimatum to lose 27 pounds in two weeks or risk losing her title."[10] Even with the latest National Institutes for Health weight guidelines, which substantially lowered previously acceptable weights using a Body Mass Index formula, a woman of 5'7" can weigh as much as 160 pounds and still not be considered overweight. However beauty queens, the role models for young girls, have to remain painfully thin. The scandal escalated as Alicia kept gaining weight. When she reached 160 pounds Donald Trump, a partner in the company that purchased the Miss Universe company, decided to call in a fitness expert to ensure that he didn't lose money on his new investment. He was quoted as stating, "We want her to stay as Miss Universe and she is working on her problem."[11] Trump, the epitome of patriarchal capitalist values who traded in his wife the way he trades in real estate, decided to hold a photo shoot while Alicia was exercising in the gym. How did this affect Miss Machado? She stated, "When I get to New York thinking they (pageant organizers) were going to help me, I find myself in a gym with eighty photographers all taking pictures and watching the little pig exercise."[12] She also claimed that Donald Trump said, "This is a perfect opportunity for us to make some publicity for the pageant. Let's take advantage of this fatty."[13] So much for the emphasis the Miss Universe organizers place on the importance of personality and inner beauty. The values perpetuated in this incident are that if you want to continue to please men and be successful in society then you have to starve yourself. This attitude serves only to reinforce the high rate of anorexia and bulimia among young women in this country. In one article Miss Machado is quoted stating, "I am not a monster."[14] Ironically, this statement is reminiscent of the famous quote from the film, *The Elephant Man*, the story of a man who was suffering from a disfiguring disease who was placed on display at carnivals and freak shows. This young beauty queen who experienced the same humiliation stopped short of continuing the quote, "I am not an animal, I am a human being."

Of course Alicia Machado could have easily shed the weight by simply hiring a plastic surgeon to use liposuction to remove it, since plastic surgery is not prohibited in the Miss Universe or Miss America beauty pageants. In fact, several Miss America contestants have used the surgeon's knife for reconstructive beauty, not to recover from any accident but to become eligible for the title of "fairest in the land." According to Naomi Wolf, "In 1989 five contestants, including Miss Florida, Miss Alaska, and Miss Oregon, were surgically reconstructed by a single Arkansas plastic surgeon."[15] Although there are pageant rules against health and race, apparently how you arrive at the standard of beauty is irrelevant as long as the visible end product fits the beauty mold. Cosmetic surgery is socially acceptable, especially among women who are indoctrinated in beauty pageant values in a culture that is obsessed with perfection.

Another issue of value is the narrow distinction between beauty queen and porno queen. It is socially acceptable to be displayed before the public as a beauty object and socially unacceptable to be displayed as a sex object. The distinction lies somewhere in the patriarchal definition of "wholesomeness" which perpetuates the ideology of the good girl versus the bad girl or, more accurately, the virgin versus the whore. This dichotomy became an issue when photographs of Vanessa Williams, Miss America 1984, appeared in *Penthouse Magazine*. The photographs contained full frontal nudity and lesbian poses.

This incident is described as "the greatest threat to the reputation and stability of the pageant" in *Miss America: The Dream Lives On*:

> [The executive committee] agreed that Vanessa Williams was a great Miss America who had made a mistake. But they had to decide who was more important: Vanessa or all future Pageant contestants? They had to consider the sponsors who put up millions of dollars. They had to weigh the national impression versus her welfare. They had to consider the implications of being labeled racist.[16]

This statement is tantamount to an admission that they had to cover their interests. How dare a woman risk losing millions of their organization's dollars? How dare a woman make a decision about the presentation of her own body and more critically how dare a *woman* do this to them? How did this unwholesome porno queen slip past them and present herself as an eligible contestant? *Penthouse* beauties are relegated to the status of bad girls and are certainly not eligible contestants. Was she less beautiful in the

Beauty pageant ethics were put to the test when Alicia Machado, the reigning
Miss Universe, had the audacity to gain weight during her reign. Photo by Peter Serling.

With light skin and Caucasian features, Vanessa Williams was "fair" enough to be the first African American woman to become Miss America. GLOBE photos.

161

nude photos than she was in the bathing suit photos? No, she was less acceptable to the patriarchal model of the good girl. In their value system it had to be a mistake since a wholesome beauty contestant would never consciously choose to pose nude. In *Beauty Bound*, Freedman states:

> Miss America must be provocative but wholesome—a pretty but pure vestal virgin, like Cinderella. Her message is, Look but don't touch. . . . Vanessa Williams, Miss America of 1984, discovered that a fine line divides the legitimate display of beauty from the illegitimate display of pornography.[17]

The section in the *Miss America* book on this scandal ends with a statement by the President and CEO of the organization, Leonard C. Horn: "We maintained our dignity, and in the intervening years, she restored her dignity."[18] The implication was that the Miss America executive committee managed to avoid being tarnished by this unwholesome creature and that Vanessa Williams had relinquished her personal dignity by exposing herself in such an inappropriate manner. However it also implies that she managed to overcome her supposed tragic flaw by making a career for herself and, more important, by marrying and having children. In their eyes, this restored her dignity because she now fills an appropriate place in a patriarchal society.

A similar distinction between beauty queen and sex queen became the subject of a lawsuit filed by 1993 Miss USA, Shannon Marketic. Miss Marketic filed charges in a U.S. Federal court against Hassanal Bolkiah, the Sultan of Brunei, alleging that she was drugged, sexually abused, and held against her will for thirty-two days in the Sultan's palace after she was lured to the country with the promise of a promotional job. Her suit also named the Sultan's brother, Prince Haji Jefri Bolkiah, and Kaliber Talent, the Los Angeles talent agency that recruited her. The Moslem Monarch is the Prime Minister, Defense Minister, and Finance Minister of Brunei and is reported to be the richest man in the world. He also is known for importing women under false pretenses for harems in which they have to entertain men sexually. In 1993, Ernesto Maceda, President of the Philippine State, conducted hearings that found that the Sultan had been enticing Filipino beauties and actresses for "entertainment" purposes. One report states that a Filipino woman jumped out the window of her living quarters in order to escape to the airport. The Sultan, who emphatically denied all charges, will not have to answer these allegations because in August 1997 Judge Consuelo Marshall, a Los Angeles Federal judge, ruled that the Sultan of Brunei is entitled to diplomatic immunity since he is a head of state. Not surprisingly, Miss Marketic is having trouble getting anyone to support her story. Other women who have gone to Brunei have told CBS 2 News that they believe Marketic is simply looking to make money by suing the richest man in the world, a man who, in their eyes, was also the most generous man in the world. Reportedly, "Even Marketic's friend, a beauty queen named Brandi Sherwood, who also took the trip, has so far not publicly supported her friend."[19] The most common reaction when one first hears of this story is: What did she expect? Did she actually think she was going to get paid $21,000 a week to do promotional work? Unfortunately the combination of beauty pageant values and extreme naiveté placed the former Miss USA in this dangerous and humiliating situation. Although there may be a thin line distinguishing beauty object from sex object in the United States there is no differentiation in Brunei, where women who preen and display themselves on stage in order to receive money and adulation are simply whores and prostitutes. Patriarchal values that have evolved in beauty pageants are so corrupt that wealthy powerful men can afford not only to demean beautiful women but also manage to elicit thanks from them for being so generous. What distinguished Vanessa Williams and Shannon Marketic is that although they participated in pageants, they did not internalize the patriarchy; this is exactly why they were the subject of sexual scandals. According to these particular values, women are seen as property of the pageant organizations or whoever hires them. When the beauty queen doesn't play by the king's rules and gets hurt either physically, financially, emotionally, or all of the above, it is assumed that she asked for it.

The Miss America Organization, which somehow manages to fit the criteria for nonprofit organization, flatters itself as the leading supporter of women's scholarships in the country. This is a sad commentary on the status of women's scholarships, especially when it is a device that is consistently used as the organization's answer to any controversial claims regarding the pageant. One needs to question the amount of money women spend on all the contests they have to win to get to the Miss America Pageant and weigh that against the amount of funding given out. This scholarship myth is promoted to pacify the public and to create a smoke screen for the sexism that is perpetuated in this contest. The organization's rationale seems to be that it is justifiable to perpetuate racism, sexism, and classism because some money is given to educate a few chosen women. No amount of money—even in the sugar-coated form of collegiate scholarships—can justify the harm being done to the integrity of American women or the minds of young girls who do not yet realize that this event commodifies and objectifies women. Even more disturbing is the issue of women who actively participate in this pageant. They are perfect examples of the damage caused by patriarchal ideals of women, including their lack of awareness about patriarchal notions of beauty, sex, youth, competition, and hierarchy. Perhaps social issues such as racism and sexism just can't compare to a year's worth of constant adoration and a trip to Disney World.

The 1996 Miss World contest, which was held on November 23rd in Bangalore, India, clearly demonstrated how American beauty pageant values are perceived differently by another culture. Major objections came from various organizations throughout Indian society. Thousands of women and men protested the event as "demeaning to our culture, devaluing to our tradition, promoting vulgarity and obscenity, and a disgrace to womanhood."[20] Others deplored the event as "capitalist exploitation of women and part of the multi-national corporations' carefully planned plundering of India."[21] Members of Akila Bharatiya Vidyarthi Parishad, the Bharatiya Janata Party youth wing, went from college to college condemning the pageant as "a cultural invasion and promotion of Western concepts of beauty, degrading to our women." The result of this action was that Bangalore colleges and schools had to be closed two days before the controversial event.[22] This beauty pageant was such a serious threat to Indian cultural values that protests became violent. "Kinay Narayana Sashikala, a member of the Mahila Jagran Samati (Forum to Awaken Women), announced a twelve-member suicide squad would immolate themselves at the pageant while the show was on."[23] They were unable to go through with the threat because of heightened police security; however, members of the group stormed a showroom and smeared cow dung on the equipment. Another group calling themselves "Indian Tigers" threatened bomb attacks. There was such outrage with the upcoming pageant that on November 14th, twenty-four-year-old Suresh Kamar, a member of the Marxist Democratic Youth Federation, committed suicide by setting himself on fire in front of hundreds of people at the Manduri train station while shouting anti-pageant slogans. If this behavior seems extreme to us it is because beauty pageants are so ingrained in American culture that it is difficult to imagine that they could provoke such powerful emotions. However, the events of the Miss World contest give us a window on how disturbingly insidious these seemingly innocuous pageants are. Although on the surface I agree with the majority of the protesters' views, an important distinction needs to be made in regard to the political agenda underlying the objections. Indian culture is very much a patriarchal society with very traditional views of women's roles in the family. The beauty pageant is offensive in India because it attacks the traditional role of women in a patriarchal society: to be mothers and housewives who only reveal themselves to their husbands. From an American feminist perspective it is offensive because it perpetuates patriarchal values that see women essentially as beauty and sex objects in a male-dominated culture. What makes this pageant so extremely threatening to Indian culture is that it represents women who have chosen a lifestyle that, although it may perpetuate sexist values, offers women a glance at an alternative to being a wife and mother. The only reason this beauty pageant is controversial in India is because it represents a clashing of two patriarchal cultures. Neither country has women's best interest in mind; they simply have different views of how women should fit into their male societies. In both places a majority of the women have internalized the values of their respective communities only to perpetuate their own degradation.

Unfortunately it took the murder of little JonBenet Ramsey for Americans to start paying attention to the disturbing values that are tolerated in beauty pageants. At the age of six she had already won several crowns, including the Colorado State All-Star Kids Cover Girl, America's Little Royal Miss, and Tiny Miss Beauty, along with a lengthy list of other beauty-related honors.

How does this relate to the Miss America Pageant? In several ways. The first correlation is that Ramsey's mother and aunt were both contestants in the Miss America Pageant, and it doesn't take a giant leap in logic to presume that they were grooming a second-generation beauty queen to follow in their high-heeled footsteps. Second, in several interviews of other child contestants it became apparent that such girls aspire to be Miss America. For example, at the age of eight, Breanna German is a veteran at beauty pageants; last year alone she was in seven pageants. Her mother is quoted in *Newsweek*: "She watches Miss America on TV and says, 'That's what I want to do.'"[24] Finally, the impact of the Miss America Pageant is demonstrated in the thousands of beauty contests held each year throughout the country. In the town of Lufkin, Texas, there are pageants for all ages including an infant division, Little Miss Lufkin, and Miss Teen Lufkin. Tiffani Green, named Miss Teen Lufkin, was quoted in a *Newsweek* article with regard to a three-year-old contestant, "She never meets a stranger! She enjoys singing and going on field trips. And she wants to be Miss America! Just think: it all starts on stages just like this one in towns just like Lufkin!"[25] Tiffany is absolutely correct. It all starts on stages in towns just like Lufkin; infants, toddlers, girls, and young women are being indoctrinated into values that exploit, commodify, and objectify—values that imply that it is permissible to display little girls in women's attire while they prance around

*Six-year-old JonBenet Ramsey in makeup, feathers, and high heels,
competing in one of many children's beauty pageants. Photo by Mark Fix,
Zuma Press.*

on stage dancing and being photographed in sexually provocative poses.
They can grow up like Shannon Marketic and unknowingly enter into a
contract that sexually enslaves them. The Miss America Pageant is the
definitive goal, the Mecca that makes the beauty circuit pilgrimage worthwhile, it is the end that justifies the means, even if the means is at the
expense of corrupting children for life.

JonBenet Ramsey. Beauty pageant values imply that it is permissible to display little girls in women's attire and to photograph them in sexually provocative poses. Photo by Mark Fix, Zuma Press.

If there is still any question in your mind about how deeply ingrained Miss America Beauty pageant values are, consider this: six-year-old Jon-Benet Ramsey was buried in one of her pageant outfits and a rhinestone tiara—the ultimate sleeping beauty.

NOTES

1. The lyrics were transcribed from the video of the televised Miss America Pageant 1995, purchased from the Miss America Organization, Atlantic City, N.J. Original lyrics by Bernie Wayne, 1955.

2. Lois W. Banner, *American Beauty* (Chicago: University of Chicago Press, 1983), p. 255.

3. Ibid., p. 269.

4. Ibid., p. 268.

5. Ibid., pp. 269–270.

6. Rita Freedman, *Beauty Bound* (Lexington, Mass.: Heath and Company, 1986), p. 196.

7. Angela Saulino Osborne, *Miss America: The Dream Lives On—A 75 Year Celebration* (Dallas: Taylor Publishing and The Miss America Organization, 1995), pp. 102–103.

8. Ibid., p. 100.

9. Ibid.

10. "Dogged by Weight Issue, Miss Universe Re-emerges in Public," *CNN Interactive* (August 22, 1996), www-cgi.cnn.com/WORLD/9608/22/newsbriefs/index.html.

11. "Weight of The World," *People Magazine,* Up Front section, February 10, 1997.

12. "Miss Universe Fed Up with Fat Discrimination," *Associated Press,* April 19, 1997, http://www.missuniverse.com/uni96.

13. Ibid.

14. "Weighty Matters," *People Magazine,* July 5, 1998.

15. Naomi Wolf, *The Beauty Myth: How Images of Beauty Are Used against Women* (New York: Doubleday, 1991), p. 267.

16. Osborne, *Miss America,* pp. 136–137.

17. Freedman, *Beauty Bound,* p. 42.

18. Osborne, *Miss America,* p. 137.

19. "Secrets of the Beauty Queen," Channel 2000 News, Special Assignment, CBS 2 News (aired May 16, 1997), http://oberon.ibsys.com/news/stories/news–970825–163019.html.

20. Choodie Shivaram, "Contested Contest: Beauty Pageant Stirs Often Violent Debate on Future of India's Culture," *Hinduism Today International,* March 1997, p. 24.

21. Ibid.

22. Ibid., p. 25.

23. Ibid.

24. Jerry Adler, "The Strange World of JonBenet," *Newsweek,* January 20, 1997, p. 45.

25. Ibid., p. 47.

Eva Kit Wah Man

8. Female Bodily Aesthetics, Politics, and Feminine Ideals of Beauty in China

There is a broad consensus in recent Western discourse that male and female bodies are not just biological facts but are historically and cultural-ly constructed.[1] This view holds that there should not be any sharp distinc-tion between being (biological) "female" and being (social) "feminine," because "feminine" represents a dissolution of self which is fragmented into a fleeting array of desires and impulses driven by symbolic and cultural propulsions that come from beyond the self.[2]

"Femininity" does not refer to part of a dichotomy between mind and body in Chinese philosophy neither because there is no such dichotomy in Chinese philosophy. I would therefore like to focus on the following two overlapping questions in the context of discussing the development of female aesthetics and the notion of a feminine ideal in China: (1) How can this development be understood within the particular historical and cul-tural context in China (and how can it be related to various factors such as economic and political situations)? and (2) Because man is the speaking subject in the Chinese patriarchal system, how do male imaginations (es-pecially those represented by the literati) construct the ideal and the aes-thetic quality in woman as the projection of their wishes or regrets and as the production of various forms of their fantasies?

I will first introduce the philosophical discussion of female beauty in the Chinese traditions. I will then present a contextual case study of the development and construction of the feminine ideal in the courtesan cul-ture in late Imperial China. This critical study will illustrate how the no-tion of female beauty in China was redefined and represented by male literati under certain political and economic changes. Last, I will outline the contemporary notion of female beauty in communist China, a notion that has departed from its tradition in order to follow the capitalist West.

The Notion of Feminine Beauty in Classical Confucian and Taoist Texts

The Vision and Other Sensations of Beauty, *Se*

The term *Nu Se* (woman color) is used to describe the beauty of women in traditional Chinese texts. It refers to the visual sense, which is believed to originate from the heart. In the old dictionary *ShuoWenJieZi*, *Se* (color) is formed when the heart manifests its feeling in *Chi* (the metaphysical sense of air), and when *Chi* expresses itself between the eyebrows, *Chi* becomes the color of physical appearance. This meaning is echoed in other Confucian texts like *Analects* and *Hsun Tzu*. Besides today's common meaning of color, *Se* in classical Chinese also refers to femaleness, the skin color and erotic qualities of a woman, which include her bodily beauty, the shape of her limbs, the gentleness of her behavior, the charm of her voice, the way she dresses and makes up, and so on. All these qualify a *meiren*, a beautiful woman. In addition to the role of the visual sense in the definition of a *meiren*, there is also the sense of touch, because the erotic factors just mentioned are perceived through sensory contact with the beholder, which produces sensory pleasure. The sense of smell also counts —the scent of women is always mentioned whenever a description of a *meiren* turns up—as does the sound of her voice.

The following are some basic criteria for female beauty listed in ancient literary and philosophy texts in both the Confucian and Taoist traditions, including *Shih Ching (The Book of Poetry)*, *Lie Tzu*, *Chu Tzu*, *Huai Nan Tzu*, and so on: young; small; slim but fleshly; soft bones; drooping shoulders; smooth white skin under colorful and tight silk underwear; clean slender fingers; long neck; broad and white forehead; long ears; dark and thick hair with stylish hairpin; thick and bluish-black eyebrows; clear and sentimental eyes; charming smiles; tall and straight nose; red lips exposing seashell-white and small teeth; relaxed and elegant bodily gestures; and finally, gentle behaviors. It is the vitality of the body that counts, the sensuous qualities and curve of which must be perceived by the integration of all our senses.

According to most of the classical writings, a woman's beauty also must be judged through (hetero)sexual sensations; that is, *meiren* is in the pas-

This painting shows the bodily features and temperament of women as they are described by traditional Taoists and Confucians. Anonymous Chinese watercolor, 19th century. Courtesy of the Gichner Foundation for Cultural Studies, Washington, D.C.

sionate eye of male lovers or admirers. The beauty of the goddess and *meiren* in classical myths and stories is grounded in male desire, fantasies, and devotion. Though the notion of beauty later departs from the realms of the physiological and sexual and pervades cultural and normative realms, it is useful to take a closer look at its sexual implications, because this dimension has never vanished.

The Sexual Connotations of Female Beauty in Taoist Texts

The sexual connotations of female beauty are explicitly discussed in classical Taoist texts. The values placed on the female physiognomy and feminine attributes reveal more than a skin-deep aesthetic judgment; they also indicate the Chinese faith in the goodness of what nature makes beautiful.[3] When scholars summarize some of the Taoist theories related to female beauty, they make judgments about female physiognomy and female gestures that facilitate sexual enjoyment and the physical benefits male partners enjoy as a result of such physiognomy and gestures.

The main recommendations given by the early Taoist texts, like *Su Nu Ching* (*The Classic of Su Nu*) of the Han dynasty (206 B.C.–A.D. 220), *Yu Fang Pi Cheuh* (*Secrets of the Jade Chamber*) of the North and South dynasties (A.D. 420–A.D. 581), *Ch'ien-chin yao-fang* (*Recipes of Priceless Gold*) (A.D. 630–A.D. 650) and so on, describe typical feminine ideals that are also the suggested requirements of an ideal female sex partner. The texts recommend that she should be young and not yet a mother, be amply covered with flesh, and have swelling breasts that fill the whole hand when held.[4] She should have silken hair and small eyes with the whites and pupils clearly defined, her face and body should be moist and glossy, her voice should be harmonious and low, the bones of her four limbs and hundred joints should be buried in ample flesh, and her private parts and underarms should be bare—but if there is hair, it should be fine and glossy. In contrast to this definition of ideal womanhood, the texts present the image of a woman with tangled and yellowish hair, a fearful countenance, a mallet-like neck, a prominent Adam's apple, irregular teeth, a husky voice, a large mouth, a high nose bridge, dull pupils, a chin with whiskers, prominent large joints, scant flesh, coarse skin, and copious rough pubic hair. The texts warned that to associate with women with these female qualities would only bring harm to a man.[5] An example is the Taoist belief that women with rough pubic hairs usually have a tough and short life and that they would not bring any luck to their male partners.[6]

The above criteria of the feminine ideal and its contrast are related to some fundamental theories about sex in Taoism, which hold that it exists for the sexual pleasure, physical benefits, and longevity of the male. The background of Taoist sexual beliefs and practices is cosmological and is generally referred to as the Yin-Yang Five-Element (*Yin Yang Wu Hsing*), which include the key elements of *Yin*, *Yang*, and *Chi* as outlined in the *I-Ching*. As is well known, the Taoist understanding of sexuality was profoundly influenced by other ancient texts, like *Huang Ti Nei Ching* (*The Yellow Emperor Classic of Internal Medicine*) written between 475 and 221 B.C., and later Taoist writings, the seventh-century *Tung Hsuan Tzu*, for example. These texts reflect a deep-rooted belief in the magical, therapeutic, and health-giving properties of sex. Sexual coupling is seen both symbolically and practically as the harmonious balancing of the *Yin* and the

Yang, preserving life through the preservation of the *Chi*. These traditions hold that *Yang* manifests as heaven and man while *Yin* manifests as woman and earth. These two elements are believed to be the polar forces of the cosmos but related to each other. Their respective sex organs possess the elemental forces. Because the penis is the *Yang* and the vulva is the *Yin*, when a man and a woman conduct sexual intercourse, the moment of orgasm is a form of metaphysical harmony that transcends the couple's corporeal existence through the fusion of the two polarities. Consequently, sex leads to a sacred experience.

According to *Tung Husan Tzu*, if one follows the natural laws of sex to the state of harmony, one's vital essence (*Chi*) will be nourished and one's life would be prolonged. Furthermore, by following a number of sequential progressions and responses during sexual intercourse, one might attain longevity. Failure to adhere to the sequence would produce illness. Thus, it was important to learn the proper procedures and to choose a partner who was cooperative and desirable. *Tung*'s sex guide, "Art of the Bedchamber," is a favorite source of such knowledge; it gained a wide following after the Tang period when it was compiled into a catalogue of some thirty basic postures. Even though the ancient Taoist texts on sex all stated that men and women should participate together in sex, it is obvious that the texts are basically male-oriented and are concerned mainly with the benefits of the males. Under the influence of the dominant Confucian patriarchal system, this bias was reinforced by the idea that during intercourse the man "chants" and the woman "harmonizes." The Taoist texts emphasize the male's nourishing intake of vaginal flow from the *Yin* element. This process further increases a man's vitality if he reserves his semen, his life force. Longevity can be achieved by reverting semen in the form of energy upward to the brain (which should be understood metaphysically rather than physiologically). This belief makes frequent and premature ejaculation a taboo. Thus, the man on the verge of ejaculation is instructed to change partners immediately or to control the woman during sexual intercourse so that he can be nourished by rich female elements. The man is also advised not to be excited prematurely by the woman's responses. Likewise, sexual monogamy is not encouraged, for if a man were to constantly control the same woman, her emission of the *Yin* element would be exhausted and her usefulness to the man would be reduced.

Sexual engagement is to be conducted in a harmonious and tranquil mood. Taoist texts generally caution against sudden and violent sexual behavior, which is regarded as improper to intercourse in terms of speed and posture; such behavior would then lead to physical afflictions. This may explain why sadomasochism is absent in Chinese erotica and is replaced instead by harmonious, cooperative, and playful sex. Now our attention should go back to the criteria for the feminine ideal. We should note that these judgments are made not only with regard to a woman's bodily characteristics, but they are also related to the sexual reaction of a woman which ultimately leads to sexual consequences for the male body. One example is that an ideal woman partner must not have a manly voice. One of the main interpretations of this is that a woman with a manly voice manifests an excess of *Chi*, which would make it difficult for her to harmonize with a man during sex. Thus, it was believed that certain bodily attributes of a woman would downgrade her beauty, as they would be inimical not only to sexual enjoyment but also to the health of the male partner. Women over forty were more likely to have many more of these negative characteristics: hearts and bellies out of order; cold, stiff, and hard bodies; smelly armpits; and spontaneous vaginal secretions. Other negative tendencies include an inclination to jealousy, bad dispositions, and eating binges.[7] In summary, I would like to cite the following excerpt from the Taoist text *Hsiu-chen yu-lu* (*Record of Cultivating the True Essence*), written in the Han dynasty (108 B.C.), as it summarizes the negative female qualities men were to avoid if they wanted a fulfilling sexual relationship and a long life:

> When mounting women one must first have a clear understanding of the "five avoidances." Women who have manly voices and coarse skin, yellow hair and violent dispositions, and are sneaky and jealous constitute the first avoidance. Those with evil appearances and unhealthy countenances, bald heads and underarm odor, hunched backs and jutting chests, and who hop like sparrows or slither like snakes constitute the second avoidance. Those who are sallow, thin, frail, and weak, cold of body and deficient of *chi*, and whose channels of circulation are out of harmony constitute the third avoidance. Women who are mad, deaf, or dumb, who are lame or blind in one eye, who have scabies, scars, or are insane, who are too fat or too thin, or whose pubic hair is coarse and dense constitute the fourth avoidance. Women who are over forty, have borne many children and whose yin is weak, whose skin is loose and breasts are slack, these are harmful and confer no benefit. This is the fifth avoidance.[8]

But is physical appearance more important than personality in determining a woman's beauty?

In the ancient Taoist myth *Su Nu Ching*, this priority is made clear when the legendary goddess *Su Nu* said the following to the emperor:

A woman's virtue is her inner beauty; her appearance is her outer beauty. First observe her skin and then observe her inner qualities. If a woman's hair is burnt black, her bones large, or her flesh coarse; if she is disproportionately fat or thin, exceptionally tall or short of an unsuitable age, then she will be barren, manly of speech, or violent and abrupt in her actions. Her private parts will be dry and her womb cold. She will leak red or white discharge and have a savage odor. This is extremely harmful to one's *yang-ch'i*.[9]

It is clear that in the old Taoist teachings, a woman's physical appearance was the primary requirement for sexual purposes, while her virtues were secondary. This echoes the Taoist philosophy, which emphasizes an affinity to Nature and regards (Confucian) moral codes as forms of constraint.

The Moral Meaning of Female Beauty in the Confucian Texts

However, it should be noted that the aesthetic objects in Chinese culture are not restricted primarily to objects of perception or physical desire. Their meaning and value have acquired spiritual, social, and material properties. The root of "beauty" in Chinese denotes material benefits and connotes wealth, abundance, longevity, vitality, good reputation, and power. The word also refers to one's behaviors and outstanding abilities of many kinds. The old Confucian teachings in *Analects* and *Mencius* relate beauty to moral practices. The sages are beautiful people, parables and analogies of which are found in *Mencius*. The following is an example:

Mencius said: "The trees of the Niu mountain were once beautiful. But can the mountain be regarded any longer as beautiful since, being in the borders of a big state, the trees have been hewed down with axes and hatchets? . . . Is there not a heart of humanity and righteousness originally existing in man? The way in which he loses his originally good mind is like the way in which the trees are hewed down with axes and hatchets. As trees are cut down day after day, can a mountain retain its beauty?"[10]

Beauty refers to the good qualities and positive dispositions in personality that define a human being. Female beauty refers to those qualities that define a good woman. When beauty is used to describe a moral saint, a righteous minister, or a kind emperor, it has transcendental, moral, and social meanings (that is, to ensure happiness and peace in a country); when it is used to describe a woman, it is subject to social norms. The old Chinese teachings for women in the Han dynasty said, "[A] man is great because of his strength, a woman is beautiful because of her weakness" (from *Nu Jie*). The term "weakness" means humility in human relations. Other words used to describe female beauty are *rou* (gentleness), *ruan* (softness), and *zhi* (innocence), all of which imply the feeling of superiority involved when one is involved with women of these qualities. These women are defined as virtuous women with inner beauty. It is interesting to see how these ideas are developed to extreme measures, praising virtuous women as saints who possess incredible moral courage that manifests the humanity for which the Confucians strive. It should be noted that the moral practice of women in the old Confucian culture stressed the virtues of chastity, piety to their parents-in-law, and marital fidelity. When a woman's behavior conformed to these ideals she was considered to have exceptional inner beauty. The more consistent women were in maintaining these virtues, the more they would be remembered in history. Records of *Lie Nu* (women of admonition) in the Han dynasty reveal how Chinese women in the old Confucian context were willing to die for patriarchal values. Numerous attempts at suicide were made by widows as protests against forced remarriages, as well as by young women whose fiancés passed away after they were engaged. The ideals of love, chastity, and marriage were internalized by women of various dynasties and actually became a type of religious cult, which ensured the success of the Confucian teachings in inculcating values in Chinese women.

We can conclude that in the Chinese tradition, as in other cultures, both the external sexual and inner moral dimensions determine the beauty of a woman, but the presentation and definition of female beauty in the Chinese context (especially under the Confucian influence) generated its own specific forms and meanings. Though Confucianism and Taoism are usually depicted as two conflicting traditions in China, they share a common philosophical background in *Tao* (the Way), and the interplay between the two maintain the so-called super-stable equilibrium of Chinese culture. The notion of female beauty comes from both traditions. The Taoist notion emphasizes natural physicality, while the Confucian beliefs stress behavior control or "inner beauty."

This is best illustrated in the courtesan culture in late Imperial China in the eighteenth and nineteenth centuries. The signification of *meiren* in that era is the result of a long history of adaptation and modification in response to political, cultural, and economic restraints. We will now turn to the development of the feminine ideal in late Imperial China, as represented in the courtesan culture.

The Development and Construction of the Feminine Ideal in Late Imperial China as Represented in the Courtesan Culture: A Case Study

Images of courtesans are various, ambiguous, and even contradictory in late imperial times. Scholars attribute this to class differences and the change of sovereignty from the late Ming dynasty (A.D. 1368–A.D. 1644) to the Qing dynasty (A.D. 1644–A.D. 1911).[11] Courtesans in that era ranged from street and brothel prostitutes who entertained men at home to high-class courtesans who could be commissioned for a trial relationship. Before investigating the ways in which a courtesan's role affected judgments about her beauty as a specific form of female beauty, it is necessary to outline the background of the social world of women at that time.

The General Life Cycle of Women in Late Imperial China

The age of six or seven was an important turning point for both sexes in late Imperial China (late Qing dynasty). For boys, it was time for formal schooling, the displacement from maternal to paternal authority, and the conferral of a formal name. For girls, it was time for foot-binding to begin. The tight painful binding of the toes and wrapping of the feet was intended to keep them the small size deemed desirable for men. This will be discussed later in this essay. Foot-binding, which began in the Sung dynasty (A.D. 960–A.D. 1279), was also a sign of social status, because it meant that the woman concerned was not available for field work or work that required physical mobility. The beginning of a woman's puberty at this age was also signified by special codes of hairstyle. For women this was also the age for formal instruction in cooking and sewing and for decreased mobility outside the home.[12] Marriage, which was arranged by parents, took place at age seventeen or eighteen for women. About 10 percent of marriages were polygamous. Marriage patterns varied according to class, depending on conditions in society, but in general, the Chinese preferred to select brides from families that were slightly lower in social status than their own. Literacy was more likely to be introduced in cities where there would be private tutors for the daughters of the elite. This education was given to prepare women to marry into better families. A lucky woman would marry into a rich family. The bride's family would provide a portion of the family estate as dowry, which would help to give the daughter honor in her husband's household and also encourage favorable treatment from the mother-in-law.[13] An unlucky woman would enter a wealthy household as a maidservant or a child concubine. Even worse was the fate of those sold into prostitution for cash, but if such girls survived and succeeded in the training, their beauty and talent would be valued and marriage or concubinage was possible.

Wives, concubines, and courtesans had to meet different role expectations. First wives and concubines had different duties. The former were the householders while the concubines were the love objects of the husbands

This painting shows the usual activities, decoration, and setting of a
courtesan house in late Imperial China. Note the elaborate dress and
hairstyles of the courtesans and the bound feet of the one engaged in sexual
activity. Anonymous Chinese painting on silk, 18th century. Courtesy of the
Gichner Foundation for Cultural Studies, Washington, D.C.

who helped to procreate for the sake of the big families. The basic responsibilities of wives were to perpetuate the race and to manage the household. They were not asked to be good lovers. Concubines were supposed to please and serve the master by different means, and they enjoyed more intimacy with the master. Courtesans—as distinct from lower-class prostitutes who fulfilled the sexual needs of clients—were literate and skilled in a variety of entertainment arts, and their services were not confined to the sale of sex.

Courtesans of high-class brothels were the only group of women besides the daughters of good families who received literacy training. They were educated because of their profession; literacy and the ability to create beautiful writing were both qualities that were required of a beautiful and cultured courtesan. Though they could produce wonderful literary work, their livelihood did not depend on it. In that era, access to women was unequal: Upper-class men had more access to women than those of the lower classes, and males outnumbered females. Intermarriages were common among the literati and the merchant class, but the elite still frequented high-class brothels to visit courtesans. The many erotic novels, prints, and scrolls that were produced in the era depicted an openly sensual urban culture in the brothels.[14] The beauty, desirable and entertaining performance, and literary talent of popular courtesans qualified them for work in high-class brothels. Literary works in praise of these courtesans therefore suggested a particular set of criteria for female beauty. In fact, some courtesans had even become honorary literati; they occupied the only place in the culture where women could openly socialize with men who were not their husbands. The most prominent among them, usually those at the upper levels of the profession, enjoyed a level of renown unattainable by any other group of women in society. To the literati, these courtesans were ideal lovers, objects of adoration and admiration, and sources of inspiration.

Though courtesanship stood entirely outside the social building blocks of kinship in Chinese society and so did not pose a real threat to the kinship structure, the profession was built securely into the structure of a Chinese society that was at once very hierarchical and surprisingly fluid. However, in the ethos of Confucian culture, courtesans could not escape the taint of notoriety.[15] Even the most famous of courtesans aspired to leave the brothel, to be purchased and "redeemed" into "respectability," and to be taken as a concubine by a wealthy or talented client.[16] Traditionally, Chinese women in their old age were entirely dependent on males and their close relatives.

The Depiction of Female Beauty in Courtesan Culture in
Late Imperial China: Painting and Writing

Nudity was a taboo in Confucian culture, which explains why it was not a common subject in Chinese art. The depiction of female bodies in traditional paintings and sculptures was linear, simple, and devoid of sensuous elements, but more details could be found in poetry and literature, especially in erotic literature. A good example is the collection of 200 linear wood-block prints related to the story and characters of the famous seventeenth-century erotic novel *Jinpingmei*. However, crude portraits of nude women were also found in paintings in albums, on porcelain bottles, and on glasses circulated in low-class brothels for the entertainment of customers in the late Qing dynasty. Literature provided more detailed and sophisticated discussions of the aesthetics of the female body, especially in relationship to courtesan culture.

Interesting analyses based on class differences could be made. Lower-class brothel culture tended to depict *Changji* (a special term that referred to prostitutes rather than courtesans, *Jinu*, which was a more decent and ambiguous term) in paintings or writings in ways that illustrated the Taoist criteria. In "pillow books" or "albums" circulated in the brothels, female bodies were quite often engaged in sexual activities, demonstrating various sexual positions to arouse desire. These activities were usually conducted in the harmonious and tranquil mood advocated by Taoists, who believed that sex was a joyful journey aimed at a sacred experience. Thus, women participating in the act of love in the paintings appeared submissive and cooperative. Late Qing erotica also reflected the criteria mentioned in classical Taoist texts for the best female bodies for sex. Some of the criteria recommended that bodies should be young, unmarried, and under thirty; they should not be full bosomed but amply fleshed, with silken hair and small eyes. Visible ribs and hair below the groin area (like leg hair) were undesirable, pubic hair should be sparse and smooth; and women should have slender limbs, soft flesh, and pure white pale skin of an elegant texture.

In quite a number of the erotic paintings of this era, male characters examined the female vulva, *yin*, which was so named because it was seen as the repository of the elemental force of *yin*. Other parts of the female body, including the breasts, received less attention and appreciation, which explained why the woman's breasts were usually bound and flat in the paintings. Facial beauty was also not of great concern, as it was not considered the center for sexual pleasure.

Foot-binding, the so-called cult of the golden lotus, is a custom depicted in late Qing erotica that most clearly illustrates attitudes toward sexual pleasure. This sexual adoration of miniature female feet represents a "Confucian patriarchal aesthetic perversion." Until the late Imperial Era, bound feet were the main feature of a *meiren*. The practice enhanced the sexual appeal of women and the intensity of sexual pleasure, but it also controlled the mobility and behavior of Confucian women and tied them to their homes. The late Qing documents contained a detailed grading system in nine categories that the literati used to evaluate a woman's bound feet. The best grade was given to small, fleshy, soft, and "boneless" female feet. Van Gulick once pointed out that it was easier for a man to lose control when they got hold of a woman's bound feet than when they got hold of her body.[17]

The erotica of this period also elaborated on the role of the golden lotus in sexual activities. Miniature feet were considered to be the sexiest part of a woman's body because they were originally designed by the dominating Confucians to act as constraints on a woman's behavior. Foot-binding soon developed into the main object of visual pleasure and tool of sexual hedonism. Beautiful women were attractive mainly because of the ways they walked and carried their bodies on bound feet. However, this tradition started to change in the latter days of the Qing dynasty. The literati and other courtesan customers of that era commented that a thin waist rather than bound feet was the fashionable trait among courtesans.[18] Later, under the influence of Western paintings and the growth of the export market, some Chinese erotic paintings in the nineteenth century portrayed prostitutes very differently. They were kissed and their breasts were fondled; their bodies were usually full-bosomed and their faces expressive. Western erotic images were supplemented with the traditional Chinese linear way of drawing. According to the detailed manuals for training *changji* in nineteenth-century China compiled by some female managers of brothels, the requirements for being popular were as follows: *Se* (beauty), which focused on artificial beauty, manners, and posture; *Yi* (art skill), which included the skill of keeping the master's company; *Qing* (emotion and affection), which demanded disguising one's true emotions with apparent sincerity; and *Bian-tai* (variation of attitudes), which required the ability to be flexible and lively in dealings with customers. These manuals reflected very different standards in evaluating courtesans in low- and high-class groups. Serious and genuine displays of emotion and poetic talent, in addition to the flirtatious wit expected of all courtesans, were requirements of the high-class courtesan.[19] We can trace the images of this group back to records earlier than the late Qing era.

At the upper level of the profession, good portraits of courtesans depicted their external appearance with most of the characteristics that satisfied the old criteria of *meiren*, but these were not the most important features. Courtesans were portrayed in a much more elegant and subtle way with simple linear brush strokes that ended in beautiful literary images. Because of the special function they served and the particular culture they lived in, there were extra requirements for a courtesan in order for her to be judged as great or beautiful. Elaborate dresses and hairstyles with flowery hairpins were necessary, in addition to bodily features and the bound feet. Detailed descriptions of dressing had always been a part of the literati's work. Since an upper-class courtesan's service was not confined to the sale of sex, the literature related to high-class brothels that flourished in late Imperial China contained few direct descriptions of the sexual performance of courtesans or the experience of the clients. This literature contained instead a detailed record of the ways the courtesans dressed and the decoration of their residence. Emphasis was put on their postures, the atmosphere of their meetings, and their artistic talent. As mentioned, most of the popular courtesans received good literary training and had the talent to write and paint. They collaborated with their elite customers to create literary works, and they read their work in public. One could say that the inner positive dimensions of a beautiful courtesan were her artistic talent and her sentimentality and emotional loyalty to her literati lovers. Thus, in the representations of high-class courtesans, Confucian criteria were applied to this group in contrast to the Taoist sexual fervor. Some of them could and did become powerful symbols of morality and virtue and were memorialized and praised by their literati fans. A great courtesan was evaluated according to her personality, talent, sensitivity, strength of character, and ability to sustain passionate and declared devotion to the man she loved.

Art historians and literary critics have analyzed the literary output and the treatment of women in late Imperial China. Wu Hung pointed out in his brilliant study that systematic accounts of *meiren* did not come into existence till the late Ming and early Qing dynasties.[20] The dominant models in literary and artistic productions, like those circulated in pinups of Qing court painting and popular New Year prints, seemed to conform to the standard, impersonal female imagery in late Imperial China. But there were also deliberate variations produced in creative ways by individual literati for personal as well as social purposes in the same period of time. Beauty that reflected courtesan culture was a good example of this kind of variation. It is different from the standard of female beauty on these New

Year prints. Courtesan images had assumed particular meanings in their own cultural contexts.

Wu correctly pointed out that according to popular writings and famous paintings in the seventeenth and eighteenth centuries, Chinese female beauty was represented within a feminine environment. Such representations were replete with details of decorative items and architectural layouts. Individual items offered static features while the architectural layouts provided the feminine environment with dynamic spatial or temporal structures and points of view. According to Wu, "feminine space" refers to a real or fictional place that is perceived, imagined, and represented as a woman. It takes figures and objects as its constituent elements, creating a spatial entity, an artificial world. These environmental elements usually were the following: particular kinds of buildings, paths, railings, trees, flowers, plants, rocks, decorative objects, painting, and calligraphy; personal attributes like clothes, ornaments, makeup, and standardized facial and bodily features; and, finally, tableaus of women engaged in typical female activities, surrounded by maids. This kind of depiction appeared long before the Qing dynasty and formed a tradition. Portraits of women produced by famous court painters like Chou Fang in the Tang dynasty already carried the structure of this kind of feminine space, though not as elaborate. A typical depiction was of groups of beautiful women playing with butterflies or engaging in various leisurely activities inside a garden. Typically, this style of portraits of women was painted on handscrolls of the Tang period, although the genre achieved its most extreme form in the early Qing period, when the lifestyle and culture of high-class courtesans, including the iconographic features of their beauty and their place in society, became a firmly established part of Chinese culture.[21]

How can one interpret the function of this feminine environment and its relation to female beauty? As mentioned, Wu suggests the concept of feminine space as a totalizing entity. In Wu's analysis, a beautiful woman was essentially the sum of all the visible forms one expected to find in her space, and that all the pre-arranged components of this environment were actually identical features of herself. One identified a woman as a *meiren* not by recognizing her face but by surveying her courtyard, room, clothes, her servants, and her frozen expression and gesture. In other words, what one found in her and in her space were numerous signifiers. On a deeper level of reading, a beautiful woman was by definition idealized, and this explained why the appearance of Chinese beauties was epitomized in classical texts by her star-bright eyes, willow-leaf eyebrows, cloud-like hair, and snow-white bosom.[22]

The "Manual of Beautiful Women" by Xu Zhen, written around the mid-seventeenth century, was a popular text to which art critics used to refer when discussing female beauty. Xu composed the iconography of an archetypal beautiful and talented woman based mainly on the lifestyles of courtesans and concubines of his time. Wu had produced a faithful translation of the ten-part iconography, including physical appearance, style, skills, activities, dwelling, seasons and moments, adornment, auxiliary objects, food, and special interests. It was a good illustration of the idealized feminine space suggested by Wu that reflected the feminine ideal in that era as follows:

1. *Physical appearance:* Cicada forehead; apricot lips; rhinoceros-horn teeth; creamy breasts; eyebrows like faraway mountains; glances like waves of autumn water; lotus-petal face; cloud-like hairdo; feet like bamboo shoots carved in jade; fingers like white shoots of grass; willow waist; delicate steps as though walking on lotus blossoms; neither fat nor thin; appropriate height.

2. *Style:* Casting her shadow on a half-drawn curtain; leaving her footsteps on green moss; leaning against a railing while waiting for moonrise; holding a pipa-guitar at an angle; glancing back before departure; throwing out an artful, captivating smile; singing and becoming fatigued from dancing.

3. *Skills:* Playing the lute; changing poetry; playing weiqi-chess; playing kickball; copying ancient calligraphy before a pond; embroidering; weaving brocade; playing the vertical flute; playing dominoes; comprehending musical pitches and rhymes; swinging; playing the "double six" game.

4. *Activities:* Taking care of orchids; preparing tea; burning incense; looking at the reflection of the moon in a gold basin; watching flowers on a spring morning; composing poems about willow catkins; catching butterflies; fashioning clothes; harmonizing the five tastes [fine cooking]; painting her fingernails with red paint; teaching a mynah to recite poems; comparing posies collected on Duanwu day.

5. *Dwelling:* A gold room; a jade-storied gallery; a door curtain made of pearls; a screen inlaid with mother-of-pearl; an ivory bed; a lotus-blossom pink bed-net; a curtain of kingfisher feathers for the inner chamber.

6. *Seasons and moments:* Flowers blossoming in the Golden Valley Garden; bright moon over a painted pleasure-boat; snow reflected on a pearled curtain; silver candles above a tortoise-shell banquet table; fragrant plants in the setting sun; raindrops pelting banana leaves.

7. *Adornment:* A pearl shirt; an eight-piece embroidered skirt; a raw silk sleeveless dress; a pair of "phoenix-head" shoes; rhinoceros-horn hairpins; hairpins made of "cold-preventive" rhinoceros horns; jade pendants; a "love birds" belt; pearl and gem earrings; head ornaments made of kingfisher feathers; gold "phoenix" head ornaments; embroidered tap pants.

8. *Auxiliary objects:* An ivory comb; a "water-chestnut flower" mirror; a jade mirror stand; a rabbit-fur writing brush; patterned letter-paper; an inkstone from Duanxi; a "green silk" *qin*-lute; a jade vertical flute; a pure silk fan; rare flowers; a volume of the *Odes with Master Mao's Commentaries* [*Maoshi*]; a rhyming book; collections of love poetry including the *New Songs from the Jade Terrace* [*Yutai xinyong*] and the *Fragrant Dressing Case* [*Xianglian ji*]; witty maidservants; a gold incense burner; ancient vases; jade boxes; rare perfume.

9. *Food:* Seasonal fruits; fresh lichee; dried fish; "kid" wine; various kinds of delicious wine; delicacies from hills and seas; famous tea from Songluo, Jingshan, and Yangxian; various kinds of pickles in clever shapes.

10. *Special interests:* Leaning drunkenly on her lover's shoulder; taking a noon bath in fragrant water; laughing seductively beside the pillow; secretly exchanging glances; picking up a pellet to shoot a yellow bird; showing slight jealousy.[23]

The content of this kind of *meiren* manual was supposed to have originated from the places where courtesan culture flourished around the late Ming and the Qing dynasties, like the southern cities Suzhou and Hangzhou. There are reasons to believe that the idealized woman described and composed in the writings and paintings of the culture was an exaggeration and idealization of some of the high-class brothel scenes in these places.

There were a number of significant coded images suggested in this representation. First, readers were reminded that such portraits of beautiful women were fictions and idealizations. The linear methods in the case of paintings were used to represent the "types" of ideal female face and body instead of individual and particular ones. The use of the metaphor of weeping willow (*liu*) had become a norm in this method to portray the "willow-branch" waist (*liuyao*) and "willow-leaf " eyebrows (*liumei*) of female features that were regarded as beautiful. Even the background and stories of the female characters portrayed were stereotyped. The *meiren* was always anonymous, enclosed in an isolated world, the object of the gaze of her male painter or author. Wu presented a good summary:

> [T]he woman in a courtesan-concubine painting is nameless and often appears in an opulent interior or a garden setting. She may be engaged in leisurely activities, but more frequently she is alone, either looking at her own reflection in a mirror or gazing at a pair of cats, birds, or butterflies. In both cases, the subtext is that she, as an "amorous beauty," is thinking about an absent lover and suffering from "spring longing." Differing from a portrayal of a palace lady, however, a "courtesan-concubine" picture often delivers a bolder erotic message. Although the painted woman rarely exhibits her sexuality openly, her sexual allure and accessibility are represented through certain gestures (such as touching her cheek and toying with her belt) and sexual symbols (such as particular kinds of flowers, fruits, and objects) that a Ming or Qing spectator would have had no difficulty understanding.[24]

Because a beautiful courtesan or concubine had to possess intellectual and artistic talents, stationery for calligraphy, books, and poetry were typically part of the ideal feminine space. This detail and the bolder erotic message of such representations reflected the special role of courtesans as ideal lovers of men and as the idealized fantasies of female beauty in the eyes of men. Courtesans satisfied both the physical desire and spiritual demand of their clients, needs that wives were not supposed to fulfill.

Another interpretaion of *meiren* painting and writing in late Imperial China was given to Qing court productions patronized by Manchu governors like Yongzheng in the eighteenth century. A form of exotic "Chineseness" was supposedly projected into and identified with the feminine space of these works. The vulnerability, passivity, excessive refinement, and the melancholic expression illustrated by the beautiful female characters were read as symbols of a lost and subordinated country that was waiting for the power of the new foreign ruler. The feminine ideal represented in late Imperial China that basically followed traditional standards (with certain elaborations) was said to have been reinvented to fulfill the desire and fantasy of the ruling patrons.[25] But aside from the particular political implications, what were the general meanings of this popular genre of female beauty in this era? How did the construct relate to the economic, class structure, and cultural factors of that time?

Deconstructing the Feminine Ideal of Courtesan Culture in Late Imperial China

I have already analyzed the transformation of the portraits of the courtesan from the late Ming to the Qing dynasties, as well as the polarization in the courtesan world into lower-class prostitutes and talented and prominent courtesans during this period. When China was taken over by the Manchurians, the political context changed the nature of the literati's identification with courtesan life. The lifestyle of famous courtesans was once said to symbolize freedom, self-creation, heroic action, and the embodiment of elite cultural ideals of the Ming dynasty. The late Ming courtesans used to be presented as the epitome of elite culture, but after the Manchurian conquest, symbols of courtesans came to represent the loss of these ideals.[26] The busy brothel area around Jiangnan and Nanjing was completely destroyed by the Qing court in the seventeenth century. Brothels resumed their business later, but in contrast to the late Ming era, prominent literati seldom published poems or essays celebrating their liaisons with well-known courtesans or took them into their homes as loving concubines. Instead, these beautiful women were seen as objects of pity. The exploitation and loneliness of the courtesan paralleled the suffering of the literati under the Manchurian sovereign; the courtesan had become a symbol of the literati's "lost world."[27] The following example, which was given by Paul Ropp in his discussion of ambiguous images of courtesan culture in late Imperial China, is an excerpt from a representative courtesan song written by a popular poet in the early nineteenth century, entitled "Sighing through the Night's Five Watches":

> With sly flirtatious glances
> > I had to encourage the guests to stay.
> When the night drum sounds the second watch,
> > The moon casts a cold shadow on the window.
> How pitiful, entertaining guests is so difficult;
> > How annoying
> > To have to talk with every guest who comes and goes.
> Tobacco and tea I serve with my own hands;
> > Maintaining friendly smiles all the while.
> What is truly frightening:
> > To encounter drunken guests at the banquet table;
> > "Ill-fated beauty" does not begin to capture the shame.

> How many days until I can escape this mire? (My God!)
>   Yet for the sake of money I have to endure it all
>
> Sadly singing, I enter the curtained bed
> Accompanying my guests;
> No matter whether young or old, he becomes my partner;
> No passion for me in this lover's tryst;
> Clouds and rain are all his doing;
> He wants to crush my flower's heart to pieces;
> We toss and turn, my agony is endless. . . .
>
> I can only
>   Muster all my strength to seem warm and compliant;
>   Pressing my cheeks against his;
>   Whispering sweet and flattering words;
>   Exhausting every bit of my cunning;
>   To swindle him out of his money. (My God!)
>   Even with the most disgusting of men,
>   I dare show no sign of resistance. . . .[28]

The poem revealed a poverty-stricken economy on the one hand, and a change of attitude regarding the life of courtesans on the other. It was well known that the Qing government reinforced orthodox neo-Confucianism while ruling China, as previous foreign rulers had done in the country's long history. This reinforcement aroused prejudices and negative attitudes toward courtesans. Throughout the Qing dynasty, it was difficult for courtesans to join the circle of those of refined letters, and the image of the courtesan changed from a member of a cultured elite to a mere erotic subject or object of hardship and misfortune, as this poem illustrates. The Confucian paternalistic and condescending views of courtesans reflected the literati's own sense of inadequacy and failure vis-à-vis the courtesans. The self-love and self-pity of these intellectuals were projected into the romanticized, pitiful, but beautiful images of courtesans. In the nineteenth century, lower-class erotic portraits of prostitutes became popular once more in the brothel districts, which flourished again later in the era albeit without their previous prestigious position.

The bodily images of the Chinese courtesan illustrate Christine Battersby's thesis that biology is a mode of discourse that cannot be separated from other symbolic codes and practices of the social networks of power. Beauty refers not to "facts" but is socially and historically constructed.[29] As Susan Suleiman has said, the question of women's bodies and women's sexuality has implications both for politics and literature, and the production of verbal constructs about them in some ways reflects and creates these relations.[30] These Chinese courtesan images also illustrate very well Naomi Wolf's analysis of the beauty myth. Wolf said beauty is actually composed of emotional distance, politics, finance, and sexual repression.[31] Ideal courtesan images in the late Qing dynasty were projections of the psychological disappointment of the literati of that era. The pretty but pitiful female images were also formed in relation to the political and ideological suppression by the Manchurian government with the aid of powerful Confucian orthodoxy. The life of courtesans working in both high- and low-class brothels had become hard because of the anti-prostitution campaign organized by the new rulers. Courtesans were no longer able to dress themselves to express ideals of beauty; they needed to dress their bodies to sell sex, most of the time against their will. Under both the Manchurian rulers and the male literati authors, courtesans demonstrated that beauty was not about women but about men's institutions and institutional power. Moreover, the representations of women in writings and paintings prove Wolf's statement that qualities a given period deems beautiful in women are merely symbols of the female behavior that period considers desirable; beauty standards are always actually about prescribing behavior rather than about appearance.

However, the feminine ideal in the courtesan culture of the late Ming and Qing dynasties also contradicts some of Wolf's analyses, whose frame of reference is in the contemporary West. Wolf said that when women show character, they are not desirable; also, that a beautiful heroine is a contradiction in terms, since heroism is about individuality that is interesting and ever-changing, while "beauty" is generic, boring, and inert.[32] The opposite is true in the case of the courtesan. Beautiful courtesan figures in late Imperial China were constructed as heroines with unique talent, vital personality, and free will. Wolf said "beauty" is amoral, that the moral lessons of male culture exclude "beauties." On the contrary, the devoted passion and loyalty of a courtesan to her male lover (who sometimes symbolized the country or its ruler) could be approved-of moral merits in the Confucian sense. Finally, Wolf said that Western culture stereotypes women to fit the myth by flattening the feminine into beauty-without-intelligence or intelligence-without-beauty; that women are allowed a mind or a body but not both.[33] Again, artistic and intellectual talent were not only treasured but were also regarded as necessary and positive in the upper level of the late Ming and Qing dynasty courtesan cultures. These contradictions only affirm that the notion of beauty is a particular cultural, social, and historical construction.

The Notion of Female Beauty in Communist China

However, Naomi Wolf's deconstruction of *The Beauty Myth* could also be applied to the general notion of female beauty in Communist China in the 1990s. The development of the feminine ideal in China after the Qing dynasty was as confusing as the modern history of the country. It is difficult to trace the notion of beauty during the first half of the twentieth century when the country was undergoing endless civil wars and the disastrous Sino-Japanese War. Discussion of beauty during this period was restrictedly led by a few elite groups of women of distinct political and social classes. After the Communists took over China in 1949, female beauty was displaced from external appearance to the love of labor, the party, and the nation. In the first thirty years of Communist China, women nationwide had their hair either tied up or cut, and the plain party uniforms suppressed every individual character or taste. Women at that time devoted their energy to economic and political practices and reforms. The plain look was to ensure that women were ready for action, and it was brought to its climax during the cultural revolution in the 1960s when nearly all the women in the country wore only blue and gray with no makeup or accessories. The only "fashion" was the shapeless socialist look, and the only exception were the brides who wore red and had their hair done for their wedding. At that time, external beauty was not important; what was important was the inner beauty of women who sacrificed themselves according to Communist ideals for the nation, the people, and the party. Women with flamboyant looks would get themselves into trouble; they would be accused of succumbing to bourgeois ideologies.

Only when China opened its door in the late 1970s did its women brighten up their appearance again. The influx of foreign economic investments brought famous brands of European fashion and cosmetics into the country. The flourishing commercial market brought new trends and colors to big cities like Beijing, Shanghai, and southern Canton areas near Hong Kong. Consumer products for women filled the country's markets in the 1980s. (It seems to be a common phenomenon that women's fashion is always the fastest sector to develop when a developing country takes off economically.) Furthermore, when the country's power structure became fluid and economic classes appeared again, fashion and looks became the necessary symbols of identity and classification. Mainland women urgently wanted a new look. Advertisements for female products were everywhere, and foreign magazines were imported and translated to promote new female images from Western culture. Because of the urge to modernize, to

羊毛织花外衣，内衬缀以褶饰的上衣及斜纹剪裁
及膝裙，属柏罗娜"Allan Chiu"赵彦纶设计系列。
发型顾问：Orent 4
化妆：Nina Ricci

A Shanghai model wearing fashion designed by a Hong Kong designer who closely follows international trends.

correct the backward past, and to forget the "wrong" history of the cultural revolution in the 1960s, contemporary discussions of female beauty in China closely followed those in the West. Women fashion models who wear European brands are the new models of female beauty.

The traditional standards of external beauty are less emphasized, and the "inner" dimensions of beauty such as moral efforts and intellectual qualities are only mentioned in the party's propaganda or in some "politically correct" publications. These publications continue some of the traditional principles of beauty: for instance, that external beauty originates from an inner beauty that aims at benevolence, commitment to one's community, self-improvement, the goal of developing a unique personality, and the idea that aesthetics is the natural principle that prevents exaggeration and the distortion of reality. However, the traditional discussion has become merely empty talk and is taken for granted. Instead, city women in China put up photos and posters of top fashion models at home and wish they could be like them. Their appearance attracts them. The following are some physical standards of beauty promoted in Shanghai women's magazines that exemplify fashion models in the contemporary Western world:[34]

(a) *Physical appearance:*

    (i) *Height:* ideally 1.74 to 1.8 meters, a little shorter than Western models.

    (ii) *Proportion:* the lower part of the body from the belly button should be longer than the upper part. The lower thigh should be a little longer than the upper thigh with the shape of the leg slim and slender. The difference between the size of the breast and the waist should be 22 to 24 cm while that between the breast and the hip should be equal or 2 to 4 cm. The shoulder should be broad enough to form a V shape at the back. The ideal shape of the head is oval; it should join the neck to form the shape of a question mark. The distance between two eyes should be one eye in length; the length of the ear and the nose should be close; upper and lower lips should be equal in thickness and red in color.

    (iii) *Others:* Hair should be smooth, healthy, and dark. Limbs should be slender. The eyebrows should be longer than the eye and tidily trimmed. Skin should be bright and soft.

(b) *Temperament*:

This is the only aspect which considers inner beauty. It is said
that the temperament of a woman is the sum of her psychological traits and her behavior. A woman's cultivation influences
her gestures, posture, and verbal expressions. The difference
from the past discussion is that now these standards have nothing to do with Confucian morality; the rationale for them rests
solely in lay psychology.

(c) *Performing ability*:

It is said that bodily movement should be rhythmic and form a
special style of one's own. It should be noted that the traditional
Chinese feminine way of movement has been replaced completely by Western forms—nothing traditional remains in the
movement style of the models though their physical bodies are
still Chinese.

Fashion is said to symbolically provide individuals with a mechanism
for detaching themselves from the past, to allow people to cope with the
present in an orderly way by helping to define what is appropriate, and to
prepare for the immediate future by providing a sense of anticipation or a
clue to emerging issues and tastes.[35] Fashion also provides consolation to
individuals because it promotes self-esteem and the language of identity. It
explodes out of enthusiasm; the fashion codes of identity always represent
leisure, fun, youth, health, open-mindedness, playfulness, energy, independence, courage, and subjectivity, no matter how controversial it could
be. Women project their self-images and fantasies onto fashion models
who from time to time appear fast, carefree, naughty, sharp, discriminat-
ing, balanced, sophisticated, coquettish, and ingenuous. With the above
explanatory notes and the historical and political contexts of China in
mind, it should not be difficult to understand why contemporary city wom-
en in China regard fashion models as a new frame of reference for beauty.
After the long turmoil of economic poverty, backward living environment,
and the turbulence of the Cultural Revolution in China, fashion works as
a form of hope for a country hungry for various forms of reform and mod-
ernization. Women turn to fashion for new identities and power. As Roland
Barthes has said, the multiplication of persons in a single being is always
considered by fashion as an index of power.[36] On the surface, the new social
role Chinese women attained in the Communist regime seems to be more

equal than ever to men because of the value of their labor contribution to the country. In fact, state policies are always unfavorable to them. Fashion may further enhance women's voice in society, which will threaten the feudal Chinese constraints on women (by liberating women's body via fashionable looks and new notions of beauty); the idea of returning to a backward Communist China (by portraying modern Western designs); and the submissive attitudes toward the "People's" Republic of China with the mandated collective behaviors (by choosing new and foreign ways of dressing and gestures). One can even interpret the new look as a silent revolution and a struggle for new identities. This is not passive but an active construction that is being initiated today by Chinese women themselves. A fashionable appearance projects the image that they are fully aware of their femininity, that they are free and sovereign, and that they make their own decisions. All these explain why women fashion models have become new feminine icons in contemporary China.

The construction is also made possible by external business investments and related promotions. Consumer culture, advertisements, popular press, television, and films all provide many stylized images of the body. It is easy then to detect the contradiction and confusion involved: the illusion of women's image built by the cosmetics, garment, and diet industries—or the so-called beauty myth essential for economic markets—is mixing with and contradicting the real working ability, growing intelligence, and fluid individualistic characteristics of contemporary Chinese women. Whereas the ability and appearance of a beautiful woman could have been in great harmony with broader social values in the past, as illustrated in the courtesan tradition, now commercial interests compete to create and define these two dimensions of women, as feminists opine.[37] Although Chinese women today are developing new self-confidence, they do not seem to be aware of the fact that one can become a slave of the fashion industry, which merely repeats the bodily constraints of past times in a new form.

NOTES

1. Moira Gatens, *Imaginary Bodies* (London and New York: Routledge, 1996), pp. 8–9.

2. Christine Battersby, *The Phenomenal Woman: Feminist Metaphysics and the Patterns of Identity* (Cambridge, U.K.: Polity Press, 1998), pp. 19–20.

3. Douglas Wile, *Art of the Bedchamber: The Chinese Sexual Yoga Classics including Women's Solo Meditation Texts* (Albany: State University of New York Press, 1992), p. 46.

4. Chinese source from "Yu-fang Chih-yao" ("Essentials of the Jade Chamber") in Te-hui Yeh, *Shuang-mei ching-an ts'ung-shu* (*Shadow of the Double Plum Tree Collection*) (Changsha, 1903), translated in Wile, *Art of the Bedchamber*, p. 100.

5. Chinese source from "Yu-fang pi-chueh" ("Secrets of the Jade Chamber") in Yeh, 1903, translated in Wile, *Art of the Bedchamber*, p. 106.

6. Ibid., p. 106, note 61.

7. Ibid., p. 106.

8. Hsi-hsien Teng, "Tzu-chin kuang-yao ta-hsien hsiu-chen yen-i" ("Exposition of Cultivating the Essence by the Great Immortal of the Purple Gold Splendor"), in R. H. Van Gulik, *Erotic Colour Prints of the Ming Period* (Tokyo: Privately printed, 1951), translated in Wile, *Art of the Bedchamber*, p. 137.

9. Chinese source from "Su Nu miao lun" ("The Wondrous Discourse of Su Nu"), translated in Wile, *Art of the Bedchamber*, p. 128.

10. Wing-Tsit Chan, translator and compiler, *A Source Book in Chinese Philosophy* (Princeton: Princeton University Press, 1963), p. 56.

11. Paul S. Ropp, "Ambiguous Images of Courtesan Culture in Late Imperial China," in *Writing Women in Late Imperial China*, ed. Ellen Widmer and Kang-I Sun Chang (Stanford: Stanford University Press, 1997), p. 17.

12. Susan Naquin and Evelyn Rawski, *Chinese Society in the Eighteenth Century* (New Haven: Yale University Press, 1987), p. 80.

13. Ibid., p. 110.

14. Ibid., p. 109.

15. Widmer and Chang, *Writing Women*, p. 43.

16. Ibid., pp. 18–19.

17. R. H. Van Gulick, *Sexual Life in Ancient China*, translated by Li and Guo (Shanghai: Shanghai People's Press, 1990), p. 287.

18. Shu Nu Wang, *ChungGuo Changji Shi* (*History of Chinese Prostitutes*) (Shanghai: ShengHuo Press, 1935), pp. 312–314.

19. Widmer and Chang, *Writing Women*, pp. 22–23.

20. Wu Hung, "Beyond Stereotypes: The Twelve Beauties in Qing Court Art and the Dreams of the Red Chamber," in Widmer and Chang, *Writing Women*, pp. 306–365.

21. Ibid., p. 326.

22. See Wu's analysis of Wei Yong's literary work, "Delight in Adornment" (flourished 1643–1654), in Widmer and Chang, *Writing Women*, pp. 325–326.

23. See Wu's translation of *Tanji congshu* (first published by Zhuo Wang and Chao Zhang in 1695, republished in Shanghai by Guji Chubanshe, 1993, pp. 141–142) in Widmer and Chang, *Writing Women*, pp. 438–439.

24. Widmer and Chang, *Writing Women*, p. 350.

25. Ibid., p. 363.

26. Ibid., pp. 19–29.

27. Ibid., p. 29.

28. The Chinese name of the poem is "Tan wugeng." It was written by Guangsheng Hua in the early nineteenth century and translated by Paul S. Ropp in Widmer and Chang, *Writing Women*, pp. 39–40.

29. Battersby, *Phenomenal Woman*, pp. 20–21.

30. Susan R. Suleiman, ed., *The Female Body in Western Culture: Contemporary Perspectives* (Cambridge, Mass., and London: Harvard University Press, 1986), p. 7.

31. Naomi Wolf, *The Beauty Myth: How Images of Beauty Are Used against Women* (New York: Anchor Books, 1992), pp. 13–14.

32. Ibid., pp. 59–60.

33. Ibid., p. 60.

34. Excerpt cited from *Fashion Show Artistry* (Shanghai: China Textile University Press, 1997), p. 29.

35. Susan Kaiser, *The Social Psychology of Clothing* (New York: Macmillan, 1990), p. 488.

36. Roland Barthes, *The Fashion System* (New York: Hill and Wang, 1983), pp. 254–256.

37. As Naomi Wolf pointed out, where modern women are growing, moving, and expressing their individuality, "beauty" is by definition inert, timeless, and generic. Wolf, *Beauty Myth*, pp. 16–17.

9. From the Crooked Timber of Humanity, Beautiful Things Can Be Made

*From the crooked timber of humanity no
straight thing can ever be made.*[1]

—Immanuel Kant

Looking at a Picture, Looking at a Person

My friend sits before me. On the wall behind her the reproduction of a Picasso painting hangs. Although familiar to me, the painting remains riveting. My gaze returns repeatedly to follow the contours of the pictured face, a flat, flesh-colored horizontally oriented oval dominated by prominent lips and one tremendous egg-like eye, an unceasingly fascinating visual site.

But my look does not similarly linger on the face of my friend. She was born with a type of dwarfism: in addition to lower limbs too short for walking, she has the physiognomy characteristic of this condition. In appearance startlingly similar to the one in the painting, my friend's face is a fleshly broad-foreheaded triangle, flattened so that it seems much like a picture plane, dominated by enormous doe eyes.[2] When her face is in profile, one eye appears to occupy almost the whole upper half of her head, very much like the immense eye in the profiled painted face.

I am drawn to dwell on the face in the painting, yet my eyes avert from the real face, even though it is closer to me. I regard the beauty of the painting, glance elsewhere in the room, anywhere other than at the face of my friend. Although both are in the room facing me, in an important sense the person and the painting are not equally visible to me.

By looking away rather than seeing my friend, I make her invisible. While doing so, I condemn myself for joining in a visual practice that sustains the stigma our culture imposes on impaired bodies. Not being

197

Picasso, Maya with a Doll, *1938. Musée Picasso, Paris. Courtesy of the estate of Pablo Picasso.*

looked at isolates people with physical anomalies, forestalling interpersonal connectedness and distancing them from social participation. Yet despite my self-indictment, my gaze is influenced not by where moral reflection advises me to look, but by the proximity of an object I don't want to see. Beauty matters, as does its absence, for moral as well as for aesthetic reasons.

Attractive Appearance and Repulsive Reality

Why is it commonplace for us to contemplate distorted depictions of faces with eagerness and enjoyment, but to be repelled by real people whose physiognomies resemble the depicted ones? More generally, what

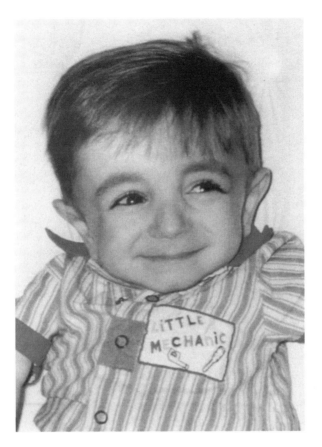

Child with osteogenesis imperfecta. Courtesy of OI Foundation.

makes perceiving pictured physically anomalous individuals so different from perceiving physically anomalous people themselves? My raising these questions has a twofold aim.

First, I aim to adumbrate aesthetic theory so as to better account for what attracts us to odd visual configurations when we take them to be artistically amended renditions of humans rather than to be actual deformed humans. A complicating factor is the lack of clarity about why some peculiarities of the human body disturb us while other, equally extreme conditions, are admired precisely because they are rare. To illustrate, we have a culture that promotes the attractiveness of certain kinds of corporeally irregular people—for instance, individuals so unusually thin as to appear emaciated; but this is no universal standard of human beauty. Polynesians admired very portly individuals. It is curious that we view corpulent people as deformed, while in some other cultures it is ultra-slim people who are regarded as defective. This kind of variation suggests that the standard against which we assess the pleasingness of any human's corporeal configuration is a constructed, or at least a culturally mediated, rather than a natural one.

Further, why, in our own culture, are kindred artificial appendages to the body regarded quite differently? Today young people admire, and many older people accept, the decorative value of noses, lips, and brows hung with rows of metal rings. In contrast, both young and old recoil at the sight of a metal hook worn to replace a missing hand. Flaccid plastic fingers made to imitate fleshly ones appear less offensive, appended to a wrist, than a functional crescent of steel. What contextualizing criteria contribute to making some corporeal configurations (for instance, brows bristling with metal rings) attractive and other (for instance, arms dangling metal hooks) repulsive?

In answering this question, I will suggest how we can theorize human beauty, as we do beauty in art, so as to savor, rather than rebuff, novelty, disproportionateness, and even crookedness in the human shape. For anomaly to present as originality rather than deviance requires a context in which we theorize the connectedness of successors with their heritage. Consequently, the relevant contextual elements will be those that influence the prescriptiveness with which individuals are obliged to conform to their predecessors.[3] Parenthetically, the understanding gained will help elucidate recent claims of disability culture promoters, who prescribe the appreciation of impaired and/or mechanically assisted bodies, urging that they are aesthetically superior to "normal" ones.[4]

Second, I also will explore whether the aesthetic process that permits—indeed, that propels—our attraction to portrayed human anomalies can be expanded so as to offset the devalued social positioning of real people whose physiognomic or other physical features are anomalous. The ensuing inquiry thus will consider whether aesthetic interventions can mitigate the deleterious influence that the deformation of an individual's personal appearance usually has on her capacity for attaining social connectedness. To enlarge our aesthetic responsiveness to real people in the way(s) this study suggests would enlarge our moral capacities.

Aesthetic Morality

Establishing the possibility that aesthetic sensibility can enhance, rather than confuse, moral conduct is important. In his influential essay "The Work of Art in the Age of Mechanical Reproduction," Walter Benjamin examines the contrasting ways in which two totalizing theories—fascism and communism—intersect aesthetic and practical principles. The former, he thinks, aestheticizes the political by making the self-alienation associated with oppression into a collective aesthetic pleasure, while the latter politicizes the aesthetic by making social ends the mainspring of art.[5] Benjamin's famous analysis thus denies a doctrine subscribed to since antiquity; namely, that the beautiful and the moral can be brought into accord.

His fear is that aestheticizing moral reflection equates acceptable social practice with the tastes of whoever exercises the strongest political influence. That is, the conduct of agents will be approved, or else condemned, depending on how pleasing the agents appear to the politically dominant regard and, furthermore, on whether so regarding them coheres with and cultivates whatever values the preeminent perspective centers. Aestheticizing moral judgment has been condemned for privileging whoever's tastes prevail in a culture, for elevating self-absorption over selflessness, and for replacing the goal of self-determination for the oppressed with pursuit of self-realization for the strongest.[6] To the contrary, in this study we will see that the aesthetic is more suited to reforming than to reiterating the exclusionary practices that currently govern our gaze and contribute to the social invisibility of odd-looking people.

Beautiful Representations and Real Ugliness

Aesthetics has a long history of addressing the phenomenon I am proposing to probe: namely, the allure of perceiving representations of objects that in themselves repel perception. Plato explains that repulsive objects are so because they are ugly, and he identifies the ugly as that which lacks the power to attract.[7] This analysis fuels Plato's well-known suspicion of the reliability of representations of physical objects, for representations can insidiously captivate our attention even though the objects they imitate are defective because they lack the power to attract. Thus, the deceptive attractiveness of artistic representations can mislead us into fantastical thinking about the capacities of their originals.

Aristotle's analysis resembles Plato's in that he too construes ugliness as the absence of the capacity to delight.[8] He applies this understanding in

Book IV of *The Poetics*, where he proposes that imitations are effective heuristic tools because perceiving them is pleasurable. Because we enjoy attending to imitations of objects that themselves deter our regarding them, he concludes that humans take pleasure in imitations. However, Aristotle insists that their accuracy is the key to making imitations that enchant, enthrall, and engross us, for we learn from them. He says: "[T]hough the objects themselves may be painful to see, we delight to view the most realistic representations of them, the forms for example of the lowest animals and of dead bodies."[9]

What puzzled Aristotle remains a challenge today. For instance, in *The Philosophy of Horror or Paradoxes of the Heart*, Noël Carroll is concerned with the same phenomenon when he observes that people who are drawn to the genre of horror "appear to seek that which, under certain descriptions, it would seem natural for them to avoid."[10] Carroll explains this phenomenon in terms of representing that which is "in some sense both attractive and repulsive," and that which correlates with "art-horror," an emotion directed at (components of) works of certain genres of art, literature, cinema and the like.[11] But this is not merely an issue in genre criticism. Carroll, like Aristotle, has engaged with a more general and more important curiosity about our experience of art: namely, why we are attracted to art which presents us with otherwise repulsive configurations.

Despite its renown and durable influence, Aristotle's account of why we are attracted to imitations of objects that themselves repel us remains unsatisfying. It is because we learn from imitations that we regard them with delight, he says. But it is hard to see how this explanation differentiates the experience of viewing dead bodies or other inherently abhorrent objects from the experience of viewing their most realistic simulations. Realistic representations are a delight to view, Aristotle emphasizes. So the realism of an imitation is no deterrent to learning from it. Quite the contrary, vivid truthfulness in representation is both a disquisitional and an artistic virtue.

So why isn't the real thing—a real dead body, for instance—an equally delightful and even more effective, and therefore even more pleasurable, heuristic object? How can a most realistic imitation corpse be the site of lessons absent in a real corpse? Of course, real corpses possess disagreeable properties that interfere with learning and defy delighting in them. They are distressingly cold and clammy to the touch, emit a stench, and cannot be disassembled without yielding unpleasant by-products.

I grant that, for these reasons, investigating a real human corpse is less congenial than studying a realistic model or drawing or CD-ROM of a body. But there usually are not similarly disagreeable tactile or olfactory sensations to be feared from attending to live but anomalously shaped individuals. Are there, perhaps, some other offensive properties that either inhere in, or are correlated with, people who are disabled and/or deformed?

As to the first of these possibilities, we should notice that if the deformations of real people are intrinsically repelling—as G. E. Moore suggests when he claims that we describe such individuals as "'ugly' to denote that of which the admiring contemplation is evil"[12]—then realistic imitations of them will be equally deformed. So these imitations should occasion comparably evil contemplative events. That is, if ugliness is either an objective property of or the epiphenomenon of one or more objective properties, we would expect accurate imitations of ugly things also to be objectively ugly. But this account is not illuminating, for rather than explaining the phenomenon we are examining, it denies the possibility that it can exist.

Yet the fact that accurate representations of ugly objects can be beautiful is referred to sufficiently often in the history of aesthetic theorizing to assign its averred factuality the benefit of the doubt. Therefore, we must conclude that ugliness is neither an objective property, nor is it an epiphenomenon of deformation or other objective anomalies, or else that ugliness pertains to being real, so that it is an objective property, but only of real things, and never of their artistic imitations or representations. As for the latter proposal, an imitated object shares all of its properties, except those that make it real, with any completely accurate imitation of itself, the excepted properties being what differentiates the original from an exact model. So, if ugliness is an objective property or is an epiphenomenon of objective properties, accurate imitations of repulsive objects will resemble their models by being equally ugly, unless their ugliness inheres in their reality itself. But this alternative is uninformative unless we further understand what reality could add to visual configurations to make them ugly.

Ugliness by Association

In this regard, the usual kind of proposal points not to anomaly itself, but rather to one or another correlate of anomaly to explain what distances us from deformation. Suppose that our realities are such that we associate deformation with some other, intrinsically objectionable property, state, or condition. To illustrate, political philosopher Iris Marion Young supposes that abjection—experiencing as permeable the boundary which separates one's self from those one takes to be inferior—accounts for the social invisibility of older people and people with impairments:

> I cannot deny that the old person will be myself, but that means my death, so I avert my gaze from the old person . . . and want to leave her presence as soon as possible. My relationship to disabled people has a similar structure. . . . Encounter with the disabled person again produces the ambiguity of recognizing that the person whom I project as so different, so other, is nevertheless like me.[13]

As Young describes it, abjection involves the realization that one could become what one beholds. The effect of this experience, she suggests, is to make encounters with people whose bodies are deteriorating or deformed disagreeable because they bring home the reality of one's own impending corporeal decay. That is, the reality of one's becoming decrepit or disabled becomes tangible in the fleshly presence of someone who is already so. Having become aware of one's jeopardy from encountering that presence, one protects one's self either by contesting or occluding it. (Parenthetically, in *Powers of Horror: An Essay on Abjection*, Julia Kristeva proposes that because what repulses us transgresses the categorical boundaries, we do not usually articulate the cause of our feeling.[14])

But it is improbable that unexceptional-looking people first identify with, but subsequently renounce their kinship to, people whose appearance is anomalous.[15] For playing out one's own deterioration has none of the familiarity characteristic of reprising either repressed or haunting earlier fears or previous bad dreams. Despite the frequency with which disabling accidents or illnesses have corroded the bodies of people one knows or has heard about, we are surprised and shocked when deformity comes upon ourselves precisely because it is in other people, rather than in one's self, that we expect to encounter it. Similarly, each of us knows she will age, yet it is in other people's faces, rather than in our own, that we readily make out the erosion of aging. Advanced age and impairment invite isolation, exclusion, or "being othered" by the dominant social group not because being aged or disabled are familiar, albeit painfully so, but rather because they seem alien, remote, impenetrable, and strange to whoever is not directly experiencing them.

Furthermore, if the appearance of real aged or disabled people is threatening because it is portentous of our own impending physical and social decline, there should be comparable menace in representations of aging or of disability. That is, it is hard to see why viewing representations or imitations of deformed or deteriorating bodies should be any less portentous than viewing real deformed or deteriorating bodies.

Similar arguments can be made for other disagreeable correlates of physical deformation: for instance, its associations with incompetence, moral depravity, and burdensomeness. All equally easily attach to portrayals of deformation. So if we explain the disagreeableness of gazing at very old or very disabled people by reference to abjection or other exorcizing reactions, we would predict that portrayals of these people must be equally disagreeable. Yet so often they are not. Consequently, the appeal to abjection and other such aversive processes to explain the interpersonal invisibility of real people with disabilities and real elderly people appears to be disconfirmed.

So far, we have considered views in which the repulsiveness of real things is attributable to their objective properties. These are accounts in which anomalous bodies that deflect our gaze induce systematic aversive responses to the disagreeableness of their real properties. For views of this kind, any disparity in attractiveness between distasteful objects and their accurate but agreeable replicas must be because the imitations are free of the deleterious properties that plague the originals. Versions of this thesis all fail because it is hard to see what ugliness is present in the configurations of disagreeable real faces and bodies that is not also so in their imitations.

Obscuring Identity by Signifying Semantically[16]

However, an alternative thesis suggests that the advantage of imitations lies not in what they omit when replicating their originals but instead in what has been added to them. That is, art enhances or embellishes images so we are attracted to replicas of visual presentations where the originals repelled us. That ugliness is defeasible in this way seems to be Kant's idea when he comments: "Beautiful art . . . describes as beautiful things which may be in nature ugly or displeasing."[17]

The history of aesthetics has seen very many theories about how art transfigures the mundane or uncomely into something beautiful. This brings us back to our initial problem. Why do we see the corporeal anomalies configured into Picasso's rendition of the human face as being beautiful but perceive my friend's facial anomalies as an unfortunate disability?

There are two main ways of explicating art's transformational power as it is manifested in the context of our problem. In the first, depicting deformed or disabled bodies in works of art typically suppresses or obscures their reality. To this way of thinking, art presents disagreeable things as something other than themselves, thus distracting us from the unpleasantness of images of impairment by assigning the representations a meaning that transcends disability. As a result of this dissimulation, artistically fashioned representations of anomalous bodies console rather than repel us.

In contrast, in the second approach, deformity itself is transfigured into something beautiful when art discloses, and even foregrounds, certain of its relational properties. That is, art has a positive transfigurative — almost a redemptive — effect on configurations we otherwise would apprehend as being ugly.

The Thesis in Disability Studies

Much has been said in respect to the first approach, not least because physically impaired and other kinds of disabled figures are common symbolical figures in literature and in art. The belief that so far has dominated the new field of disability studies is that disability is used in literature and the arts to signify something other than itself. This conspiratorial interpretation of why disability so often is exhibited in art when it is concealed in life prompts many disability studies scholars to complain about art's exploitation of the figure of disability.

To illustrate, literature scholars David Mitchell and Sharon Snyder launch a volume on the cultural study of disability by characterizing the record of representing disability in the visual and literary media as a history of "metaphorical opportunism."[18] That is, they appeal to a "pervasive cultural and artistic dependency on disability" as evidence that our culture colonizes and exploits people with various kinds of impairments, or at least their images, in order to nourish non-disabled people's fictions about their own perfections.[19] The indictment they tender incorporates several key contentions.

First, it assumes that disability cannot be other than disruptive or transgressive of the social order. Because current social organization is structured to marginalize people in virtue of their corporeal or cognitive anomalies, Mitchell and Snyder argue, the prospect of their full social inclusion or participation is unsettling. However, their second point is that the fictionalized frailty and vulnerability of impaired individuals typically is found to be artistically felicitous by the public because it portrays the disabled as too weak to thrust themselves into ordinary civil and commercial life, and thereby forestalls their being too threatening. The third component of the charge applies a moral template to this artistic device; namely that the prominence of the trope exacerbates the stereotyping of people with disabilities and entrenches the real-life conditions that curtail their access to social opportunity.

Mitchell and Snyder further argue that, when represented in literature and art, deformity is veiled by being treated as broadly symbolic of disempowerment. In literature and art, they claim, disability is used as the stereotypical signifier of the disempowerment of all those, whether impaired or not, whom the dominant society excludes and oppresses:

> [T]he disabled body also serves as the raw material out of which other socially disempowered communities make themselves visible. [But] once the [deformed] bodily surface is exposed as the . . . facade that disguises the workings of [dominant] class norms, the monstrous body itself is quickly forgotten . . . [which] further entrenches the disabled as the "real" abnormality from which all other non-normative groups must be distanced.[20]

Signifying defeats aversion, they think, by disconnecting representations of impairment from their disagreeable models and assigning them more appealing meanings. For, of course, people are not repulsed by disagreeable-seeming things when it is evident that they are not what they seem.

In this politicized account of the artistic use of disability, signifying not only diminishes people with disabilities but also privileges people who are not disabled by serving a therapeutic purpose for them. In its usual assignment as a signifier, Mitchell and Snyder insist, disability represents undeserved misfortune. This usage creates what they call the "representational double bind of disability."[21] That is, the limitations of people with impairments are put on display to be manipulated by others in order to assuage societal guilt. Consequently, non-disabled people identify disability with affliction in order to congratulate themselves on their own superior assets.

It might be expected that they would do so as readily when confronted by a truly afflicted person as by the representation of one. But, as exemplified by the analysis pressed by Mitchell and Snyder, the prevailing analysis in disability studies admits—indeed, insists on—the difference between the real world, in which the disabled encounter indifference or worse, and artistically constructed worlds, in which they are represented as being showered with benevolence and protection. In such a politicized account, sympathetic portrayals of disability allow the non-disabled public to respond benevolently to depicted disability, thereby relieving public uneasiness about the realities of the treatment accorded to the disabled. Because of its role in inducing such therapeutic experiences for the non-disabled, artistic and literary representations of impairment acquire an appeal that is absent in their originals. Regrettably, in doing so they also distance disability itself.

More Mechanisms of Marginalizing

Mitchell and Snyder also believe that there is yet another way in which the manner art and literature represent disability systematically obscures its realities and therefore makes it palatable as a trope or figure, though not as a fact. They say that images of disability are used to call attention to the general repressiveness society visits on people who are different from those of the dominant group.[22] Disability thus becomes a placeholder or marker for the suffering of other groups which are of greater concern to the audience. Representations whose unpleasant particularities are obscured because they are vehicles for larger meanings of this sort are understandably intriguing. But such signifying reprises the averted glance that disregards, and thus veils veridical experiences of, disability. For if this is really the prevailing way in which disability functions in art and literature, its uses are thoroughly figurative and, consequently, fail both to illuminate the actual experience of disability and to expand non-disabled people's appreciation of it.

To illustrate, no medium has the potential to exhibit disability more realistically than film, and there are clear cases in which films use disability to signify the oppression of other groups. For instance, in the 1951 film *Bright Victory* (based on a 1945 Baynard Kendrick novel called *Lights Out*), a racist soldier is blinded and, when he is rejected the way he himself has rebuffed black people, decides he has more in common with blind black veterans than with the non-disabled whites in his hometown. Here, according to the prevailing disability studies view, disability stands in for race, and the insulting treatment to which the blind veteran is subjected signifies the fate of whoever falls away from the dominant physical norm.

As the film's meaning is interpreted by cinema theorist Martin Norden,[23] the hero's blindness paradoxically enlarges his vision precisely because he now distinguishes his friends on the basis of their conduct rather than their color. From the prevailing disability studies perspective, this plot is exploitative because it magnifies the incapacities of disability for symbolic purposes: "[T]he blinded vet is unable to 'see' skin color, [and] the folly of his own racial intolerance, until the end of the film."[24] Mitchell and Snyder deplore such signifying: "[D]isability seldom has been explored as a condition or experience in its own right; instead, disability's psychological and bodily variations have been used to metaphorize nearly every social conflict outside its own ignoble predicament in culture."[25] For them, *Bright Victory* is exploitative, at least if it is understood along the lines of Norden's reading.

Countering the Prevailing View

Literature and art undoubtedly present many stereotypical figures of disability, age, and illness. But enumerating them is far from demonstrating that they make disability presentable by diverting attention to more palatable meanings. That impairment is shown in a work of art or literature does not entail that it operates as a trope. Not all manifestations of impairment in the movies are identically meaningful. For instance, there are cases where an actor's actual impairment becomes, of necessity, his character's impairment without signifying or representing anything beyond itself. The severe arthritis which impaired Lionel Barrymore's mobility means nothing more than it is. At a time when no one in a wheelchair could be admitted to medical school, Barrymore the wheelchair-user was the wheelchair-using Dr. Gillespie in fifteen Dr. Kildaire films that unobtrusively refer to his condition but neither emphasize nor metaphorize it.

Another kind of case in which disability does not signify beyond itself involves the familiar early-day cinematic device of the chase or running scene. Representations like this serve as a main event in such productions as *The Lost Child* (1904), *The Legless Runner* (1907), *The One-Legged Man* (1908), *Story of a Leg* (1910), *Legless Acrobats* (1910) and a collection of similarly titled films, in all of which a one-legged or legless individual runs rings around his unimpaired pursuers.[26] Some of the figures in these films are remarkably reminiscent of the impaired form of the crippled man on the furthest left in Breughel's famous painting *The Beggars*, lithely suspended on his crutches, his lower limbs starkly terminating at the ankles. Yet another example is the famous scene in *The Best Years of Our Lives*, in which the armless actor Harold Russell removes first his shirt and then his prosthesis. The scene tests both his girlfriend's and the audience's acceptance of his reality. "No matter how good a performance an actor gave of a man without hands," wrote director William Wyler about the casting, "an audience could reassure itself by saying, 'It's only a movie.'"[27] In these and many other instances, disability is made noticeable—and sometimes takes center stage—without being made into something other than itself.

Although characters with disabilities often are assigned stereotypical roles such as the Sweet Innocent, the Tragic Victim, the Noble Warrior (or Noble Wounded Veteran), and Abased Avenger, these familiar filmic figures are not usually people with disabilities. It seems odd to hold that, for instance, the Sweet Innocent with a disability Mary Pickford plays in *Stella Maris* is a more concealing and therefore exploitative signifier than the Sweet Innocent without a disability she plays in so many other films. And no renunciation of family by a character with a disability is as high-mindedly self-sacrificial as the self-abnegation of the non-disabled heroine Mildred Pierce. (Ironically, this icon of maternal feeling who sacrifices everything, including her own identity, for her ungrateful daughter is the role most associated with Joan Crawford.) So a more plausible analysis of the artistic representation of disability than that art illegitimately capitalizes on disability is that audiences are partial to suffering heroines, and illness and death are among the many kinds of events which plausibly can be used as plot devices to occasion the characters' suffering.[28]

Nor are disabled bodies indisputably the ones most often obscured or concealed by art and literature. Nor is diverting attention beyond the particularities of the depicted body the most malignant instrument of aesthetic oppression. There are many other candidates.

Varieties of Hegemonic Depiction

As bell hooks reminds us, "[F]ew American artists have worked with the black female body in ways that are counter-hegemonic. . . . [W]ithin sexist racist iconography, black females are most often represented as . . . caretakers whose bodies and beings are empty vessels to be filled with the needs of others." For hooks, hegemonic depiction is fully frontal so as to induce a colonizing gaze, whereas counter-hegemonic depiction shrouds the body and turns it away.[29] Thus, for hooks, exposure rather than concealment is the preeminent instrument of cultural tyranny. Veiling the black female body by representing it as indifferent or resistant to the scrutiny of others is emancipatory. She praises the images of the photographer Lorna Simpson "because so many of them are not frontal images. Backs are turned, the bodies are sideways, specific body parts are highlighted—repositioned from the start in a manner that disrupts conventional ways of seeing and understanding black womanhood."[30]

From these examples, we can see that whether an artistic mode of representing socially marginalized people elevates or diminishes them is not a matter of the inherent character of the artistic representation, but rather is determined by extrinsic considerations; namely, the political and practical manifestations of their repression. To understand this point, it is useful to consider how it emerges more generally in social analysis. For example, the feminist legal theorist Kimberle Crenshaw argues that feminism's "singular focus on rape as a manifestation of male power over female sexuality" is "an oversimplified account and an ultimately inadequate account" because it ignores the institutionalized difference between white and black women.[31] Crenshaw illustrates by pointing out that, during slavery, black women's parenting of their own children was under constant threat of disruption; after emancipation, they continued to be employed to raise white women's children, putting their energy into nurturing other women's children to earn basic subsistence for their own.

Thus, representations of womanhood rooted in white feminine experience cannot help but miss the meaning of references to roles in which black women traditionally have been devalued. It is not only whether, but also the way in which, sexuality, procreation, and nurturing are valued that affects their meaning for both black and nonblack women.[32]

Black women typically have had access to sexual, procreative, and nurturing roles, but the social construction of their race has devalued their participation in them. hooks tells us: "In general, in this culture, black women are seen and depicted as down to earth, practical, creatures of the mundane."[33] In contrast, the social construction of disability commonly prevents women with disabilities from assuming procreative and maternal roles, even in the belittling assignments typically reserved for black women.[34] Paradoxically, portraying black women in these roles reprises the social practice that oppresses them, but failing to portray women with disabilities in these roles is equally dismissive. This point suggests one of the complications of imagining that representing disability in art and literature is a broad signifier of oppression: namely, that depictions that disclose disempowerment due to disability are often the inverse of those that reveal other kinds of disempowerment. For instance, if depicting a woman with a disability other than frontally is oppressive, while depicting a black woman frontally is oppressive, and so on, the difficulties of supporting interpretation that correlates ways of depicting with oppression are formidable. In such an interpretive frame, no rendering can be counted on to maintain its import from the depiction of one marginalized group to the depiction of any other.

Veiling Disability or Showing It

Taken together, these observations cast grave doubt on the contention that artistic renditions of impairment are attractive because they categorically direct our attention away from disability and thus shadow rather than illuminate it. The counter-examples offered here are just a few drawn from a very replete catalog which demonstrates that it is hyperbolic to characterize the history of representing disability in art as one of "metaphorical opportunism."[35] Misinterpreting representations of disability this way emanates from reading deterministically from the society, which incontrovertibly disregards individuals on account of their disabilities, to art, which clearly does not do so.

Both in life and in art, disability is closely associated with negatively value-laden states like suffering. But no one supposes that similarly connected conditions like slavery and poverty are categorically concealed and metaphorized, rather than revealed and interrogated, in the various artistic media. For were this the case art would be so much less able to elucidate the human condition, and therefore so much less valuable, than its reputation attests. Granted also that art sometimes invokes disability as a signifier. But disability often is shown simply for what it is by the artistic media. Contrary to the account in which representing disability involves manipulative semantic signifying, artistic representations which show disability as it is effectively elicit our delight despite the painfulness of viewing their originals. How this is so is our yet-unanswered question. But we should observe that, in the course of our discussion so far, politicizing the aesthetic has not helped to clarify why painted corporeal anomalies can be beautiful when similarly configured real bodies are not so.

Embattled Identity and Syntactic Meaning

We have found no basis for categorically taking riveting (or, for that matter, pedestrian) artistic representations of deformed or impaired humans to be signifiers that systematically divert regard from disagreeable to agreeable meanings (although some may do so). But there is another diversionary role disability is reputed to play in art: namely, as "one of the instrumental devices of . . . [artistic] production."[36] The disability studies literature does not pursue the difference between the previously discussed semantic role and this syntactic one, for these are equally politically suspect from the prevailing perspective in disability studies.

However, in this syntactic role "disability is more than a background. . . . [I]t is . . . the basis on which the 'normal' body is constructed. . . . [D]isability defines the negative space the body must not occupy, according to Lennard Davis."[37] As Rosemarie Garland Thomson explains in *Extraordinary Bodies: Physical Disability in American Culture and Literature*, the "subject position of cultural self [is] the figure outlined by the array of deviant others whose marked bodies shore up the normate's boundaries. The term normate usefully designates the social figure through which people can represent themselves as definitive human beings."[38]

Politicizing or Aestheticizing the Syntactics of Disability

This syntactical analysis admits of two importantly different versions, although recognition of their distinctness does not usually surface in disability studies scholarship. The first version internalizes the politicized processes of disability oppression to the experience of art, explaining that when (human) bodies are represented in art, their significance is the product of an inescapable conceptual struggle which places normalcy and disability in irresistible conflict. In contrast, the second, aestheticizing version holds that normalcy and disability not only are concordant but are vitally so.

The first version assumes that art which represents the body relies on a syntactical process whereby "the 'normal' body always is in a dialectical play with the disabled body. . . . [O]ur representations of the body are really investigations of and defenses against the notion that the body is anything but a seamless, whole, complete, unfragmented entity."[39] Thus, what is normal is thought to have no identity absent its relationship to its own absence; that is, its identity depends on its contrast with impairment: "[T]he disabled figure operates as a code for insufficiency, contingency, and abjection—for deviant particularity—thus establishing the contours of a canonical body that garners the prerogatives and privileges of a supposedly stable, universalized normalcy."[40]

Casting disability as a component of a binary construes it as a discrete concept but one that nevertheless is interdependent with the concept of normalcy. In this binary relation, normalcy operates as the superior term, while disability is the inferior and consequently the repressed one. Representing disability thus is supposed to exhibit deficiency by necessity, because representations of disability always invoke what they are not. Indeed, the principle that unifies or consolidates normal bodies is their wholeness, a concept understood as being oppositional to impairment.[41] Although whole bodies are privileged by being valued over disabled ones, neither can be discerned without reference to the other. So although the standard of normalcy is imposed on discourses of disability, not the least through the assumption that normalcy is a state disabled people covet, discourses of normalcy themselves are vitalized by the energy with which both non-impaired and (unenlightened) impaired people disclaim disability. In this view, the discourse non-disabled people impose on everyone makes commonplace or typical corporeal configurations definitively desirable and anomalous ones definitely unwelcome.

Normalcy in bodies thus is both understood and embraced by means of the identical process by which disability is denied or distanced. For to refer to disability as a lack and to impairment as an absence implicitly cites normalcy as regulative. So we can think of represented disability as one of the elements of a binary dynamic occurring within the work (that is, as a term in a syntactic production of meaning), rather than as pointing to or otherwise signifying something outside the work (that is, as a term in a semantic production of meaning). There are several points to be made in favor of this oppositional analysis, but also something to be said against it.

Disability as a Binary Opposite

First, proposing that representing disability initiates a dynamic explains the power of this category of appearances to engage our attention. Second, the representations emit this energy by showing disability to be itself and not another thing; in this analysis, they can do so regardless of the likeness's particularities because there can be no simulation of disability that fails to fall away from normalcy. Third, this account situates the disruptiveness occasioned by disability within the work of art rather than in the world. The anomalous pictured face Picasso painted is unexpected. That is, it is not the face normally found in the paintings of Raphael, Rubens, and Renoir. Thus, the work itself is disruptive because it is seen as supplanting or transcending normal art; namely, the art of Raphael, Rubens, and Renoir. Similarly, Harold Russell's upper torso, with the harness that affixes his metal hooks, is explicitly oppositional to the physiques of heroes previously pictured on the screen. The image of Russell's composite body signals that the normalcy represented in *The Best Years of Our Lives* will be a postwar or newly challenging normalcy, not the complacency of the pre-Hitler era. Art shapes, and therefore can reshape, which appearances seem familiar and commonplace, as well as which strike us as strange and disturbing.

There are, nevertheless, several drawbacks to viewing normalcy and disability as definitively locked in struggle. The most obvious is that conceptualizing their relation this way constructs a dualism that tends to force all cases into one or the other category or camp. Representations must show their originals as normal or else as deviant; they must present either normalcy or its transgressive, defective opposite. However, to bind the significance of disability to such a structure impoverishes it by reducing it to a confrontation between privilege and inferiority and thus rendering it unresponsive to the pluralism inherent in diversity. Furthermore, this analysis is intolerant of borderline cases because their undecidability defeats the binary dynamic.

If disability is identified as oppositional, the product of a binary dynamic, what it is cannot help but be a function of (the opposition to) oppression. That is, in this theory, disability inescapably is in disadvantageous contention with normalcy. Conceptualizing disability this way forestalls, by definition, the possibility of its transcending limitation and necessarily mires it in deficit. However, normalcy and disability need not be antithetical. The privilege of being normal is that one has a claim on having one's commonness respected; the equivalent, and compatible, privilege of being disabled is acknowledgment of a claim to having one's difference respected.

Prizing Novelty More Than Normalcy

Both of these points indicate the virtue of seeking another analysis of the meaningfulness of the dynamic between normalcy and disability, an analysis which explains why normalcy appears to be a regulative ideal affecting our social responses to other people's corporeal configurations, but not of aesthetic reactions to representations of those same bodies. Mitchell and Snyder approach an important thought regarding this, but almost immediately back away. Their volume, they say, "seeks to demonstrate that disabled bodies and lives have historically served as the crutch upon which artistic discourses and cultural narratives have leaned to ensure the novelty of their subject matter."[42]

Subsequently, however, they avoid grappling with the notion of novelty by eliding it with deformation and distortion. In doing so, they revert to worrying about literature's "often hazardous complicity in the 'ideology of the physical,'"[43] by which they mean a way of thinking that "constructs an imaginary bridge between bodily differences and individual abilities . . . [and] seeks to lure the reader/viewer into the mystery of whether discernible defects reveal the presence of an equally defective moral and civil character."[44] Of course, if one assumes that advantage always lies in being normal, the slope from novelty to blemish is well greased. But unlike life, in art normalcy seldom is prized. Novelty rather than normalcy, and uniqueness rather than usualness, are the aesthetic desiderata.

That singularity emancipates imagination and frees the exceptional individual from the expectations to which the group is held is an artistic commonplace. In the last century, this understanding was expressed in women's literature by the figure of the invalid. From Harriet Martineau's *Life in the Sickroom: Essays. By an Invalid*[45] to Charlotte Yonge's *The Clever Woman of the Family*,[46] confinement to the couch empowers women by freeing them from reproductive roles and thereby redefining their productivity as intellectual. Generally, for members of groups whose social oppression severely limits their opportunities, being normal is not categorically less limiting than being impaired.

Making Impairment Powerful

Art can make impairment powerful. This idea occasionally surfaces in disability studies, but it is treated as an exceptional manifestation rather than as a familiar achievement of art. In this regard, Rosemary Garland Thomson observes that three African American writers (Ann Petry, Toni Morrison, Audre Lord) create characters whose "disability neither diminishes nor corrupts . . . [but instead] affirms the self in context [and] augments power and dignity . . . [thereby] inspiring awe, and becoming a mark of superiority."[47] For these writers, "difference, not sameness, is (the) principle of identity. Being outside the ordinary is both essential and emancipatory in . . . self-definition."[48] Their characters flaunt rather than conceal their physical differences in a way that repudiates the primacy of "normalcy, wholeness, and the feminine ideal."[49] The character's "extraordinary body disqualifies her from the restrictions and benefits of conventional womanhood, freeing [her] to create an identity that incorporates a body distinguished by markings . . . of their individual and cultural history."[50]

The upshot, according to Thomson, is that "disabilities, then, are not metaphors for lives twisted by oppression, but the identifying, affirming, and valued manifestations of bodily uniqueness and personal history."[51] The extraordinary body becomes "a site of historical inscription rather than physical deviance."[52] To understand the import of this last remark, it will be useful to return to our original case, the attractive representation of a homologous, but repulsive, original.

Transcending the Normate

We view neither anomalously configured pictured faces, nor homologous real faces, with an innocent eye. Each face we view is limned by its lineage and kin; these factors outline what is expected of it and what it is expected to be, that is to say, what is normal for it. Why, then, does the normal hold so much less sway in art than in life? We see a painted face in cubist style as beautiful, but see a similarly configured fleshly face as deviant. Noël Carroll tells us that "the anomalous nature of [objects of art-horror] is what makes them disturbing, distressing, and disgusting. However . . . the very fact that they are anomalies fascinates us."[53] Yet, unlike what is the case for art, even for art-horror, the perception of real anomalous humans distances rather than beguiles us.

To understand why these cases diverge, we may begin by adverting to a time when they did not. As is the case for much truly novel art, it was not unusual for the initial reception of such paintings to duplicate the aversion with which real faces similarly configured are received. For instance, when Caravaggio started painting from dead bodies, art viewers were shocked because his depictions were "too real/natural." The famous painting by Thomas Eakins, *The Gross Clinic* (1875), was rejected by jurors from an exhibit in the "art" section and hung in the "medical" section.[54] What eventually altered apprehensions of them so that they attract rather than repel attention?

Critic Michael Kimmelman advances a strategy for accommodating to, and enjoying, the shock of the new in art.[55] He recollects a remark by the pianist and essayist Charles Rosen, in *The Frontiers of Meaning*,[56] who "demonstrates how we may actually be sickened when something is truly unfamiliar to us, when it thwarts our expectations."[57] The initial shock evoked by novel art, Kimmelman observes, "isn't specifically about grotesque or horrible . . . effects. It's about incomprehension."[58] What then permits configurational anomaly to transcend incomprehension and become attractively lucid when it pertains to the artistic representation of people? And is the strategy appropriate for confronting the shock we experience in perceiving extreme configurational anomalies in real people?

Thomson gestures in the direction of a response. She remarks that, in art, anomaly can "neutralize alienation and repugnance [in order] to highlight the potential for an iconoclastic liminality that can accommodate new forms of identity."[59] To put it plainly, innovative art calls into question the prescriptive authority of the historical contingencies that shape our expectations and thereby augments what we previously have imagined to be normal, even—indeed, especially—what we consider normal in regard to art itself.

That anomaly presents as originality rather than deviance thus depends on the way we conceptualize the connectedness of successors with their heritage and, specifically, on the prescriptiveness with which individuals are obliged to conform to their predecessors. To embrace art, yet be respectful of its history, is to comprehend how historical precedent can be of consequence for future art without commanding conformity. Art's history has been theorized in various ways that facilitate the firm but free connecting of novel objects with their aesthetic predecessors. Art's history thus receives rather than repudiates new forms of identity, for art's history is interpretive, not coercive.

Beautifully Crooked

Is it possible for human history to do so as well? My friend sits before me. On the wall behind her the reproduction of a Picasso painting hangs. What theorizing of human beauty would facilitate my perceiving her face as enlivening, rather than depreciating, the human collective in a manner similar to the ways in which theorizing permits me to see the innovatively painted face as invigorating art?

Aesthetics makes available a variety of applicable proposals for bringing novelty and precedent into contiguity for this purpose. Accepting any of these requires recognizing that (some) anomalous people advance our comprehension of humanity as (some) novel objects expand our conceptualization of art.

To view the particularities of my friend's face as attentively as I do the painting, I must appreciate her both as an original and also as an heir to human biological history. Parenthetically, as we learn more about genetics and the variables affecting human's inheritance of various corporeal traits, we have become more sensitive to the errors of simple-minded Darwinian functionalism. Further, molecular biology is giving us techniques to intervene therapeutically at the genetic level. In principle, gene transfer technology will make such matters as whether or not an individual inherits blue or brown eyes, or is bald rather than hairy, or has the triangular face characteristic of osteogenesis imperfecta as much a matter of human artifice as Picasso's portrayal of his model with dark rather than light hair and eyes.

We must discern how expansive and inclusive beauty should be. It is the impoverished political understanding of beauty that prevails in disability studies, not the imaginative aesthetic understanding of beauty for which I have been arguing, that prompts Thomson to caution that "aestheticizing disability . . . precludes analysis of how these representations support or challenge the sociopolitical relations that make disability a form of cultural otherness."[60] Our discussion should put this kind of worry to rest. Understanding how beauty really matters quiets concerns about the aestheticizing of interpersonal conduct by showing that aestheticizing disability elevates otherness to originality, thereby defeating the hegemony imposed by "normal" socio-political relations.

NOTES

1. From Immanuel Kant's "Idee zu einer Allgemeinen Gesichte in Weltburger-lichter Absicht" (1784). Translation by Isaiah Berlin in *The Crooked Timber of Humanity: Chapters in the History of Ideas* (Princeton: Princeton University Press, 1998).

2. My friend has a genetic condition called osteogenesis imperfecta congenita. To learn more about this condition, contact the Osteogenesis Imperfecta Foundation, 804 W. Diamond Ave., Suite 210, Gaithersburg, Maryland, (301) 947–0456.

3. I have addressed this process as it occurs in the history of art and literature in

some of my previous work. See especially "Once upon a Time in the Artworld," in George Dickie, Richard Sclafani, and Richard Roblyn, ed., *Aesthetics: A Critical Anthology* (New York: St. Martin's, 1989); "The Story of Art Is the Test of Time," *Journal of Aesthetics and Art Criticism* 49, no. 3 (Summer 1991); "Has Her(oine's) Time Now Come?" *Journal of Aesthetics and Art Criticism* 48, no. 4 (Fall 1990); "Pure Historicism and the Heritage of Heroines: Who Grows In Phillis Wheatley's Garden?" *Journal of Aesthetics and Art Criticism* 51, no. 3 (Summer 1993); "Vincent's Story: The Importance of Contextualization in Art Education," *Journal of Aesthetic Education* 28, no. 3 (Fall 1994).

4. D. Martin, "Disability Culture: Eager to Bite the Hands That Would Feed Them," *New York Times*, June 1, 1997, Week in Review Section, p. 1. In this article, Martin interviews individuals who identify with the new "disability culture." The affirmation that impaired and/or mechanically assisted bodies are aesthetically superior to normal ones appears to be a response of some people with disabilities to their exclusion from normal social opportunity and participation. When "disability culture" is understood oppositionally—that is, is delineated in terms of the rejection of people with disabilities by normal society and their consequent rejection of normal social standards—the most attractive and successful individuals from a disability perspective are those who are the most visibly impaired and use the most intimate assistive equipment (such as catheters and ventilators).

5. Walter Benjamin, "The Work of Art in the Age of Mechanical Reproduction," in *Film Theory and Criticism: Introductory Readings*, ed. Gerald Mast and Marshall Cohen (London: Oxford University Press, 1974), pp. 612–634.

6. Terry Eagleton, "From the Polis to Post-Modernism," in *The Ideology of the Ideology* (Oxford: Blackwell, 1990), pp. 366–417.

7. Plato, *Hippias Major* 288c–289b; 289e; 290cd; 296a. Of course, what is thought to be ugly, or for that matter beautiful, has evolved over the many centuries since Plato. For an excellent account of assessments of ugliness regarding the human shape, see Robert Garland, *The Eye of the Beholder: Deformity and Disability in the Graeco-Roman World* (Ithaca: Cornell University Press, 1995).

8. Aristotle, *Nicomachaean Ethics* I, 8. Cf. *Politics*, IV,11,1295b 6–9; De part. an.I,5, 645a 6–7.

9. Aristotle, *The Poetics*, 4,1448b 11–13, reprinted in Stephen David Ross, ed., *An Anthology of Aesthetic Theory* (Albany: State University of New York Press, 1987), p. 71.

10. Noël Carroll, *The Philosophy of Horror, or, Paradoxes of the Heart* (New York: Routledge, 1990), p. 160.

11. Ibid., pp. 27–42. Carroll takes horrifying monsters to exemplify the kind of artistic component toward which feelings of horror are directed.

12. G. E. Moore, *Principia Ethica* (Cambridge, Mass.: Harvard University Press, 1962), p. 208.

13. Iris Marion Young, *Justice and the Politics of Difference* (Princeton: Princeton University Press, 1990), p. 147.

14. Julia Kristeva, *Powers of Horror: An Essay on Abjection* (New York: Columbia University Press, 1982).

15. Carroll's *Philosophy of Horror* presents compelling arguments against the view that we identify with things that horrify us.

16. To signify is to mean, so when one speaks of a work of literature as "signifying," one is speaking broadly of its having meaning. Used transitively, to signify is to denote, that is, to have semantic meaning. However, used intransitively, to signify is, more generally, to mean.

17. Immanuel Kant, *The Critique of Judgement*, 48, trans. J. H. Bernard (London: Macmillan, 1914), p. 195.

18. David Mitchell and Sharon Snyder, *The Body and Physical Difference: Discourses of Disability* (Ann Arbor: University of Michigan Press, 1997), p. 17.

19. Ibid., p. 12.

20. Ibid., p. 6.

21. Ibid.

22. Ibid.

23. Martin Norden, *The Cinema of Isolation: A History of Physical Disability in the Movies* (New Brunswick, N.J.: Rutgers University Press, 1994), pp. 181–182.

24. Ibid., p. 180.

25. Mitchell and Snyder, *Body and Physical Difference*, p. 12.

26. Norden, *Cinema of Isolation*, pp. 19–25.

27. William Wyler, "No Magic Wand," *Screen Writer*, February 1947, p. 6.

28. Anita Gates, "Ready for My Fade-Out, Mr. DeMille," *New York Times*, June 21, 1998, sec. 15, p. 29.

29. bell hooks, *Art On My Mind: Visual Politics* (New York: The New Press, 1995), pp. 95–97.

30. Ibid., p. 98.

31. Kimberle Crenshaw, "Demarginalizing the Intersection of Race and Sex: A Black Feminist Critique of Antidiscrimination Doctrine, Feminist Theory, and Anti-racist Politics," in Alison Jaggar, ed., *Living with Contradictions: Controversies in Feminist Social Ethics* (Boulder: Westview Press, 1994), p. 47.

32. Ibid., pp. 39–52.

33. hooks, *Art on My Mind*, p. 97.

34. Anita Silvers, "Disability," in *Blackwell's Companion to Feminist Philosophy*, ed. Alison Jaggar and Iris Marion Young (Oxford: Blackwell, 1998), pp. 330–340; Anita Silvers, "On Not Iterating Women's Disabilities: A Crossover Perspective on Genetic Dilemmas," in *Embodying Bioethics: Feminist Advances*, ed. Anne Donchin and Laura Purdy (Lanham, Md.: Rowman and Littlefield, 1998); Anita Silvers, "Reprising Women's Disability: Feminist Identity Strategy and Disability Rights," *Berkeley Women's Law Journal* 13 (1998); Tom Shakespeare, Kath Gillespie-Sellis, and Dominic Daies, eds., *The Sexual Politics of Disability* (London: Cassell, 1996); Karin Barron, "The Bumpy Road to Womanhood," *Disability & Society* 12, no. 12 (Spring 1997): 223–224.

35. Mitchell and Snyder, *Body and Physical Difference*, p. 17.

36. Ibid.

37. Lennard Davis, "Nude Venuses, Medusa's Body, and Phantom Limbs: Disability and Visuality," in Mitchell and Snyder, *Body and Physical Difference*, p. 68.

38. Rosemarie Garland Thomson, *Extraordinary Bodies: Physical Disability in American Culture and Literature* (New York: Columbia University Press, 1997), p. 8.

39. Davis, "Nude Venuses," p. 68.

40. Thomson, *Extraordinary Bodies*, p. 136. Despite thinking that disability "operates as a code," Thomson makes clear in a subsequent discussion ("Disabled Women

as Powerful Women in Petry, Morrison, and Lorde: Revising Black Female Subjectivity," in Mitchell and Snyder, *Body and Physical Difference*) that it should not be assumed to be a trope (p. 265).

41. Davis, "Nude Venuses," passim.

42. Mitchell and Snyder, *The Body and Physical Difference*, p. 13.

43. Ibid.

44. Ibid.

45. Harriet Martineau, *Life in the Sickroom: Essays. By an Invalid* (Boston: Leonard Bowles and William Crosby, 1844).

46. Charlotte Yonge, *The Clever Woman of the Family* (1865; reprint, New York: Virago, 1985).

47. Thomson, "Disabled Women as Powerful Women," p. 250.

48. Ibid., 241.

49. Ibid.

50. Ibid.

51. Thomson, *Extraordinary Bodies*, p. 125.

52. Thomson, "Disabled Women as Powerful Women," p. 241.

53. Carroll, *Philosophy of Horror*, p. 188.

54. Thanks for these examples to editor Peg Brand, who adds that "In spite of our repeated exposure to the work of Cindy Sherman, her large photographs of the mid to late 1980s—with mud, blood and vomit—are still hard to look at." Personal communication, 1998.

55. Michael Kimmelman, "How the Tame Can Suddenly Seem Wild," *New York Times*, August 2, 1998, Art Section, p. 35.

56. Charles Rosen, *The Frontiers of Meaning* (New York: Hill and Wang, 1994).

57. Kimmelman, "How the Tame" p. 35.

58. Ibid.

59. Thomson, *Extraordinary Bodies*, p. 247.

60. Ibid.; and Thomson, "Disabled Women as Powerful Women," p. 112.

PART THREE

Body as Art

Hilary Robinson

10. Whose Beauty? Women, Art, and Intersubjectivity in Luce Irigaray's Writings

What I am going to try and talk about today, often in the form of questions, stands at the meeting point of the properties of physical matter and an elaboration of sexualized subjective identity that has still to be thought through and put into practice.[1]

This statement by Luce Irigaray could indicate a discussion in a woman artist's studio. We could be contemplating her practice. We could be at the site—the meeting point of the properties of physical matter and an elaboration of sexualized subjective identity—of her enunciation through that practice. This essay explores the implications of Irigaray's discussion of the concept "beauty" for that site. Her writings indicate moments of strategic or structural possibility from which women can create beauties appropriate to their subjectivities, and outline how becoming subjects, women, and mediating the resultant subjectivity is in itself to create beauty. Although in Western culture the Symbolic has a phallocentric syntax and what is read as beauty of body and beauty in art are products of phallocentric structures,[2] nonetheless moments of resistance and disruption can be discerned in contemporary artworks by women. It is against the backdrop of Irigaray's reconfiguring of "beauty" that I discuss some of these works.

Whose "Beauty"?

Luce Irigaray's essay "How Can We Create Our Beauty?" is published in *Je, Tu, Nous: Toward a Culture of Difference*, a book of short polemic essays, each focused on a particular aspect of Irigaray's thinking in order to introduce it to a wider audience and demonstrate its politics.[3] This essay can work as an indicative reading, pointing to areas in Irigaray's broader work that are important for developing radical discourses and practices of art. Irigaray begins by positing her argument in words which are a challenge to many of us who are involved with contemporary art practices. This terminology can even appear naive for a number of reasons. Most of us making or working with art will have assimilated, for instance, Adorno's discussion about the impossibility of lyricism after Auschwitz, or the way an avant-garde-ist principle of *épater les bourgeois* has disintegrated into postmodernist horror-chic, or a feminist-realist impulse to "tell it like it is," or possibly even the desire for catharsis which can only be achieved at the resolution of a certain order of narrative. At first, Irigaray appears either to ignore or be unaware of the impact of each of these issues for contemporary art practice. She writes:

> Very often, when looking at women's works of art, I have been saddened by the sense of anguish they express, an anguish so strong it approaches horror. Having wanted to contemplate beauty created by women, I would find myself faced instead with distress, suffering, irritation, sometimes ugliness. The experience of art, which I expected to offer a moment of happiness and repose, of compensation for the fragmentary nature of daily life, of unity and communication or communion, would become yet another source of pain, a burden.[4]

Irigaray uses the rest of the essay to outline in four main points why she thinks women make images of pain and how women could create beauty. First, she puts herself into the discussion by pointing out that she too deals with pain in her work, but states that she attempts to do so in what she calls "a literary style" to cushion any potential sense of dereliction in the reader. At the same time she will look for something positive—something for which, she says, women, "who have a tendency to identify only with what they lack, their shortcomings,"[5] sometimes criticize her. She says that showing the negative

> is positive and necessary given that it was meant to stay hidden. The portrayal of suffering is, then, for women an act of truthfulness. It's also akin to an individual and collective catharsis. . . . Daring to manifest publicly individual and collective pain has a therapeutic effect, bringing relief to the body and enabling them to accede to another time. This doesn't come as a matter of course, but it may be the case for some women.[6]

She likens the anguish represented to that of (unspecified) masked figures in Greek tragedy who were subjected to fate.

Irigaray's second point is that having children is a most wonderful creativity. However, within the "male social order" there is a particular obligation to do it; and further, a distinction is made between creation, which is reserved for men, and procreation, which is deemed of a lesser order. She suggests that "there would seem to be confusion now between the beauty of the work [of childbirth] and its definition within a between-men civilization in which women no longer have a recognized right to engender spiritual values."[7]

The third point is stated bluntly: "[A]s women, we have thus been enclosed in an order of forms inappropriate to us. In order to exist, we must break out of these forms."[8] This may have one of three consequences. First, it may destroy us: "[I]nstead of being reborn, we annihilate ourselves." Second, it may show us what flesh, and therefore what colours, we have left: "I think colour is what's left of life beyond forms, beyond truth or beliefs, beyond accepted joys and sorrows. Colour also expresses our sexuate nature, that irreducible dimension of our incarnation."[9] The third possible consequence of breaking out of the inappropriate order of forms which encloses us is that women may rediscover their identity and forms, forms which are "always incomplete, in perpetual growth, because a woman grows, blossoms and fertilizes (herself) within her own body."[10]

The fourth and final main point of "How Can We Create Our Beauty?" concerns the representation of a "female divine." The between-men culture disallows women's expression of meaning. Just as a child is not an abstract or arbitrary sign, so too for women "meaning remains concrete, close, related to what is natural, to perceptible forms."[11] In what is called pre-history, women participated in civil and religious life and were represented as woman-goddesses (not only as mother-goddesses). Today, lack of divine representation leaves women in a state of dereliction, without means of designating or expressing self, or of identifying and respecting mother-daughter genealogies.

From this essay, then, there are three salient points for discussion: (1) the very broad issues of flesh, body, their representation, and female morphology; (2) the nature of female creativity and subjectivity; and (3) the representation of what Irigaray terms the "female divine" and its inevitable adjuncts, "universality" and "transcendence." Running through these discussions, as they unfold into Irigaray's wider writings, are two others: 4) the necessity for productive acknowledgment of female genealogies (two-way interchanges between mother and daughter, and its concomitant, exchanges between women) and; 5) in very close relation to this, a notion of fulfillment or "becoming" for women. Without any of these points, women's beauty is not possible: indeed, in conjunction they would be productive of and allow for the performativity of women's beauty. It is thus clear that anything approaching "an Irigarayan aesthetic" will not be found in the reproduction of certain methodologies in the studio, or adherence to one or another "style" of imagery. Irigaray's discussion of beauty therefore, and my discussion here, is *not* about defining a new aesthetic, *nor* is it an essentialist notion of a female aesthetic which has been overshadowed by a male aesthetic, and which only requires a light to be shone on it in order to become visible. For Irigaray, "beauty" for women is a potential state of being which can only come about as a result of rethinking political and cultural discourse. Her discussion of beauty is about making possible an order of discourse which would in and of itself, and inevitably, be productive of beauty. It is a discussion which requires the reader to think differently: to rethink what might be productive of beauty, and what might constitute the transcendental and the universal.

Reflection, Self-Image, Beauty

In "Divine Women," Irigaray quotes Ludwig Feuerbach as saying "God is the mirror of man," adding:

> Woman has no mirror wherewith to become woman. Having a God and becoming one's gender go hand in hand. God is the other that we need absolutely. In order to become, we need some shadowy perception of achievement [*besoin du pressentiment d'un accomplissement pour devenir*]; not a fixed objective, not a One postulated to be immutable but rather a cohesion and a horizon that assures us the passage between past and future, the bridge of a present *that remembers*, that is not sheer oblivion and loss, not a crumbling away of existence, a failure simply, to take note.[12]

Feuerbach's comment adds to the complexity of the structure which rests upon a fundamentally simple premise: phallocentric structures build man's subjectivity upon his "seeing" everything around him as other of his same. Most important for this discussion, it means that he has constructed what I will term the representation, "Woman," and projected it upon women. But it also means that, certainly in patriarchal, Western, Judeo-Christian or Helleno-Christian cultures, man can create God in his own image. This other idealized "other of his same" (as distinct from the deformed "other of his same," the representation, "Woman") then functions as the horizon of his possibilities, that necessity for a "becoming" into subjectivity. For patriarchal man, the "other of his same" functions for his subjectivity like a mirror, and Irigaray has indicated that "Representation can dispense with and supplant the role played in the real life of the senses by the mirror."[13] But if women do not have an horizon of possibilities, an enunciative divine, then one of the things that is needed is a movement the other way:

> The impotence, the formlessness, the deformity associated with women, the way they are equated with something other than the human and split between the human and the inhuman (half-woman, half-animal), their duty to be adorned, masked, and made up, etc., rather than being allowed *their own* physical, bodily beauty, their own skin, their own form(s), all this is symptomatic of the fact that women lack a female god who can open up the perspective in which their flesh can be transfigured.[14]

In addition to a move toward recognizing the potential for a representation that is an horizon of possibilities, we need also to move toward its necessary corollary: a representation that is "in the real life of the senses" that allows for such an horizon; a self-image in a real-life mirror and elsewhere. There are clear implications here for art practices (representational practices) by women; not only how women image themselves, but how they image each other, how they image womanliness and femininity: becoming a woman. I think that what Irigaray does in following this argument through without being proscriptive about the nature of practice is to offer indicative analyses of the structures by and through which women represent themselves in the broadest sense (initially to themselves, but not exclusively).

In "Divine Women" Irigaray performs such a move (from an horizon of possibilities in the divine to one in the spirit *through* the body) in her account of women's relation to their own self-image in the mirror, and to their beauty: "Women have rarely used their beauty as a weapon for *themselves*, even more rarely as a *spiritual* weapon. The body's splendor has rarely been used as a lever to advance self-love, self-fulfilment."[15] Without being able to see their self-image (to represent it to themselves) as beautiful, there is no potential for women to recognize or develop a representation which is an horizon of possibilities that are appropriate for them; such a horizon would necessarily include a possibility of beauty for women, a female soul, and a female divine. Following this point, Irigaray works through the problems of self-image for women in a patriarchy, and the credible potential self-representation. (I distinguish here between women's relation with self-image, by which I mean in particular the visual image in the mirror, and self-representation in the broad sense indicated above, including how women represent that self-image to themselves: how they see the image, allow for and develop its potential as an horizon.) I shall follow these arguments through, taking Irigaray's discussion in five sections.

Section One

> *Maternal beauty has been glorified in our religious and social*
> *traditions, but womanly beauty for centuries has been seen merely as*
> *a trap for the other [que séduction pour fair tomber l'autre chez la*
> *femme amante]. The transfiguration of a female body by beauty, the*
> *active share that the woman can have in that transfiguration, are*
> *today often misunderstood. Perhaps they have been forgotten. Beauty*
> *is not presented or represented as the spiritual predicate of the flesh.*
> *Yet, it is not impossible to imagine that a body can be, can above all*
> *become, intelligent or stupid, that our relation to corporeal love can*
> *be actively aesthetic or passively abject [soumis], reduced: for*
> *example, to a pseudo-animality (animals themselves are beautiful in*
> *their sexual displays; bestial is an animal quality negatively*
> *attributed to man), or to motherhood, with its associations to bodily*
> *deformity and the link often made between it and chastity.*[16]

Beauty in women, as it is understood in Western patriarchal culture, is
found in the two extremes of the representation, "Woman": the/his mother
and the/his mistress, the virgin and the whore, the beautiful object of
contemplation and the woman subjected to the phallocentric gaze. This
has been well charted, not least through feminist research and works such
as Julia O'Faolain and Lauro Martines's *Not in God's Image*. They have
collected passages from the early teachings of the Church such as this from
Tertullian:

> And so a veil must be drawn over a beauty so dangerous as to have brought
> scandal into heaven itself, so that before God, in whose eyes it is guilty of
> the angel's fall, it may blush in the presence of the remaining angels and
> give up the licence to show itself and hide even from the eyes of men.[17]

Mary was the model of beauty for women, but as mother and virgin, not as
woman. Mothers were encouraged to emulate her as much as was possible.
Marina Warner includes in her eloquent charting of the mythic figurations
of Mary the following modern prayer for girls: "Most blessed Virgin Mary
. . . your life of faith and love and perfect unity with Christ was planned by
God to show us clearly what our lives should be. . . . [Y]ou are the outstanding model of motherhood and virginity."[18] Olwen Hufton has collected a
seventeenth-century French prayer recommended by the church for wom-
en in labor which begins: "Oh Mother of the holiest one of holies who
approached nearest to his divine perfection and so became mother to such
a son."[19] But to place women as mothers by creating an ideal who is figured

as a mother rather than as a woman is to reduce women; and to structure an ideal of motherhood which has bodily failure built in to it (she conceived without sex, and she did not die but was taken body and soul into heaven) is to reduce still further any possible sense of becoming women. As it is, and with this impossible ideal, Irigaray reminds us, the motherly body is often considered deformed (and thus shameful in its relation to the ideal) and has to remain chaste (the closest approximation to the patriarchal definition of Mary's virginity).

The language that Irigaray uses in her discussion of female beauty and women's self-images in the mirror intertwines terminology of corporeality with that of Christianity, particularly Catholicism. While exposing the maintenance mimesis expected of women in Western patriarchy, she performs an act of productive mimesis[20] upon this terminology in order to work toward a sense of spirituality or the divine for women, which issues from a sense of female beauty. A sense of womanly corporeal beauty is part of this, and thus so too is a woman's comprehension of beauty in her self-image. In this introductory passage, Irigaray talks of "the transfiguration of the female body by beauty" and the possibility that beauty can be "the spiritual predicate of the flesh." We already consider other emotional and intellectual aspects of the body; why, then, is it impossible to think of the spirituality of the female body?

Section Two

> *Female beauty* [la beauté féminine] *is always considered as finery* [parure] *ultimately designed to attract the other into the self. It is almost never perceived as a manifestation of, an appearance of, a phenomenon expressive of* [qui dit] *interiority—whether of love, of thought, of flesh. We look at ourselves in the mirror to please someone, rarely to interrogate the state of our body or our spirit, rarely for ourselves and in search of* [en vue de] *our own becoming.*[21]

Feminine beauty is *une parure*—that most feminine of finery, a word used in France in relation to (for example) the frivolity of food trimmings, bridal wear, and the innate floweriness of spring. Innate, frivolous, up for consumption, and feminine, it is both a trap—indicative of intentionality and concealment—and surface, not speaking of the profundity and interiority of body and spirit. We are back in the realm of the two-dimensionality of the phallocentric representation, "Woman": surface, with an illusion of depth. The relationship that women *as* the representation, "Woman" have with the mirror at present is one of maintenance mimesis *of* the representation, "Woman": to please, to reproduce the allure that the other has in the eyes of the same. We cannot become subjects in this representational economy; we cannot become women. When we look at images of ourselves, in the mirror and elsewhere, we *look at ourselves as* the representation, "Woman." We *represent ourselves to ourselves* as the representation "woman." The Symbolic does not have a syntax for articulation and representation of a woman's subjectivity (the hole in its scopophilic lens). So, caught in a representational economy which can only recognize the phallocentric representation, "Woman," we cannot yet see, read, understand or create our self-image in a different syntax, as subjects, women.

Section Three

> The mirror almost always serves to reduce us to a pure exteriority—of
> a very particular kind. It functions [il intervient] as a possible way to
> constitute screens between the other and myself. In a way quite
> different from mucuses or skin, living, porous, fluid differentiations
> and the possibility of communion, the mirror is a weapon of frozen
> [glacée]—and polemical—distancing. I risk only my double to love. I
> do not abandon or give myself as body, flesh, as immediate—and
> geological, genealogical—affects. The mirror signifies the constitu-
> tion of a fabricated (female) other [d'un(e) autre fabriqué(e)] that I
> shall put forward as an instrument [enjeu] of seduction in my place.
> I seek to be seductive and to be content with images of which I
> remain the artisan, the artist.[22]

In the dominant ways of seeing in Western culture, the flat mirror structures representational and interpretive possibilities, as we have seen. As guarantor of the "subject," it is also guarantor of the other of his same. A screen for projecting onto, it maintains this "otherness," it maintains a distance without a possibility of mediation and disallows the play of couples. Thus the representation, "Woman" is fixed, frozen (*glacée*): the mirror is *la glace*—the ice-glass-mirror—not *la psyché*, the soul-mirror, or the *miroir ardent*, the burning mirror. A woman, always already elsewhere than the representation, "Woman"—her double—can never enter fully that play of the couple, can never, as the representation, "Woman" fully risk love. How can she when her subjectivity is elsewhere? The representation, "Woman" created by patriarchal man, is re-created in a process of maintenance mimesis by women. This is her stake in the patriarchal game of representation: to create the seductive *parure*. This is her art. How can there be room here for her to make anything else as art? This does not mean that she will not make "art": but that the "art" she makes will embody aspects of the phallocentric representation, "Woman" and not the woman's subjecthood, her subjectivity.

Section Four

> *I have yet to unveil, unmask [démasquée], or veil myself for me—to veil myself for self-contemplation, for example, to retouch myself with my gaze so as to limit my exposure to the other, but also to again be in touch with [retoucher] my own gestures and garments, thus to re-nest (into) my vision and contemplation of myself. Which is not a kind of cold narcissism, but rather a way that I can supply extra help and assistance, as an adult, to the different houses, the different bodies that have borne me, enveloped me, rocked me, embraced me, wrapped themselves around me. . . . The mirror, and indeed the gaze, are frequently used as non-tactile weapons or tools, which break off the fluidity of touch, including that of the gaze.[23]*

If *la parure* is a covering of finery and trimmings for the representation, "Woman" then those I will term "the subjects, women," must have garments which are different and with a different relationship to the gaze. In "The Poverty of Psychoanalysis," Irigaray describes the function of the dance of the veil:

> In many traditions [it] is the sexual and religious rite *par excellence*, a dance with a mystery and a cosmic reality that is at once prior to and beyond any already-constituted subjectivity. The scene is played out by the goddess-mother [*la déesse-mère*] or the woman-lover [*amante*], the gods and the universe. It does not cover nothingness; it attempts to pass through illusion towards the act/gesture of creating or begetting the world.[24]

This leads me to understand the use of the word "veil" in the above passage as indicating two ontological directions: not merely a choice of being clothed or not. "I have yet to unveil, unmask" I see as an acknowledgment of having yet to remove the covering that is *la parure*, the representation, "Woman," the masquerade required within patriarchy: to remove the surface plan/e or screen of the mirror. With "I have yet to . . . veil myself *for me*" a difference in the veil is indicated: note that she says "veil" and not "re-veil" after the unveiling. I understand this as referring to clothing oneself with the vestments that are the Symbolic syntax appropriate to one's subjectivity,[25] and thus to have a screen/veil of mediation, whether of the subject with herself or of intersubjectivity. This is a veil that allows the self-contemplation of the subjects, women; and it also sets limits on that subjectivity and choice about marking those limits. It is a veil which allows touch to return to the gaze, rather than one which retains the gaze as abstract, specular, evaluation. This is not the frozen auto-erotics projected onto the representation, "Woman" by an economy of sameness, but a subjectivity to which amorousness, touch, vision, and history have been returned, and in which they are returned to each other.

Section Five

> Though necessary at times for separating, the mirror—and the gaze when it acts as a mirror—ought to remain a means and not an end to which I yield. The mirror should assist, not undermine my incarnation. Generally it reflects back [renvoie] nothing but superficial, flat images. There are other means that generate volume better than specular reflection [le reflet spéculaire]. To work at beauty is at least as much a matter of working at gestures as the relationship to space and to others as it is a matter of cross-examining, usually with anxiety, your mirror. The mirror freezes our becoming breath, our becoming space. Our becoming bird, perhaps? Though it may at times help us to emerge, to move out of the water, the mirror paralyzes our energies [élans], our movements, our wings. What protects me from the other and allows me to move toward him or her is more often the plotting out of a space of air [l'aménagement d'un territoire d'air] rather than the interposition of mirrors and ice-glasses [glaces] whose cutting edge always threatens to turn against me. After the totally enveloping waters of our prenatal time, we have to construct for ourselves, bit by bit, an envelope of air for our time on earth—air in which we can breathe and sing freely, in which we can spread our appearances and movements. Once we were fishes. We are destined to become birds. This will not happen without opening and mobility in the air.[26]

Luce Irigaray is not discarding mirrors. A sense of immediacy is intensely problematic for women, who have not had an appropriate Symbolic syntax through which to mediate themselves and their subjectivity. Then a sense of separation is necessary, and mirrors can assist. But assist they must, not hinder; at present, they do not assist women's becoming and their subjectivity. In phallocentric structures, they fix women as the representation, "Woman," freeze them into an anxious, speculative relationship with their own self-imagery. Irigaray suggests that beauty is to be found in our gestural relationships with space, with other subjects. Space—air—is necessary for breath, life, and movement. Beauty will be found in our becoming the subjects, women, for which air and space is necessary. It does not reside in the anxious relationship of the representation, "Woman," with her image *as* the representation, "Woman" in the mirror; caught in a closed circuit, a maintenance mimesis of the phallocentric gaze.

Relational Identity, Intersubjectivity, and Objects of Mediation

As might be imagined, mediating subjectivity is far from being the same process for each gender, not least because men and women have a different relation to the Symbolic in our present culture. Thus what is necessary is not only a sense of identity and its limits, but a more active sense of identity: what Irigaray calls a *relational identity*, a subjective identity which recognizes that each gender has its own particular problems to overcome to achieve intersubjectivity and thus attentiveness, both with other subjects of its own gender and other subjects of the other gender: "Such a relation [of attentiveness] can only come about if man renounces the domination of nature and of the economy of subjectivity, and if woman has the ability to govern her nature so that she becomes subjectivity."[27] Men must acknowledge that their subjectivity has limits; while women must realize their subjective identity (their identity as subjects) and, therefore, their need for subjective mediation:

> Men *and* women must modify their relational identity. Certainly, women "spontaneously" privilege the relation between subjects and men the relation to objects. The feminine subject constructs itself through a relation to the other, the masculine subject through the manufacture of objects and worlds starting from which it is possible for him to exchange with the other. Let us say the woman must learn to put some objectivity susceptible to being shared between *I* and *you*: this relation must not remain, for her, at the level of need and of subjective immediacy, otherwise the *you* risks disappearing as *you*. The man, on the other hand, needs to rediscover the other as subject beyond his universe of objects. What the one and the other lack in order to realize their relation is a dialectic between subjectivity and objectivity, at the same time proper to each and common.[28]

In this passage, Irigaray returns us to the highly pragmatic nature of this relationship; indeed (to treat it pragmatically), it could serve as an analysis of the crisis of representation in the art world. Historically, women artists have had to make work which can be seen to be a maintenance mimesis of the patriarchal languages of men, while at the same time that work has been written about *as if it were* a symptom of their *immediacy as women* (a phenomenon well-charted within feminist art history). More recently, the apparent breakdown of the visual languages of art has served only to present the father-son power struggles of the maintenance mimesis in a slightly altered guise. The space that seems to have opened up for developing subjectivities is still, for men, about the production of the object (often as spectacle) and not about developing an awareness of the other subject and the possibilities of inter-subjectivity. The market keeps excelling itself, not only (and most clearly) with palpable objects (paintings, sculptures, etc.) but with the selling of objects of little or no monetary value (Richard Long's stone circles; David Mach's sculptures made from wire coat hangers, matches, etc.) and the marketing of body art (from Pietro Manzoni's canning of his breath and shit to photographic documentation of performance work being promoted to the level of artwork itself—and always on the behalf of the performer being photographed, not the photographer). Aspects of conceptual work could be considered as avoiding this; but some which clearly rely upon a degree of intersubjectivity, such as Sol LeWitt's wall drawings and Lawrence Weiner's descriptive statements, nonetheless compromise this by only being available *as objects* on the market. They can only be accessed once they have negotiated the market (been sold) and have been reproduced by the owner. All of these correspond to Irigaray's identification of men's patterns of "communication":

> For men's teleology implies rather an abandonment of immediate communication—of inter-subjectivity and dialogue—in order to set off in quest of an *oeuvre* (in which they usually alienate themselves) and, among other things, a spiritual journey compelled by a transcendence appropriate to their ego.[29]

For women, the situation is slightly different. Of course, some are still permitted a place through their maintenance mimesis of patriarchal languages; and in some cases their work is still written about as a symptom of their immediacy. For others, particularly those who acknowledge their gender, the expression of a subjectivity through an appropriate Symbolic syntax has become an issue—even if it is one they appear at once to close. Tracy Emin, for example, with her video monologue about an abortion, and her creation of confessional rooms, furniture, quilts, and so forth, depoliticizes—or even undoes the politics of—feminist work of the 1970s by copying the surface style of that work while ignoring its collectivity, its political intent, and its responsibility to its audience.

Other cases appear more ambiguous. Janine Antoni's performance *Loving Care* (1993) is one such case. Having dipped her long hair in *Loving Care* hair dye—rumored to be the brand used by her mother—Antoni then proceeded to "mop" the floor of the gallery with it. One understanding of this work could be that Janine Antoni was performing a mimesis of the 1950s works of Yves Klein which involved painting the naked bodies of women models, then using their bodies to make marks.[30] It could be argued that it is a productive mimesis; she reasserted a female genealogy (the link with her mother and with earlier works by feminists such as Mierle Laderman Ukeles) which bring to mind the irony of the product name, "Loving Care"—it is, after all, a product to aid women in performing the masquerade, femininity, and not about loving the subject, woman. It is also a highly ironic reference to "women's work" (the "loving care" of usually unseen tasks of cleaning) and to Jackson Pollock's action painting. But another understanding can be gleaned from the photographic documentation. Here are images of a woman turning herself into an object—or maybe abjecting herself—before the speculative gaze of the viewers. If this is what happened (I was not present at the performance) then either way—object or abject—she denies any possibility of articulating her subjectivity and of an attentive, intersubjective, presence from (and relationship with) the audience.

There is a problem with achieving an intersubjectivity between women to which Irigaray returns on a number of occasions. Between a woman and a man there is the irreducible difference of gender:

> [B]etween a man and a woman there's a negative, a type of irreducibility that doesn't exist between a woman and a woman. Let's say between a man and a woman the negativity [*la négativité*] is, dare I say it, of an ontological, irreducible type. But between a woman and another woman it's of a much more empirical type and, furthermore, can only be understood and can only live in the ontological difference between man and woman. It's complicated.[31]

Irigaray holds that gender difference and gendered subjectivity work across other forms of difference. The subject's recognition of difference and of the other subject is rooted in the experience of sexual difference and its irreducibility. For a subject, woman, to recognize the difference that is another subject, woman, she has first to be a woman—to have her subject-

Janine Antoni, Loving Care, 1992. "I soaked my hair in hair dye and mopped the floor with it." Detail of performance at Anthony D'Offay Gallery, London. Courtesy of the artist and Luhring Augustine Gallery.

hood—and secondly to have a relational identity—to have an awareness of her limits, and that the other subject is irreducible to herself. The subject, woman, is still more likely to reduce the other subject, woman, to herself than she is to reduce the other subject, man. This has more to do with identity than with identification; by which I mean that it is a matter of ontology, of the relation to origin and the subsequent relationship with the mother:

> The possible discovery of their identity . . . poses a major problem of subjective relationships. Woman has a direct inter-subjective relationship with her mother. Hers is more an *inter-subject* economy than an economy of subject-object relations; it is thus a very social and cultural economy that has doubtless led to interpretation in which women are seen as the guardians of love. This subjective economy between mother and daughter can be partially translated into action [*en gestes*]. . . . But that is not enough. Woman must be able to express herself in words,

images and symbols in this inter-subjective relationship with her mother, then with other women, if she is to enter into a non-destructive relationship with men. This very special economy of woman's identity must be permitted, known and defined. It is essential to a real culture. It means supporting, not destroying, the mother-daughter relationship.[32]

It is not so much that what is needed here (between mothers and daughters, and then between women) is a re-assertion of limits; what is necessary is an insertion—a bringing into play—of objects. To become the subjects, women, cries out for mediation between women. Irigaray suggests this when discussing the interaction of the woman analyst and the women analysand:

> When it is a matter of *analysis of women, between women*, this path has to be invented, created. . . . Our grammar remains foreign to this becoming of feminine *jouissance*, which loses its self-affection and the possibility of speaking its name therein.
> Unable to create their own words, women remain and move in an immediacy without any transitional, trans-actional object. They take-give without mediation, commune without knowing it with and in a flesh they do not recognize: maternal flesh not reducible to a reproductive body, more or less shapeless amorous matter to which there could be no debt, no possible return.[33]

So there is a fundamental need for women to create objects in an appropriate syntax; objects that function trans-actionally between them in order to achieve a form of intersubjective mediation. Indeed, in her list of highly pragmatic recommendations to aid the creation of space between mothers and daughters, Irigaray suggests "Between mother and daughter, interpose small handmade objects to make up for losses of spatial identity, for intrusions into personal space."[34] Evidently not tokens to assuage guilt after traumatic rows, these objects are the development of a Symbolic—and symbolized—syntax in the mother-daughter relationship; one that will create the third space of mediation, and prevent women from collapsing back into immediacy.

To extrapolate from this, therefore, the art object *between* women can then be understood as a means of attending to an intersubjective relation *if* we recognize it as a gift of a means of mediation between subjects, rather than as a stand-in for the objectness of the other, as phallocentric man does with his production of objects. There is a risk, however:

> How can women—especially amongst themselves—refrain from taking from this gift the means to palliate their dereliction through a more or less immediate and paradoxical mimetic identification? This operation

turns the donor inside out before there is any gift-object and closes the path of the taker; a gesture which involves a sort of capitalization of the mucous membrane, an exteriorization of what is most inner.[35]

A woman may make an object—an artwork—as a means of mediation and offer it in all good faith as a space through which mediation can occur. But this does not guarantee that the woman to whom it is offered will be a subject able to accept and produce intersubjective relationships between women or able to be attentive. This risks an injury to the subjectivity of the woman who gives the space/object. In part, this risk may be ameliorated by the nature of the enunciation, the presenting of what we can call the gift-space/object. We can look here at the offer of love. Irigaray explains her use of the phrase "I love to you":

> I love to you thus means: I do not take you for a direct object, nor for an indirect object by revolving around you. It is, rather, around myself that I have to revolve in order to maintain the *to you* thanks to the return to me. Not with my prey—you become mine—but with the intention of respecting my nature, my history, my intentionality, while also respecting yours. Hence, I do not return to me by way of: I wonder if I am loved. That would result from an introverted intentionality, going toward the other so as to return ruminating, sadly and endlessly, over solipsistic questions in a sort of cultural cannibalism.[36]

Irigaray is here suggesting an approach to an intersubjective mediation through the phrase "I love to you." If we take this as a model for extended forms of intersubjective communication, then it suggests practices of enunciation—of creating intersubjective objects—that neither reduce the other subject to an object nor use them to reflect back one's subjectivity. If I then further extrapolate from this to the making of art, it suggests a practice which is respectful of the subjectivity of the artist (i.e., which is not a maintenance mimesis but instead aids the woman artist in becoming the subject, woman) and which is offered as a mediation between attentive subjects, not a spectacle through which to win approval. "Attentiveness" here is thus actively two-way, not only about the audience, woman. For the artist, it is not only about the private, studio practice of making her work, but also about the broader aspects of enunciation through the making of art: the practices of the market, exhibiting, documentation, criticism, teaching or lecturing, and so forth. This suggests that women artists continue to get more attentive to these practices *as* practices (that they get more "difficult"?) and make the shift from treating their artworks as objects of distance (as galleries tend to) to treating them as objects of mediation, or, rather, objects through which mediation can happen. It means taking further responsibility for the work, whatever its material nature: in particular, painstaking exactitude over the installation of work, but also, for example, in the heart of the gallery system. insisting upon a veto—and making positive suggestions about—other aspects of the gallery's activity.[37]

Imaging Beauty

Luce Irigaray takes the discussion of the representation of women's bodies back to representations of women-goddesses:

> In those ["pre-historical"] days women were represented [*représentent*] as goddesses: not only as mother-goddesses—the only ones subsequent eras accepted—but also as women-goddesses. This is particularly evident in the fact that women-goddesses are beautiful, slim, and their sex marked by a triangle (as for mother-goddesses) in which the lips are drawn; all this was to be wiped out by what followed. Their divinity doesn't depend upon the fact they can be mothers but upon their female identity, of which the inter-enter-opening of the lips [*l'entre'ouverture des lèvres*] are an affirmative expression.[38]

Irigaray indicates that these representations of goddesses were not reduced to representations of mother-goddesses. A concept of the divine appropriate to woman is not located in the representation of her ability to be a mother, but in its representation of her *as a woman*. It would be easy to assume that the kind of artworks which might be a contemporary development of this form of representation would include many of the goddess images produced from the 1970s onward as a result of the women's movement. However, a large number of these enact a simplistic reversal of the phallic languages we have been taught—a more general trap, of which Irigaray is aware:

> From a feminine locus nothing can be articulated without a questioning of the symbolic itself. But we do not escape so easily from reversal. We do not escape, in particular, by thinking we can dispense with a rigorous interpretation of phallogocentrism. There is no simple manageable way to leap to the outside of phallogocentrism, nor any possible way to situate oneself there, that would result from the simple fact of being a woman. And in *Speculum*, if I was attempting to move back through the "masculine" imaginary, that is, our cultural imaginary, it is because that move imposed itself, both in order to demarcate the possible "outside" of this imaginary and to allow me to situate myself with respect to it as a woman, implicated in it and at the same time exceeding its limits.[39]

We can see in a brief examination of two artworks how some artists, in attempting a feminist development of goddess imagery, have assumed that there is a "simple manageable way to leap to the outside of phallogocentrism," and how others have attempted "to demarcate the possible 'outside' of this imaginary and to . . . situate [themselves] with respect to it as a woman."

A work such as Cynthia Mailman's *Self Portrait as God* (1977) falls into the former category. The centrally placed figure in this 9-foot-high painting is well over life size. The figure is painted in a symmetrical standing pose and using a perspective that increases the illusion of height of the figure; the effect is of an all-powerful being who literally and metaphorically looks down upon the viewer. Although the figure is naked and we see the lips of her vulva, any potentially revolutionary disruption of the viewer's relationship to the figure is immediately undone by the pose, the perspective, and by the style of painting. Flat areas of color are articulated with hard-edged borders and use of line. The overall effect is of a phallic goddess, the one who knows, sees, and judges all, who maintains a fixity of position; the viewer too has to maintain a fixed (subordinate) position in order to be in relationship with her. (I can't help feeling also that there is displayed here by the artist—in what is after all a self-portrait—at best an overweening ambition and at worst a representation of sublime arrogance.) Irigaray has warned about how we explore goddesses:

> I am far from suggesting that . . . we have to regress to siren goddesses, who fight against men gods. Rather I think we must not merely instigate a return to the *cosmic*, but also ask ourselves why we have been held back from becoming *divine women*. . . . But all this must be done in the context of entering further into womanhood, not moving backwards. If we resist hierarchies (the man/woman hierarchy, or state/woman, of a certain form of God/woman, or machine/woman), only to fall back into *the power* [*le pouvoir*] of nature/woman, animal/woman, even matriarchs/women, women/women, we have not made much progress.[40]

In this painting, Mailman has fallen back into these retrogressive power structures. There is no space for mediation between the subjects, women, and her/their divine; there is no intersubjectivity, no reassertion of female genealogies. We have here an equivalent to a Christian representation of an Old Testament God, or a Zeus, in a woman's body; a maintenance mimesis of phallocentric structures of representation and patriarchal structures of religion.

Yolanda López's *Portrait of the Artist as the Virgin of Guadalupe* (1978) presents an interesting contrast as it has some strong similarities with Mailman's painting: both are two-dimensional works, both are self portraits, and in both the figure is centrally placed, frontally posed against a background which represents infinite space. The López, however, is an oil pastel drawing and just 24" high; the outlines are necessarily a little fuzzy because of the pastel; and the figure carries a cloak-like cloth which billows around her, giving a sense of dynamic interrelation with space. It is significant that the figure is seen straight on (rather than illusionistically towering over the viewer) and active: She runs out of, or through, or is creating as she runs, the energy field which encircles her. Her eyes are partially closed by her very human grin, so the viewer is not fixed by her gaze into a spatially or emotionally static relationship with her.

The Virgin of Guadalupe is a national symbol to Mexicans and a symbol of cultural identity to Chicanas like Yolanda López. In herself—the Virgin Mary as a Mexican—she begins to undo some of the Eurocentrism of Catholic symbolism; but she is still very much an interceder and is maintained in a particular position in the Catholic patriarchy-hierarchy of imagery. She is

> the mark of a people's favour with God and thus boosts their confidence in the Church. At the shrine of Our Lady of Guadalupe, all the strands of Catholic devotion since the departure of the Reformed Churches are gathered together in their most characteristic form. . . . Her shrine is the best loved of Catholic Mexico. She was declared patroness of the country in 1754 by Pope Benedict XIV, and of the Americas in 1910. She is dark-complexioned like an Indian. . . . During the Mexican revolution, the Royalists fought under the standard of *La Virgen de los Remedios*, the ancient palladium of Cortes' conquering army, which he had brought with him from Alcantara. The independents marched under the banner of Our Lady of Guadalupe.[41]

By representing herself as Guadalupe, Yolanda López asserts a Chicana cultural identity; by representing Guadalupe as a physically and spatially dynamic contemporary woman, López discards the role of interceder; by showing her holding a snake, López refers back and across cultures to pre-Columbian religion and to the Cretan snake goddess; by then placing this image as the center of a triptych which also images her mother and grandmother, López asserts a genealogy which modulates across time and space, both within each image and across them, wresting the imagery away from the Catholic church in an exploration of the matrilinear and the divine. She has written about this:

> I looked at Guadalupe as an artist, as an investigator of the power of images. I was interested in her visual message as a role model. Essentially she is beautiful, serene, passive. She has no emotional life or texture of her own. She exists within the realm of magical mythology sanctified as a formal entity by religious tradition. . . . Because I feel living, breathing

Yolanda López, Portrait of the Artist as the Virgin of Guadalupe, *1978.*
Detail of The Guadalupe Triptych. *Oil pastel on paper, 30 inches x 24*
inches. Courtesy of the artist.

women also deserve the respect and love lavished on Guadalupe, I have chosen to transform the image. Taking symbols of her power and virtue, I have transferred them to women I know. My hope in creating these alternative role models is to work with the viewer in a reconsideration of how we as Chicanas portray ourselves. It is questioning the idealized stereotype we as women are assumed to attempt to emulate.[42]

For Luce Irigaray, the abstract is a human product which is completely arbitrary in its relation to the human body. This is expounded upon in most detail in "Flesh Colors"[43] which starts with an examination of the psychoanalytic scenario, where sound (the spoken word) is prioritized over light. The gestures and colors within that scenario are spoken of when the spoken word fails—for example, the gestures of the hysteric are only commented upon because of her muteness or verbal incoherence. Because sound moves more slowly than light, "psychoanalytic practice becomes an exercise in patience,"[44] a soporific experience, where the subject risks sinking into a colorless demented language of arbitrary forms. Lying down increases this risk, because the subject no longer needs a sense of balance, which encourages an artificial, arbitrary—abstract—reality. This model is one that echoes across all of Irigaray's work on writing, on the abstract and the arbitrary, and which informs her thinking about the cultural, social, political, and religious roles accorded the body.

Frequently in Western culture the abstract is referred to as objectivity, but this is a delusion, as Irigaray has outlined:

> This abstractness and the loss of that concrete, sensual immediacy that was always Hegel's point of departure block the passage from subjective into objective, from objective into subjective. Hegel sought to keep faith with nature but to do this one must pass through that question of sex and the spirit. The increase in so-called objective cultural effects produced by an inadequate dialectic of subjective and objective risks burying us under its spiritless shell, overwhelming us with its pestilential waste products.[45]

Alphabetical writing is fundamentally implicated in this; as Irigaray affirms, it developed as cultures shifted from women goddesses to mother-of-sons goddesses; from goddesses to gods; from oral histories to written histories; from living with nature to hierarchical domination of nature; and as financial systems were developed. Underlying this is a phallocentric structure which sees woman not as different but as other of the same. This is itself a form of abstraction:

> Cultures have forced us to repress the female genealogies. This means that we have entered into a kind of historical mania made up of forms that

are balanced in an artificial game of contradictions (the two poles are contained within sameness).[46]

And as a result our culture is constructed from

resemblances, abstracted from the body instead of expressive of it, that form a system of mimicries that allow me to say that I am like the other sex without in fact there being any correspondence with the same living forms, the same relations to sounds, to colors.[47]

These "resemblances, abstracted from the body instead of expressive of it" can, I think, begin to account for the shift Irigaray notes from the representation of women goddesses to mother-of-sons goddesses:

During the period when there were female goddesses, the woman's sexual organs always appear in the representation of the bodies of women, particularly goddesses, and not merely in the form of the triangle indicating the womb, but also in the form of the labia, an inscription which will later be erased. The cult of goddesses who are exclusively mothers, and mothers of sons, is a late episode in the history of women. In the symbolism of social exchanges, it is accompanied by the representation of the woman's sexual organs as the figure of the triangle representing the womb and standing as a symbol of the maternal function.[48]

The triangle alone represented women reduced to mothers; the representation "Woman," without her ontology recognized, without her relation to origin represented. The triangle plus the labia represents the woman goddess, and the possibility of mediation for the subjects, women. Neither of these representations could be confused with Realism, and it becomes clear that Irigaray, in decrying abstract representation, is not implying that we return to forms of Western Realism in art. That which is expressive of the body, after all, has to be a form of mediation, not a form of illusion. Considered this way, the rigid structures of two-dimensional, illusionistic Realism could be considered as "resemblances, abstracted from the body instead of expressive of it."[49]

Irigaray's comments on the excision of women's genitals from the scene of representation in phallocentric "art" are comparable with slightly earlier comments made by Suzanne Santoro in her artist's book, *Towards New Expression*. In the short text in this image-based work, Santoro first discusses a graffito on a wall in Rome of a penis, a vulva, and drops of semen being collected in a cup:

The penis and the semen were drawn with force and the cup for the care and preservation of the semen was given great importance. On the other hand there was the subordinate and mystified presence of the female

Book cover by Suzanne Santoro. Per Una Espressione
Nuova [Towards New Expression] *(Rome: Rivolta
Femminile, 1974).*

genitals, the usual crack-hole, hole-crack. . . . When I saw how this
subject had been treated in the past, I realized that even in diverse historical representation it had been annulled, smoothed down and, in the end,
idealized. . . . We can no longer see ourselves as if we live in a dream or
as an imitation of something that just does not reflect the reality of our
lives. . . . The substance of expression is unlimited and has no established
form. Self expression is a necessity. Expression begins with self assertion
and with the awareness of the differences between ourselves and others.[50]

Santoro's aim through the bookwork is (as the title suggests) to begin to work toward what we might call (after reading Irigaray) a syntax appropriate to women. She does this through the delicate and spare selection, editing, and juxtaposing of photographic images in this intimately scaled book (each page is approximately 16 cm × 11 cm). The images are of the vulva, the labia, the clitoris; of women's genitals seen from the front, with the outer and inner lips visible above the "Y" formed by the tops of the thighs; of the "Y" as represented by artists such as Cranach and Raphael, missing the representation of the lips; of Greek statues; of shells; and of flowers. Santoro makes explicit her aim of encouraging women toward expression through an appropriate significatory system:

> The placing of the Greek figures, the flowers and the conch shell near the clitoris is a means of understanding the structure of the female genitals. It is also an invitation for the sexual self expression that has been denied to women till now, and it does not intend to attribute specific qualities to one sex or the other.[51]

Notoriously, the Arts Council of Great Britain (as it was then called) removed *Towards New Expression* from an exhibition of artist's books touring Britain in 1976–1977, after it had been selected and included in the published catalogue. In an article written about the affair, Rozsika Parker contrasts this censorship with the inclusion of Allen Jones's artist's book *Projects*.[52] In a manner consistent with the rest of his work, this contained images of women taken directly from sado-masochistic fetish magazines, where the women are heavily "clothed" with harnesses, belts, gags, and skin-tight leather, and often have props such as whips. Their bodies are then further stylized by Jones to provide shiny surfaces, improbably small waists, and so forth, but their genitals are never represented. It was about Jones's work that Laura Mulvey had expounded her theory of fetishism (that the fetish displaces the sight of women's genitals), and Parker cites this in order to explain why the Arts Council of Great Britain was able to include the Jones book while justifying their exclusion of Santoro's

> on the grounds that obscenity might be alleged. . . . We are willing to defend obscenity on the grounds of artistic excellence but considered that in this case the avowed intention of the book was primarily a plea for sexual self-expression.[53]

We can expand Parker's understanding of this censorship as a result of phallocentric man's need to remove women's genitals from his sight and see Santoro's work as part of that broader cultural and ontological threat to phallocentric man which Irigaray identifies. Santoro's work is a threat not because it images women's genitals but because it is a strategic response, developed from within the political, collective site of the women's movement,[54] to what Irigaray identifies as the "need . . . to work out an art of the sexual, a sexed culture."[55]

In Luce Irigaray's use of the term, "beauty" cannot be subdivided into different categories that each require differing criteria for their evaluation. For her, corporeal beauty, spiritual beauty, and beauty in art are all linked; the aesthetic, the ethical, the political, and the ontological are inextricably related. The beautiful is not abstract, nor is it an objective category. It is deeply subjective — of the subject, and of the structuring of subjectivity; it is the becoming of a sexualized subjective identity through its appropriate mediation, attempts toward which can be uncovered in some extant artworks by women. In short, to become the subjects, women, is to become beauty.

NOTES

1. Luce Irigaray, "Flesh Colors," in *Sexes and Genealogies*, trans. Gillian C. Gill (New York: Columbia University Press, 1993), p. 153.

2. Irigaray's work is heavily informed by (and deconstructive of) Freudian and Lacanian psychoanalysis. I am using the term "Symbolic" here in the psychoanalytic sense, where it indicates the realm in which the subject mediates his or her subjectivity and understands the world around him or her self. I will retain the capital letter in order to distinguish this usage from both the everyday and the art-historical usage. Likewise, "phallocentric" indicates the psychological structures built around the phallus as primary signifier which inform what in political terminology would be called a patriarchal culture. For good introductions to feminist usage of psychoanalysis, see Patricia Elliot, *From Mastery to Analysis: Theories of Gender in Psychoanalytic Feminism* (Ithaca, N.Y.: Cornell University Press, 1991); Rosalind Minsky, *Psychoanalysis and Gender: An Introductory Reader* (London: Routledge, 1996); Elizabeth Wright, ed., *Feminism and Psychoanalysis: A Critical Dictionary* (Oxford: Blackwell, 1992).

3. Irigaray, "How Can We Create Our Beauty?" in *Je, Tu, Nous: Toward a Culture of Difference*, trans. Alison Martin (London: Routledge, 1993), pp. 107–111.

4. Ibid., p. 107. Nowhere does she indicate which works these may be.

5. Ibid., p. 108.

6. Ibid.

7. Ibid., p. 109.

8. Ibid.

9. Ibid.

10. Ibid., p. 110.

11. Ibid.

12. Irigaray, "Divine Women," in *Sexes and Genealogies*, p. 67. I would like to note

that there is an echo here of Lacan's "mirror phase" and critiques of it; an echo which will recur through this section. To engage with this fully would, again, be necessarily technical, lengthy, and tangential to my aim, which is not to chart the differences between Irigaray and Lacan. Such a project would be of more interest in a psychoanalytic-historical context, but is not really of interest here. So I would like to leave Lacan's work in the status of being symptomatic of the phallocentric structures that Irigaray is trying to undo, rather than present it as over-determinedly causal of her work.

13. Irigaray, *Speculum of the Other Woman,* trans. Gillian C. Gill (Ithaca, N.Y.: Cornell University Press, 1985), p. 95.

14. Irigaray, "Divine Women," p. 64.

15. Ibid.

16. Ibid., pp. 64–65.

17. Tertullian, *De Virginibus Velandis,* quoted by Julia O'Faolain and Lauro Martines in *Not in God's Image: Women in History* (London: Virago, 1979), p. 144.

18. From Dermot Hurley, ed., *Marian Devotions for Today Based on the Second Vatican Council* (Dublin, 1971), quoted in Marina Warner, *Alone of All Her Sex: The Myth and Cult of the Virgin Mary* (London: Pan Books, 1985), p. 68.

19. From *Dévotions particulièrs pour les femmes enceintes* (1665), quoted in Olwen Hufton, *The Prospect before Her: A History of Women in Western Europe,* vol. 1: *1500–1800* (London: HarperCollins, 1995), p. 183.

20. Irigaray differentiates two *mimeses* in Plato: "To simplify: there is *mimesis* as production . . . and there is the *mimesis* that would be already caught up in a process of *imitation, specularization, adequation,* and *reproduction.* . . . It is doubtless in the direction of, and on the basis of, that first *mimesis* that the possibility of a woman's writing may come about." *This Sex Which Is Not One,* trans. Catherine Porter with Carolyn Burke (Ithaca, N.Y.: Cornell University Press, 1985), p. 131. Hence my terms "maintenance mimesis" and "productive mimesis."

21. Irigaray, "Divine Women," p. 64. Translation modified.

22. Ibid., p. 65. Translation modified.

23. Ibid. Translation modified.

24. Irigaray, "The Poverty of Psychoanalysis," trans. David Macey, in *The Irigaray Reader,* ed. Margaret Whitford (Oxford: Blackwell, 1991), p. 87. Translation modified.

25. Luce Irigaray talks of the double syntax within the Symbolic; at present, the phallocentric syntax is virtually the only one at play, and the syntax appropriate to women is almost unknown. See "Questions," *This Sex Which Is Not One,* pp. 119–169.

26. Irigaray, "Divine Women," pp. 65–66. Translation modified.

27. Irigaray, *I Love to You,* trans. Alison Martin (London: Routledge, 1996), p. 46.

28. Irigaray, "Thinking Life as Relation: An Interview with Luce Irigaray," interview by Stephen Pluhacek and Heidi Bostic, trans. by Stephen Pluhacek, Heidi Bostic, and Luce Irigaray, *Man and World* 29, no. 4 (1996): 355.

29. Irigaray, *I Love to You,* p. 100.

30. Dan Cameron makes the link between this piece and the Yves Klein works in *Janine Antoni: Slip of the Tongue,* ed. Nicola White and Brenda McParland (Glasgow and Dublin: Centre for Contemporary Art and Irish Museum of Modern Art, 1995), p. 45.

31. Irigaray, "'Je—Luce Irigaray': A Meeting with Luce Irigaray," interview by

Elizabeth Hirsh and Gary A. Olson, trans. Elizabeth Hirsh and Gaëtan Brulotte, in *Women Writing Culture*, ed. Gary A. Olson and Elizabeth Hirsh (Albany: State University of New York Press, 1995), p. 160.

32. Irigaray, *Thinking the Difference: For a Peaceful Revolution*, trans. Karin Montin (London: Athlone Press, 1994), pp. 19–20.

33. Irigaray, "The Limits of the Transference," in *The Irigaray Reader*, trans. David Macey, p. 105.

34. Irigaray, *Je, Tu, Nous*, p. 49.

35. Irigaray, "The Limits of the Transference," p. 110.

36. Irigaray, *I Love to You*, p. 110.

37. I do not wish to point the finger at individuals, but my personal experience of working as a critic and art administrator suggests that the epithet "difficult" is more readily applied by curators to artists who are women than to artists who are men; indeed, the man who is exacting about the context in which his work is presented may be described as "committed" or "professional." I would read this as symptomatic of two things: first, the problematic of phallogocentric representation of "Woman" and second, the strategies some women use to disrupt or open up the structures of various gallery situations.

38. Irigaray, *Je, Tu, Nous*, pp. 110–111. Translation modified.

39. Irigaray, *This Sex Which Is Not One*, pp. 162–163.

40. Irigaray, "Divine Women," p. 60. Irigaray is meticulous in her usage of the two words for power: *le pouvoir* and *la puissance*. Here, the masculine *le pouvoir* re-enforces the patriarchal nature of power structures that must not be thoughtlessly reinstated.

41. Warner, *Alone of All Her Sex*, pp. 302–303.

42. Yolanda López, quoted by Shifra Goldman, "Contemporary Chicana Artists," in *Feminist Art Criticism: An Anthology*, ed. Arlene Raven, Cassandra Langer, and Joanna Frueh (New York: HarperCollins, 1991), p. 199.

43. Irigaray, "Flesh Colors," in *Sexes and Genealogies*, pp. 153–165.

44. Ibid., p. 153.

45. Irigaray, "The Universal as Mediation," in *Sexes and Genealogies*, p. 142.

46. Irigaray, "Flesh Colors," p. 160.

47. Ibid.

48. Irigaray, "Questions to Emmanuel Levinas," in *The Irigaray Reader*, p. 178.

49. It also accounts for patriarchy's (and patriarchal capitalism's) ability to exchange women through the structure of the representation, "Woman"—which is, after all, an abstraction: "Woman's price is not determined by the 'properties' of her body—although her body constitutes the *material* support of that price. But when women are exchanged, woman's body must be treated as an *abstraction*. The exchange operation cannot take place in terms of some intrinsic, immanent value of the commodity. It can only come about when two objects—two women—are in a relation of equality with a third term that is neither the one not the other." Irigaray, *This Sex Which Is Not One*, p. 175.

50. Suzanne Santoro, *Per Una Espressione Nuova/Towards New Expression* (Rome: Rivolta Femminile, 1974), unpaginated. *Ce sexe* was first published in France in 1977, but other similar comments appeared in *Speculum* in France in 1974. I do not wish to suggest any direct influence one way or the other.

51. Ibid.
52. Rozsika Parker, "Censored," *Spare Rib* 54 (1977): 43–45.
53. Ibid., pp. 44–45.
54. Ibid., p. 44.
55. Irigaray, "Each Sex Must Have Its Own Rights," in *Sexes and Genealogies*, p. 3.

Kaori Chino
(TRANSLATED FROM THE JAPANESE BY REIKO TOMII)

11. A Man Pretending to Be a Woman: On Yasumasa Morimura's "Actresses"

The "Actresses" series by Yasumasa Morimura brutally exposes the position, attitude, or stance we assume when we see this body of work.[1] The viewer's one-sided gaze, inflicted upon the women Morimura has impersonated, is repelled and hurled back to the viewer as the pointed questions: "Who are you?" and "What is your position?"

You yourself, not an abstract human being, are being interrogated here. It is easy to speak lofty ideas while casting ourselves as objective transparent beings: disappearing borders, the self in flux, anti-essentialism. . . . However, it is not an abstract narrator who manipulates language but an actual you defined by your sex, gender, and sexuality who is being questioned in front of Morimura's "Actresses."[2]

Readers who purchased the inaugural issue (August 1994) of *Panja*, a monthly magazine for young adult males, must have been flabbergasted when they turned to the five-page end-of-the-magazine special feature, entitled "Descent of Actresses."[3] What they found, in a full spread, was the nude Marilyn Monroe posing in front of that familiar backdrop of red drapery . . . no, not her, but the naked Morimura, striking a Monroe-esque pose. Artificial breasts, demonstrating that the artist is not a member of womankind, are attached to his chest by a brassiere-like device, as if to flaunt their false nature. Morimura must have specifically selected this image of Marilyn for *Panja*'s first issue because his Marilyn was based on

Yasumasa Morimura, Self-Portrait (as Actress)/Red Marilyn. *Courtesy of the artist.*

the photograph that served as the cover of the very first issue of Hugh Hefner's *Playboy* in 1953.[4] Yet, while *Playboy*, the magazine packed with pinups of naked women, fulfilled its slogan "Entertainment for Men" by successfully arousing the masturbating heterosexual male, Morimura's nudes obviously did not entertain men. For the next year, Morimura's monthly impersonation of an actress in the "Descent of Actresses" series never failed to make the "most boring" list that was compiled each month based on readers' questionnaire responses. Very few expressed their support for his series. With the twelfth actress, Elizabeth Taylor, published in the July 1995 issue, Morimura's "Descent of Actresses" series was ended after a year as originally planned.

I, as a woman, in no way know what kind of reaction was effected by Morimura's work in the mind of an average male reader who must have thought he was simply buying a magazine widely available at any convenience store. Morimura himself wrote in an essay that accompanied the final installment:

> How have you the readers reacted to my one-year series? Reactions varied: Some have wondered why they should look at a man's nude body, some others have felt uncomfortable, yet some others have thought it bizarre. But what I have sought for more than anything else was "beauty."

This remark allows us a glimpse at the kinds of readers' responses and the artist's view. Comments conveyed to Morimura not only from *Panja*'s readership but also by his own friends and acquaintances seems to have amounted to one word: "weird."

I, as a woman, find Morimura beautiful. For example, his Catherine Deneuve, lifting her face from the bed as in *Belle de Jour*, looks so gorgeous, her frayed blond hair included. How especially delicate and exquisite the fingers of Deneuve/Morimura are. Lit by bluish-white light from the right, the hands are softly folded and imbued with emotion, underscoring the grace of Deneuve/Morimura as a cunning prop.

On the other hand, some works from this series also make me chuckle. In the following pages, I find the dazzling Deneuve/Morimura at, of all places, the Myoshinji temple in Kyoto. The twin Deneuves/Morimuras, one sitting back on her/his feet and the other standing next to her/him in a tea ceremony room, both stare at me. What Morimura calls "Oh! France" and Japan meet here. [*Translator's note*: O-Furansu with an honorific prefix "o" somehow mocks the cultural status of France.] Or Sylvia Kristel, shrouded in purple underwear and seated in that famous cane chair as in *Emmanuelle*, is more radiant than ever, surrounded by golden, shimmering ornaments. As I examine the scene more closely, however, I realize that all these props are, stupefyingly, Buddhist adornments, which situates Morimura in a Buddhist temple's main hall, with him posing like a statue of the half cross-legged meditating Bodhisattva. Giggling spasms run through my body. Then there is Vivien Leigh, in a dark green dress made from curtains as in *Gone with the Wind*, who casts a stern glance, raising her right eyebrow. Aware as I am that Morimura's snare awaits me, I cannot help bursting into laughter. The story has it that Morimura, whose right

Yasumasa Morimura, After Catherine Deneuve 1.
Courtesy of the artist.

eyebrow arches when he grimaces, was ecstatic to learn that Vivien Leigh's eyebrow did exactly the same.

   In order for these strategies to be successful in making readers laugh, Morimura has to be beautiful. The viewer should be able to recognize in Morimura, even only for a moment, the glory of the actress who used to shine on the screen and titillate her audience's fantasy. Otherwise, the image will fail to incite laughter through a rift between the two figures. And Morimura is overwhelmingly beautiful.

Yasumasa Morimura, After Sylvie Kristel 3. *Courtesy of the artist.*

Beautiful yet funny—my twofold reaction is far from the "weird" impression that Morimura's friends and acquaintances had. Granted, people can react to his series in various ways; however, a casual survey among my friends and acquaintances indicates that no woman said "weird" but many described him as "beautiful," while most men sneered or clammed up. At work here must be not so much simple differences due to one's sex as complex divergences due to one's gender and sexuality.

Morimura, by impersonating Caucasian actresses in the "Descent of

Yasumasa Morimura, After Vivien Leigh 3. *Courtesy of the artist.*

Actresses" series, transgresses the borders previously perceived to be self-evident such as Japan versus the West and women versus men. Or rather, he nullifies the borders and laughs them away. He further attempts to nullify the borders between men and women in the series dealing with such Japanese actresses as Shima Iwashiwa and Momoe Yamaguchi. Indeed, the border between men and women appears to be nullified in these works in which Morimura impersonates actresses.

However, Japanese viewers (problematic as the word "Japan" or "Japanese" may be, I am tentatively using it here) who are (made to

Yasumasa Morimura, After Shima Iwashita. *Courtesy of the artist.*

be) familiar with Edo and Kyoto culture are well aware that the male impersonation of the female—that is, men pretending to be women— is not unusual; it is a historically sanctioned practice in Japan.

Many "traditional arts" have excluded women, starting with the well-known practice of the *oyama* actors who have played women in Kabuki theater. In Noh, male actors have performed female roles in many plays, wearing a variety of masks ranging from *koomote* (signifying the young noblewoman) to *hannya* (representing the woman turned into a demon by her rage and jealousy). In terms of Kyoto's imperial and court culture, men began pretending to be women as early as in the Helan period (794–1192 C.E.). A renowned instance is Ki no Tsurayuki's *Tosa Diary* (*Tosa nikki*) in which he expressed his feelings under the disguise of a female author. "Imagining female emotions," male poets, in countless instances, composed *waka*, the traditional 31-syllable poem. Thus, the convention of "men pretending to be women" is considered to have been established quite early in the genre of poetry. Such celebrated classic poets as Ki no Tsurayuki and Fujiwara Teika all created their "impassioned" pieces of poetry while pretending to be women. Yet, it has been in principle unthinkable for women to pretend to be men in their poetry-making, unless they entered another world as into a painting to live dissociated from this world.

In relation to this, we may also turn to the so-called women's hand (*onnade*) and men's hand (*otokode*), respectively designating the use of Japanese *kana* alphabets and Chinese characters, and the ways they were used by men and women in the Heian period. Since this, of course, involves the issue of class as well, our discussion is limited to those who belonged to the ruling class. While women in general were only allowed to use the women's hand, men enjoyed the license to use both the men's hand and the women's hand depending on the occasion; that is, the former in the public domain and the latter in the private domain. In the genre of painting, especially screen and wall painting that served as a marker of each room's function within a whole architectural design, the rule goes that paintings with Chinese subjects (*Kara-e*) were used for public spaces and Japanese subjects (*Yamato-e*) were used for private spaces. This indeed constituted an utterly inequitable practice in which men could freely go back and forth between "the public = China (*Kara*) = masculinity" and "the private = Japan (*Yamato*) = femininity," whereas women were confined to "femininity." In other words, gender meant for men a convenient device which could be adopted in accordance with men's use.

Since I have already discussed elsewhere the question of why men in the ruling class wanted to be women,[5] I will not go into any detail here. Suffice it to say here that the huge "center" of "*Kara* = China" played a major role in the phenomenon. As early as the tenth century, Japanese men in power used two different genders—"masculinity" and "femininity"—appropriate to their purposes and tried to regulate both genders. This practice, as a result, gradually alienated Japanese women, who could only exist within "femininity."

In the framework of "Japan," the male impersonation of the female has historically been performed as an established convention. A part of "tradition," however, it was never meant to constitute a protest against the "mainstream." Although it must typically be undertaken in the private domain—in the back room, so to speak—not in the public realm, men's impersonation of women has been sanctioned by society, in a sense, as an accepted mannerism. Thus, Japanese viewers must not have been as shocked as Western audiences when they saw Morimura, a man of color, slip into Manet's *Olympia* and lay his naked body on the bed where the white courtesan once was placed. After all, didn't Morimura gain fame in Japan after his notoriety, achieved among the white race, was imported back to his native country?

To my surprise, in spite of the country's cultural history, certain people in contemporary Japan abhor the male impersonation of the female with utmost sincerity. The reactions of the male readership to Morimura's "Actresses" more than anything else point to this phenomenon. The strict gender differentiation established in modern times perhaps completely wiped out the earlier male self-awareness of the elasticity of gender. Or, perhaps, they are comfortable to see the famed *oyama* actor Tamasaburo in drag because it fits the practice of "tradition = *Yamato* (Japan)," while they feel uneasy to watch the same practice coming from the context of the "West = New *Kara* (China)."

As long as the power relation between men and women is inequitable, the male impersonation of the female must be looked at cautiously because it unjustifiably deprives women of femininity or simply reinforces the unequal power relation. Some of Morimura's actresses pique my suspicion. For example, let us look at an earlier (1991) work entitled *Elder Sister*, whose excessive embellishments include such French brand articles as a Louis Vuitton umbrella and a Hermes scarf, as well as certain curious and inexplicable hybrids as a Chanel suit with a Louis Vuitton pattern and a Chanel-Courreges bag. If this image makes us laugh, who is being laughed at here? The answer is those women who mindlessly pursue brand-name objects, not the artist himself, who appears to be laughing with us at brand-obsessed women. He laughs at them because, I suspect, he has no sympathy whatsoever toward the woman he is impersonating. The love that permeates Morimura's "Actresses" series, the zest that drives the artist to impersonate his beloved subject to the smallest detail, is absent in this image. In this work, Morimura is as beautiful and, in some ways, as funny, but we cannot laugh at it in innocence.

So some of Morimura's works make me skeptical. Some others, such as

Yasumasa Morimura, Elder Sister, *1991. Courtesy of the artist.*

those with gilded men and women in period costumes, render me tongue-tied in my effort to decipher his images. The "Actresses" series may also involve ambivalence and deviation. Nobody can say for sure that Morimura the male artist never intends to rob "femininity" in this series.

Even if he did, Morimura's "Actresses" series is a very important body of work that strikes a critical chord in this heterosexual female author. It provides me with pertinent clues when I explore such questions as how the work receives and repels the viewer's gaze and how it can possibly affect society in any substantive ways.

When I visited the Andy Warhol exhibition held at the Vancouver Art

Gallery in the fall of 1995, I became very uneasy in front of the famed Marilyn Monroe series. Although I had seen these familiar Marilyns numerous times in reproduction before, the Marilyns hung on the wall filled me with stirrings of an unpleasant feeling. The subtle texture of the silk screens perhaps induced a sensation different from the impression I had when seeing the flat reproductions. I do not quite know why. But, at any rate, I was hurting, stung by the sight of these Marilyns with bright greens and yellows rudely painted on her faces.

Everybody now knows of Marilyn's pitiful life. Flattered as a "pretty actress" and a "sex symbol" and consumed to the last piece of her flesh, she died at the young age of 36. Very likely, with these images Warhol wanted to point to the fact that the film industry and society at large treated her badly. Roughly applied colors on her faces may well signify the violence inflicted on her. However, just as police questioning and examination of a rape victim by trial lawyers cruelly amount to the second rape, Warhol's Marilyns are, to my eyes, another second rape.

When the viewer looks at Warhol's Marilyns, s/he sees various colors along with their rough applications. The viewer's gaze traces the color patches, thus repeating the violating acts and raping Marilyn again and again. It is possible that Warhol may not have been so conscious of the "masculine gaze" exercised so conspicuously by the viewer—the violent gaze of heterosexual men and the pleasure that it (probably) incites in them. Perhaps the artist himself did not cast the violent "masculine gaze" on her. However, doubtless those who have purchased Marilyns as a commodity, those who have looked at them in reproductions or at museums, have repeatedly enjoyed, consumed, and raped her images. Exposed to the gaze of those who see it, the image of Marilyn that Warhol created will never cease to be an object of rape.

It should be noted that Warhol also created many other portraits using a similar technique. Still, I found the gaze focused on the Mao Zedong series at the Vancouver Art Gallery to be as violent, though not as sexual; this explicitly involves the dimension of race. On the other hand, strokes that may induce the demeaning gaze were carefully removed from the portraits of Queen Elizabeth and Jacqueline Kennedy. Above all, in one self-portrait, I saw Warhol himself placed in a lovely setting that would entice the viewer only to admire the artist. In comparison, it is clear how badly the Marilyns were treated, with her faces irreverently painted, which greatly aroused the consumer's appetite and the viewer's sexual desire as well.

My intention here, for all the analysis, is not to accuse Warhol of any wrongdoing. I am simply examining the problem of the viewer's gaze; more generally, I merely intend to present a case study to demonstrate that a discussion of a work of art can include the issue of the viewer's gaze as well as the work itself. When we see from the perspective of the gaze, we will begin to understand aspects of the work previously invisible to us. This applies to Warhol, Morimura, and Cindy Sherman alike.

From the 1970s to the 1980s, Cindy Sherman photographed herself playing a wide range of roles conferred on women by society: female stereotypes that have repeatedly been represented in films and photography and mass media; lonely-looking, beaten, or erotic women in whom we sense some stories. In Sherman I observe a clear will to critique the gaze of society at large that has treated women only as "helpless," "objects to be seen," and "sexual."

Yet, whatever Sherman's intention may be, whatever claim she may be staking, her work, upon being created, becomes a commodity subject to the gaze. The representation presented by Sherman as a critique of the female stereotype is destined to be savored, devoured, and consumed as another female stereotype. No one can stop the process of commodity consumption. As long as one tries to critique the female stereotype by using the female body, the work falls prey to the violent masculine gaze of heterosexual men in the consumerist society, offering them the "pleasure of seeing." Unless one follows a direction similar to Sherman who, in her recent works, daringly represented the harrowing grotesquerie, one's work, whatever representation one seeks to produce, is bound to become an object of heterosexual male desire—as long as one uses the flesh of the female body.

This brings us back to Morimura's "Actresses" series.

Morimura's "Actresses" are beautiful. That is why the viewer is momentarily seduced by that Marilyn Monroe, that Sylvia Kristel, the fourteen-year-old Jodie Foster who played Iris the hooker in *Taxi Driver*, the impassive, sexually manipulated Jane Fonda in the B movie *Barbarella*, the Faye Dunaway who died in a pool of blood, sprayed by a rain of machine-gun bullets in the final scene of *Bonnie and Clyde*. . . . One famous scene after another comes back to the viewer's mind. Men who toy with beautiful actresses at their will in their fantasy.

The next moment, however, their fantasy is interrupted. The violent masculine gaze cast by heterosexual men, eager to enjoy, devour, and consume the images of actresses, encounters not a female body but Morimura's male body, by which it is repelled. Their gaze is now transformed into piercing questions, asking them "Who are you?" and "What is your position?" The fact that men do not constitute the abstract human being but that men and women each share one half of humanity is revealed. In fact, the heterosexual male cannot possibly make up one half of humanity but less than a half. They hardly represent humanity as a whole; they have arrived at their values on their own. These facts, known to everybody but previously concealed, are visualized in their totality in Morimura's "Actresses" series. The urge to avert their eyes from these facts makes men express a negative feeling: "Weird."

Morimura has accomplished what women could not. Morimura receives the violent masculine gaze often aimed at women with his exposed body, then the next moment laughs it away, and finally nullifies it. Morimura in his "Actresses" series sides with women not merely in his appearance but in his thought.

The situation of "Japan" today that surrounds the sex of us, the women, is becoming increasingly unbearable. "Hair nudes," or photographs of completely naked women with their pubic hair visible, and similar illustrations are printed in newspapers and magazines, which, because they are looked at in commuter trains and other public places under broad daylight, are not hidden from children's eyes. The streets are flooded by pornographic comics that objectify women; young boys grow up reading them. As long as we live in this country, most of us do not have many options. Enraged as we are by Japanese men who buy Asian women's bodies, we, the Japanese women, cannot entirely write off our country's men. We are trapped in our present circumstances, scarcely breathing fresh air.

In these dark days, Morimura's "Actresses" series offers us a rare occasion to laugh innocently. His "Actresses" lightheartedly laugh away the violent masculine gaze of the heterosexual male that lusts for female bodies and utterly snubs it. The representations of "Actresses" impersonated by Morimura create a site where women and men (excluding the violent straight male,[6] but including the gay male) who suffer gender-related repression under the Japanese patriarchy and have a hard time living their lives unexpectedly meet as comrades. Until the day comes when the kind of men who find Morimura's "Actresses" series unpleasant and disturbing become extinct, this body of work will continue to assert its relevance in Japan.

NOTES

This text was originally published both in Japanese and English in *Morimura Yasumasa: The Sickness unto Beauty: Self-portrait as Actress* (Yokohama, Japan: Yokohama Museum of Art, 1996), pp. 131–135 (Japanese), 157–162 (English). Minor modification was made to the text, including the exclusion of some photographic references.

1. As I prepared this text, I benefited from my conversations with the artist Yasumasa Morimura and professors Norman Bryson and Yoichi Ohashi. I wish to extend my sincere gratitude to them.

2. Judith Butler points out that gender (defined culturally, socially, and historically) precedes, and even defines, biological sex. See Judith Butler, *Gender Trouble: Feminism and the Subversion of Identity* (London and New York: Routledge, 1990). In light of this argument, it becomes difficult to consider sex as a self-evident fact. Although I agree with her, I wonder if we lose something important once we acknowledge that sex is also artificially constructed and no essence of "woman" as such exists. Given the present condition of an inequitable male-female power relation, a sense of solidarity among women appears to me to be still important. I would caution that with all its legitimacy, "anti-essentialism" as a discourse could be exploited to repress the weak. In any case, I am making my argument here on the premise that sex and gender can be considered different.

3. I wish to thank two editors who discussed with me the "Descent of Actresses" series first published in *Panja* by the Fusosha publisher: Nobuo Kaneko, *Panja's* deputy editor, and Kunio Yoshie, the freelance editor charged with the production of the series. [*Translator's note: Panja* is made by transposing "Ja" and "pan" of "Japan."]

4. See Shunji Ito, *Ratai no mori e: Kanjo no ikonogurafi* (*To the Forest of Nudes: Iconography of Emotions*) (Tokyo: Chikuma Shobo, 1985). My discussions of Marilyn Monroe and Cindy Sherman draw in part on this book.

5. See Kaori Chino, "Nihon bijutsu no jenda" ("Gender in Japanese Art"), *Bijusushi* 43, no. 2, cumulative issue number 136 (March 1994), pub. by the Japanese Society for Art History; "Gender in Japanese Art," trans. Joshua Mostow, *Aesthetics* 7 (1996), pub. by the Japanese Society for Aesthetics.

6. I am not, of course, arguing that every heterosexual male inflicts an aggressive, violent gaze on the female body at all times.

12. "A New Kind of Beauty": From Classicism to Karole Armitage's Early Ballets

The Ideal of Beauty in Ballet

Following Kant, the Russian-French ballet critic André Levinson states in his 1922 essay "Some Commonplaces on the Dance" that "it [is] difficult to define beauty."[1] A few years later, in his seminal 1925 essay "The Spirit of the Classic Dance," Levinson remarks that "the dancer is a machine . . . for manufacturing beauty," suggesting that it is in the dancer's body, rather than the choreographer's composition, that the beauty of ballet may be found.[2] Although Levinson refers to ballet's "logic" of "creating beauty by *organized dynamism*" and its "spirit of order and discipline," implying that both the dance composition and the dancer's technical prowess might provide grounds for discovering beauty, in neither essay does he establish specific criteria for defining or gauging beauty in ballet—in performance or composition.[3] He seems, like Kant, to think of beauty as subject to no prescriptive formula but rather as particular to each object. One can recognize free beauty when one sees it, but one can't conceptualize it.

And yet, in his attempt for the first time "to formulate specifically the laws of this art on its own ground, . . . to portray the intrinsic beauty of a dance step, its innate quality, its esthetic reason for being," Levinson does lay down the basic principles of ballet, or classic dancing, that many historians, theorists, and critics since his time have used repeatedly as a framework for discussing how ballet as an art form generates its own kinds of beauty in specific works.[4]

According to Levinson, the three basic principles governing ballet are verticality, the five positions of the feet, and the turnout of the body (especially the legs). These are the constraints that define and limit classic dancing. By verticality, Levinson means not only the upright carriage of the individual ballet dancer, but also the very "configuration of motion in space" oriented along the vertical frontal plane of the proscenium arch.[5]

Turnout, or the rotation of the legs outward from the hips, was also a result of the move to the picture-frame proscenium stage. Dance historian and theorist Lincoln Kirstein calls turnout "the bedrock of ballet style and practice," and he explains that it is the means through which the human body achieves theatrical legibility—it allows "the frontal plane of the dancer's body [to face] his audience in its maximum silhouette."[6] Turnout also permits the dancer total freedom of lateral, forward, backward, and diagonal movement while still facing front; Levinson observes that "instead of being restricted to a simple backward and forward motion . . . many motions otherwise impossible are thereby facilitated."[7] And turnout creates a perspectival, rather than foreshortened, view of the dancer's body within the proscenium picture frame.[8] This constraint, Levinson argues, proves to be the exact opposite of a restriction, for it leads to a state in which "the dancer is freed from the usual limitations upon human motion."[9]

The five positions of the feet are, in a sense, a logical extension of turnout, since they constitute the various relationships between the legs as, rotated, they line up (first position), cross (fifth and third positions), or separate (second and fourth positions). The five positions allow the feet to navigate without collision, arranging themselves parallel to one another as the legs move in a variety of directions.[10]

Added to these three principles or constraints are the generative possibilities facilitated by elevation (including aerial work like jumps and leaps) and pointework, or dancing on the tips of the toes (for women).[11] And resulting from these restrictions and possibilities are the qualities of equilibrium, symmetry, harmony, and unity of line, made all the more arresting because of their contingency—because in ballet, unlike in static art forms such as sculpture and architecture, they are achieved, disturbed, and found again in the flow of motion.

The presence of the three principles adumbrated by Levinson does not, in itself, constitute beauty; most experts would agree with Levinson that all ballet dancing, beautiful or not, is grounded at least in these principles. But it is widely believed among dance critics that the perfect achievement of these principles of the dancer's technique typically contributes to the beauty of the work. Levinson states that the difference between the athlete or the mechanical doll and the dancer is that "the technique of a dancer . . . is physical effort constantly informed by beauty."[12]

Critics look for another quality when they judge ballet beauty: a perfect line. Kirstein refers to beauty in ballet in compositional terms as deriving from eighteenth-century principles of naturalness in art, making reference to William Hogarth's analysis of the serpentine "line of beauty," which supplies "composed variety," rather than the monotony of simple straight lines.[13] But, perhaps because in a temporal art (where composition is constantly shifting) it is difficult to pinpoint formal aspects of visual pleasure, far more often beauty in ballet is associated with the body of the dancer—with technique and its perfect achievement. Most dance critics use the term "line" quite differently than Hogarth did, to speak of the harmonious, dynamic alignment of the dancer's body, rather than the shape of the dance's overall composition. Echoing Levinson's difficulty in delimiting beauty in dance, dance critic Robert Greskovic observes that "line is something you come to recognize, even when you can't quite define it." He approaches a definition, however, calling line "an internal dimension, a sublime inner connection of all the physical aspects that make up a dancer's physique . . . something far greater than a mathematical whole." And, he continues, "line is able to ground external surfaces with inner understanding. Great dancers with impeccable line . . . [show] themselves to us in a supremely internalized, unending harmony."[14]

Beauty and Morality

The beauty of ballet is not based only on formal principles, however. For many it has an added moral dimension. Stéphane Mallarmé called ballet "that catalyst and paradise of all spirituality."[15] Ballet is, first of all, derived from Renaissance court entertainments in which every posture, gesture, and movement had its emblematic political and metaphysical meaning. The stress on vertical carriage that characterizes ballet technique is rooted in the noble deportment required of Renaissance and Baroque courtiers, and that postural verticality itself has deep-seated moral associations that reach back to classical Greece. In his discussion of slavery in the ancient world, Bernard Williams points out that Aristotle tried to justify slavery by claiming that "nature aims to make the bodies of free men differ from those of slaves, the latter adapted in strength to necessary employment, the former upright and not suited to such work."[16] Thus ballet's verticality has an ethical dimension whose origins are sociopolitical. Associated with the elite ruling classes of Europe from the Renaissance to our day, it is based on political hierarchies and moral traditions that equate beauty of outward or physical form with both nobility and inner goodness.

But beyond the ancient Greek idea of nobility manifested in the upright posture that was invoked in early modern times, it is easy to see how, in the Christian (and more specifically Catholic) French and Italian cultures in which ballet was born and initially flowered, verticality could take on religious as well as moral connotations. One looks upward to find God, and the vertical body aspires heavenward. Verticality suggests spirituality as well as nobility, for in Christian cosmology spirits rise to join God and the angels, who dwell in the upper regions of space, in heaven. Verticality may, in fact, be seen as a form of grace. By the late nineteenth century, evolutionary concepts about "man's" upright posture, separating humans from animals, added another layer of meaning to vertical carriage.

For the Russian dance and art theorist Akim Volynsky, the vertical is the basic principle of ballet. In *The Book of Exultation* he explores the social and moral meanings of the vertical orientation of human bodies, though—understandably, for a dance theorist writing in Soviet Russia in 1925—he stresses the socially and politically ethical over the religious aspects of the erect body. He notes that Kant "emphatically asserted standing upright as an act of the spirit that overcomes the natural state and raises man above nature." He points out that to the ancient Greeks, "to see straight, to speak straight—all this is at once pictorially sensible and heroic. An upright city is a city of good and high morals that rests firmly on its foundation in a state of political and economic welfare." And he tells us that "the Romans demanded that the heart burn as a flame, high and heavenward." He concludes that "only in ballet do we possess all aspects of the vertical in its exact mathematically formed, universally perceptible expression. Everything in ballet is straight, upright, as a taut string that sounds a high note."[17]

Just as the postural and pictorial principle of verticality has profound moral and even spiritual meanings for many interpreters of dance, so too has the balletic principle of turnout taken on ethical implications. For Volynsky, the openness of the turned-out body is analogous to the "increased intimacy, warmth, and meaningfulness" of the open palm of the hand, and even more crucially, to the very act of seeing, of observation, that occurs when we open our eyes. When the eyes are truly open, "the act of will, set in motion, tears the veil from the eyes and makes possible the observation of beauty. Beauty demands of us a certain enrapture, a stubbornness of observation, eyes turned outward to the light and reality." Thus, Volynsky claims, when in ballet "insofar as the body turns in every direction and opens 'outward,' it becomes susceptible to radiations of the spirit and an instrument of ardor." The turned-out leg "reveals closed surfaces that had been hidden in darkness. And everything appears pure, harmonious, and exultantly bright." But this exposure is not, for Volynsky, erotic or pornographic. "This glowing transport is . . . of a higher nature. . . . Only he can experience it . . . who opens wide all the gates, windows, and vistas of his soul, turning them 'outward.'"[18]

The British dance critic Adrian Stokes expands Levinson's formal scrutiny of turnout into the moral realm. For Stokes, it is turnout that is "the essence of ballet," and not only for the sake of the technique that allows the dancer to show "as much of himself as possible to the spectator." In Stokes's view, this is not simply a matter of aesthetic form, for it implies a salutary, almost religious disclosure. When the ballerina's cavalier turns her as she stands on pointe, he writes, "she is shown to the world with the utmost love and grace."[19]

Stokes also extends Levinson's contrast between the inward turning of Asian dance and the turnout of Western ballet into the moral realm, arguing that turnout serves metaphorically to symbolize the openness and outwardness that he sees as embodying European values. If the dances of Indian, Javanese, and other non-Western cultures express, for Stokes, "the absorption of strength, the building up of a reserve of vitality, a kind of inner recreation" in which "the dancer is drawing to himself the strength of the outside world," European dances "show a dissolution of mystery." Like European visual art, Stokes claims, ballet projects outward from the body. "The same fixity without distortion and without sternness, the same outwardness, is the hall-mark of our art, a steady revelation that calls to mind the open face of the rose or smooth mountains in unbroken sunlight. . . . We like to have the mystery cleared, to see our feelings laid out as something concrete and defined."[20] He explains: "In ballet the human passions are expressed by the gradual uncontorted curves and straight lines of the extended human body. There is no residuum, no veil. The human body is purged of atmosphere. All is shown."[21] The British critic Alastair Macaulay further elaborates Stokes's argument when he writes:

> The classicism that we recognize in ballet seems to have originated in twin principles: the idea we find in Homer that embedded in the human is something divine and that the gods are active in human warfare and human love and human conduct; and the idea we find in Genesis that God created humankind in God's own image. Is that so when we look at the different classicism of Javanese culture? What I don't see is that outwardness of impulse, that openness, the sense that the body radiates

into infinity. There is a more inward concentration that has different moral suggestions for all of us.[22]

The moral significance of the human body's geometry, exemplified by the Vetruvian man, is the classical image that rules this conception of ballet. Even when the limbs move in opposition or the shoulders tilt away from the hips in contrapposto, the dancing body in ballet is fundamentally open and symmetrical. And although its turned-out posture may be unnatural in relation to our movements in everyday life, the classical dancing body makes turnout look easy, graceful, and natural.

Finally, the special balletic terrain of pointework by women dancers also lends itself to moral metaphors. Levinson devotes only a few sentences to pointework, but he clearly suggests that it conjures a spiritual meaning closely related to verticality: "[W]hen a dancer rises on her points, she breaks away from the exigencies of everyday life, and enters into an enchanted country—that she may thereby lose herself in the ideal."[23] The near-impossibility of walking, running, and balancing on the very tips of the toes makes the ease with which the ballet dancer moves seem miraculous, even magical; standing on pointe effects in the spectator an extraordinary awareness of an equilibrium that seems superhuman, buoyed by grace. And moving quickly on pointe creates the impression of an ethereal, immaterial body in flight, calling up images of angels and other holy spirits (though of course pointework has also been used in the service of unholy spirits, such as the vampire-like Wilis in *Giselle*).

The Grotesque Tradition

Although the theorists and critics I have cited so far have been at pains to describe and account for the beautiful and the classical in ballet, most of them acknowledge that there has always been a place for classical values to coexist with anti-classical, or grotesque, elements within the art form itself. In thinking about the relationship between the balletic bodily canon[24] of beauty and its opposite, I find the Russian literary critic Mikhail Bakhtin's study of the grotesque body in *Rabelais and His World* suggestive. Bakhtin contrasts Renaissance values of beauty in the human form (derived from classical ideals) with the medieval, folkloric, "grotesque" (and, one might add, peasant) body. For Bakhtin, the classical body is smooth, finished, closed, and complete, in contrast to the grotesque body, which is rough, uneven, unfinished, open, and full of apertures—and therefore, in the classical view, "hideous and formless."[25] In ballet up to the twentieth century, the conflict between these two sets of values held up the classical body as the political and moral ideal and the grotesque body, though at times formally more interesting, as a threat to the classical norm.

Ever since the birth of ballet during the Renaissance, sinister mythological characters, witches, wizards, furies, evil fairies, madmen and madwomen, and humans transformed into animals, as well as exotic (non-Western) characters and peasants, have provided dramatic tensions in the story lines. These tensions were formally embodied in the contrast of "inappropriate," grotesque bodily canons—often angular and asymmetrical—to the symmetrically balanced, classical form. Dramatically speaking, evil made incarnate in the form of physical monstrosity (the grotesque body) posed a threat to the reign of virtue in the form of the classical body; as the classical body triumphed, virtue's dominion was ultimately strengthened or restored. For instance, in *The Sleeping Beauty*, the evil fairy Carabosse, danced by a man in travesty, violates classical lines in multiple ways, from her overly large scale to her asymmetrical, bent-over, turned-in posture. Even in Romantic ballets that seemed to end in the tragic defeat of the virtuous—like *La Sylphide*, in which Madge the witch destroys the hero James—the classical body remained the ideal.

Thus in ballet, deliberately breaking the classical bodily canon has traditionally signaled social or moral malignancy first and foremost. It has also served to express negative emotions such as anger and jealousy, or to signal situations of chaos and disorder. Finally, it has marked the exotic or picturesque, in the form of character dancing (or balleticized folk dances) by the lower classes. In character dancing, angular shapes and turned-in body postures may not have stood for evil, but they nevertheless hinted at Otherness: either Oriental mysteries or rustic crudities. Even when bucolic life was idealized as robust, as in the Romantic ballet, its earthiness was expressed in grotesque terms, breaching the decorum, elegance, and grace of the noble classical ballet line. Until the end of the nineteenth century, these various forms of grotesque embodiment derived their meaning in the context of and in contrast to the classical norm that regulated definitions of beauty in the human form, whether in painting, sculpture, or dance.

The history of ballet in the twentieth century, however, has been punctuated with calculated infractions of the classical bodily canon for other purposes, especially that of expression. Perhaps inspired, or perhaps challenged, by modern dancers' rejection of the balletic principles of verticality and turnout, choreographers like Michel Fokine and Alexander Gorsky at the turn of the century sought a greater range of expressivity, while still remaining within the domain of ballet, through the use of turned-in stances and a variety of steps and gestures previously excluded by the strict ballet vocabulary. For Fokine, fascinated by unclassical notions of beauty culled from non-Western and modern art, the first principle of "the new ballet" should be "to create in each case a new form corresponding to the subject, the most expressive form possible for the representation," without following pre-ordained rules.[26]

Vaslav Nijinsky went even further, introducing extremely awkward bodily shapes and contorted movements into his ballets. The ballerina Tamara Karsavina writes that in *L'Après-midi d'un faune* and *Le Sacre du printemps*, "Nijinsky declared his feud against Romanticism and bid adieu to the 'beautiful.'" She describes the posture Nijinsky asked her to achieve in *Jeux*, a ballet of modern life based on a tennis game and a sexual triangle, as follows: "I had to keep my head screwed on one side, both hands curled in as one maimed from birth." Although she records her irritation at and incomprehension of Nijinsky's demands at the time, reflecting later on Nijinsky's work in her autobiography Karsavina suggests that the choreographer, however inarticulate about his own aesthetic program, was surely influenced in *Jeux* by Italian Futurism and by Filippo Marinetti's vehement rejection of beauty and of the masterpieces of past art.[27]

George Balanchine, schooled in Imperial Russia but thoroughly American in his taste, tampered differently with the rules of ballet. Balanchine opened ballet up to a spectrum of steps and movements alien to the pure classical style (including modern dance and African American jazz dancing[28]), departing in surprising ways from the traditional vocabulary, from canonical body shapes, and even from the tempi of classical ballet. Yet dance critic Edwin Denby observed that Balanchine had developed "a largeness of expression" in his dancers that showed "the kind of beauty classic ballet is by nature about." In his 1953 essay "Some Thoughts About Classicism and George Balanchine," Denby writes, "Classic ballet . . . tries to be as wonderful as possible in its own beautiful and voluntarily limited way, just as does any other art. What correct style exists for, what it hopes for, is a singular, unforeseen, an out-of-this-world beauty of expression." Balanchine's attention to "continuity in motion," Denby argues, "develops in his dancers a gift for coherent, vigorous, positive, unsimpering movement, and a gift too for a powerful, spontaneous rhythmic pulse in action."

> Clear, sure-footed dancing travels through space easy and large, either in its instantaneous collective surges or in its slow and solitary paths. So space spreads in calm power from the center of the stage and from the moving dancer and gives a sense of human grandeur and of destiny to her action.[29]

The image of the female dancer, especially, that Balanchine created—slim, long-legged, with a jutting hip and elegantly angled wrists—was that of a runway model. His distortions were anything but ugly. Rather, even during the pre-feminist era of the 1940s and 1950s, they defined a contemporary vision of glamorous and assertive female beauty.

A New Kind of Beauty for Our Time

Unlike Fokine, Nijinsky, or Balanchine, Karole Armitage was not necessarily fated to work only in the arena of ballet. When she began her career as a choreographer, she was a member of the Merce Cunningham Dance Company, one of the major modern dance companies in the United States. Although trained in her youth by a New York City Ballet dancer and a veteran of several years spent performing a Balanchine-dominated repertory in the Geneva Ballet, by 1978—when she created her first piece, Ne—she had been dancing with Cunningham for two years and was equally immersed in downtown New York avant-garde culture and the art-punk-music scene.

Armitage's early pieces—Ne (1978), Do We Could (1979), Objectstacle (1980), and Vertige (1980), took off from a recognizably Cunninghamesque technique, using a foundation of classical principles—verticality, turnout, and the five positions—in the lower body and a flexible upper torso and freely mobile arms. But her dances also toyed with extremely unclassical possibilities. In Ne, the stiff-legged, knock-kneed, pigeon-toed stance nearly brought all movement to a halt. The reckless aggression of Vertige, a duet for Armitage and guitarist-composer Rhys Chatham, vehemently threatened verticality as Armitage repeatedly lurched dangerously off balance and scrambled all around the musician, worrying him like a mosquito and disrupting his performance by reaching over to untune his guitar as she flippantly turned the pegs. Armitage says that at the time, inspired by punk music, she "went into the studio and started making distorted and dissonant, raw movement to correspond to that sound and those ideas." She describes her movement as "[retaining] a regal center from classicism," but adds that "basically, I was taking all the rules from the classical canon and breaking them. If they said keep your shoulder down, I would bring it up. And if the hand was supposed to be elegant, I was taking it into angular types of shapes and adding extra planes and angles to the whole body." And she explains, "The reason I did this is because I thought it was a new kind of beauty, one that demanded a kind of passion, because it had a troubled spot at the center."[30]

In *Drastic Classicism* (1981), Armitage seriously began her systematic critique of classical movement. Still working in the idiom of a Cunninghamesque technique that, while based on the classical principles of verticality and turnout, does not make use of pointe technique, she opened up a front-line attack on the matter of line. Armitage's publicity materials describe *Drastic Classicism* as "a strictly choreographed violation—and amplification—of virtuosic dance technique, with a rock rhythmic structure in which constant tension between restraint and clarity vied with drastic, passionate impulses."[31]

Through a variety of strategies, Armitage conspicuously framed her distortions and deformations of the elegant classical line. As the dancers calmly executed straightforward, rhythmically precise classroom exercises (i.e., the building blocks of ballet and of Cunningham's technique, in which the control over the body necessary to achieve perfect line is practiced daily), wild, out-of-control movements suddenly seemed to take over

Drastic Classicism, *choreographed by Karole Armitage. Armitage is the dancer on the far right. Photo © 1981 by Johan Elbers.*

their bodies. It was not so much as if they were possessed, but as if they had been repressed, and now were throwing off the shackles of that stifling regime. High-voltage, unbridled social dancing moves straight from the Mudd Club seemed to have invaded the ballet studio. Arms flailed, legs crossed over in the extreme; dancers lunged off balance, ran at full speed, made fighting gestures, and jumped on the musicians with whom they shared the stage. There was a general spirit of willful, bratty (mis)behavior threading through dance images of incredible speed, power, and extreme beauty. And that defiant misconduct was not just expressed by, but was also on a deep moral level constituted by, the drama of the imperiled vertical and the tortured line. While the classical core of the dance seemed to survive a battering in ways that spoke metaphorically of human dignity in the face of a daily assault on the senses in contemporary life, its ferocious tone and rebellious energy implied that no principle is fixed or can be taken for granted but must be tested for its merits.

The punk style of the loud, dissonant music (by Rhys Chatham) as well as of the childlike costumes and dark lighting (both by Charles Atlas) drenched the dancing as well. It underscored metaphorically the theme of a youthful revolution against all self-styled "civilized" values. And yet, as dance critic Arlene Croce put it: in *Drastic Classicism*, "classical values that were flayed alive stayed alive."[32] As in Fred Astaire's drunk dances, it was clear that despite the frenzied pacing and the nihilistic gestures, nothing here was chaotic or unplanned. Without exquisite technique, the dancers would fall down instead of balancing off-kilter; their feet would tangle instead of nimbly crisscrossing at lightning speed.

The painter David Salle, who would later become Armitage's fiancé and collaborator, has said of seeing her dance at this time, "It wasn't simply the fact that Karole's dancing was extreme, which it was, that made it interesting. She is very long-limbed and had amazing extensions and the ability to appear as though all four limbs were working in contradictory ways, but also with complete visual harmony. The fact that it was wild and extreme was simply a condition, one of its conditions." In other words, Salle noticed that Armitage achieved perfect line (that is, visual harmony) despite the extreme tests to which she put the classical bodily canon. Echoing Denby's remarks on Balanchine, Salle observes another aspect of Armitage's classicism when he says what he saw in her work of this period was "an image of a woman who was looking at fate unafraid. This image was not created with acting . . . but with a controlled *barrage* of steps."[33]

One year after the Paris Opéra Ballet commissioned her to create GV–10, in which she worked with both the Opéra's modern dance group and its

The Watteau Duets *with Karole Armitage and Joseph Lennon.*

ballet troupe, Armitage moved squarely into the arena of ballet in terms of technique, if not in terms of institutional affiliations, with *The Watteau Duets* (originally titled $-p = \frac{\partial H}{\partial q}$, 1985). With this dance, she introduced extended pointework into her choreography, although she continued to present her work at various downtown New York venues known for post-modern choreography (as well as at clubs, galleries, and rock festivals). Above all *The Watteau Duets* was a concentrated exploration of two important ballet conventions: the pas de deux (or duet form), and pointework.

The dance has six sections. In each, Armitage and her partner (originally Joseph Lennon) wear unusual, even fantastic costumes. They range from a black leotard and tights under a breastplate in one section and boxer shorts and undershirt in another for him to a diaphanous apricot negligée with satin toeshoes dyed to match in one section and a white T-shirt, black tights, white anklets, and black patent leather shoes with five-inch stiletto heels for her. The dance is performed to live music by David Linton—primarily percussion, it seems based on military marches with Scottish bagpipes—and intermittent taped musical quotations from Stravinsky, Handel, Verdi, and Wagner. The partners, in black leotards and tights trimmed with leather cuffs, headbands, and boots, greet each other in a formal, ritualistic moment like two medieval jousting opponents and then begin about an hour's worth of intense interaction. Always erotic and intense, each section of the dance varies partly because the dancers change costumes, but also because of affective tone: formal, haughty, tender, playful.

Croce, though enthusiastic about the piece, remarks that the dancers "didn't contribute . . . to the lore of the pas de deux—their 'erotic' number was essentially a variation on Nijinsky's *Faune*, and later they added variations on the *Agon* pas de deux."[34] What Croce seems to have missed, however, is the deliberateness of the reflexive allusions to ballet history, especially to Balanchine. The allusions to *Agon*, especially, are not derivative, but rather are obviously quite conscious quotations.[35] (In 1982 Armitage choreographed *Slaughter on MacDougal Street*, an homage to Balanchine's jazz ballet *Slaughter on Tenth Avenue*. She had never seen the Balanchine ballet but was inspired by seeing photographs of a recent revival.) In *The Watteau Duets*, Armitage invokes a history in order to interrogate and elaborate it. Armitage assertively takes the leading role in the pas de deux even more than Balanchine's ballerinas do, in a way that is conspicuously marked. If in *Agon* the man manipulates the ballerina, here the ballerina (man)handles her partner, directing the action, calling the shots, pushing him away and pulling him into position. Thus she makes manifest and calls into question the relations of the sexes in the tradition of the ballet pas de deux as well as in society.

It's no secret that the standard ballet pas de deux, however chastely danced, is about the sex act. But in *The Watteau Duets* the slightly sadomasochistic aspects of the *Agon* pas de deux (and so many other ballet pas de deux) are heightened, brought to the surface, and made explicit by the leather accessories in the first section and by the tortuous, contortionist methods the dancers use to maneuver one another. Too, there are many other overtly sexual elements: Armitage's spread legs and grinding hips; a moment when she climbs onto and straddles her partner's back; another moment when, as she stands over him and he reclines on the floor (one of the allusions to *Agon*), he raises and lowers his leg repeatedly as his foot flexes, comically indicating a phallus becoming erect; not to mention her patent leather high heels (purchased in the red light district of Paris). All these details unmistakably signal a frank carnality that most earlier ballets, even those considered shocking in their time, only gestured toward. But these signs, verging on the pornographic, are mixed with icons of ravishing, transcendent beauty recognizable from the ballet canon—the perfect plumb line of verticality repeatedly achieved in the face of off-balance jeopardy as Armitage stands suspended upright, balancing on one pointe; a hand held outward with palm open in a gesture of greeting; the familiar and beloved supported arabesque, reminiscent of *The Sleeping Beauty*, in the first section; the slow lifts of the leg in *grands battements* that show off Armitage's elegantly long, turned-out limbs and exquisite equilibrium as she stands steady in one high-heeled shoe; her arms circling her head like rose petals. This iconography of balletic beauty exalts the often shocking sexual imagery, moving it into the realm of the spiritual and the moral. Armitage has spoken about the influence of Hindu temple sculpture and tantric yoga, which merge the erotic and the holy, on her choreography in one of the sections of *The Watteau Duets*.[36] But certainly the dance conjures up modern as well as archaic passions, especially in its contemporary look and its unflinching postfeminist exploration of conflicts, competition, and desire between men and women.

Although Armitage does not wear pointe shoes in every section of *The Watteau Duets*, it is a dance that celebrates and investigates pointework, whether done in toe shoes, high heels, or the strange combination of stilts and cothurni, attached to two semicircular frames that form the shape of a large skirt, which Armitage wears in the final section. Armitage's pointework is descended from the "steely toe" of the nineteenth-century Italian ballet, later absorbed into the Russian tradition, and also perhaps from the stabbing steps of Bronislava Nijinska in her 1923 feminist ballet *Les Noces*, rather than from the soft, ethereal tradition of the French Romantic ballet. She seems, as well, to move on pointe precariously, like a tightrope walker —not through lack of technique but as a result of the daring, extreme positions of her legs and torso. Armitage has stated that she sees pointe shoes "as weapons."[37] That implies both technical prowess and erotic frisson.

Judging her pointe technique "a mite tense" and yet, because of her work with Cunningham, connected to a wider range of leg movements, Greskovic writes that, nevertheless,

> the lack of complete ease in her pointes works *for* the drama of her choreography, not against it. Simultaneous to occupying her place in the

very real present of longstanding ballerinadom, Armitage also shows us something from the other end of that lineage—the early stages in the long-gone past, where pointework was experimental, raw, rare. Armitage reveals something of the actual struggle necessary to keep all the figure's weight on the toetip of the foot.[38]

In her utter contemporaneity—her chic style, her use of art-rock music, her explicit sexuality, and her strenuous postmodern inspection of previous techniques—Armitage seemed in *The Watteau Duets* to invent ballet utterly anew, to locate and reframe ballet's beauty for a jaded era when it seemed nothing could be novel or surprising.

Croce had earlier written that "in its over-all effect, 'Drastic Classicism' was . . . a retrieval of classical dance values from their irrelevant mold of decorum." And she explains:

> Decorous music, decorous costumes, decorous body positions and shapes were thrown out, together with the notion that all these should be decorously related. Relations were expressed . . . but not decorously. . . . [There was] something that we could identify as Armitage's own discovery—the annihilative fury of rock music as a scourge analogous to the flaying of the systematic and the habitual in the dance.[39]

In 1986, Armitage took up the question of ballet decorum even more directly in *The Mollino Room*, a thirty-minute work commissioned by the American Ballet Theatre under the direction of Mikhail Baryshnikov. The ballet featured Baryshnikov, a lead couple, and an ensemble; Baryshnikov, always dancing alone, often brooding, seemed to be marginalized by the group, although—given his star status—one could also see the ballet as literalizing the adage "It's lonely at the top." Indeed, Armitage intended the ballet to be a portrait of the multiple aspects of Baryshnikov's public persona: "as our greatest male dancer; as a classicist in search of contemporary style; as a movie star; as head of ABT, with all the responsibilities that fall on him; and as a performer who's reached the age of 38, and can't help but wonder about his artistic future."[40] Salle (who had recently entered the realm of theatre design with his set for Kathy Acker's play *Birth of a Poet*, directed by Richard Foreman with music by Peter Gordon) designed the decor for *The Mollino Room*—a series of backdrops both abstract and figurative, depicting large-scale objects: men's shoes, a tea service, and a fishing reel—and the costumes.

The use of the dancers—Baryshnikov as soloist, then a lead couple, then four ensemble couples—was so academic that it almost seemed Armitage was drawing attention to and commenting on ballet's institutional hierarchy with dry irony. And, for the most part, the movement vocabulary

The Mollino Room, *choreographed by Karole Armitage with decor and
costumes by David Salle. Photo © 1987 by Johan Elbers.*

was classical. Greskovic comments, "The travels and in-place posings of
the soloists are always distinguished by some definition of limb or append-
age that acknowledges the special geometry of academic dancing (and this
includes the eccentric angles and twists that Armitage intermittently imposes in her plainly classical inventions)."[41]

At the time she was working on *The Mollino Room*, Armitage had
declared that "my own interest now is almost exclusively in ballet."[42] She
remarked that the ballet vocabulary "was figured out over three hundred
years by some very intelligent people, and I think it is wise to use all those
years of thinking, rather than to start in the poverty-stricken position of
zero." She explained that whereas in her earlier work she had wanted to
break the rules, now she was interested in "[making] a classicism about our
time."[43] In this she seemed to share a twin path with Salle, whose complex,
disjunct paintings are monumental in scale and clearly rooted in classical
forms, but are also suffused with eroticism (often centering on the female
body) and with references to art history, popular culture, and contemporary everyday life.

But if *The Mollino Room* was classical in movement terms, Armitage slyly breached opera-house decorum in other ways. The program note stated that the ballet took its title from the twentieth-century Italian architect and designer Carlo Mollino, who celebrated "bad taste," suggesting that this champion of kitsch was a precursor to the generation of postmodernist painters, musicians, performance artists, and choreographers who came of age in the 1980s. *New York Times* critic Jack Anderson declared, "For an example of bad taste, one need go no further than the ballet's own accompaniment." Although the first and third movement were set to difficult music by Paul Hindemith, the second movement was danced to a 1960 comedy routine by Elaine May and Mike Nichols—"My Son, the Nurse"—in a recording in which one can hear the comedians losing control, giggling, and trying to re-establish their composure to resume the routine with their usual deadpan wit. Clearly, in the routine May and Nichols intend to ridicule the stereotypical Jewish mother's notorious desire that her son become a doctor. But Anderson points out that "the dialogue's mockery of the honorable profession of male nursing and the self-satisfied sniggering of its performers might well draw the wrath of sexual liberation groups if this sketch were to turn up in a club today."[44]

Salle has commented that what he understood the May and Nichols routine to be about was "improvisation, the making of humor—that is, *meaning*, before an audience in an unexpected way. . . . [I]t created a metaphor for creativity," and, moreover, he remarks "that Nichols and May, with their sheer creative brilliance, could have been reduced to a sign for *gender roles* makes me want to laugh and cry."[45] However, given the homage to Mollino that frames the ballet, this apparent gaffe could be also be read as deliberate in its politically incorrect outrageousness, as indeed signaling gender roles, not in the way that Anderson and other critics thought offensive, but rather, by laughing rudely at those who uphold traditional gender stereotypes. Among the dancers' three changes of costume were 1950s-style Bermuda shorts for the men and cartoon-like false breasts for the women—costumes that comically underscored the heterosexual imperative and the strong gender divisions underlying every aspect of ballet, from its choreography to its social institutions. On the one hand, Armitage choreographed a lusciously erotic duet for the lead couple. On the other hand, she simultaneously poked fun at the "ballet boys and girls" who always populate the ballet stage—both the characters in the ballets and the dancers who portray them docilely, never questioning the stereotypical gender roles they enact.

Seen in this light, in a post-Stonewall, postfeminist era, Armitage herself seems to be engaged in ironizing "My Son, the Nurse" as a comic success, and thus in criticizing the sexist and homophobic culture of the 1950s and early 1960s that would find male nurses hilarious. That is, by showing in a vulgar way—one that contrasts shockingly with the refinement of the dancing—how the comedy routine (and in general ballet) subscribes to unenlightened values regarding sex and gender, she unmasks ballet's hypocrisy, even while loving its ways of moving. She seems to say bluntly to the opera-house audience, "Yes, it's beautiful, elegant, and satisfying to watch. But don't you also see that ballet is about sex but doesn't admit it? Don't you see that ballet costumes salaciously reveal the body's erogenous zones even as ballet calls itself high art, not pornography? Don't you see that ballet 'boys' and 'girls' are stuck in impossibly old-fashioned, false gender codes?"

The Morality and Politics of the New Beauty

Armitage has stated, "Manners, style, morality, point of view—one leads to the other through musicality. As someone else has said, dance is not only entertainment, it is truly a spiritual question."[46] Since ballet's beauty, as I have indicated, is deeply connected with the body and the issues of morality surrounding the body, it's not surprising that Armitage's ballets, which feature the bodies of unruly women, have often been criticized on moral grounds. Dance and art critic Jill Johnston wrote of *The Mollino Room* that it brought "a certain traditional, and reactionary, trend in the culture of the '80s into focus. With their considerable skills [Armitage and Salle] service a pre-feminist world view, projecting sharply demarcated sex differences which are rooted in the male gaze and the female as object. This is a world view preeminently represented by the classical ballet." Johnston chastised Armitage for her "exhibitionism and female posturing," suggesting that this inappropriate behavior called into question the choreographer's lineage as a postmodern choreographer and speculating that, since modern dance is matriarchal, perhaps Armitage's "partnering and posing and deference to the male" locate her squarely in the patriarchal ballet tradition.[47] Performance art critic Jacki Apple wrote of *The Tarnished Angels* and *The Elizabethan Phrasing of the Late Albert Ayler* (both 1987), "Armitage claims to be a feminist, liberating the female image in ballet. A pretentious conceit on her part! . . . Armitage's women are still sexual cartoons. . . . Gender definition in Armitage's scheme of things is both regressive and oppressive."[48]

And yet, seen from the vantage point of the 1990s, Armitage's cartoon representations of gender codes mark her as a harbinger of what is now identified as postfeminist, "bad girl" art. In the exhibition catalogue essay for the sister shows *Bad Girls* and *Bad Girls West* held, respectively, in New York and Los Angeles in 1994, curator Marcia Tanner writes that bad girls are "truly unruly women who threaten to turn the social order upside down," and she characterizes their art work as "[seducing] the viewer via humor, the bracing shock of freedom unleashed by its unexpected, often subtle subversion of accepted rules, and its projection of countervailing versions of experience." Unlike the programmatic, often humorless politically correct work of an earlier generation of feminist artists, bad girls "invite the viewer to see and think beyond stereotypes and simple either/or oppositions, to imagine a more inclusive, various, and funny world." Unlike good girls, who "don't rock the boat . . . don't talk openly about their own sexual proclivities and erotic fantasies . . . don't invent their own jokes, don't mock truths held to be self-evident," bad girls "flout all these precepts. As Cyndi Lauper sings, these 'girls just wanna have fun.'"[49] Bad girls make transgressive art that revels in taboo content, that trades in stereotypes precisely in order to turn them on their heads, that uses the shock of impropriety and the politically incorrect to make its points, and that rejects the puritanism of early feminism to embrace all sorts of pleasures—bodily, visual, and intellectual—and to fashion a new kind of beauty.

Outrageous and beautiful in their way, Armitage's reworkings of the ballet choreography of a long line of male predecessors function simultaneously as tongue-in-cheek parody, serious critique, and loving homage. Johnston disparages Armitage as somehow betraying feminism as well as her own identity as a woman in choosing to work in the male world of ballet choreography rather than the female domain of modern dance. But it seems to me that Armitage made that choice expressly to bring a postfeminist sensibility to a world in which images of women predominate and yet are usually made by men. Like Madonna's videos of the same period, Armitage's dances of the 1980s show contemporary young women who are figuring out their lives; they're angry or hostile or just generally in charge. If the dances show conflicts between men and women, it is also true that the women often best the men. Lynn Garafola is one of the few dance critics who has written directly about Armitage's feminism:

> Gutsy, sexy, streetwise, [Karole Armitage's women are] big-city teens who go to seamy discos and pick up boys their mothers would never approve of and have sex for the fun of it. When the going gets rough, they know how to call it quits. With a shrug that seems to say, chalk that one up to experience, these brave new girls pick themselves up and move on. . . . When it comes to sex Armitage's women are as independent as Amazons, even if they happen to like men. . . . Again and again, they show us their spunkiness.[50]

Armitage recalls that "the real reason that I became attracted to dance was seeing photos in *Life* magazine of New York City Ballet. There were these gorgeous dancers who looked like a garden of tropical flowers, both very artificial, daring to be that beautiful, controlled, and warm at the same time."[51] For the generation of feminists who emerged in the 1960s and 1970s, female beauty was suspect, for it simply pandered to male desire. And for the modernist artists of that period, beauty in art had long since been banished. But for Armitage's generation, already empowered by the political gains of feminism on the one hand, and engaged in a postmodernist challenge to the values of artistic modernism on the other, beauty in art and in the female body could once again be appreciated. If Armitage was drawn, as a child, to the beauty and glamour of ballet, her own interventions into the history of the art form have given that beauty a new, more complex face. Her unabashed love of ballet's beauty (especially its female beauty) and its erotic display, combined with her intelligent interrogation of the grounds for that beauty, her historical references, and her witty irreverence, wickedly and triumphantly reclaim the art form for our postfeminist times.[52]

NOTES

1. André Levinson, "Some Commonplaces on the Dance," *Broom* (December 1922), reprinted in *André Levinson on Dance: Writings from Paris in the Twenties*, ed. Joan Acocella and Lynn Garafola (Hanover, N.H.: Wesleyan University Press/University Press of New England), p. 32. Noël Carroll argues for Kant's influence on Levinson in "Theater and Dance: A Philosophical Narrative," *Dance Chronicle* 15, no. 3 (1992): 317–331.

2. André Levinson, "The Spirit of the Classic Dance," *Theatre Arts Monthly* (March 1925), reprinted in Acocella and Garafola, *Levinson*, p. 48.

3. Levinson, "Some Commonplaces," pp. 32, 34.

4. Levinson, "Spirit," p. 43.

5. This Levinson sees as a break from a "'horizontal' conception of the dance, based on outlines and figures marked by the feet of the dancer on the floor—what you might call his itinerary" (Levinson, "Spirit," p. 45).

The vocabulary and technique of academic ballet were born in the Renaissance courts and retain the courtly, vertical carriage they inherited from noble deportment and such other physical techniques as fencing. But the visual interest of horizontally oriented, geometric floor patterns of court entertainments, designed to be seen—as if from a bird's-eye view—by spectators seated in balconies, came to be replaced in the seventeenth century by a composition more suited to the picture-frame shape and frontal orientation upon which the proscenium was based. It is as if the plane on which the dance activity took place was raised perpendicularly from the horizontal flatness of the floor to the vertical flatness of the window; it is as if dancing had been a carpet, full of interesting figures, that was suddenly hung on the wall like a tapestry, for better viewing.

6. Lincoln Kirstein, *Movement and Metaphor: Four Centuries of Ballet* (New York: Praeger, 1970), p. 5; Lincoln Kirstein, *Dance: A Short History of Classic Theatrical Dancing* (1935; reprint, New York: Dance Horizons, 1969), p. 187.

7. Levinson, "Spirit," p. 46.

8. Levinson remarks that "The turning outward of the body increases [the dancer's] space to an extraordinary degree, . . . multiplying to an infinite degree the direction of the movement as well as its various conformations. It surrounds the vertical of the body's equilibrium by a vortex of curves, segments of circles, arcs; it projects the body of the dancer into magnificent parabolas, curves it into a living spiral; it creates a whole world of animated forms that awake in us a throng of active sensations." "Spirit," pp. 46–47.

9. Levinson, "Spirit," p. 46.

10. Ibid.

11. Ibid., p. 47.

12. Ibid., p. 44.

13. Kirstein, *Movement and Metaphor* [see note 6], p. 11.

14. Robert Greskovic, *Ballet 101: A Complete Guide to Learning and Loving the Ballet* (New York: Hyperion, 1998), pp. 151–52.

15. Stéphane Mallarmé, "Ballets," in *Mallarmé: Selected Prose Poems, Essays, and Letters*, trans. Bradford Cook (Baltimore: Johns Hopkins University Press, 1956), reprinted in *What Is Dance?: Readings in Theory and Criticism*, ed. Roger Copeland and Marshall Cohen (Oxford: Oxford University Press, 1983), p. 113.

16. Bernard Williams, "Necessary Identities," in *Subjugation and Bondage: Critical Essays on Slavery and Social Philosophy*, ed. Tommy L. Lot (Lanham, Md.: Rowman and Littlefield, 1998), pp. 10–11. Williams cites Aristotle, *Politics* 1254b27 seq. He points out that Aristotle cannot fully justify his claim, since, Aristotle admits, "the opposite often happens, and some people have the bodies of free men and others the souls."

17. A. K. Volinsky [*sic*], "The Book of Exultation," trans. Seymour Barofsky, *Dance Scope* 5, no. 2 (Spring 1971): 18–20.

18. Ibid., pp. 24, 26–28.

19. Adrian Stokes, "The Classical Ballet," in *To-night the Ballet* (London: Faber and Faber, 1935), reprinted in Copeland and Cohen, *What Is Dance?*, pp. 244–45.

20. Ibid., pp. 245–47.

21. Ibid., p. 247.

22. Alastair Macaulay, "What Is Classicism? International Critics Look at Javanese Bedhaya," in *Looking Out: Perspectives on Dance and Criticism in a Multicultural World*, ed. David Gere (New York: Schirmer Books/ Simon and Schuster Macmillan, 1995), p. 147.

23. Levinson, "Spirit," p. 47.

24. I use the term "bodily canon" to denote a set of standards for approved images of the body, as well as for authorized behaviors, stances, shapes, postures, and gestures.

25. See Mikhail Bakhtin, *Rabelais and His World*, trans. Helene Iswolsky (1968; reprint, Bloomington: Indiana University Press, 1984), pp. 19–30.

26. Michel Fokine, "Letter to *The Times*, July 6, 1914," reprinted in Cyril W.

Beaumont, *Michel Fokine and His Ballets* (1935; reprint, New York: Dance Horizons, 1981), p. 146.

27. Tamara Karsavina, *Theatre Street* (1931; revised paperback edition, New York: E. P. Dutton, 1961), pp. 236–37.

28. See my articles "Balanchine and Black Dance," *Choreography and Dance* 3, no. 3 (1993), reprinted in my *Writing Dancing in the Age of Postmodernism* (Hanover, N.H.: Wesleyan University Press/University Press of New England, 1994), pp. 53–69; and "Sibling Rivalry: The New York City Ballet and Modern Dance," in *Dance for a City: Fifty Years of the New York City Ballet*, ed. Lynn Garafola and Eric Foner (New York: Columbia University Press, 1999), pp. 73–98.

29. Edward Denby, "Some Thoughts About Classicism and George Balanchine," *Dance Magazine* (February 1953), reprinted in Edwin Denby, *Dance Writings*, ed. Robert Cornfield and Willam MacKay (New York: Knopf, 1986), pp. 440, 433, 438–439.

30. *South Bank Show: Karole Armitage*, London Weekend Television, producer and director David Hinton, 1985.

31. Performing Artservices, "Karole Armitage: Narrative Biography," Press Kit, 1985.

32. Arlene Croce, "Closed Circuits," *New Yorker*, January 30, 1984, reprinted in Arlene Croce, *Sight Lines* (New York: Knopf, 1987), p. 165.

33. *Salle: An Interview with David Salle by Peter Schjeldahl* (New York: Vintage Books/Random House, 1987), p. 44.

34. Arlene Croce, "Modern Love," *New Yorker*, April 29, 1985, reprinted in Croce, *Sight Lines*, p. 255.

35. On *Agon*, see my extended analysis in Sally Banes, *Dancing Women: Female Bodies on Stage* (London: Routledge, 1998), pp. 194–211.

36. *South Bank Show.*

37. Quoted in Robert Greskovic, "Armitagean Physics, or the Shoes of the Ballerina," *Ballet Review* 13, no. 2 (Summer 1985): 79.

38. Ibid., pp. 79–80.

39. Arlene Croce, "Think Punk," *New Yorker*, March 9, 1981, reprinted in Arlene Croce, *Going to the Dance* (New York: Knopf, 1982), p. 351.

40. Quoted in Alan M. Kriegsman, "A Dancer's Circle: Karole Armitage and ABT's 'Mollino Room,'" *Washington Post*, April 10, 1986, p. C4.

41. Robert Greskovic, "The Past, the Present, & the Future: American Ballet Theatre & the Kirov," *Ballet Review* 14, no. 2 (Summer 1986): 68.

42. John Mueller and Don McDonagh, "Making Musical Dance: Robert Irving, Richard Colton, Kate Johnson, Karole Armitage," *Ballet Review* 13, no. 4 (Winter 1986): 39.

43. *South Bank Show.*

44. Jack Anderson, "Dance: Baryshnikov in 'The Mollino Room,'" *New York Times*, May 18, 1986, sec. 1, pt. 2, p. 68.

45. Quoted in *Salle*, p. 55.

46. John Mueller and Don McDonagh, "Making Musical Dance," p. 44.

47. Jill Johnston, "The Punk Princess and the Postmodern Prince," *Art in America* 74, no. 10 (October 1986): 24–25.

48. Jacki Apple, "The Los Angeles Festival: The Armitage Ballet," *High Performance* Issue #39, Vol.10, no. 3 (1987): 32–33.

49. Marcia Tanner, "Mother Laughed: The Bad Girls' Avant-Garde," in *Bad Girls* (New York: New Museum of Contemporary Art; Cambridge, Mass.: MIT Press, 1994), pp. 48, 51. Tanner cites the Lauper song as follows: *Girls Just Want to Have Fun*, music and lyrics by Robert Hazard, New York, Sony Tunes, Inc., 1983. Recorded by Cyndi Lauper, 1983.

50. Lynn Garafola, "The Armitage Ballet," *Dancemagazine* 62, no. 11 (November 1988): 80.

51. *South Bank Show.*

52. Thanks to Noël Carroll, Neil Donahue, and Robert Greskovic for their help with this essay.

Peg Zeglin Brand

13. Bound to Beauty: An Interview with Orlan

> *I show images which almost make us blind. My work stands between*
> *the folly of seeing and the impossibility of seeing.*
>
> —ORLAN (October 1998)

Orlan is a French performance artist whose work on beauty elicits shock and disgust. Beginning in 1990, she began a series of nine aesthetic surgeries entitled *The Reincarnation of St. Orlan* that altered her face and body, placed her at risk in the operating room, and centered her within certain controversy in the art world. Undergoing only epidural anaesthesia and controlling the performance to the greatest degree possible (given that a surgeon does the actual procedure), she "choreographs" and documents the events. In 1993, one portion of a five-hour surgery, *Omnipresence*, was broadcast live to the Centre Georges Pompidou in Paris and Penine Hart Gallery in New York while Orlan interacted directly with critics and viewers watching on monitors.[1] Another performance was based in part on a text written by the French philosopher, Michel Serres, that asked:

> What can the common monster, tattooed, ambidextrous, hermaphrodite and cross-breed, show to us right now under his skin? Yes, blood and flesh.[2]

Orlan's aesthetic surgeries are integrally bound to beauty: more particularly, standards of feminine beauty codified in the art of "the great masters" of Western Europe, beginning with the Renaissance. By means of actual surgery—filmed in graphic detail—Orlan has altered her face to resemble a composite computer-generated image combining the chin of Sandro Botticelli's *Birth of Venus*, the forehead of da Vinci's *Mona Lisa*, the lips of Gustave Moreau's *Abduction of Europa*, the eyes of a Fountaine-bleu School *Diane Chasseresse*, and the nose of Gerard's *First Kiss of Eros*

Orlan, The Reincarnation of St. Orlan/Omnipresence. *Scene from the operating room during Seventh Plastic Surgical Operation, November 21, 1993. Duration of performance: 5 hours; transmission: 1 hour. Courtesy of Sandra Gering Gallery, New York.*

and Psyche.[3] A template functions as the imagined Orlan: a technologically created composite of virtual beauties—where "virtual beauty" is defined as beauty "being in essence or effect, not in fact; not actual, but equivalent, so far as effect is concerned." Virtual beauty substitutes for, yet is not in fact, real beauty. The actual Orlan, photographed during and after surgery, has realized each projected change: forehead, eyes, chin, and lips. Her project appropriates past norms of feminine beauty that were codified by revered artists but critiques them as well: both the control such norms wield over women and the subordination of women's bodies in marriage, commerce, and art within patriarchal cultures. The ongoing artwork, *Reincarnation,* alters the physical body of Orlan but will also include a new name (and a legal change in identity).[4] This is Orlan—*literally* at the cutting edge.

More recent work by Orlan consists of dozens of radically altered self-portraits, realized in large-scale color photographs, called *Self-Hybridation*. In this series, she extends the notion of a template that operates as a guide for computer-generated identities but leaves the surgeon and operating room behind. Allowing for multiple transformations into visages that seem to originate in another time and place, these "portraits" are hybridized personae, unique constructions of past and present. The guiding role played by feminine beauty in *Reincarnation* is replaced by genderless norms of beauty in *Self-Hybridation*: norms held by both men and women as well as by members of various classes within the ancient Olmec and Maya civilizations. In these images, Orlan is pictured with crossed eyes, jewel-encrusted teeth, an enlarged nose, or a deformed skull. To our eyes, she does not look beautiful. Yet she brings to our attention the power of beauty to emerge and operate within a culture, even one so far removed from our own.

Her work has elicited debate from an amazing array of interpreters including physicians, psychologists, art critics, artists, philosophers, cultural critics, Women's Studies scholars, and technophiles. As her performances are critiqued, a hierarchy of penetrating questions has emerged, beginning with the most basic, Is it art? and eventually taking more historical and contextual routes: How does her work relate to "Body Art" of the 1960s and 1970s, created primarily by male artists? What role does the graphic depiction of blood and flesh play and how does it relate to religious strictures about the sanctity of the body? How is aesthetic surgery different from cosmetic surgery? And most important, what is the role of beauty?

I have been fascinated for years by the work of Orlan: the controversy caused among art world critics, the abhorrence and rejection expressed by some feminist scholars, and the complex philosophical issues raised about the interaction of mind and body and what constitutes a person's identity. For these reasons, I welcomed the opportunity to engage her in conversation where she generously shared her thoughts. I feel that two themes emerged that place her art squarely within recurring debates in the aesthetics and politics of bodily representation: (1) There is no one (universal) ideal of beauty, yet (2) we are bound to beauty in how we see ourselves and our relationships to others. When Orlan claims (in the opening quote) that images of her work make us blind and stand between the folly of seeing and the impossibility of seeing, she links together issues vital to perceiving art — what invites us (in) to look — to the way our assumptions and beliefs help mold what we *think* and *want* to perceive. Most people find the graphic display of a scalpel cutting through flesh nearly impossible to view. Yet, as in horror films or documentation of actual accident scenes or surgeries, we

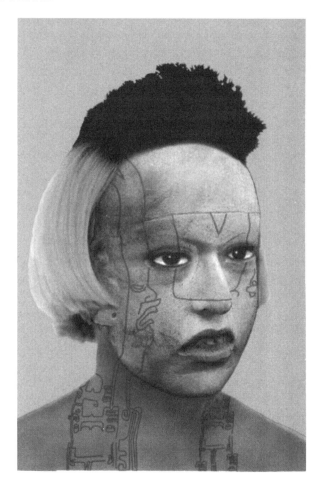

Orlan au Masque Olmèque. *Digitally processed image,*
1998. Courtesy of the artist with the collaboration of Pierre
Zovile.

are drawn in to gaze, often more than once. Similarly, we may be horrified
by the thought of babies' skulls being deliberately malformed in the name
of beauty, yet we are curious as to how it would actually look. The folly of
looking—of wanting to see what is horrible—is Orlan's stock in trade. The
irony is that her exploration of beauty takes us down the grisly path one
must travel in order to achieve beauty—causing us to subvert standard

philosophical notions of aesthetic distance and aesthetic appreciation.[5] She brings us to the discomfort of a cutting edge which we aesthetically, and sadistically, enjoy.

Bound to Beauty: *Reincarnation*

> *I am not against cosmetic surgery at all. I am against the way cosmetic surgery is used. . . . It all comes down to this: The "envelope" [body] is not very important; I can change it if I want. The body is just like a costume, a bag.*

Early on in Orlan's project (1991), French psychologists, critics, and artists devoted an entire issue of a psychoanalytic publication to the relationship of her work to psychopathology and aesthetics, concluding that she was indeed sane and that her performances were art.[6] American critic Barbara Rose argued in favor of art status based on "two essential criteria for distinguishing art from nonart, intentionality and transformation."[7] Feminist psychoanalytic writer Parveen Adams wrote about the "new space" opened up by Orlan's surgeries. When the skin of her cheek, for instance, was lifted off her face during surgery, it created a space between the skin and what lay beneath. She interpreted the meaning of this physical space metaphorically: as the space between what is customary and what stands in contrast—the horrifying unknown; as the space between the inside and the outside. For her, the revelation of Orlan's work is the underlying "emptiness of the image":

> It is here on the operating table that castration occurs, not in the act of cutting, not in the drama of the knife, not in the barely suppressed frenzy of it all, but in the space which is opened up. . . . Something flies off; this something is the security of the relation between the inside and the outside. It ceases to exist. . . . There is an emptying out of the object.[8]

Another feminist, Kathy Davis, approached the physicality and the meanings it evokes quite differently, coming at it from the perspective of a scholar seeking explanations for the increasing number of women who undergo routine modes of cosmetic surgery—procedures antithetical to certain feminist sensibilities.[9] Her explanation of cosmetic surgery as a means of overcoming feelings of inferiority continues to cause controversy among feminists.

When it is assessed within the same context, Orlan's work emerges as behavior that can be read simultaneously as feminist *critique* of beauty practices today and feminist *utopia* where modern technology, as in standard cosmetic surgery which is designed to improve a woman's looks, brings about empowerment. Since Orlan does not attempt to become more beautiful or attractive, and has, in her words, come to look somewhat "monstrous," her performances are clearly distinct from cosmetic surgery. They are instances of what she calls "aesthetic surgery" and they result from a variety of complex intentions.

Since 1990, the year of Orlan's fortieth birthday, she has undergone nine surgeries, calling her work Carnal Art in contrast to the 1960s–1970s Body Art that captured the documented performances of Vito Acconci, Chris Burden, and Dennis Oppenheim and the four Austrian Actionists including Herman Nitsch, Gunther Brus, Otto Muehl, and Rudolf Schwarzkogler.[10] Seeking to explain the differences between her work and the Austrian Actionists who claimed to be exploring the motif of sexual and erotic identity in the style of Egon Schiele and Oskar Kokoschka, she wrote the Carnal Art Manifest: a series of definitions and observations on her work.

> Carnal Art is self-portraiture in the classical sense, but realized through the possibility of technology. It swings between defiguration and refiguration. Its inscription in the flesh is a function of our age. The body has become a "modified readymade," no longer seen as the ideal it once represented.[11]

As in traditional self-portraiture, the body is the subject matter of her art, but she also uses her physical self—her bodily flesh—to embody her depiction. No canvas, stone, or paper is used here! Unlike traditional painting or sculpture by which self-portraiture is achieved through a depiction or expression of the image of the body, she literally becomes (or transforms herself into) the *self* that is portrayed. Her portrayed self is both *de*-figured (destroyed, deconstructed) and *re*-figured (repaired, replaced). The body is the medium, but the physical attributes she borrows from Botticelli, da Vinci, and other artists are symbolic of characteristics *not* visible on the surface, that is, of personality traits or psychological characteristics. Each personage—Venus, Diana, Psyche, Mona Lisa, and Europa—is chosen for some quality each figure embodies or represents:

> They all have some of me. Psyche is always sticking her nose into things. Diana traveled a lot; she is a goddess who doesn't surrender to men. Botticelli's Venus has the drive of birth. And Mona Lisa? A beacon, . . . the most enigmatic in all history of art. She is unavoidable.[12]

As with performances by other artists, actors, and dancers who use their own bodies, she initiates and executes her plan. Agency and control are essential to the process; and the meaning of her work, and its ultimate empowerment, comes from her manipulation and appropriation of past icons of beauty. Unlike cosmetic surgery which is done to enhance the appearance of a person's face or body, however, she highlights the process, not the results. Borrowing from Duchamp, she calls the body a "modified" —not ideal—found object. It is not ideal nor can it ever achieve idealization; the beautifying surgery of modern technology, based on one's own projections, imaginings, or fantasies, is basically futile. Orlan offers herself as living proof: in the name of art.

> My work is all about my own image, which is supposed to represent today's standards of beauty, as well as some "counter-standards," because these two bumps [on the forehead] are like a counter-standard of beauty today.

Orlan is referring here to the two silicone implants in her forehead, intended to resemble the forehead of the Mona Lisa. She has become an odd combination: an attractive woman with unnatural bumps, highlighted —for the sake of making them more prominent than they might ordinarily be—by two shades of frosted gold makeup. Her hair is bright yellow and black and she sports yellow and black eyeglasses. With no eyebrows, her forehead is even more prominent. Black lipstick and fingernail polish complete the look. The gaze she returns to onlookers is penetrating and intense; one could even say that there is beauty in her eyes, evidence that only *some* of her features have been changed to contrast with today's standards of beauty. She reports on how people react to her in public:

> If you can't see me and someone describes me and they say, "This is a woman with two bumps," you'll think that I'm a monster and that I'm not pleasant: that you can't communicate with me. If you see me, however, it's different. And in my normal life—in the bus, in the subway, in the street—it ends up being very difficult for me. All types of people want to speak with me, look at me.

Orlan both appropriates and comments on male artists as she places herself within the history of how women are visually represented *by* men as codified by centuries of practice within the art world. As a composite of borrowed (false, virtual) beauty, she places her *self* as art within the context of the everyday world around her. But she also brings us face to face with the realities of how beauty standards function in art and advertising to motivate women to undergo dangerous cosmetic surgery simply for the sake of looking better. She questions the motivation of women who seek a

Portrait of Orlan. © 1997. Courtesy of the artist with the collaboration of Pierre Zovile.

simple "fix" to their physical problems: sagging breasts, crow's feet, thick thighs. Her claim—"One thing is sure: it is through cosmetic surgery that men can exert their power over women the most"—reminds us that technology has made this possible and that, in the past, where male artists held the paintbrush and controlled the representation of women in the realm of high art, now male surgeons hold the scalpels and control the tucking, sucking, and erasing.

Such power can be overt, as in the case of a male surgeon operating on a female patient, or it can be more subtle. Some feminists, like Naomi Wolf, argue that women are duped "victims" of "the beauty myth"—pressured against their wills to undergo expensive and dangerous procedures in order to look better according to the ideals promoted by the male-dominated fashion industry and its massive advertising campaigns.[13] In contrast, Kathy Davis asks why women should refrain from such procedures *if* they end up feeling better, more confident and self-assured. At issue is justified skepticism about basic motivation: For whom is the woman undergoing surgery? Is it for a husband, male lover, the fashion industry complex? Or is it (really) for herself?

Orlan realizes the futility of answering such questions like these that lie at the heart of feminist disagreements about cosmetic surgery. In truth, no one can answer them *except* the person undergoing the actual procedure and even then, like artists reporting artistic intentions, s/he may be self-deceived or deliberately untruthful. As she clearly states, Orlan is not against *all* cosmetic surgery but rather against *the way it is used*. She disapproves of women submitting their autonomy to the preferences of men. This manifests itself on several levels. First, on a personal level, Orlan's manipulation of past codes of feminine beauty enables her to feel control, agency, and a new sense of identity and empowerment. Second, on a symbolic level, her simultaneous appropriation and critique of past art's historically encoded norms of beauty is an instance of feminist activism; she attempts to show, by example, that the legacy of masculine portrayals of feminine beauty precludes women's full agency and control. In appropriating the power inherent in the very act of creating the image, she wrests control away from men who help set the standards and enshrine them in oil on canvas. It is a political act that goes beyond art-historical significance. Hence the interest in her work by persons in the medical and health-related professions.

Orlan explicitly ties the uses of cosmetic surgery to the need for persons to reassert or reactivate an individual sense of identity:

> In the past, women, and men too, had a much shorter life expectancy; women often died in childbirth. And very often, people, once they've reached seventy, wind up with a face they don't recognize as theirs any longer. There is a loss of identity because they no longer recognize themselves. They are alien to themselves. And I think that, in this case, when it is too difficult to feel "other," there is cosmetic surgery.

Until the time when we find "injections or drugs to cure facial disfigurement or disease," the only option—other than to do nothing and risk loss of one's sense of self—is cosmetic surgery. She cites an example close to home:

> Recently, I was with a friend who is, I don't know, sixty-five or something like that, and she feels fine. She is married and happy with her husband. But she was telling me—it's very odd—she felt very healthy and had a lot of energy; still, people would say to her, "Oh, you look so tired." She would answer, "No, I'm not tired. I feel good." But you couldn't tell that she was fit anymore. She simply looked tired. And at first, she would tell me that she'd always been against cosmetic surgery but that now she couldn't stand people telling her that she looked tired when she wasn't. "I am not tired or sick and I want people to know and to see for themselves," she said. I think that by now, she's had surgery. It was for her social life, her normal life, but her herself too.

She contends that although cultural norms encourage us toward possibilities to educate, expand, and even alter and control our minds, we are not similarly encouraged toward physical changes. Recent trends of tattooing or body piercing seem innovative and experimental, yet they lack originality and lapse into mere conformism.

> For example, many people said to me: "But your bumps, it's the same thing as tattoos or piercing." But for me, it's a very different thing because very often, those who do piercing do so to differentiate themselves from others. In fact, their intention is mainly to join a different group, another tribe, to "resemble." It's becoming a new kind of conformity. That's the danger.

Several people have suggested she try meditation or Zen techniques instead of changing her physical features. Her response brings us back to the issue of who she *is*, internally, in spite of her appearance: "I can change images of myself and still have this kind of radiance that some inner quality or strength allows me to have."

Perhaps this explains her disdain for a young Belgian fashion designer, Walter Van Beirendonck, whose initials, WLT, come from his nickname, "Wild and Lethal Trash." He has fashionably appropriated Orlan's bumps on both male and female runway fashion models as well as her rhetoric. For instance, one of her statements has been "Remember the future," and his statement is "Kiss the future." Orlan laments, "I don't want the imitation; I don't want to be the model."

> Fashion has caught up with me. I mean that a great number of designers, American or French, find inspiration in my work. And there's one in particular, called WLT, who has made a lot of fashion shows with models on whom he put the same bumps I have, but these were made out of materials like latex or cinema make-up.[14]

She complains that he is imitating her implants simply to copy her, not to assert any individual sense of self or identity nor to make any sort of original artistic statement. This, too, is the problem with women who undertake surgery for the "wrong" reasons and why such reasons are attributed to *her* when she undergoes surgery:

> A lot of women are very self-conscious; they want to look like the most beautiful women, like the supermodels we see on commercials or in magazines. So, when the critics hear "cosmetic surgery" in relation to my performances, they inevitably assume that I want to be the most beautiful woman, that I want to do as Michael Jackson does, or Cher, or I don't know who.

Clearly this is not her goal, and she is "absolutely opposed" to any one standard of beauty or any notion of a timeless or universal ideal of beauty. Her fight against the visual icon of Venus—"the image I fight against the most"—was motivated by surgeons attempting to tell her *how* to proceed "correctly" with what they thought would be typical cosmetic surgery:

> I had some surgeons tell me, "Your nose must be at a thirty degree angle, your chin here with respect to your forehead." They showed me very precise pictures and some geometrical percentages, and so on and so forth. They would tell me: "This way is fine, you will be attractive; otherwise, you aren't fuckable." Really! Plastic surgeons didn't really understand what my intentions were, and I had to go to the States, where I met a woman surgeon, a feminist, to get what I wanted.

Her problems may come as no surprise to those familiar with the world of cosmetic surgery which, like medicine in general, is dominated by men. Magazine and newspaper ads routinely advocate surgery as a site "where art and science meet," that promise women they will still be them*selves*, only enhanced: "You. Only better." One Web site, for example, advertises such procedures as breastlifts, lipsuction, rhinoplasties, facelifts, and other procedures against the visual backdrop of two classic works of art: an Ingres painting of nude women in a Turkish bathhouse and a small insert of Michelangelo's image of God infusing life into the hand of Adam![15] Given that men are now undergoing surgery at increasing rates, Orlan finds her work caught in the subtle politics of the role good looks play in the lives of powerful *men* in the art world:

> It's very difficult for my work to be understood in art milieus because very often, the collectors—the people who have money, power, and who have almost all had cosmetic surgery—call my work "shameful." They are ill at ease because they've already taken care of everything [i.e., their own looks].

To call her work "shameful" also raises ethical and religious questions similar to those asked about the work of Andres Serrano (creator of the controversial photograph, *Piss Christ*) and other artists. In the Manifest, Orlan seeks to contrast her motivation from that of typical surgery:

> Carnal Art is not against aesthetic surgery, but against the standards that pervade it, particularly, in relation to the female body, but also to the male body. Carnal Art must be feminist, it is necessary. Carnal Art not only engages in aesthetic surgery, but also in developments in medicine and biology: questioning the status of the body and posing ethical problems.

She articulates the political and subversive role of the artist:

> Carnal Art asserts the individual independence of the artist. In that sense it resists givens and dictates. This is why it has engaged the social, the media (where it disrupts received ideas and causes scandal), and will even reach as far as the judiciary (to change the name of Orlan).

And in contrast to the imitative fashion designer WLT, originality and playfulness play an important role:

> Carnal Art loves parody and the baroque, the grotesque and the extreme. Carnal Art opposes the conventions that exercise constraint on the human body and the work of art. Carnal Art is anti-formalist and anti-conformist.

It is the opposition to constraints on the body—again a case of agency and control—that inevitably raises the issue of the pain she endures at the conclusion of her performances. She neither seeks nor condones it:

> As distinct from "Body Art," Carnal Art does not conceive of pain as redemptive or as a source of purification. Carnal Art is not interested in the plastic-surgery result, but in the process of surgery, the spectacle and discourse of the modified body which has become the place of a public debate.

Technology allows her to explore and exploit advances over the past several decades in aesthetic surgery and in medicine and pain control. As she notes, any presumption that the body is sacrosanct is already outmoded in medical circles:

> Many people are against cosmetic surgery because it corresponds to an influence of our Christian religion, at least in Europe: one should not alter one's body, one should accept oneself as one is. But I think that a lot of taboos concerning the body are going away, including that one. We realize that we can alter our body and that when we grow older, it seems normal to change a patella here, or put a plastic hip there, and there are no problems, physical or psychological. On the contrary, we feel better.

For Orlan, the step to extending this argument to elective changes in physical appearance is a small one:

> We still think that if we change our appearance, the sky will fall down on our head! It goes along with the idea of doing something against nature. But I'm happy to take an extreme position on this, even if it's not genuine: I hate nature. Because I don't know where the switch is that forces me to die, for instance. I don't know how to switch it off, and this is what nature is: Life is a killer. . . . Nature represents everything that locks me in, that applies force on me, that bothers me.

She cites four examples: (1) growing up as an adolescent, unable to stop the natural process of developing breasts and pubic hair—"I couldn't stop it; it was against my will"; (2) later, several times when she became pregnant—"It was so unbelievable at first that I thought that my will alone would cause me to abort; but it didn't, nature kept it going"; and (3) now, at middle age—"I can't stop that thing which takes me closer to death." Perhaps her most convincing example, however, is (4) control of pain. She recalls an anecdote about a family acquaintance:

> Recently, I was having a conversation with a woman in my family who wanted to deliver her baby with an epidural shot but shortly before she was due to give birth, called me to say: "You know, Orlan, actually I've decided to do things the natural way, normally. It will be an important experience in my life. I have to know what it's like."

Orlan's response was swift and certain, arguing by analogy:

> It's so ridiculous because if we go to the dentist's to have a tooth pulled out, just before going, we don't say: "Hey, I wonder what it would be like to have it done without a shot? Maybe it would be an experience, maybe it would be interesting, natural!"

Thus, unnecessary pain is a form of *uncontrolled* nature that "bothers" her, that "locks" her in and "applies force." Anything outside one's control—death, pain, physical maturation, and pregnancy—are "natural"; they take place in spite of our resistance. From a philosophical point of view, it is interesting to note that these are all bodily processes and that Orlan's views about the body end up aligning her with some of the most influential dualist thinkers like Plato and Descartes. The most tenacious doctrines of male-dominated philosophy include those that hold that persons consist of mind and body, that the body is far inferior to the mind, and that man (and in nearly all cases men exclusively and not women) are defined by the rationality of their functioning minds. It has been only recently that feminist philosophers have challenged the legacy of Western philosophy, searching for ways to rescue the body, which was previously seen as an impediment to knowledge, and to secure status and integrity for the emotions, which were seen as an antithesis and impediment to reason. Is it conceivable that Orlan's attention to the body is a feminist philosophical activism as well? Although there is no space to pursue it here, future philosophical investigations into Orlan's assumptions would prove fruitful, especially in light of Plato's *Symposium,* in which the eternal and intangible Form of Beauty is first perceived and appreciated *in* the body through sexual attraction.

Orlan's thoughts on the body as "envelope"—changeable without limit —remind us that we live in an age of startling technological advances that enable us to control nature more than ever before. It is logical, then, to extend the category of what is natural (given to us by nature) to the body and its parts that cause us unhappiness or dissatisfaction, especially the changing, aging body. Cosmetic surgery is one means of alteration now available. The body and face given to us by nature can easily be changed. Consider the case of the Barbie "clone"—a woman with an extremely high (in fact, MENSA-level) IQ who has undergone eighteen surgeries to resemble the famous Barbie doll in order to improve her social life (so she says); or the many women who undergo breast implants; or numerous girls who choose to get nose jobs to mask undesirable ethnic traits.[16]

The religious implications of Orlan's views about nature, natural pain, and pain in childbirth have led some to consider her work as blasphemous. She places her pain in the broader context of women's pain as it has been recorded in scripture and religious doctrine:

> The famous "You shall deliver in pain" is still deeply fixed in women's minds, just as religions dictate: Suffering is prestigious, it means you'll get to Heaven, it's good. To me, suffering is a mere alarm signal that goes off when our body is sick; we don't need more suffering. So, this is my first goal concerning suffering: to show that suffering is uninteresting. In fact, the times we live in are wonderful, for we are overcoming pain; at least we can control it.

She elaborates in the Manifest:

> Carnal Art finds the acceptance of the agony of childbirth to be anachronistic and ridiculous. Like Artaud, it rejects the mercy of God. Henceforth we shall have epidurals, local anaesthetics and multiple analgesics. Hurray for morphine! Down with the pain!

In addition, she highlights the difference in attitudes toward pain management in France and the United States:

> My work is not about standards of beauty alone; it is also on physical pain, in Europe and particularly in France. I believe that, concerning pain,

things are different where you're from. For instance, in hospitals in France, most of the time, they don't give palliative care. When people die, they are left in agony for days without the morphine or drugs that would alleviate the pain.

Thus pain management operates as an issue of medical ethics as well as an issue for women in childbirth since both are involved with control over one's body, whether male or female. Carnal Art is the site where these concerns come together:

Carnal Art does not inherit the Christian Tradition, it resists it! Carnal Art illuminates the Christian denial of body-pleasure and exposes its weakness in the face of scientific discovery. Carnal Art repudiates the tradition of suffering and martyrdom, replacing rather than removing, enhancing rather than diminishing—Carnal Art is not self-mutilation.

Her goals, then, are both artistic and political:

I am one of those women who fought a lot to defend the right to have an abortion (at a time when women who had abortions were hunted down like witches) and to use contraception. My work is not feminist in its artistic dimension alone; I have also worked a lot in the political arena. That's why I also work among women, because the idea that childbirth has to be painful is still widespread. And in my mind, this is ludicrous.

Her intentions are insistently feminist, in spite of being misunderstood and alienated in what she considers a hostile atmosphere in France:

You do not realize how widely feminism is accepted in the States. But in France, if you declare: "I am a feminist" or if people think you are, well, your career as an artist might as well be over. People won't pay attention to you any more.

She recounts two instances as evidence:

Something quite extraordinary happened: There was an exhibition held in Beaubourg and there were guidelines for the art historians who wrote in the catalogue. One of them was told not to use the word "feminism." I was not part of this exhibition and somebody told me, literally, "Your work is too feminist." In another case, the cover photo for a catalogue for an exhibition in Italy has a woman on all fours! That's Europe for you. I don't think you would find this in the States.

In addition, she cites examples where the public and critics from the art world have misunderstood her explicitly stated feminist intentions:

First, I was on a television show with Madonna. It was a program about sex, provocation, and religion. On this program—it was a fake live program with an audience of maybe five hundred people—I said that my nose was natural, that I never had any surgery on my nose, and that if one day I do, it will be very, very big (like the Mayas). Still, at the end of the program, three people in the audience, three young women, came up to me. It was quite comical. They put their hands on their noses and said to me: Do you see how ugly our noses are: so long, so big! We want a nose just like yours. Tell us, who is the surgeon who did it? We want exactly the same nose.

Now another story, because the most difficult thing about my work is to make myself understood, because my work goes against our customs, our habits, to such an extent that people cannot see it; all they hear is "cosmetic surgery." When I came back from the States with my bumps which, at the time, were much bigger—there's since been a physiological change —one of my friends told me: "I'll make a deal with you; I'll throw a huge welcome-back party in your honor in a night club called Le Palace but in return, I want you to allow me to organize a press conference, so that at last, the press will stop saying stupid things about your work." And I agreed and found myself in front of about sixty international journalists, and I told them, "Look at my head! Will you stop saying that I want to look like Venus, which is the image I fight against the most? For me, this is what I want to debunk. And stop saying that I want to look like Mona Lisa. You can see it's not true. Do you understand now?" Afterwards, more than fifty percent of the headlines in the press read, "She wants to be the most beautiful woman," "She wants to look like Venus," or "She wants to look like the Mona Lisa." Headlines! At times it is irritating; at other times, it is amusing, but what is terrible for me is that now a whole movement has started. Namely, some art historians took what had been said in the popular press, elaborating some big theories that were all wrong. Even in one of my catalogues, one that was done quickly in Italy and that I didn't have a chance to proofread, an art critic wrote about my ideal of beauty, etc. It's just unbelievable. It's crazy. It's very difficult.

Orlan's frustration with viewers' misunderstanding of *Reincarnation* is understandable given her explicit denial that she intends to improve her physical appearance with cosmetic surgery. Such circumstances have led her to move in a direction that is less likely to be misinterpreted and which places *Reincarnation* within a broader spectrum of exploration. Moving away from Western European standards of feminine beauty and her own reconfiguration based on Diana, Psyche, Venus, Europa, and the Mona Lisa, recent work explores an expanded notion of beauty while simultaneously infusing technology with a more prominent role.

Bound to Beauty: *Self-Hybridation*

Orlan's *Reincarnation* series can now be placed within a broader cultural and historical context in light of more recent work that features computer-generated self-portraits with Olmec and Mayan features:

My new work is a global survey of standards of beauty in other civilizations and at different periods in history. I start with the pre-Columbian
civilizations and will eventually study Africa and Asia.[17]

In *Self-Hybridation*, Western European standards of feminine beauty no
longer function as virtual beauty that inspires actual surgery. Instead, computer-generated self-portraits become examples of virtual beauty that allow
the artist to pursue a range of "multiple, evolving, mutating identities":

> I am not like most transsexuals, for instance, who have a mental image of
> themselves that they want to resemble at any price. To my mind, everyday
> results are not important. It's not my problem, and what I like is multiple,
> evolving, mutating identities, not one fixed identity with an image you
> want to resemble.

This new phase of techno-art enables her to transform self-portraits
into dozens of images that seem to spring from another time and place:
hybridizations of past and present, the real and the imagined. The role of
beauty in these works differs from that in *Reincarnation* since Orlan adopts
the norms of beauty from the past, shaping her own computer image according to ancient cultural codes of Olmec and Maya symbols of regal and
supernatural power, thereby becoming on-screen (and in printed photograph) a hybrid of virtual beauty.[18]

What sorts of refigurations does Orlan create? First, she borrows two
distinct styles from the Olmec tradition. One comes from giant basalt rocks
called "Colossal Heads" from the Gulf Coast region of Mexico, some of
which measure seven to twelve feet in height and weigh five to twenty tons.
They are believed to be individualistic portraits commemorating male
rulers, expressing respect and honor. Volcanic in origin and thus a manifestation of earthly power, the placement of the heavy stone—eventually
located miles away and at higher elevations than their original source—is
a testament to the ruler's organizational power to coordinate the many
people needed to transport them to a place of veneration. Stylistically, the
faces were round, full, curvilinear, and naturalistic:

> The heads represent adult males wearing close-fitting caps with chin
> straps and large, round earplugs. The fleshy faces have almond-shaped
> eyes, flat broad noses, thick protruding lips, a slight frown, and down-
> turned mouths.[19]

The other Olmec style was quite different. Found in life-sized masks—
often made of jade and placed on top of the deceased ruler's face upon
burial—as well as on much smaller maskettes, faces were generally more
abstract, geometrical, and idealized. Human and animal images, and com-

posites of the two, as in the case of the human jaguar (also a representation of the Olmec Supreme God), were routinely depicted.[20] The facial mask became the repository for the ruler's likeness: not in terms of specific physical features that captured resemblance, but rather in symbolic patterns of proportion and symmetry that captured a ruler's *inner* transformation, thus revealing the true nature of the wearer. The masks of one particular period, from 900–600 B.C.E., are described as "spiritually ecstatic faces" designed "to represent the soul within" by means of the "beauty of geometric shapes."[21] One example of this time period, an illustrated incised mask made of white and gray jadeite, seems to provide the inspiration for one of Orlan's hybrid faces which adopts conventions from the two Olmec styles: broad forehead, elongated skull, almond-shaped eyes, large curved nose with enhanced bridge, full lips, down-turned open mouth, elongated ears, and facial line drawings. The following explanation offers guidance on the incised line drawings of the illustrated Olmec figure as well as the hybridized face of *Orlan au masque Olmeque*:

> Made legible by the red pigment rubbed into the fine lines, the incisions are divided into four major elements: an irregular, rectangular cartouche surrounding the right eye, a T-shaped element below the right eye, and vertical bands on either side of the face. . . . The profile heads of the cartouche recall the T-shaped monoliths of Teopantecuanitlan. The encircled double merlons suggest the portal and passage to the supernatural realm. The triple-pronged element between them may be a cloud motif and symbol of the celestial realm. The cartouche may then be understood to represent an enclosed court, a sacred precinct in which the wearer of this mask was a ritual performer. These incisions speak to the shamanic empowerment of both the mask itself and its wearer.[22]

Thus Orlan becomes, through computer-generated images, a composite of two distinct Olmec styles as well as a hybridization of past and present. She creates a hybrid which replicates the process of hybridization crucial to sustaining the ancient culture. Art objects like masks were seen as animate: more than just art objects, they were links with primordial power. The predominance of human forms in specific idealized proportions sought to convey the character of the ideal ruler and his role within society, a society whose welfare was in his hands. One of his main responsibilities was to feed his people and since the principal crop was corn (maize), its role in the culture's representations was recognized as a central life force of the earth and the ruler. Hybridizations of corn successfully carried out by the Olmec people required not only an extensive knowledge of plant reproduction but also considerable ingenuity. Maize, the great Mesoamerican

Incised Olmec mask, 900–600 B.C.E. *White and gray jadeite with red pigment, 17 cm (height) x 16 cm (width) x 9 cm (depth). Courtesy of Justin Kerr.*

staple, could only reproduce with human intervention and it is postulated that the women were the gardeners who performed such tasks.[23] Olmec scholars now consider such hybridizations to have functioned at a metaphorical level as well, that is, like composite figures of human and animal, they represented a symbolic synthesis of two life forms made more powerful as one.

This theme was also replicated by the Mayas, who depict in some of their illustrations the combination of two sexes into one deity. One example is an Earth or Moon God/Goddess which is half male, half female. Even more notable is the divine nature of Lord Pacal, designated as both male and female, whose features—known to us from a tomb sculpture from the mid-seventh century B.C.E.—are also replicated by Orlan.[24] Consider this description from an art history text:

> A stucco portrait of Lord Pacal found with his sarcophagus shows him as a young man wearing a diadem of jade and flowers. His features—sloping forehead and elongated skull (babies had their heads bound to produce this shape), large curved nose (enhanced by an ornamental bridge, perhaps of latex), full lips, and open mouth—are characteristic of the Maya ideal of beauty. Traces of pigment indicate that this portrait, like much Maya sculpture, was colorfully painted.[25]

Other Orlan images offer many variations: some showing the Maya nose, another with crossed eyes, and another with filed-down, jewel-encrusted teeth. This collection of images (available on CD-ROM) is a type of catalogue of her work, and as she notes, is "not definitive" but is rather open-ended; "It's possible here to do many things." Humor even plays a

Orlan Pacal de Palenque. *Digitally processed image, 1998. Courtesy of the artist with the collaboration of Pierre Zovile.*

Lord Pacal, from his tomb in the Temple of Inscriptions,
Palenque. 17th century, stucco. Museo Nácional de
Antropología, Mexico City.

role, as Orlan pictures herself with Olmec and Maya features with rollers
in her hair. This points to the consistency in her underlying message of
both appropriation and critique. The egalitarian nature of the standards of
beauty employed by Orlan (that operated for both men and women) also
draw our attention to issues of class as well as gender. She explains:

> The main idea is to study the deformations of the skull found in the
> Olmecs and the Mayas. They would put a wooden frame on the baby's
> head as soon as he was born, in his crib, and for the first three years of his
> life, this frame would be tightened until the fontanel was firm, so that the

skull is permanently oblong. Such deformations were found in all social classes in the Mayas, on both men and women. There was no difference.

Orlan remarks, "It wasn't a religious thing; it was an aesthetic thing." As she notes, the Maya also appreciated crossed eyes.

> They would place a ball of wax or clay on the baby's nose until the child squinted. There were other criteria of beauty such as filing down teeth and having them inlaid with diamonds, jades, or precious stones. And another study is about Mayan noses. Dignitaries wore false noses for ceremonies: long noses starting from the forehead, with a large bump.

Transforming computer-generated images of herself along Mayan lines again highlights the malleability of her own facial features and the "multiple, evolving, mutating identities" that result. Like *Reincarnation*, she is less interested in the product than the process. *Self-Hybridation* highlights the process of experimenting and manipulating virtual beauties, so much so that in her recent exhibitions, viewers are allowed to actively participate in the process of experimenting with individual features of her "interactive 3-D clone" which ask questions of viewers by means of Aztec riddles on parts of the body.[26] She encourages viewers to repeatedly "hybridize" her image, thereby empowering them with agency to change her looks. They come to share firsthand in the ancient Olmec process of cultivating hybrids, creating twentieth-century virtual beauties of their own.

Given the emerging interest in virtual reality in recent art, it is noteworthy that Orlan has been preoccupied with these issues since 1990. In her early work, computer technology fabricated the template of various norms of western European feminine beauty as inspiration for self-exploration through actual surgery. Beauty was "lifted" from paintings of the past while it was simultaneously critiqued. The computer-generated image of a face incorporating past beauties was virtual, but the surgery and pain were real. In *Self-Hybridation*, technology to create virtual beauty becomes primary. Olmec and Maya standards of beauty, power, and agency function as inspiration but also as a visible means, as created masks of virtual beauties: as metaphor for inner strength achieved through transformation.

As Orlan pursues the process of creating "multiple, evolving, mutating identities" we are drawn into how "the spectacle and discourse of the modified body has become the place of a public debate." She underscores the futility of the philosophical search for one universal standard of beauty while she undermines the security of personal identity that rests solely on one's looks. Most of all, she encourages us to ponder the extremes: the impossibility of seeing (the horror of Carnal Art) and the folly of seeing (the playfulness of techno-art). Philosophy shows that we have defined ourselves as *rational* human beings that privilege mind over matter; but history shows we are *emotionally* bound to elusive, impossible ideals of beauty manifested in the physical body. Technology may ultimately show us that in our folly, the only beauty we can ever (really) attain is virtual.

NOTES

Unless otherwise indicated, all quotes of Orlan's speech are from the interview she did with me in Paris, France, on October 8, 1998.

I would like to thank Dr. Emita Hill for invaluable help with translation during the interview, and Chad Langford for his skillful transcription and translation of the recorded conversation. Thanks also to Carolyn Korsmeyer for helpful suggestions on an earlier draft.

1. For over an hour, she answered faxes. Her current gallery in the United States is the Sandra Gering Gallery. In addition, there are several others in Europe and one in Israel.

2. Additional text from Michel Serres's *Tiers-Instruit* reads: "Science talks of organs, functions, cells and molecules, to acknowledge that it is high time that one stopped talking of life in the laboratory." See Miryam Sas, "The Doyenne of Divasection," *Mondo 2000* 13 (Fall/Winter 1995): 109.

3. The plan to alter her nose to that of Psyche has not yet been realized.

4. Part of the plan is to adopt a new legal name at the completion of the series of surgeries.

5. For a discussion of how Orlan's graphic images both repel and attract (thereby causing viewers to experience them both disinterestedly and interestedly) and how a viewer's cognitive predisposition may affect such viewing, see my essay, "Disinterestedness and Political Art," in *Aesthetics: The Big Questions*, ed. Carolyn Korsmeyer (Oxford: Basil Blackwell, 1998), pp. 155–171.

6. *VST, Revue Scientifique et Culturelle de Sante Mentale* 23/24 (September-December, 1991). Two of the essays are descriptions of three of the first five operations, written by the attending surgeon, Dr. Cherif Zahar.

7. Barbara Rose, "Is It Art? Orlan and the Transgressive Act," *Art in America* 81, no. 2 (February 1993): 87.

8. Parveen Adams, *The Emptiness of the Image: Psychoanalysis and Sexual Differences* (New York and London: Routledge, 1996), pp. 153–154. Orlan plans another surgery in the future. Although it is not a part of the *Reincarnation* series and is as yet unscheduled, she speaks of a surgical event in which she will defy the traditional connection between an "open" body, pain, and suffering. In her Carnal Art Manifest, she wrote: "I can observe my own body cut open without suffering! I can see myself all the way down to my viscera, a new stage of gaze." In our interview, she notes that our "old" bodies—receptors of old ways of thinking—must overcome the natural reaction "that when we see an open body, this body is not necessarily dying, due to war, torture,

or sickness; that today, an open body does not have to be a suffering body." When asked what she intends to open and why, she points to her underarm and replies: "I plan to have a large opening here, because here, we have hair; it looks like the genital area, and I can place my head very close and have close-ups of myself smiling, laughing, or reading, when my body is open." Calling it "an operation of opening and closing of the body"—she plans to be awake throughout and to block the pain by means of a local anaesthetic. She adds, "Maybe it will take place in the year 2000; I'm ready to stop having surgery. I don't want to have surgery all my life. I'd like to stop having cosmetic surgery."

9. Kathy Davis, *Reshaping the Female Body: The Dilemma of Cosmetic Surgery* (New York and London: Routledge, 1995) and "'My Body Is My Art': Cosmetic Surgery as Feminist Utopia?" *The European Journal of Women's Studies* 4, no. 1 (February 1997): 23–37. Davis is professor of Women's Studies at Utrecht University, the Netherlands.

10. Schwarzkogler reportedly bled to death after cutting his penis; it was discovered later that the event was a fake. His work has been called "staged photography." See Rose, "Is It Art?," p. 87.

11. The Carnal Art Manifest is an unpublished manuscript.

12. From a 1991 interview by A. C. Remond, *France-Soir*, February 12, 1991.

13. For only a small sampling, see the writings of Susan Bordo, *Twilight Zone: The Hidden Life of Cultural Images from Plato to O.J.* (Berkeley: University of California Press, 1993); Naomi Wolf, *The Beauty Myth: How Images of Beauty Are Used against Women* (New York: William Morrow, 1991); and Sandra Lee Bartky, *Femininity and Domination: Studies in Phenomenology of Oppression* (New York and London: Routledge, 1990).

14. Valerie Steele mentions Van Beirendonck in her "Letter from the Editor," in *Fashion Theory* 2, no. 2 (June 1998): 109. In the same issue, author Kate Ince discusses Orlan's art in relation to skin (the covering of the body) and fashion. "Operations of Redress: Orlan, the Body and Its Limits," pp. 111–128. Ince is writing a book-length manuscript on Orlan.

15. The latter is from the Web site of The Aesthetics Center (the Banis-Derr Center for Plastic Surgery) located at www.aesthetics.org/.

16. One report notes a decline in these numbers based on the current desire of women to retain "a natural look," in contrast to past decades. "They're not trying to erase their ethnic background anymore," said a Park Avenue surgeon. In addition, insurance coverage is less extensive. Jane Gross, "As Ethnic Pride Rises, Rhinoplasty Takes a Nose Dive," *New York Times*, January 3, 1999, sec. 4, p. 2.

17. A number of these works were exhibited in "Out of Portrait" in October 1998 at the exhibition space of Espace D'Art Yvonamor Palix at FIAC (an exhibit of 150 galleries) and at Yvonamor Palix Gallery (from November 1998 to January 1999), both in Paris.

18. The earliest Olmec society began around 1200 B.C.E. and lasted into 400 B.C.E. It was the first major Mesoamerican civilization, extending from central Mexico (near Mexico City) into northern Central America, where some of the earliest agricultural settlers located in the Andean region of South America. The earliest Maya civilization arose around 1000–300 B.C.E., gaining its own identity in 300 B.C.E.–250 C.E. in southern Mesoamerica (Guatemala, the Yucatan peninsula, Belize, and the eastern part of

Honduras and El Salvador). It peaked 250–900 C.E. and endured until the Spanish Conquest in 1500 C.E. The influence of the Olmecs on the Maya was particularly widespread between 1000–300 B.C.E. but the two cultures still maintained distinct artistic styles and goals. See Marilyn Stokstad, *Art History* (New York: Harry N. Abrams), pp. 445–447.

19. Ibid., p. 448.

20. Caroline E. Tate cites evidence from Beatriz de la Fuente in an essay, "Art in Olmec Culture," in *The Olmec World: Ritual and Rulership*, ed. Michael D. Coe (Princeton, N.J.: Princeton University Art Museum, in association with Harry N. Abrams, 1995), p. 47.

21. Ibid., p. 59.

22. A mask with incisions is described in Coe, *The Olmec World*, p. 268. Another mask, not pictured here, contains a V-shaped cleft which is also utilized by Orlan. The cleft is an interesting element, described by Coe on p. 154 as follows:

> The extension at the top of the head is broken, but the beginning of a V-shaped cleft can be seen. The meaning of this motif, a defining attribute of the Olmec style, is much debated. Various interpretations have been offered, i.e., that it is the result of a blow to the head from an axe, the fontanel of a newborn baby, the furrow of a jaguar's head, or the split in the skin of a toad beginning the molting process. It is read as a "generalized deity head" or symbol of fertility, perhaps the corn plant itself, or the parted earth from which the plant emerges, a symbol of passage from the terrestrial to the supernatural realms. The V-shaped cleft appears in so many different contexts that it cannot represent an attribute of a specific deity, but it is an all-powerful one for a shamanic ruler to appropriate and incorporate into his own image.

23. David A. Freidel, "Preparing the Way," *The Olmec World*, p. 4.

24. See the Codex illustrations associated with the tomb of Lord Pacal in James C. Gruener, *The Olmec Riddle: An Inquiry into the Origin of Pre-Columbian Civilization* (California: Vengreen Publications, 1987), pp. 271, 276.

25. Stokstad, *Art History*, p. 454.

26. More information on *Self-Hybridations* can be found online at: http://www. cicv.fr/orlan. The exhibit is not yet scheduled for the United States.

Contributors

SALLY BANES is Marian Hannah Winter Professor of Theatre History and Dance Studies at the University of Wisconsin–Madison. She is the author of several books on dance and performance, most recently *Dancing Women: Female Bodies on Stage* and *Subversive Expectations: Performance Art and Paratheater in New York, 1976–85*. She is past president of the Society of Dance History Scholars and of the Dance Critics Association.

SUSAN BORDO holds the Otis A. Singletary Chair in the Humanities at the University of Kentucky. Her books include *Unbearable Weight: Feminism, Western Culture, and the Body; Twilight Zones: The Hidden Life of Cultural Images From Plato to O. J.*; and *The Male Body: A New Look at Men in Public and in Private*.

PEG ZEGLIN BRAND is an artist and Assistant Professor of Gender Studies and Philosophy at Indiana University. She is co-editor with Carolyn Korsmeyer of *Feminism and Tradition in Aesthetics* and is currently working on a book entitled *Parodies as Politics: Feminist Strategies in the Visual Arts*.

NOËL CARROLL is Monroe C. Beardsley Professor of the Philosophy of Art at the University of Wisconsin–Madison and President of the American Society for Aesthetics. His most recent books are *A Philosophy of Mass Art* and *Philosophy of Art: A Contemporary Introduction*.

KAORI CHINO is Professor of Japanese Art History at Gakushuin University. She is co-editor with Takaaki Kumakura of *Women? Japan? Beauty?* She co-edited *Art and Gender: The Asymmetrical Regard* with Tokiko Suzuki and Akiko Mabuchi.

ARTHUR C. DANTO is Johnsonian Professor Emeritus of Philosophy at Columbia University. He is the author of many books in the history of philosophy and aesthetics, including *Embodied Meanings; After the End of Art;* and *Selected Essays,* volume I: *The Body/Body Problem,* and volume II: *Philosophizing Art.* He is art critic for *The Nation* and has written extensively on the arts for numerous publications such as ARTFORUM and ARTnews.

MARCIA MUELDER EATON is Professor of Philosophy at the University of Minnesota. She is the author of several books and articles in aesthetics and philosophy of art. She has served as President of the American Society of Aesthetics. She has been a visiting scholar and lecturer in Europe, China, Canada, and the United States.

ELEANOR HEARTNEY is an internationally published art writer. She is a contributing editor to *Art in America* and *The New Art Examiner* and author of *Critical Condition: American Culture at the Crossroads.* Her forthcoming book is *Movements in Modern Art: Postmodernism.*

KATHLEEN M. HIGGINS is Professor of Philosophy at the University of Texas at Austin. She is author of several books, including *Nietzsche's Zarathustra; The Music of Our Lives;* and (with Robert C. Solomon) *A Short History of Philosophy.* She is also editor of *Aesthetics in Perspective.*

EVA KIT WAH MAN is Associate Professor and Associate Course Leader in the Humanities Program, Hong Kong Baptist University. She has published thirteen books in Chinese and numerous articles in English and Chinese on comparative aesthetics, comparative philosophy, and feminist studies.

DAWN PERLMUTTER is Assistant Professor of Art and Philosophy at Cheyney University of Pennsylvania. She is the author of numerous articles and co-editor of *Reclaiming the Spiritual in Art.* Her current research involves the development of a philosophical theory of violence and has resulted in a book entitled *Postmodern Idolatry: Ritual Uses of Blood in American Culture.*

HILARY ROBINSON, formerly an artist, now lectures in the history and theory of contemporary art to studio students in the School of Art and Design, University of Ulster at Belfast, Northern Ireland. She is currently editing an anthology entitled *Feminism/Art/Theory 1968–1998.*

ANITA SILVERS, Professor of Philosophy at San Francisco State University, is the co-author with Mary B. Mahowald and David Wasserman of *Disability, Difference, Discrimination: Perspectives on Justice in Bioethics and Public Policy* and co-author with Margaret P. Battin, John Fisher, and Ronald More of *Puzzles about Art.* She has co-edited four volumes and authored more than seventy essays in ethics and bioethics, aesthetics, feminism, disability studies, and public policy. Silvers was California's Distinguished Humanities Scholar in 1978 and in 1989 was the first recipient of the California Faculty Association's Equal Rights Award for her work in making higher education accessible to people with disabilities.

PAUL C. TAYLOR is an Assistant Professor of Philosophy and Adjunct Assistant Professor of American Ethnic Studies at the University of Washington. He works principally in the areas of aesthetics, Africana philosophy, pragmatism, and social and political philosophy. He is working on a book entitled *Pragmatism and Race.*

Index

Italicized numbers refer to illustrations.